RUDOLPH MATAS

RUDOLPH MATAS

A Biography of one
of the great pioneers
in surgery

ISIDORE COHN, M.D.
WITH HERMANN B. DEUTSCH

Doubleday & Company, Inc.
Garden City, New York
1960

Library of Congress Catalog Card Number 60–9471

This volume is affectionately
dedicated to my wife
ELSIE W. COHN
whose devotion and confidence
have been a source of encouragement
for the past fifty years.

PREFACE

Professor Rudolph Matas was my teacher. His devotion to the ideals inherent in the practice of medicine and his catholic interests stimulated his associates to endeavor to serve the community and the profession to the extent of their ability. His interest in me personally, which was continuous from the day of my entering the field of medicine until his death, will ever be a source of great satisfaction. As time went on I became a confidential friend to whom he entrusted responsibilities which he felt that time would not permit him to complete. Years ago, when I first suggested that I be allowed to be his biographer, he demurred because, as he expressed it, "you would be too partial." I assured him that I would try to tell the story of his life in a factual way, uninfluenced by personal partiality. In order to help me he placed all of his personal correspondence and personal diaries at my disposal. Free use of this material has been of the greatest service.

Fifty-four years of personal contact and observation have contributed to an understanding of his character, habits, and attitudes. The public did not know him intimately, because of his almost cloistered life.

In the preparation for this adventure I had the constant enthusiastic support of my wife, Elsie Cohn, and the co-operation of Hermann Deutsch, whose experience as an author and editor, aided by his facile pen, has brought to fruition a dream for me.

I am indebted to many people for helpful material, notably Miss Mary Louise Marshall, Mrs. Hathaway Aleman, Dr. Garland Taylor, Mr. John Hall Jacobs, George Logan, and to Charles L. Dufour, for invaluable assistance in the laborious task of correcting galley proofs. Many others have given helpful suggestions. To Mrs. Mildred Dennery and Mrs. Martha Disimone, the stenographers, I owe a special debt of gratitude.

I am especially grateful to Mr. Lee Barker, of Doubleday & Company, the publishers, for consideration and understanding.

It is my sincere hope that this portrait will enable others to appreciate one whose contributions were of value to the entire human race.

ISIDORE COHN

PROLOGUE

She sat beside her baby son's crib on the gallery of their weathered house, a small woman stubbornly trying to deny the years that swept her past the middle thirties, haunted always by the fear that her physician husband, ten years her junior, might at any moment abandon her for a newer love as lightly as he discarded one scheme to make himself wealthy for a newer and still gaudier venture.

She looked out beyond the crest of a low levee to the empty expanse of river where no steamboat had passed for days. This time her solitary vigil might be very long. Her husband had ridden off to New Orleans, fifty twisting miles downstream from Bonnet Carre, to retrieve what he could of the ruins of his latest, and for a time most successful, get-rich-quick project.

He had tried to explain it to her. As plantation physician he had been taking his pay for some time not in Confederate paper money but in molasses. This he converted into rum by running it through a home-built still with a capacity of eighteen barrels daily, forty gallons to the barrel, and every gallon readily salable at sixteen dollars, now that the Union blockade had halted imports from Jamaica. All had gone well till Farragut captured New Orleans; the commanding general who took over the city, already known as "Beast" Butler, had at once prohibited the operation of stills by Confederates.

So, the doctor explained, he must go to the city. He must impress upon General Butler that he, a Spaniard, was a neutral. If even this did not succeed in gaining permission to continue his distilling bonanza,

9

he would ask safe conduct for a herd of cattle to be sold to the civilian population, chafing because blue-clad Union troops had all the meat they wanted while the citizens of New Orleans had none.

Of course, he went on, he would then have to secure from Governor Thomas Overton Moore, who had retired to a temporary capital at Opelousas, permission to bring the herd through Confederate territory to the Union lines, but that would readily arrange itself. He would return as soon as possible. Meanwhile she was to keep herself and their child in good health and good cheer.

The son she had borne him a year and a half earlier was the joy of his exuberant father's heart. What a little man! Already he looked out on the world with awareness and understanding. This was not simply an illusion of paternal pride. On the contrary, it was, he assured his wife, a physician's objective appraisal.

And now he must be off to argue with General Butler, or with the General's brother, Andrew, the question of his rights as a Spanish neutral. Had she packed into his saddlebags the razors, fresh linens, and all else that might be needful?

She bade him go with God. Hopelessly bewildered by endless talk of neutrals and Confederates and Unionists, she was clear on one point only: the little boy asleep in the crib beside her was the strong tie that bound her volatile husband to his family. He might cast her aside for a newer love, but never would he abandon the son in whom he saw himself fulfilled. Nothing else mattered; not the isolation imposed upon her by alien speech and alien ways which cut her off from the settlement's normal chattering companionship; not the conjectures about which way the tides of war might flow; not the doctor's perennial schemes for amassing riches.

Mechanically she waved a plaited swish of sweet-flag leaves over her baby's crib, paused in mid-gesture, then leaped to her feet. Above the willows and cottonwoods on the *batture* dense smoke writhed skyward. She knew at once that this must be the Yankee fleet.

Pros and cons of the conflict of which this was a part lay beyond her understanding. But the fleet that steamed almost into the low-riding sun as vessel after vessel turned the broad bend, the enormous plumes of smoke, the banners snapping above burnished water, the deep-throated chuff of laboring engines—all this was splendor. She raised the baby high so that he too might share the magnificent sight.

She could not know that nearly a century later, his mental faculties undimmed, this baby, born before Lincoln became President, would look back from the atomic age, recalling a glimpse of Farragut's fleet as the first real memory of a life that made him one of the greatest surgeons the world has ever known.

RUDOLPH MATAS

CHAPTER I

Had Don Quixote been born in Catalonia instead of La Mancha; had he been caparisoned in Natty Bumppo's buckskins, Hopalong Cassidy's chaps, and Young Doctor Malone's surgical gown instead of rusty armor; had he bestridden not Rosinante's saddle but Jay Gould's seat on the Stock Exchange; and had his dreamy romanticism been leavened with flashes of authentic genius, the result would have been an almost photographic likeness of the incredible physician-adventurer who Americanized his name with the signature "Dr. N. H. Matas."

We are given a clear insight into what motivated this rolling stone of pharmacy, finance, errantry, and medicine. Late in life, berating himself without stint for earlier failure to compile a record of his ancestry, he penned a revelatory chronicle in English under the title of "A Few Remarks on the Genealogy and Biography of Dr. N. H. Matas." Only the first segment of this work was committed to what is now rusty brown ink. Even as a fragment it must be classed as an extraordinary mélange of fact and fable, humility and vainglory, candor and self-serving gloss. It speaks of "the doctor" always in the third person. One is bound to regret that it remained unfinished.

Technically, "Dr. N. H. Matas" was Narciso Areu y Matas. Areu was the family name of his father, Matas the maiden name of his mother. His "Few Remarks on the Genealogy and Biography" are at pains to explain that the Catalonian word *areu* means "heir," but that in the original Latin the word for heir would be spelled with an *he*, as in *hereditas*. Therefore, he—the doctor—decided early in life that the

13

family name which had been Areu at least as far back as the War of the Spanish Succession, should thenceforth be written "Hereu."

In time this Dr. Hereu came to the United States, where the custom of following the family name with that of the mother's family is unknown. Weary of having to explain to French-speaking New Orleans in the 1850's that "Narciso Hereu Matas" should be addressed as "Dr. Hereu" he finally gave up the struggle and became Dr. Matas, though he continued for some years to be Hereu on official documents and in the city directory. However, his son, born four years after his sire's arrival in the New World, was formally christened Rodolphe Matas and is so inscribed on the register of the old Jesuit church in New Orleans.

The parents of "Dr. N. H. Matas" were Manuel Areu Casals and Paula Matas Vilardell, to whom he was born on March 5, 1837, in the village whose Catalonian name, Pont Major, is shown as Puente Mayor on Spanish maps. In politics, customs, and speech, Catalonia has always been stubbornly nonconformist. In the war that followed Louis XIV's efforts to place his grandson, Philip, on the throne of Spain, Catalonia sided with the Dutch and English against Spain and France. Her capital, Barcelona, was not subdued until a year after her Dutch and British allies had conceded victory to Louis and his Bourbons.

In that struggle, a Catalan named José Areu Masoliver, son of Lorenzo, is known to have participated. His great-grandsons later fought in the interminable Carlist and Separatist uprisings. Like their progenitor, they were peasants, tilling the Val d'Aran in the Pyrenees, tending flocks of goats whose hides they manufactured into wineskins and canteens for the army.

One of these descendants, Benito Areu Balado, besought for his son, Manuel Areu Casals, the hand in marriage of Paula Matas, a patrician who could trace her ancestry back through eight generations to the Bernardo Matas whose son, Juan, married Esperanza Puig in 1586. Paula's father, Narciso, had served as mayor of Pont Major, as had his father, José Matas Vila, before him. Her father's brother, Juan, was secretary and archivist to the bishop of Gerona. The family was wealthy, owning many fields, large olive groves, an oil mill, a soap factory, and a pottery.

The suit of a peasant for the hand of such a blue blood was all but unthinkable. Had Paula's mother, Magdalena, been alive, the match between her daughter and a goatherd's son would never have been entertained, much less consummated. But Magdalena was long since in her grave, having died early, as her grandson put it in his memoirs, "of a fright." Her husband, the one-time mayor, remarried.

He seems to have held some socially mutinous but genetically sound ideas about the value of exogamy. Hence, gently reared Paula became the wife of a sturdy scion of peasant stock. Their first-born, a son, was rejoicingly christened Narciso after the grandsire who had sanctioned the match. Their ceremony was held in the church of Sta. María in Pont Major, shortly before the family moved to Gerona, the provincial capital.

Paula's sacrifices in marrying Manuel were genuine enough. As his wife she had to forgo all the luxuries to which she had been accustomed in her father's home, performing even the most menial household tasks herself. One may suspect that it was she who insisted they move from the village to the city, so that her son might enjoy the advantages of urban schooling. In his case the infusion of yeoman blood seems to have vindicated the elder Narciso's views. The boy's mentality and physique were both outstanding, not merely by his own admission—he was quite candid on that score when compiling his memoirs—but as documented by the facts of his subsequent career.

In his "Few Remarks" he says of himself that "he was always at the head of his class and carried for five years the highest prizes and honors in his examinations. He was the pet of his professors and all students felt proud of his company. . . . His moral character was perfect and [in] his physical development [he was] a strong, robust young fellow."

That was after he had advanced from elementary school to the college of San Felipe Neri to prepare himself for eventual admission to the University of Barcelona, where he planned to study pharmacy. Meanwhile, his ambition was furthered by Dr. Vivas di Colonnas, second husband of one of his mother's sisters, who took him into his home, relieving Manuel and Paula of the future cost of his education and upbringing. He likewise made him an apprentice at the Vivas pharmacy, where he worked two hours every evening before retiring to his studies.

His instructors' tenuous hopes of dedicating Narciso to the priesthood were dashed during his fifteenth year. At this time, according to his memoirs, "the first impressions of love began when he met a young lady named Rita Rimbau who became equally fond and infatuated with him." This affair of the heart had not progressed very far when Paula abruptly sickened and died.

The loss of his mother dealt Narciso a profound shock. Above all he wanted to leave Gerona, where everything reminded him of the immutable reality of his bereavement. One of his mother's sisters, Narcisa Burgaria, invited him to be her guest for the summer at San Felíu de Guixols on the coast. There a schoolmate introduced him to a local celebrity, Tomás Jorda, recently returned from New Orleans to visit his birthplace. Jorda, world traveler and adventurer, claiming descent from a crusader who barely escaped drowning in the River Jordan and hence adopted the name borne by his descendants through all the centuries that followed, became Narciso's idol.

Through him he met the great man's sister, Teresa, and instantly Rita Rimbau was banished from his heart. Still speaking of himself in the third person, he notes that "while he was talking to said Tomás Jorda a lady with long black hair crossed the room, and without having been introduced to her and without even having seen her face or knowing whether she was married or single, ideas struck his mind that she would be his wife. The same idea struck the lady that night, as she often confessed to him, which seems to prove the destiny of God's creatures."

Tomás painted glittering pictures of far-off New Orleans and of opportunities to amass wealth. When he urged Narciso to follow him and establish a drugstore in the New World after completing his education, the boy was enthralled. The older man was soon to leave Spain, taking ship at Barcelona. Narciso pleaded to be told when this journey was to begin, so that he could accompany his hero as far as Gerona on the way. The fact that Teresa, "the lady with long black hair," would also accompany her brother to the port of embarkation, made the journey doubly delightful. Nothing, Narciso vowed, should keep him from joining Tomás at New Orleans.

The boy and the lady with long black hair kept up a decorous correspondence while he completed his studies. Both families recognized Narciso as Teresa's accepted suitor. They would be married as soon as, at nineteen, he was graduated from the University of Barcelona. When he emigrated to America to seek his fortune, Teresa would accompany him as his bride.

Yet in its very inception the marriage was star-crossed. When the contract was being executed, nineteen-year-old Narciso discovered to his horror that his bride-to-be was twenty-nine. At once he perceived physical blemishes and disfigurements in what had heretofore always seemed to be flawless beauty. He found himself caught up in emotional turmoil. All night he walked the Paseo, struggling with himself. Love had fled, but he had given his word to wed the girl. What must he do?

He records that early one morning in this troubled time, he encountered his first love, Rita Rimbau "weeping profusely" as she too walked aimlessly along the Paseo. Neither could utter a word. Still weeping, they parted without so much as a syllable of farewell. This may or may not be factual. It is the sort of thing an aging gallant, looking back along the years, might well regard as legitimate adornment for a spot of soul-searching. Certainly no explanation of the momentary reappearance of the young lady of Gerona on the beach at San Felíu is offered.

Be that as it may, Narciso resolved the conflict between love and obligation by declaring that "he had given his word of honor to marry her and . . . he considered it his duty to marry her as promised." When he returned to the Jorda home from his walk along the beach, Teresa was instantly aware of something amiss. In response to her questions Narciso told her, with a teen-ager's surrender to the dramatic moment, that though love had been quenched by the discovery that she was ten years his senior, he had "given his word and would die rather than break it." The "Few Remarks" also include here the quaint notation that this "explanation [was] found not entirely satisfactory to her."

Nonetheless, they were married on San Narciso's day, October 27, 1856, in the church of San Narciso at Gerona. One is bound to sympathize with Teresa. First, the groom informed her candidly that he married her solely to maintain his given word. Then, during the feasting, dancing, and merrymaking which followed, the groom's brother, Manuel, "took very ill." The groom thereupon packed off his bride to spend her nuptial night in solitude at the home of her Aunt Narcisa while he kept watch at his brother's bedside.

Not until two or three days later, by which time it is to be supposed Manuel's *Katzenjammer* had subsided, did the newlyweds leave for Barcelona by stagecoach, embarking there for Havana, where they spent the *luna de miel* as guests in the home of the Forto family, who were cousins of brother-in-law Jerónimo Jorda, before continuing their journey to New Orleans.

There Tomás welcomed them at the levee, took them by carriage to the home of another of Jerónimo's Catalonian friends, Francisco Sambola, proprietor of a macaroni factory, who assured them after the courtly Spanish fashion, that his house was theirs until such time as they might be settled in an establishment of their own.

Narciso had planned to seek employment immediately in a drugstore, working there while learning English and studying medicine. However, Tomás insisted that they buy a pharmacy of their own. He supplied funds for the purchase of a *boutique* at one of the *Vieux Carré*'s principal intersections—Toulouse and Bourbon streets—where the legendary French Opera House was soon to rise and would be opened two years later.

Since his knowledge of English was not yet even rudimentary, Narciso decided to postpone his matriculation in the newly organized New Orleans College of Medicine, whose initial session had begun a month or so prior to his arrival. Instead, he received special instruction in pharmacy from Dr. Isaac L. Crawcour, entering the medical school at the opening of its second year of existence, in November 1857.

Here he took two courses, each of five months' duration, receiving the degree of Doctor of Pharmacy in 1858 and Doctor of Medicine in 1859. Various considerations had decided him to enter the new medical school rather than the well-established Medical College of Louisiana which would one day become Tulane University. For one thing, the new school was installed in a building immediately opposite a great charity hospital; it established the first dispensary or outpatient department in the Deep South; and it organized a lying-in department through which students could attend patients in their homes with the assurance that the professor of obstetrics would give prompt assistance if difficulties were encountered.

Teresa had become pregnant in 1857, was overjoyed at the prospect of giving her young husband an heir, wishfully hoping that he, now bound only by ties of duty which had been not too willingly assumed, might become lover as well as spouse. In the spring of 1858 she gave birth to a daughter. They named the baby Teresita. Narciso described her as beautiful and healthy, but she sickened and died within a matter of weeks. Teresa, suffering from abscesses of both breasts, could not nurse her. The Negro mammy who had been called in apparently cared little for the small charge entrusted to her. The baby died, Narciso records almost casually, "from bad milk and carelessness of the nurse."

In other respects, however, the couple prospered. The pharmacy was a success from the start. Tomás was in no hurry to have his investment repaid, the business throve and gave full-time employment to two clerks in addition to the services of the proprietor. Narciso and his wife came down with yellow fever in the first hot weather of 1859, but survived both the disease and its treatment and were now among the fortunate *immunisés* who could face future summers without fear.

A graduate physician, Narciso enjoyed a general practice which centered about his pharmacy. Nonetheless, he was plagued by an itch to challenge destiny more boldly. The Vieux Carré was crowded and populous, but many physicians practiced there already. This was not yet the case in the American *faubourg*, upstream from Canal Street, behind whose development a group of Anglo-Saxon financiers had jointly put their talents and capital. If he established a pharmacy and a medical practice in this budding new *faubourg*, adjoining whose residential and business fringe were many plantations, he could become rich. Planters paid well for medical service not only to themselves, but to those valuable and perishable properties, their slaves.

Teresa, it may be assumed, would not favor such a project, though she did not actively oppose it. Dissolution of the partnership between her husband and her brother in the *Pharmacie* Hereu would necessarily do away with one of the ties that held Narciso to her. On the other hand, she was by now all too well aware how passionately her young husband chafed against restraint.

Perhaps it was just as well, therefore, that the decision was taken out of their hands, even though disaster made the choice for them. Returning afoot from the neighborhood of the Poydras Market one night, after Narciso had taken Teresa there to show her the uptown location where he wanted to strike out for himself, they found that their existing pharmacy had burned to the ground during their absence.

The building had been insured by Jorda; but, since he was the venture's sole financial backer, all insurance money went to him. Under the circumstances, he not only raised no objection to his brother-in-law's proposed uptown venture; he helped to underwrite the Hereu Pharmacy at Baronne and Hevia Streets in the American section.

Patients and customers alike were slow to take advantage of the new medical center's facilities. Those who had come to Dr. N. H. Matas when his office was in the Vieux Carré refused stubbornly to seek his services beyond the pale above Canal Street.

Teresa's new isolation in a neighborhood where only English was spoken was eased by the welcome discovery in the following spring that she was once more pregnant. She was on the point of pleading with her husband to return to more familiar surroundings when he dashed off on a new tangent: a project that would bypass the dragging wait for wealth.

Tomás had introduced him one night at the theater to Norbert Louque, a sugar planter whose estate lay in St. John the Baptist parish at Bonnet Carre. That area's fertility had been wonderfully enhanced during the spring of 1850 when part of the levee had suddenly given way at floodtime. A brown torrent raged through the abruptly opened breach. But it deposited rich new loam—the cream of a continent's topsoil—in its wake.

The Louque's plantation physician was anxious to move back to the city. No planter with a large slave investment could afford to be without medical service. Mr. Louque would furnish Dr. Matas a comfortable house and two slaves to tend it, in addition to paying an impressive salary. Over and above that would be the fees Dr. Matas would earn as medical practitioner to the non-slave plantation personnel and their families, and to the settlement of Bonnet Carre, up and down the winding River Road.

Narciso accepted the offer with alacrity. Surrender of his incipient uptown practice involved no hardship, financially or scientifically. In all likelihood the opportunity to gain knowledge and experience in caring for a large plantation's medical requirements outweighed even the monetary consideration. Was it not near Donaldsonville, just upstream from Bonnet Carre, that the brilliant pioneer surgeon, François Marie Prevost, had performed on a female slave the first Caesarean section which saved the lives of both mother and child?

Narciso told Teresa they would embark within the week by steamboat for their new home on the Louque plantation. She accepted the decision unquestioningly. Any community with a church where she could make a novena, asking that the new baby be a boy, would encompass virtually all she demanded of life at the moment. She also prayed each night for the miracle, kneeling beside the bed with the filmy mosquito bar draped from its tester, her great, dark eyes upraised to the ivory crucifix above the vigil light. There she poured out her heart to *María Santísima*, one sorrowing woman confiding to another the haunting fear that unless a man-child were born to survive the perils of infancy her husband might forsake her.

May came, and with it the omen of high water, as on distant mountain ranges the snows of winter began to melt. Feeling new life quicken within her, Teresa viewed the rising river without alarm. Had not her husband assured her this levee would not fail, as had its more primitive, weaker predecessor?

The summer of 1860, with its mosquito clouds and fevers, dragged to a conclusion. On September 12, in the house Mr. Louque had set aside for them, her physician husband and a slave woman delivered Teresa of a lusty son. Her first clear perceptions on emerging from the blankness of agony were her husband's kiss and his murmur, lips against her cheek, that a new life had begun for them. She, the mother of his son, was the sole object of his adoration. The baby—he wrote years later in his memoirs—"was the fruit of a true love and happiness from his parents. Everything concerning the first love was forgotten by the doctor, and his love and happiness with his wife [was] now real, genuine, and the love of his son had no limits."

This was all that mattered to Teresa. At last she felt herself secure as Narciso Hereu's wife. The talk of sectional strife and bitterness that became ever more general as September merged into October, with its opening of the cane harvest, meant literally nothing to her. Narciso's talk of Black Republicans and Secession and Lincoln and a Little Giant had no interest for her even after the electoral college met in December and it was proclaimed officially that Abraham Lincoln would be inaugurated as president in March.

Though the countryside seethed with the revolt implicit in Lincoln's assumption of office, plantation life remained for a time superficially serene. White children and pickaninnies alike went into the swamps to cut canes of wild bamboo, stacking them in great heaps on the levee so that they might dry by Christmas Eve. That was when they were put to the torch. The joints exploded like firecrackers as flames licked upward, and there was much capering and hand clapping and laughter.

Yet only a week later New Year's was celebrated more soberly. The legislature was being called into session at New Orleans to authorize a convention that would formulate, the resolution under which Louisiana would secede from the Union. "Cump" Sherman, president of the new State Seminary of Learning established near Alexandria only a few months earlier, quit this position to resume his commission as a major in the Federal army. Mississippi seceded within the week. Louisiana followed suit.

A Louisianian, son of a St. Bernard parish family of sugar planters, General Pierre Gustave Toutant-Beauregard, gave the command to fire on Fort Sumter, and explosions followed as the flames licked upward. War had become a commonplace of the plantation's daily life when, in January of 1862, Narciso bundled his wife and sixteen-month-old son aboard a steamboat at Bonnet Carre landing, and journeyed downstream to New Orleans, where the child was baptized in the Church of the Immaculate Conception on Baronne Street. The infant's sponsors were Tomás Jorda and Rose Marsal; the officiating priest was the Rev. J. J. Duffo, S.J.

Decades later, when Narciso, setting down his "Few Remarks," came to this particular autobiographical milestone, he noted "the name Rudolph was selected by his father out of the enthusiasm experienced from reading *The Mysteries of Paris.*"

Thus the physician whose contributions to the advancement of surgery during the ensuing century would be hailed in every quarter of the globe as the work of one of mankind's great benefactors became the namesake of Rodolphe de Gerolstein, fictional hero of Eugene Sue's greatest blood-and-thunder romance. There had been quite an argument before Narciso had his way because, as a Catholic, the baby should have been given the name of a saint. But Narciso insisted, declaring that beyond doubt there must have been a German saint named Rudolph, and finally carried his point. Teresa had to be content with dedicating her son to her own patroness.

On the baptismal certificate issued January 31, 1862, in French-speaking New Orleans, the infant's name was inscribed as Rodolphe, the father's as Narcisse, and the mother's as Thérèse. In course of time Rodolphe would be anglicized to Rudolph Matas, a final metamorphosis from seventeenth-century beginnings with the Catalonian patronymic of Areu.

CHAPTER II

Just before the onset of cool weather, about the time of Rodolphe's second birthday, he and his mother left Bonnet Carre for New Orleans and the home of his Uncle Tomás. During the ensuing year he would see his mercurial sire no more than twice, as day followed monotonous day. If the weather was fine, his mother carried him with her to church. In the cool of the evening he was wheeled along Esplanade Avenue in the leather-faced miniature Concord buggy which was his perambulator.

Twice a slim, well-knit stranger visited the Jorda home and made a great to-do over Rodolphe. The visitor's slenderness gave an impression of finely tempered strength, despite *en brosse* barbering which a much later generation would dub a crew cut. Black hair matched the meticulously tended mustache and the wisp of goatee.

Though directed to address this stranger as *papá* or *papacito*, Rodolphe could not identify with the family circle anyone so rarely encountered. His father's absences, of course, were due to the fact that at long last the fortune of which he had dreamed was all but in his grasp. Thirty years later he was to set down the words: "The idea of having or possessing wealth to a man of family gives the courage to his heart to go through the most arduous enterprise and it gives him valor also to face the most dangerous situation." Since he was then seeking to present this phase of his past in a wholly favorable light, he did not amplify these observations by adding that in such a situation a man of family might conceivably also divest himself of scruples and

23

let the end justify the means. Many decades later his son, then approaching his ninetieth birthday, said: "My father became a Yankee overnight."

From May 1 to December 15, 1862, the Union military force which occupied New Orleans was commanded by General Benjamin Franklin Butler, Massachusetts attorney, who was particularly embittered at the time by a series of galling rebuffs. A vain man, he had urgently requested President Lincoln to exchange his commission as a volunteer for one in the regulars. Lincoln did not refuse; he merely did not comply.

This may well have engendered both the extraordinary harshness of Butler's regime and the documented rapacity with which he used his position to fill his personal coffers. Since he was never prosecuted it must be assumed that technically he operated within the law. Since he was abruptly replaced after a treasury agent, George Dennis, reported to Secretary Salmon P. Chase that Butler was "using his position to engage in mercantile speculation and had already made considerable shipments north on private account," it must also be assumed that the ethical aspects of his transactions outraged even those partisans who ordinarily would have been heavily prejudiced in his favor. Only an understanding of the Butler *modus operandi* can keep the second—and unfortunately final—installment of Narciso Matas's unfinished autobiography from being a mere huggermugger of romantic absurdities.

The uncontested facts are that in the spring of 1860, when he became Louque plantation physician at Bonnet Carre, he not only lacked substantial means but was deeply in Tomás Jorda's debt; that when he left Louisiana for London and Paris, only three years later, he had a fortune of more than $100,000.

With the seas closed to her by Union blockade and the River in Union hands, the New Orleans of 1862—an almost wholly commercial community with no industrial potential to speak of—was in the position of a bank whose vaults are sealed against withdrawals and whose doors are closed against fresh deposits.

The flow of trade promptly shifted to Texas; specifically to Brownsville, some thirty miles up the Rio Grande from Port Isabel, and to their opposite numbers on the Mexican side of the stream, Matamoros and Bagdad. "The city throve," a WPA guidebook says of Brownsville, "as merchants and army contractors came to take advantage of its warborn commerce. . . . The roads northward were crowded with an almost continuous stream of wagon trains, bringing cotton, wool, and hides [to the port] and carrying medical and military supplies to the [Confederate] army distribution centers at Shreveport and Marshall."

During 1862, next to no effort was made by the Union's military department of the Gulf, under Butler, to halt this traffic.

When taking over the city, Butler had issued assurances of full protection, both in their persons and their possessions, to neutral aliens and "loyalists." In a metropolitan seaport there were naturally many of both. Says his apologist-biographer Parton: "General Butler's brother, Col. A. J. Butler, who found himself by the action of the Senate without employment in New Orleans, and having both capital and credit at his command, embarked in the business of bringing cattle from Texas to the great advantage of the city and his own considerable profit." The army quartermaster's chest being empty, "General Butler placed all the money of his own which he could raise at his disposal."

From Narciso Matas's "Few Remarks" it appears that just at this very time he journeyed westward from New Orleans for cattle, with Texas as his announced destination. Returning, he sold the cattle in Butler-dominated New Orleans at a profit—the figures are Narciso's —of $40,000, not to mention the collateral fact that brother-in-law Tomás Jorda, who had advanced $4000 in Confederate currency toward the enterprise, received $4000 gold in return. Narciso subsequently made at least two round trips between New Orleans and Texas by boat, once with two shiploads of flour, wagons, tobacco, rum, and other valuables.

To assume that he did all this in competition against, rather than in collaboration with, the Butlers would be entirely too naïve. We know to the day when he came back from the West with his first drove of cattle. He speaks of reaching the Mississippi River at Donaldsonville just after Federal naval forces shelled and burned it. Some of the ruins were still smoldering when he arrived. This was August 9. In short, three months after Butler's advent in New Orleans, Narciso had purchased and delivered to New Orleans a drove of cattle (having previously shut down his still), after securing from General Butler (or from his brother; it amounted to the same thing) assurances of freedom from Union molestation in bringing the herd to the city. He also obtained from Louisiana's Confederate governor, Thomas Overton Moore, a safe conduct through Confederate lines.

After receiving Governor Moore's permit, Narciso returned to New Orleans, where "he exposed fully his plan to Tomás Jorda who, seeing the certainty of his success of the enterprise, requested him to take $4000 in Confederate money and have this invested like his own at his own risk." Narciso then set out for Texas from Bonnet Carre in a sulky. We are asked to believe that en route he encountered a herd of a thousand cattle at Opelousas and bought them on the spot, paying $1000 additional to "one colored man who was in charge of the expedi--

tion. It was wonderful how two men and one boy could drive the
whole herd through the bayous and rivers safely." In view of the fact
that in crossing from Opelousas to Donaldsonville two men and a boy
had to put these cattle over the Atchafalaya River and the far-flung
swamp through which it meanders to the Gulf, the doctor's estimate of
the feat as "wonderful" is something of an understatement. Yet it pales
into insignificance beside his subsequent report of swimming the entire
drove across the Mississippi without loss of a single head.

"At daybreak," chronicles the autobiography, "the doctor had mounted
guards six miles above and below the [Donaldsonville] landing to
watch [for] and report the approach of gunboats. He crossed, the horse
swimming to the other side of the river and the sulky in a boat. At
a moment's notice they drove all of the cattle into the deepest part
of the Mississippi River, and with two boats the men guarded safely
all of the cattle to the other side of the river where the doctor was
waiting. To swim across the big river without losing a single head of
cattle looked marvelous."

The animals were then herded to a fenced enclosure at Bonnet Carre.
After a day with his wife and baby son the doctor engaged other
drovers and moved his beef to an enclosed pasture at Kennerville,
some fifteen miles upstream from New Orleans. Here the animals
were sold in small lots to butchers.

It is obvious from even the most cursory reading that in a number
of respects this account simply does not hang together. For example,
who really financed the enterprise? Jorda, Dr. Matas's wealthy patron,
put up only $4000; someone else must have supplied at least $30,000
more, and the supposition that Narciso Matas could have set aside
such a sum out of his plantation practice, plus a few months of rum-
distilling profits, challenges belief. For that matter, the young doctor's
own figures of eighteen 40-gallon barrels a day at $16 a gallon—
in other words, a daily gross of $11,500—are fantastic.

And what of the cattle, so providentially encountered at Opelousas,
Louisiana's temporary capital and military G.H.Q.? Governor Moore had
proclaimed he would hang without trial anyone found in possession
of a Butler cattle pass. Let us assume, nonetheless, that Dr. Narciso
Matas, holder of such a permit, managed, by concealing the fact or
by an appeal on behalf of the suffering civilians of New Orleans, to
secure a Confederate safe-conduct. But what could account for the
immunity of whoever was driving those 1000 beeves through the very
heart of the Confederate-held Opelousas area before Narciso came into
the picture so opportunely?

On the other hand, no one disputes the fact that General Butler's
brother Andrew, "who found himself by the action of the Senate with-

out employment in New Orleans," but with plenty of credit and capital on his own account or the General's or both, "embarked on the business of bringing cattle from Texas." Financing the venture would present no difficulties, nor would the business of marketing the cattle, once they reached New Orleans. The only hitch would have been: "How can we, who will buy and sell the cattle, get them from the Texas border through Confederate lines?"

At this juncture, Dr. Narciso Matas appears in General Butler's headquarters, proclaiming himself one of the neutral aliens who were promised full protection of person and property. He speaks Spanish— and Texas is less than a generation removed from being part of Spanish-speaking Mexico. But beyond all these advantages, Narciso already has or can procure from Governor Moore a safe conduct through Confederate military lines for himself and for cattle dedicated to the relief of Confederate civilians. Wouldn't Andrew Butler, who is "shrewdly and ably arranging" all such details for his brother, welcome Narciso with open arms, and, what is more to the point, open money-bags?

Years pass. In New Orleans the name of "Beast" Butler is still anathema. An aging physician-adventurer, having sought his fortune in many lands, prepares to cast anchor in New Orleans to live out whatever further span the fates vouchsafe him in companionship with his beloved and now famous son. In the year of the Alaska gold rush he undertakes to set down his version of what befell in 1862. Would it not be natural for him to expunge, by whatever means can be called to hand, any intimation that he had once made common cause with the still hated Butlers? Would he not strain every effort to show that the fortune he reaped in those days was acquired through personal dicing with danger and not by collaboration? And would this not account for the discrepancies which made his "Few Remarks" a somewhat less than coherent chronicle of bygone events?

Narciso's share of the cattle profits was, by his own statement, $24,000 in gold; a tidy return, indeed. Yet the venture was not repeated. "Jealousy began to be plainly manifested," one reads in the "Few Remarks," "and he thought prudent not to risk the enterprise a second time." Yet he immediately shifted to other enterprises and activities involving infinitely greater hazards of loss in blood and treasure. In the light of almost a century's passage, there is room for the conjecture that "jealousy" might have manifested itself in Governor Moore's refusal ever to issue another safe-conduct to anyone shown to have acted for and with the Butlers.

That precious pair of patriots, and especially Andrew, were now systematically trading not merely with speculators, but with the enemy, to their own enrichment. Grant was going into winter quarters at Newellton, preparatory to throwing a noose about Vicksburg the next spring and throttling the Confederacy there. Marshall, Texas, and Shreveport, Louisiana, cheek by jowl on the Red River, became the South's principal distribution centers for military matériel, received by wagon train from Brownsville-Matamoros. In general, each enormously profitable cycle was begun by loading a ship at New Orleans with salt, flour, or medical supplies—the three items whose lack was most acutely felt by the Confederate military. The boat was then dispatched to Port Isabel or Bagdad, and its cargo lightered ashore or ferried up-river to Brownsville.

Here it was sold to speculators—boom-time Brownsville swarmed with them—or loaded into wagon trains and hauled overland to Shreveport or Marshall, where it was exchanged, either by barter or sale, for cotton which the same wagon trains brought back to tidewater on the return journey. This was stowed in ships which carried it either to Old or New England, where famished spinneries clamored for supplies of staple. The cotton was purchased with Confederate paper currency, referred to disparagingly as "shinplasters." It was sold for gold. Even when paid for at Boston in greenbacks, the difference in exchange values afforded a dazzling additional profit.

Narciso records he bought $30,000 in Confederate currency in New Orleans on learning it could be exchanged for $15,000 in gold at Brownsville and set out for that port in September 1862. He had relinquished his Bonnet Carre position; at least, he never returned to the Louque plantation and so must have brought his wife and baby to her brother's home in New Orleans soon after closing out the cattle business in August.

Arrived at Brownsville, he discovered that the local market for Confederate currency had plummeted. No whit discouraged, he bought a horse and set out for the interior to purchase cotton with his capital, instead of exchanging it for gold at the new depressed rate. If his account of the journey is to be credited, hair-raising adventures were met at almost every turn of the road to Corpus Christi. He described in vast detail how he was twice held up but escaped with the $30,000 in his saddlebags, though he was armed with no weapon more formidable than a double-edged pocket knife.

At length he reached Alleyton, where he met several former Catalonians, among them one Galzerán, whose offer of assistance he gladly accepted. It is not clear from the "Few Remarks" whether, with Galzerán's help, he actually bought $24,000-worth of cotton and stored it with Galzerán's brokers until he should send back a wagon train for it; or whether, on Galzerán's advice, he deposited the money with the brokers. In all probability it was the latter.

When he set out to ride back to Brownsville, his Alleyton friends urged him to go armed and gave him a revolver. Since one of their servants was being dispatched to Monterrey anyway, they insisted that he ride along with the doctor as a sort of bodyguard.

Safely arrived at Brownsville, the doctor crossed to Matamoros, where by now he had made a number of close friends among a colony of former Catalonians. The names of José and Luis San Román, Dimas Barreda, Fulgencio Armendais and Manuel de Liano are among those most frequently encountered. He practiced medicine very successfully, but ultimately applied to the American (i.e., Union) consul for assistance in returning to New Orleans. Through that official's intercession place was found for him aboard a Union military transport vessel, another very revealing footnote on the relations between him and General Butler. The three-day passage between Bagdad and New Orleans passed without incident, "but," reports the autobiography, "it was again dangerous and full of excitement. The *Alabama* (a Liverpool-built privateer, commanded by Admiral Raphael Semmes, which destroyed sixty-six Union ships before she was finally sunk off Cherbourg by the *Kearsarge*) had just passed, and sunk the transport *Hatteras* . . . as a neutral, the doctor was simply a spectator, but he knew too well that if [the *Alabama* were encountered] he would run the same risk as the others. Very fortunately, the *Alabama* did not come in the course."

After a tender reunion with his wife "and his dear little boy whose absence had caused many sad moments especially at hours of danger," he bought a schooner, changed her registry from American to Mexican, loaded her with flour, and sent her on to Brownsville with instructions to the captain to sell the vessel there after discharging her cargo. The captain had a good offer for the schooner but held out for a higher figure, tried to cross the bar without a pilot, ran aground, and had to jettison the flour, which suffered extensive water damage. Nonetheless, it was sold for $18 gold a barrel, having cost only $7.00 in Confederate paper. But what was left of the schooner barely sufficed to cover the cost of salvage.

In evaluating this narrative, an unsolved mystery is encountered at this point. On the record, Narciso had no more than $4000 when he returned to Brownsville from Alleyton. Of his original $30,000 he had spent or deposited $24,000 for cotton. Travel expenses, including such items as purchase of a horse, would more than account for the remaining $2000. Obviously, $4000 would not have sufficed to buy a schooner, equip her, and load her with flour; yet that was only the beginning of his current investment. He followed the ill-starred schooner in the packet boat *Red Fox*, on which he had loaded corn, bagging, cordage, twelve fully equipped wagons with harness, and a large consignment of Havana cigars. It goes without saying, therefore, that he was not the sole backer of this latest and, despite continuing misfortunes, most profitable undertaking.

Not long thereafter, the Union government finally yielded to the clamor of protest against what General Butler was doing in New Orleans and replaced him with General Banks as commander of the department of the Gulf.

Early in 1863 back home in Lowell, Ben was still urging brother Andrew to wind up their business along the Gulf, and Dr. Matas at Matamoros was trying to save his cotton from Union forces, Confederate forces, and various embattled Mexican factions. Each side tried to burn all cotton awaiting shipment in order to keep it from falling into the hands of the opposition.

Meanwhile, Andrew Butler encountered no end of difficulties, now that General Banks was in military command. On February 1, 1863, he wrote to brother Ben at Lowell: "I have drawn for $274,683 to pay 829 hlds. tobacco shipped to New York. I am closing up as fast as possible, but have innumerable obstacles thrown in my way." A fortnight later he wrote again that "I will not be able to leave for 20 or 30 days. It will take that long to wind up. They seize everything that comes from below, and it takes from one to eight days to get it past that bulletheaded commission. But it will pay me something for all the drawbacks and charges."

The same obstacles were thrown into Narciso Matas's path, but on the personal side he fared much better with those among whom he practiced medicine at Matamoros when not guarding his cotton against hostiles. A German whom he restored to health paid him a fee of $300 gold. Beyond doubt his Mexican friends sought to persuade him to cast his lot among them permanently; a renowned practicing physician might well be called by Maximilian, after that worthy had been crowned emperor, as now seemed certain with Bazaine holding the capital. Why not? Had not Maximilian himself once summoned a Dr. Louis de Wecker to Miramar all the way from Paris and urged him to remain at court? Earlier this same Frankfurt-born, Austria-naturalized, Vienna-educated Parisian had been personal physician and traveling companion to Count Stroganov, gayest of the Czar's playboy cousins and godfather to a recipe for cooking beef in sour cream. Inclusion of a personal physician in one's entourage was in that era one of the fashionable perquisites of royalty and the peerage.

But young Dr. Matas was as doubtful of Maximilian's success as he was of the Confederacy's victory. His primary concern was to convert his cotton into cash or credit. Some of it finally went aboard one steamer, bound for Liverpool, some of it into another vessel which appears to have been lost at sea. The howling northers of early spring interposed endless delays to all operations for lightering cargo from shore to ship. Despite a violent storm, he accompanied some ships' officers in a lighter to the steamer *Barcelona* to cash a warrant on her purser. "It was raining and cold like ice," relates the autobiography. "The lighter called loud to the men of the steamer but nobody appeared. Finally in one of those big jumps of the lighter the doctor got hold of a rope on the steamer and in a minute he found himself with fingers and hand nearly frozen hanging over the sea being impossible to go any further. At that supreme moment the thought of his wife and his little son came before him and making a supreme effort he succeeded in calling the attention of the watchman of the steamer who immediately put a rope around him and with the help of other seamen hoisted him up to the steamer. . . . As soon as the weather allowed the lighter to come out after four or five days he took the money and went ashore," since the *Barcelona* was not putting in at New Orleans. "A small schooner was the only thing he could get and he went aboard of her, reaching New Orleans after six days navigation until at last he could see and embrace once more his little boy and his wife."

His account of the episode is brought to a close with the following reflection:

"The hardships, dangers, privations, and moral suffering experienced [during] that unfortunate trip to Brownsville can hardly be believed. It requires a combination of fatal circumstances such as have been described to produce such terrible effects. It is only by a man having a most strong constitution, courage, youth, and hope that they could be successfully resisted. The idea of having or possessing wealth to a man of family gives the courage to his heart to go through the most arduous enterprises and it gives him valor also to face the most dangerous situations. Few men who go today to the Klondike gold fields will have to face more suffering and dangers than what the doctor met in this unfortunate trip."

Narciso must have engaged in some prolonged soul-searching before deciding where next to settle. First, of course, he must go to England; a substantial fortune awaited him at Liverpool, where the cotton he had bought at Alleyton and shipped from Matamoros was finally sold. But after that, whither?

Return to New Orleans? A community seething with bitterness against anything and anyone tainted with Butler association? Assuredly not; and just as assuredly, not to medical practice at Bonnet Carre where plantation fortunes had been wiped out and no planter could have further interest in chattels of which the Emancipation Proclamation had permanently deprived him.

Return to Matamoros and the Catalonian expatriates who had welcomed him to their closely knit coterie? No; Mexico was in the throes of a three-way civil and foreign war which would obviously be worsened if Maximilian ever swallowed Bazaine's fiction that he had been summoned by popular demand to become Emperor of a supposedly fallen Republic.

We must not lose sight of the fact that Narciso was at this time only twenty-six years old, with a fortune in his pocket and a son at his side. What more natural than a desire to parade both before Gerona and San Felíu? With Teresa and Rodolphe he embarked at New Orleans for Havana in the late summer of 1863 and revisited brother-in-law Jerónimo's cousins who had been their hosts in the honeymoon days of 1856. From Havana they took ship for New York; from New York for Liverpool, where a financial balance was finally struck. Then on by ship to Spain's Mediterranean coast, to bask in the flattering admiration, not untinged with envy, of family and friends, admiration for one who had dared greatly in lands beyond the seas, returning with visible proof that there the streets must indeed be paved with gold.

CHAPTER III

During the Second Empire, Paris became the world's foremost center of science, learning, and the arts. Charles Louis Napoleon Bonaparte, who called himself Napoleon III, may indeed have been the visionary fop to whom contemporaries referred derisively as Moustachu, or Napoleon the Little. But avid to win for himself at least a reasonable facsimile of the veneration in which France had enshrined his uncle, he laid himself out to be all things to all Frenchmen.

His domestic policy coupled a WPAish program of government construction projects with "cheap bread," by way of assuring what passed for prosperity among the masses. But he catered to other echelons of the body politic as well. To win the support of financiers and merchants, he extended and liberalized credit. To gain adherents among the aristocrats, he maintained the most lavish court in Europe, thus allaying their fears of possible sans-culotte resurgence, however much they might look down their noses at beautiful Eugénie in the role of Empress.

Finally, to curry favor with the clerical and scholastic elements, he gave them back at least nominal control of the colleges. In consequence, they made unprecedented progress, especially in the field of medicine. Students and practitioners flocked to Paris from all quarters of the globe for certificates, licenses, *ad eundem* recognition, and other learned degrees. Among them in 1864 was Dr. Narciso Matas.

The several *écoles, instituts,* and *académies* of the University were scattered along the left bank of the Seine, opposite the island on which

Julius Caesar had bluntly decreed Lutetia to be the capital of Gaul. Roman profiteers built magnificent villas along stone roads that led from this section to the Mediterranean. Naturally, Latin continued to be its everyday speech. Indeed, even within the past hundred years, professors and pupils conversed only in Latin throughout what is still called the Latin Quarter.

Its Broadway, Piccadilly, Via del Corso, Ringstrasse—in short, its Main Street—was the Boulevard St.-Michel. Hard by the point where this thoroughfare crossed the Boulevard St.-Germain, Narciso engaged the apartment to which he brought his wife and son. Hereabouts dwelt the more affluent students, artists, and savants. Starvelings among the poets, musicians, and painters lived along narrow, crooked streets in a section where newcomers, eager to be shocked, were invariably shown the house which the Marquis de Sade had occupied when not in prison for publishing appallingly pornographic novels.

Both Narciso's family and Teresa's had tried to dissuade him from going to Paris. It was their idea he should settle in Gerona, or at least no farther away than Barcelona, as a practicing physician. Why Paris for instruction? they demanded. Had he not already learned what the schools could teach? Had he not practiced for half a dozen years? Besides, where in all France was there to be found a physician to compare with Barcelona's world-renowned Dr. Letamendi?

Certainly the resumption of his ancestral name, Hereu, must have appealed strongly to Narciso's love of the dynastic. But in no other respect could a man of his temperament have brought himself at that time to consider a day-in-day-out routine of cupping patients for fevers, attending women in labor, extracting decayed teeth, and otherwise sinking back into dull provincial practice of the sort from which his departure—or dismissal—from Norbert Louque's plantation at Bonnet Carre had liberated him.

It was Teresa who insisted the time had come to strike root, to enter their son in a good school, and, above all, to keep him there; and where better than in the dear, familiar soil that had given them birth? Little Rodolfo's upbringing would inevitably suffer if he were transplanted every few months. She too wanted to maintain constant friendships, with no more lonely vigils in some alien land while her husband dashed off in quest of who knew what. They had amassed enough to assure them of security. Why risk it to seek still more?

For a time he let her have her way, listening tolerantly without receding from his avowed resolve to broaden the scope of his medical knowledge by a year of specialized study in Paris. At length patience gave way to resentment. What could she offer by way of recompense for the dullness she wanted him to accept forthwith? All too obviously her outlook, like her physical appearance, was becoming more and more that of a woman nearing the forties, whereas he, a man of twenty-seven, still responded to the hot pulses of youth.

At the time of their marriage he had accepted the disparity in their ages not because of desire, but to fulfill an obligation. Nonetheless, he would never agree to quench for all time the bright fires of his young manhood simply because Teresa was growing old; not when a wide and wonderful world held out the thrill of the unexpected and the unknown. With curt finality he put an end of further discussion of their course. They would go at once to Paris.

The pension he selected as their dwelling place was ideally situated for both of them. In the shadow of the reopened Sorbonne, it was also within easy walking distance of the *Ecole de Médecine*, the *Ecole Pratique*, half a dozen hospitals, and on the Rue Jacob both the *Charité* and the clinic of Louis de Wecker. This was the brilliant surgeon of whom Narciso had first heard in Matamoros as onetime personal physician of Maximilian. He had finally cast aside the easy luxuries of court appointment to study in Berlin under Albrecht von Graefe, the world's foremost pioneer of eye surgery, a brilliant zealot of experimental science who literally worked himself into the grave at forty-two years of age. Under his tutelage de Wecker also won renown; it was to him that Narciso Matas applied for instruction.

Teresa had merely submitted—not agreed—to her husband's decision to leave Gerona for Paris. During the tedious journey she reminded him in a hundred petty ways that she came because of compulsion rather than desire to remain at his side. Yet even she found their new home at the pension on the Boulevard St.-Michel agreeable. The churches of St.-Julien-le-Pauvre and St.-Séverin were almost cheek by jowl with their dwelling place. Notre Dame was but a few blocks away on the *Ile de la Cité*. Almost immediately around the corner was an *école des enfants*, not yet known by Froebel's designation of "kindergarten," where, two or three mornings a week, little Rudolph, as he was ultimately to be named, regardless of baptism, could play group games, sing, and weave bright paper mats with other children. He was soon jabbering French as though he had never lived anywhere but along the Seine.

This was the year in which he and his father discovered one another. Up to that time Narciso had seen so little of his son that the child merely represented fulfillment of the flesh-of-my-flesh yearning inherent in all men. As for the boy, he had theretofore known his sire only as a slim, swiftly moving adult who bobbed up unexpectedly and briefly from time to time as part of the household, and then vanished as abruptly and inexplicably as he had come. In a sense, they had all been together during the long sea voyage. But his mother had been sick in their cabin most of the time and his father had remained almost constantly in the smoking room. During this fortnight of association they had actually been less of a family unit than before. In London, to be sure, his mother had recovered, and his father had let him run riot in a toyshop, buying for him whatever he wanted, despite Teresa's scandalized protests. But through it all there had been no link of shared affection to bind them.

In Paris, however, there sprang up between father and son a mutual devotion. More and more frequently, the two went on rambling walks in the late afternoons, enchanting excursions utterly unlike the staid outings on which he accompanied his mother. She always took him first to church and then perhaps to some small playground square. Here he might occasionally roll a hoop or participate in decorous games of tag with other children. But for the most part his mother required him to sit primly at her side on one of the wooden benches which rimmed the circular walks of crushed stone, where starchily uniformed *bonnes* flirted with conscripts.

Somewhere in the Paris of that year one such *bonne* wheeled in his perambulator an infant for whom Paris in time would name a little square that was destined to replace one wing of Hôtel-Dieu, adjoining the church of St.-Julien-le-Pauvre: the Square René-Viviani. The year-old baby of 1864 would serve France as premier half a century later, when Sarajevo triggered what was ultimately known as the First World War. Yes, and among the medical students Narciso met casually was a youthful Georges Clemenceau. As *Le Tigre* he would succeed Viviani in the premiership.

Naturally, none of what the future thus held in store leavened the insipid sameness of Rudolph's outings with his mother. By contrast, walks with his father were all the more adventurous. When they visited Notre Dame it was not to genuflect and light tapers but to converse with the gargoyles, to whom, one by one, young Dr. Matas ceremoniously introduced his son. Their favorite was The Philosopher, so named because he was obviously a mixture of raven and parrot and hence blended wisdom with loquacity. They further agreed they could never come to any semblance of friendly terms with a gargoyle Narciso called "surly old Cerberus," conceding he had only one head but insisting his ill temper sufficed for the conventional three, as evidenced by the fashion in which he growled and snarled stonily at everyone he could see from his cornice.

The boy yearned to possess a gargoyle or so of his very own, and for once his mother, quite possibly misled into accepting this as evidence of interest in the church, bought him some miniature plaster replicas.

He was delighted, but unfortunately forgot them after placing them on a bench in the park that same afternoon. However, his father more than compensated for this bereavement by buying him a small white rabbit at a pet stall in the market. They conceded that, as a substitute gargoyle, he had fully as much right to a name as the stone originals, but were never able to agree on one. Consequently, the bunny remained his own *cher 'ti' lapin* even after he was no longer *petit* but had waxed fat on the lettuce leaves and carrots Teresa grudgingly provided for him.

On other occasions his father would tell him wonderful stories as they strolled through the city. Once, for example, they came across a group of children noisily playing at seesaw. Just such a scene in just such a place, and quite possibly in this selfsame park, had led to a great medical discovery, Narciso said. A young physician named Laennec had seen some children press their ears to one end of a seesaw plank while another of their playfellows tapped the opposite end with his finger tips. The sound was inaudible to bystanders, yet those whose ears were pressed against the wood could hear it plainly. Hastening to the Necker hospital—and one day his father would take Rudolph there—Laennec fashioned the world's first stethoscope, a wooden rod, one end of which could be pressed against a patient's chest while the physician held his ear firmly to the other. This, explained Narciso, had simply revolutionized the science of medical diagnosis because of the clarity with which heartbeats and lung sounds became audible.

The boy remembered these stories with a retentiveness that amazed his father. True, Narciso had always said his son was no ordinary child. Even as a cradled infant his glance had been meaningful. But never had he expected such talents as he now revealed. Often in the evenings, just before bedtime, Narciso would disassemble for him the large papier-mâché-and-plaster model of a human eye which he and his fellow students used in laboratory work.

"*Tu vois ça?*" he would ask, pointing. "*Ça, c'est la cornée!*"—or "*la pupille*," or "*l'iris*," as the case might be. Rudolph would dutifully repeat the proper designation and later, when asked "*Qu'est-ce que c'est?*" would give the proper response, capering about the room at his father's words of praise in a delight too vast to be contained in his small body.

It was not always the inanimate model which figured in these tours de force. Narciso and his classmates had made an arrangement with one of the butchers at Les Halles Centrales, the market beyond the Louvre, newly completed as part of Napoleon III's public works program. The meat seller gathered for them the eyes of slaughtered sheep, cattle, and pigs. These they would take to the home of one or another of the study group, frequently the apartment of Narciso, and there they would practice the delicate techniques of de Wecker and Galezowski, a brilliant Pole whose clinics they also attended.

Ocular surgery had entered a new era with von Graefe, who viewed the medical shibboleths of his day with little of the reverential awe customarily accorded them. Among other things, he was one of the first to deliver his lectures in German instead of Latin. One of the greatest advances he pioneered was the surgical treatment of cataract. For centuries prior to his time, this malady had called for "couching." A bluntly pointed rod was thrust into the eyeball, and with it the clouded, opaque lens was pushed to one side, away from the pupil, which thereafter gave passage to unfocused light rays. Even as late as the 1860's, itinerant charlatans still wandered from village to village, couching cataracts along the roadside for pay whenever patients presented themselves.

Von Graefe, and after him his disciples, surgically removed an opaque lens, cutting through the iris to make room for its passage. They invented new lancets and other instruments to aid them in their work and reduced postoperative eye degeneration to a fractional minimum of that which followed couching. With rapt attention, the students who flocked to Paris in this era watched de Wecker and Galezowski—who, incidentally, were almost rabidly jealous of one another—as the masters went about their delicate work in the amphitheater of clinic and hospital. As nearly as might be, they emulated these techniques faithfully with the eyes of slaughtered sheep and cattle, standing about the living-room tables frock-coated and bearded, just as did their preceptors in the operating room, and even smoking cigars while they wielded their surgical instruments, for the belief was still widely held that smoke acted as a fumigant.

Occasionally, after the students returned from lectures or clinical demonstrations and practiced on eyes from the slaughterhouse, Narciso would call his small son into the room; pointing to one part of a dissected eye, he would ask what it was. "*La cornée*," or "*l'iris*," the child replied unerringly. It would be difficult to say which of the two Matas males was more swollen with pride over the applause these achievements evoked.

As might be expected, Teresa was bitterly opposed to having a room turned into a dissecting parlor but realized that this was another of the burdens she was fated to bear. Even so, she found Paris a much pleasanter abiding place than she had anticipated. Certainly it was more to her liking than the mosquito-swarming, flood-menaced River Road at Bonnet Carre or the periodically fever-ridden and tumultuous life of New Orleans, where she had not even troubled to learn French.

Now, however, she acquired enough of the language to chat with other matrons in the little squares where children played decorously about the crushed-stone walks, or in the Luxembourg gardens which she could reach from her pension by a short stroll along the Boulevard St.-Michel. Occasionally engaging a fiacre, she would have herself and Rudolph driven out to the Bois de Boulogne. She could afford such minor extravagances, though she still haggled over every sou with the stall keepers at the market and would buy none of the trumpery toys Rudolph wanted, reminding him of the gargoyles he had so heedlessly lost the very day she bought them for him.

As a matter of course, Teresa was bewildered by the war talk she heard on every hand. In this respect Paris apparently differed no whit from Louisiana, except that now the figure of special omen was someone called Bismarck instead of someone called Lincoln. Apparently discord was everywhere; everywhere, that is, except in serene, peaceful San Felíu de Guixols. If only she were younger, and pretty enough to maintain more of a hold on her husband's capricious fancy, she could insist that they return to Catalonia. Each passing day made more evident her inability to bridge the widening rift between her husband and herself. All the tender things he had said that hot and dreadful September evening after he and a slave woman delivered her of their son were now forgotten. Perhaps if baby Teresita had not died of bad milk and worse nursing, perhaps if she could bear him another child—but why spin foolish dreams? To hold Narciso she must rely on a father's love for his son; he no longer felt even affection for his wife.

Naturally, Rudolph had no foreboding of what such a situation must bring in its train. Nonetheless, he made his first poignant contact with tragedy at this season. Returning to the apartment from an outing with his mother, he discovered that his *cher 'ti' lapin* had vanished. The slatted hutch stood forlorn and empty, its leather-hinged door sagging wide. For days the pension was an abode of mourning. Narciso's offer to buy another rabbit was rejected.

Then, quite miraculously, the *cher 'ti' lapin* reappeared. One morning when Rudolph arose he discovered his darling back in its cage, fat and torpid as ever, wobbling its nose over some lettuce leaves and occasionally flicking a pinkly translucent ear. His shrill welcome to the returnee was nothing short of rapturous; neither then nor later was he aware that *la pupille* of one albino-red eye was substantially larger than its mate. Even had this come to his notice, it must be doubted he would connect the circumstance with his father's long-cherished ambition to perform a practice iridectomy on a living creature and not merely on slaughterhouse refuse.

Toward the close of his study year, a chance meeting brought Narciso into contact with a young man destined to play a larger role in four-year-old Rudolph's future than any other individual encountered during the European sojourn. This was Edmond Souchon, of New Orleans, a modishly bearded youth who had come to France in 1860 to study medicine. Eruption of Civil War hostilities deprived him at one stroke of means either to return to his blockaded homeland or continue his stay abroad.

He had begun his studies under the busiest surgeon in Paris, Alfred Velpeau, of whom Oliver Wendell Holmes once said that a sound head above a pair of wooden shoes was infinitely better than a wooden head whose owner's feet were shod in finest calfskin. When the war marooned Souchon, Dr. Velpeau found him a minor position at the Charité. It paid approximately $20 a month, by grace of which, as Dr. Souchon confessed in a published memoir many years later, "I was starving to death as slowly as I could."

A curious sort of coincidence saved him from transmuting a figure of speech into hard reality. As he was donning his hospital apron early one morning, a visitor inquired in English whether Dr. Velpeau was about and was as delighted to receive a fluent English response as he was cast down by its import, for Souchon informed him Dr. Velpeau was absent not merely from the hospital but from Paris on a fortnight's vacation.

Thereupon the stranger introduced himself as Dr. Marion Sims, a New York surgeon. Learning that his vis-à-vis claimed New Orleans as his home, and sensing a sudden cooling of prior cordiality, he hastened to add that his birthplace was in Alabama. His purpose in coming to Paris, he continued, was to demonstrate before Velpeau a new operation which almost invariably rectified vesicovaginal fistulae, theretofore considered irremediable.

A fortnight later, with Souchon as interpreter, this request was formally laid before Dr. Velpeau, who, though openly skeptical of the American's claims, finally put at his disposal a charity patient on whom he could demonstrate his instruments and techniques. The result impressed even the most biased of Paris' medical reactionaries. Sims was accepted by the local faculty and was subsequently called to treat sufferers in many of the courts of Europe.

Some two years later Edmond Souchon came to the end of his financial tether. There was simply no further possibility of continuing both his studies and his existence on a total income of $20 a month. In desperation he appealed to Dr. Sims, who, in thanking him for his services years before, had urged him to "call on me if I can ever be of help to you." Making a frank statement of his situation, Souchon asked for the loan of a dollar a day until such time as he could complete his medical education or re-establish connections with his family in New Orleans. Protesting that this would be too little, Sims insisted that the stranded student accept two dollars a day. They compromised on a dollar and a half.

"The check came every month, no matter where [Dr. Sims] was, in France, England, Germany, or America," Dr. Souchon wrote long afterwards. "He made such a deep impression on me by his goodness, his gentleness, that for many years of the early part of my life he was the model and the guiding star I strove to follow." He also named his only son, who succeeded him as a physician, Marion Sims Souchon.

Souchon's contacts with Narciso Matas in Paris, however brief and casual, must have been anything but friendly. Certainly no fiery partisan of the Confederacy could have entertained any feeling of cordiality for one who had collaborated with the rapacious Butler brothers in the occupation of New Orleans. In all likelihood he never met Narciso's four-year-old prodigy of a son. Yet a baker's dozen of years later, when Edmond Souchon was demonstrator in anatomy at the University of Louisiana, one of his most brilliant pupils would be Rudolph Matas. And many years later still, Marion Souchon's son, a second Edmond, would attend the lectures of Dr. Rudolph Matas when the latter was Tulane University's professor of surgery.

Even had not the hostility of partisanship kept the two young men—Matas and Souchon—from becoming friends in Paris, Narciso's completion of his apprenticeship under de Wecker put an end to further contact between them. The certificate de Wecker gave him attested to the excellence of his work during the year of training and vouched for his qualifications to practice ophthalmology. Its receipt also posed the peremptory question: "Whither now?" Should he remain in Paris where he would have to compete with the world's most renowned specialists in a relatively narrow field? That was obviously impracticable, as would also be the case, and for much the same reason, in Berlin and Vienna or London.

The idea of returning to New Orleans merited not even a moment's serious consideration, though Tomás Jorda had invited him to do so. With the city still under military occupation (this would not be lifted for nearly fifteen years) he probably could not even secure official permission to resume residence there. In any case, the population would be implacably bitter against collaborationists.

Well, then; if not Europe or Louisiana, what of Matamoros-Brownsville? His many friends in the Catalan colony there, notably the San Romans, would gladly make a place for him. But even considered as one community, the twin border cities were too small to support a specialist in ophthalmology. Though he derived an income from invested capital, he would still have to resume the drudgery of general practice there, thus setting his newly acquired skills pretty much at naught.

But why not the northeastern area of the United States? Certainly Dr. Sims had made his mark and his fortune there, after migrating to New York from Alabama. The region was populous and wealthy enough to provide a highly remunerative practice for a specialist who possessed a Paris certificate. Had not Georges Clemenceau fled thither when his political views brought him into conflict with the reigning clique? A graduate physician, Clemenceau was nonetheless supporting himself well by teaching French and writing news dispatches for *Le Temps* of Paris. Narciso put the proposal to his wife. What would she think of moving to New York or Philadelphia?

She was not slow in giving him her reply. Taking full advantage of the fact that he could not dash off without her unless he also left his son behind, she delivered an ultimatum. If he went anywhere but to Catalonia, he would go alone. She had accepted the year in Paris, but only because she believed that at its end they would return to their homeland. If he insisted on some wild excursion into the blue, well and good. She would not accompany him; and since he could not assume the responsibilities of caring for a small child on his adventurous travels, he would have to provide the means by which she and their son could live decently at home during his absence. She was well aware of his indifference toward her as a woman. She knew what she knew. But certainly he would not let their son become a dependent on the bounty of relatives, and so the case was that he could remain in Catalonia with his wife and son, or he could bolt alone to any part of the world he chose.

Narciso gave in. It was the last time he would do so. Actually he had no overwhelming convictions at this time about wandering afar. Barcelona, seat of a brilliant and ancient culture, was no village in which a man of eager intellectual curiosity would stagnate. Moreover, his heritage of blood and spirit had been bequeathed to him by Catalonia. Why should not the son who would carry that heritage a generation further be reared as a Catalan?

So it was decided. They would return first to Gerona and after appropriate family reunions would settle in Barcelona. Teresa took charge of the matter of packing their possessions for the long railway journey. While she went fussily about this task, Narciso took his son on farewell rambles over the familiar left-bank scenes they might perhaps never revisit.

As a matter of course, they paid several courtesy calls on The Philosopher, perched high among his fellow gargoyles on the cornice of Notre Dame. They strolled down the rue de l'Ecole de Médecine, Narciso explaining that it had once been a Roman road, where later the Guild of Barber-Surgeons maintained their headquarters, they being permitted to practice minor surgery, principally leeching and bloodletting, once regarded as sovereign palliatives for almost any ailment. And here, on the corner opposite the Ecole de Médecine, was the very house in which Charlotte Corday had murdered one of the architects of the Terror, Jean-Paul Marat, by stabbing him while he was or was not—Narciso said there were two stories of the incident—in his bath.

He also redeemed his promise to take Rudolph to the Necker hospital, which should be maintained as a shrine, since it was here that Laennec had fashioned the world's first stethoscope. Rudolph must be careful to remember all these scenes, for someday—who knew?—he might be sent to Paris to study medicine. The world was at sixes and sevens. With endless Carlist revolts seeking to oust Isabella from the Spanish throne, and Napoleon III making emperors in Mexico, the future was indeed uncertain, though in America the Civil War was at last wearing to a close. Perhaps when all the bitterness was forgotten they might return to New Orleans for a visit with Uncle Tomás. Meanwhile, he must be a good boy and learn well the lessons he would be taught when he went to school that fall in Barcelona.

In addition to the few pieces of furniture which were nailed up in wooden boxes and the garments which were packed in a tin trunk with a domed lid and the polished ebony case in which Narciso's precious instruments were stowed, Teresa filled a hamper with food to be taken along on the journey. She did not trust her husband's assurance that trains stopped at mealtimes where passengers could dine at railway stations, inexcusable as the tedious length of their journey might be.

"It is fantastic nonsense," he raged, "that in this day and age one who wishes to travel from Paris to Madrid must go around one end or the other of the Pyrenees, either by way of Irún on the west or Port Bou on the east. The time is coming, and soon, when there will be a track straight across the mountains, through one of the passes, probably Somport. If it was in operation now, we could cut down our journey by two-thirds. In the first place, I will have to go to Madrid anyway, after we get home, to secure my license from the University's medical faculty and the government. In the second place, there is already a railway line from Madrid to Barcelona."

However, the weary journey was accomplished at long last, though they traveled first to Toulouse and then to storied Carcassonne and Perpignan and finally to Port Bou, in the home province of Gerona

and on the very threshold of San Felíu. There Teresa and little
Rudolph remained, while Narciso journeyed on to Madrid to comply
with official licensing formalities. On the way back he stopped at
Barcelona to make a binder payment on the purchase of a home and
to present himself before the great José de Letamendi who would
take him under his wing, personally and professionally, as one of the
resident physicians of Catalonia's ancient capital.

CHAPTER IV

When Narciso Matas brought his family to Barcelona in 1865 it was with every intention of settling there for the balance of his days. He purchased a commodious house near the Rambla on the Street of the Princess, remodeled one of its ground-floor apartments into a surgery which included waiting and consultation rooms, and resumed the family name of Hereu. In short, to the entire satisfaction of all concerned, and particularly of his family and Teresa, he undertook a permanent return to the land of his birth.

Yet within two years he was back in New Orleans, striving valiantly but without either understanding or success to help stay the progress of a dreadful yellow-fever epidemic. Within a matter of months after that he was once more a general medical practitioner in Matamoros-Brownsville, which he soon left for Arizona, where, until a year or two before his death, he sought fortune in various mining ventures. He never again revisited his birthplace. Indeed, he never again set foot on European soil. His ashes are entombed in New Orleans' Metairie Cemetery.

How far should one probe to determine a cause for so abrupt a reversal of what set out to be an established way of life? By 1867, two years after leaving Paris, Narciso was fully reintegrated, a native Catalan returned to his homeland with wealth and wisdom acquired in the far places of earth. Not only that, but the city's greatest man, Dr. José de Letamendi—physician, professor, writer, painter, composer—was his patron.

Narciso's son, five-year-old Rodolfo Hereu y Jorda, who had been baptized Rodolphe Matas in New Orleans, was enrolled in the school of his mother's church parish where, except for a minor block in the area of arithmetic, he again became known as an infant prodigy.

Moreover, Teresa had ceased to complain. Ninety years later her son recalled that she seemed happier during that brief Barcelona interlude, than he ever knew her to be thereafter or theretofore. Perhaps she even became reconciled to her obvious inability to rekindle the embers of Narciso's ardor. But she had at least made good her veto of his proposal to wander about the world. Not only were they settled, as all respectable, God-fearing families should be; their abiding place was but a few kilometers distant from San Felíu de Guixols, and, thanks to the rail line from Barcelona to Perpignan, Teresa could visit her family as often as she chose.

Also, she could and did make frequent pilgrimages to Montserrat, shrine of the dark Virgin, *la Patrona de Cataluña*, high on the mountain which was supposedly cloven at the time of the crucifixion. Finally, in Barcelona as elsewhere along the Costa Brava, the winters were balmy; yet Teresa was not walled off in the isolation that had been her portion in Louisiana, nor was she subject to that region's mosquito-swarming twilights, the menace of floods, and the ever recurrent epidemics of yellow fever, to which she was now immune, though so many others—her little son, for one—were not.

Yet almost overnight we find Narciso once more penniless, delving for a fresh start in America, his son in bondage to schools where English was the speech of the classrooms, his wife a blank, unsmiling presence in the home where before long she would bear him another child.

The immediate cause of this turnabout is plain enough. But its prime mover was Clovis, first convert to Christianity among sovereigns of the Salian Franks. One of his bequests to posterity was a code of laws, most of which dealt with criminal jurisprudence, but one of whose provisions prohibited the inheritance of property by a female.

In time, this one provision became "the" Salic law, and specifically banned accession to a throne through the female side of any royal family. But the seventh Ferdinand repealed the Salic law in 1833, in order to pass the throne on to his three-year-old daughter, who grew up to demonstrate that she had inherited most of the worst vices of her forebears. Her accession to the throne precipitated the four strife-torn decades known to history as the Carlist wars. In order to distract attention from the reeking lasciviousness of her court and from the Carlist ferment, she encouraged chaotic speculation in a new and expanding enterprise: the development of steam railroads.

At first the railroad fever passed Narciso by. Lost in admiration of José de Letamendi's many talents, he was more engrossed in emulating this brilliant patron than in the quest for wealth. It is difficult even yet to gauge de Letamendi's stature. His biographers were rhapsodic rather than objective, and the scope of his scholarship almost defies credence in this age of specialization.

It is related, for example, that, though unschooled in the casuistry of the age-old controversy between advocates of free trade and those who demand high protective tariffs, he listened for two days to a debate on this subject and then wrote so masterly a summation of the various arguments that it was used for years as a textbook.

Later in life, after he had served a term in the senate at Madrid, where he found the climate unsuited to his health, he nonetheless painted and presented to the Augustine fathers at the Escorial a tremendous mural in recognition of the first public rendition by them of a *Dies Irae* of his composition. One of the final achievements of his old age was the development of a technique long used in surgery as a precursor of local anesthesia.

Narciso and de Letamendi would have been drawn together by personal gravitation in any case. But what brought them into almost immediate close association was a series of anatomical paintings de Letamendi had recently completed in heroic scale. One of them represented the form and anatomy of a human eye. Narciso urged the artist to send this and a painting of the musculature of a human leg to the Exposition at Paris, where Napoleon III was engaged in one of his final bids for international recognition—a world's fair. De Letamendi fell in with the idea and was naturally gratified by the acclaim and the medals which this gained for him.

Narciso had hoped to specialize in ophthalmology, but de Letamendi's opinion that this would not prove feasible, even in as large a community as Barcelona, was soon borne out. Despite his Paris certificates and other degrees, and his backlog of capital, Dr. Hereu y Matas was called on more and more for the type of general practice he had hoped to escape. Nonetheless, he energetically negatived a suggestion that he operate a pharmacy in connection with his medical work.

One of the principal discussion topics of the day throughout the world was railroad development. In the United States fabulous inducements were being offered for the promotion of new routes— alternate sections of land, free station sites, tax exemption, and the like. To mid-century Europe in general, and to Spain in particular, railroads were what motor-car manufacture was in the United States during the first decades of the 1900's, with a *bouquet garni* of the stock-market craze that drew margin money from scrubwomen to bucketshops in the latter 1920's and the pyramid-club pandemic of the early 1950's.

Narciso had carefully surveyed Spain's transport problem; out of the knowledge thus gained he took pains to point out the obvious need for a tunnel through some pass in the Pyrenees, since a direct rail route between Paris and Madrid—the two most important capitals on the Continent—was essential. In the new era of steam and steel, a major detour around a relatively minor obstruction in the terrain was no longer tolerable. The mountains could be crossed at Huesca or Lérida and probably a dozen other passes besides. No more than regard what Sr. de Lesseps was doing in Egypt! A modern canal to bypass a marine detour around the Cape of Good Hope—a vastly more difficult project than a Pyrenees tunnel—was on the point of completion. It would be opened any day now, and its backers would become richer than Croesus. Investments of that sort in a vital improvement of global transportation differed from mere speculative gambling on the *lonja* as day differs from night.

Attention to such matters, a growing practice, and his association with de Letamendi left Narciso less time for companionship with his son than he had enjoyed in Paris. However, family outings were frequent enough. Sometimes these were drives to one of the nearby coastal resorts in the carriage the doctor had to maintain for his house calls. Rodolfo found such excursions little to his taste, even when their goal was one of the hill suburbs in an area called, as he frequently reminded his schoolmates, the Serranéa de Matas.

Far more intriguing were visits to the vineyard of a Jorda kinsman north of the city. Family and friends were conveyed along the Rambla and beyond its swiftly growing suburbs to hedgerowed country lanes and at last to their relative's estate, where much highly spiced food and much music and dancing were the order of the day.

Best of all, however, was the harvest season, when workers trudged in from the terraced slopes with white and purple grapes in great flat baskets which they emptied into what Rodolfo felt was the largest wooden vat in the world. Then off with shoes and stockings and so into the vats, where the children tussled and jumped up and down on the pungently aromatic grape bunches, laughing at the feel of the wet pulp between their toes.

The fact that such vineyard experiences remained sharp and vivid in a great surgeon's memory for so many years bears more eloquent witness than the testimony of contemporaries to the basically uneventful character of the life led by the Matas family during its stay in the house on Barcelona's Street of the Princess. Outstanding among his recollections beyond this were merely his mother's apparent contentment with their lot, and a small boy's preoccupation with such major events as All Saints' Day observance or the gaiety of Epiphany—Twelfth Night, January 6—when the three kings, coming to pay homage once more to the Christ child, stop along the way to distribute sweetmeats, toys, and other gifts to mortal children who obeyed their parents, studied their lessons, and were otherwise well behaved during the preceding twelvemonth.

The day of *Los Reyes* with its cakes, pomegranates, and presents, was a much more enjoyable festival than *Todos Los Santos* with its visits to churches, even though play centers were set up for the children. Here Rodolfo managed to come to grief, for he was rather an awkward boy; descending a chute, he rolled to the bottom instead of sliding and thus lost some religious medals his mother had that day bought for him. This entailed a sharp rebuke, in which his loss of miniature Notre Dame gargoyles in a Paris playground was also reviewed in some detail.

But it was a good life, and Rodolfo won the admiration of his elders by his fluency in three languages: French, Spanish, and Catalan. He even knew a few words of English and on one occasion astounded Dr. de Letamendi by correctly identifying the various features of that famous scholar's huge painting of the human eye.

Rodolfo's father was particularly expansive in this period, conducting the household extravagantly on a scale Teresa often mentioned with disapproval. But Narciso waved her protests aside, declaring they stood on the threshold of an open treasure cave rich enough to rouse the cupidity of an Arab prince. All his capital was now invested in a railroad; not just in railroad securities generally on the Exchange, where the unthinking *chusma* gambled feverishly in shares as another might gamble with dice, but in one particular railroad company which projected a direct line across the Pyrenees.

There was a contractual agreement—signed, sealed, and delivered— with a French concern, under the terms of which the Spanish partners would build a line north from Lérida to Sort, through the Segre, Noguera, and Palonesa valleys. This was no more than child's play, 125 kilometers at the most and much less if a few tunnels were driven. The French parties to the agreement already had a rail line in the Ariège valley, south from Toulouse. The French, therefore, needed only to extend this line beyond Tarascon to Ax-les-Thermes. After that nothing remained to be done but construct a connecting link through the main ridge of the mountain chain along a pass just east of Andorra. That would be a joint enterprise, and surveyors were already running their field crews along the route. With a direct rail line from Spain's largest port, Barcelona, into France, why—their fortunes were made, enough to free them for all time from concern for future security.

Month after month the ebullient young physician thus continued to speak of the golden tide they were foresighted enough to have caught at the flood. He was delighted to learn of another, and in a sense competitive, tramontane venture in Franco-Spanish rail construction, a route through the Canfranc Pass via a proposed international tunnel. All the railroads that could possibly be built would still fall far short of filling the need, he maintained.

There is no evidence that Dr. de Letamendi was caught up in the prevalent speculative mania. His remarkable analytic faculties must have clearly foretold the imminence of another period of governmental chaos. Without doubt he brought up this omen in his talks with Narciso, arguing that if Serranistas succeeded in overthrowing the queen, the numberless railroad subventions her ministers had issued during the era of recklessly encouraged wildcat promotion might not be worth the seals attached to the documents. Would it not be wise, therefore, to wait until some sort of stable government had been re-established?

To all such arguments Narciso had a ready counter. Every political party—liberals, *borbonistas*, *apostólicos*, or whatever they chose to call themselves—favored railroad expansion. No matter who held power in Madrid, the rail lines would be completed because this was essential to national welfare.

Yet in time his confidence began to wane, and he spoke with increasing bitterness of the hidebound fixity of the military mind. Everything Narciso and others had said about the need for rail construction stood uncontroverted. Yet both in Spain and in France the cabinet ministries and the general staffs were taking the position that direct rail communication across the natural rampart of the Pyrenees would make it easy for aggressors to launch hostile troop movements. Not only did they veto the projected construction programs as such but they kept the gauge of French and Spanish rail trackage at odds for almost fifty years more.

Naturally that tumbled the precariously balanced, point-down pyramid of Spanish rail speculation into a jackstraw pile of bankruptcy. Narciso lost literally everything. Even had this not been the case, his was not the temperament to settle down to a life constricted by the relatively meager income of a general practitioner which would thenceforth be his portion if he remained in Catalonia. Teresa yielded to the inevitable when he announced his decision: they would return to America forthwith, so that he might amass another fortune there.

It is a pity the doctor gave up the labor of writing his "Few Remarks" before that fascinating chronicle reached this chapter in his

biography. How, for example, did he and his wife come to their understanding after the collapse?—the brilliant, quixotic physician-adventurer, just turned thirty, and the embittered *Señora esposa*, now forty,
who had said that if ever he fared forth again from their homeland
he must go alone?

To have remained behind at the time she made this declaration
would have been unpalatable, of course. But at least Narciso would
have provided well for them, if only as a matter of personal pride.
However, should she now refuse to accompany a penniless spouse,
she would have to appeal to her relatives or his for such bare necessities
as food and shelter. Indeed, even if Narciso remained in Barcelona,
they would be dependent for a time on the direct assistance of their
kinsfolk.

On the other hand, if they all went to New Orleans together, Tomás
Jorda would see them through. He was, after all, not merely a man of
business. His principal income, which was large, stemmed from his
position as Louisiana representative of the Cuban National Lottery,
in an era when such enterprises were accepted as a normal phase of
Louisiana's prodigal way of life. Since they must seek assistance in
making a fresh start, by all means let it be from Tomás, who was in
a sense under obligation to them, since Narciso had helped him to turn
a handsome profit on cattle and cotton transactions aforetimes; and
if she must lose face, let it be among strangers rather than among the
friends and relatives with whom she had been reared and to whom
she had returned as a wealthy matron.

She made a final pilgrimage with little Rodolfo to the shrine of
la Patrona de Cataluña on Montserrat in the late spring of 1867. With
her husband and son she journeyed to San Felíu de Guixols to bid
farewell, not merely to the members of her family but to the one spot
on earth that was dearest of all to her. Alone she walked to the
promontóry from which she could see the blue and gold panorama of
the coast, set against the dark green background of cork forests and
olive groves, that the image of this beloved scene which perhaps she
would never again revisit might remain with her always.

Returning to Barcelona, Narciso took passage with his family on a
paddle-wheel steamship which was equipped with sails for auxiliary
propulsion. His was not a nature to hold attachment for any particular
spot in a world the rest of which he still wanted very much to see.
As for the journey, it was merely a workaday means to an end. But
seven-year-old Rodolfo Hereu y Jorda, soon again to become and remain Rudolph Matas, savored to the uttermost the fascinations of the
first sea voyage of which he could retain reasonably coherent memories.
These ranged from the "stock farm" he visited from time to time with

his father—the pens on the afterdeck where cattle and sheep were kept for slaughter as needed—to the incessantly plunging pistons in the engine room. Luxury liners had not yet reached even the blueprint stage. Narciso's stateroom for three was a cubicle with barracks-type bunks set one above the other and pitcher-bowl-slop-jar plumbing.

They halted briefly at Madeira and again at Havana, where they had time to go ashore for a day and meet two Jorda cousins—the Forto brothers—who were serving with the army and, having survived attacks of yellow fever to which they were thenceforth immune, planned to settle in Cuba after their enlistments came to an end. No doubt both Teresa and her husband wondered at this decision. Late in August Cuba was not the paradise it could be during January. Lack of anything remotely resembling municipal sanitation, lack even of adequate water supplies—they found it cost as much as thirty cents "oro" to have a shirt laundered—meant that personal cleanliness was on a par with the unpaved and undrained streets, markets, and living areas.

For the most part the streets themselves were used as sewers; during seasons of heavy, tropical rains, privies were emptied into the open roadways so that the filth might be carried into the harbor by the surface flow of rainwater. In fact, a dozen years hence, young Rudolph Matas would be one employee of an American Yellow Fever Commission which would report officially that "in many streets of Havana itinerant chamber-pot vendors plied a prosperous trade . . . these conveniences were daily used by many, the contents emptied into the streets, and there concealed by a thin covering of loose dirt. Nothing more stinking, nasty, and unwholesome than the privy system of Havana and of Cuba can be conceived."

Moreover the swarming mosquitoes were worse, if anything, than those of New Orleans. Though she wept at parting from her cousins, even Teresa was happy when their ship put once more to sea, where the salt tang of clean winds replaced the fetid stenches of the Pearl of the Antilles. Then, after two days, the blue Gulf water that surrounded them abruptly became brown, and they found themselves within sight of the Balize with two pilot boats racing toward them. Slowly they entered the river's mouth and proceeded upstream to the head of the passes and beyond that point to the quarantine station established twelve years earlier—two large buildings and one small one, interconnected by boardwalks on pilings above the marsh; a hospital, a warehouse, and living quarters for the physician in charge.

That functionary grew professionally friendly with Narciso as soon as he learned the visitor's identity. New Orleans, he related, was in the throes of one of the worst yellow-fever epidemics in the city's history—and all because of greed. Heretofore vessels had been held at Quarantine for ten days; if no sign of yellow fever appeared among those aboard, the ship was permitted to proceed to the city's wharves. But the merchants and shipowners—all wealthy and influential—had compelled the authorities to rest content with disinfection. Cargo holds were fumigated with burning sulphur, all fabrics or other porous materials were treated with weak solutions of carbolic acid. Thus in a matter of hours the vessel could move on upstream. . . . Yes, and there would be no less than some 4000 deaths from yellow fever in New Orleans this year before cool weather brought remission from the summer's scourge.

At the Canal Street levee Narciso and his family were met by Tomás Jorda and Anthony Sambola. The latter would put them up at his home until they could find suitable and reasonably permanent quarters. This they learned during the short carriage drive through an inert city. Nowhere was a crowd congregated. Mule cars on Canal Street trundled along with no more than one or two passengers aboard. No noisy throngs milled about the Royal Street intersection, where big sporting saloons catered now to a mere handful of customers.

Narciso would find much to do, both Anthony and Tomás assured him. As always during such sieges, the city's physicians were woefully overworked. And yet, they seemed impotent to lessen the harvest which Bronze John—current journalese for Yellow Jack—reaped from the crowded city during his visits.

Little Rudolph found time heavier on his hands than ever before in his short life. He was not allowed to leave the house or mingle with other children. The reek of burning sulphur and of crude carbolic acid which had been spread over the filthy streets from sprinkling carts, hung over everything. The silent house, the deserted thoroughfares, the lack of anything approaching the city's wonted liveliness—all these combined to create an air of general desolation.

The boy could do little more than wander about the quiet house, going from one darkened room to another. Everywhere the curtains were drawn, the shutters securely closed, so that no breath of air brought even a semblance of relief from the oppressive, humid heat. His mother would not even take him with her to church, and his father was never more than briefly in the house, night or day.

Neither of his parents was present when he first felt the onset of lassitude and then a terrifying headache. When Teresa returned she found the child in the grip of a hard, shaking ague.

CHAPTER V

Teresa bundled her small son into all the blankets she could find, removing only his shoes before putting him to bed in the enormous fourposter with its filmy mosquito bar of bobbinet. Her only thought was to warm him, regardless of the stifling heat of a New Orleans September. Was he not shaking with cold? Unwittingly, she thus hit upon the very expedient to which every physician of the era resorted in an effort to induce diaphoresis, profuse perspiration designed to "break the fever."

In the ever-deepening resentment she harbored toward Narciso she found him guilty of marking the child of her heart for death. His follies had brought them to this pass. He alone was to blame. Nonetheless, he could do more than she to snatch the boy back from the grave. All that lay within her power was to wait and pray, pray and wait. Since her husband was visiting God knew how many patients in God knew what parts of the city, she could not even dispatch a messenger in search of him.

With steadily mounting desperation she realized he probably would not even return at noon for a mouthful of food and a moment of rest, though a skillet of *grillades* and a pot of grits were ready on the stove, so that food could be set before him along with a glass of iced rum, lime juice, and sweetened water. Every ablebodied physician in New Orleans customarily remained on his rounds in those dreadful autumn days until exhaustion claimed him. A grisly total of 3107 deaths from yellow fever would be entered in the ledger of the city's vital statistics

55

for 1867, before the onset of cool weather put an end to the scourge for another season.

And still no one had any real knowledge of what caused such visitations. This year, to be sure, the outbreak could be traced to the arrival from Havana of Mrs. Hooper, wife of the captain of the bark *Florence Peters*, which docked on June 22 at the Algiers levee, after a ten-day detention at quarantine. A week later Mrs. Hooper died of yellow fever in a New Orleans boardinghouse. Her death was the first of thousands, and no one knew how it triggered the epidemic which followed.

Teresa understood little of her husband's irate diatribes against the entire medical fraternity because of their ready acceptance of explanations which to him plainly failed to explain. At every opportunity he labored the point that physicians and sanitarians knew not one whit more about the cause, transmission, prevention, and therapy of yellow fever than did their forerunners nearly two centuries earlier in 1693, when the first positive appearance of such an epidemic in the United States occurred, not along the semitropical, miasmatic Gulf marshes but in Boston.

By now it was well established that the plague had been brought to the Atlantic seaboard from Africa in slave ships and had appeared there sporadically for fifty years before its initial incidence in Havana or along the Gulf. How, then, clamored Narciso, could it originate only in the filth of local gutters or in the "morbific miasmata" exhaled when swamp soil was exposed to the air? Yet these and other equally infirm beliefs all had their passionate adherents—and with each recurrent visitation the stricken turned in disconsolate faith to their blindly groping physicians who purged, induced profuse sweating, "purified" the privies with sulphate of iron, sluiced the vicinity of each patient's dwelling with disinfectants—and waited for late autumn's first chill to end the epidemic.

So Teresa prayed while the minutes crept by and flies buzzed torpidly about the darkened and oppressively humid bedchamber. She brushed these away mechanically, as she had once waved a swish of plaited sweet-flag leaves over her baby's crib at Bonnet Carre. From time to time she placed her palm lightly on the child's forehead. Appalled by its heat and unnatural dryness, she wrung out white clothes in cologne water and bathed his temples. And all the while, in the intervals between prayers and ministrations, bitterness against her husband ate its way deeper into the core of her being.

Then it was borne in on her that in at least one respect her prayers had not fallen on deaf ears. Contrary to custom, Narciso made one of his rare noonday halts at home for a few moments of rest, and at long last she could find release for taut nerves in a storm of sobs. The responsibility was no longer hers alone. Wailing, she begged Narciso to do something for the *chiquito* who was so sick, who babbled unintelligibly as he tossed from side to side, who moaned in piteous appeal as waves of dreadful pain wracked his small body.

It will be recalled that in the biographical fragment of "Few Remarks" he wrote thirty years later, Narciso recorded how the thought of his "dear little son" had given him courage to meet whatever dangers might beset him. However, it was now not he, but the dear little son, who stood in peril of his life. One can all but feel the chill clutch of panic that must have seized him on beholding at a glance the all too familiar details he had noted in so many patients, helpless in the realization that at least a fourth of those to whom he ministered were doomed. Yet it is no less obvious that he must have mastered his emotions in that same instant, for he took immediate charge as the father stepped aside for the physician.

"Send for Dr. Armand Mercier at once," he directed. "Then heat water—there is hot water on hand already? Excellent! Bring me the foot bath and whatever other blankets are in the house. Is there powdered mustard?—— Then send to the pharmacy for a couple of pounds at once, or go fetch it yourself. We must have it immediately."

Teresa hastened to do his every bidding. Meanwhile he divested Rudolph gently of stockings, shirtwaist, underwear, and other items of clothing in which his mother had put him to bed, being careful to undress him without too greatly disturbing the blankets in which the boy was swaddled.

Long before Dr. Mercier arrived, Teresa had returned from the *boutique* with her precious packet of powdered mustard. Narciso tossed a double handful of this into the tin foot tub, reduced it to a paste with cold water, and then poured in scalding hot water until the tub was three-fourths filled. Lifting it onto the bed, he maneuvered it carefully beneath the blankets which now housed Rudolph like a tent; as tenderly as possible he immersed the boy's feet in the steaming infusion. He winced as the child shrieked but kept the little feet in the tub, to which he added a pint or so of almost boiling water from time to time as the bath cooled.

When Dr. Mercier finally entered the sickroom, he nodded approval of what had been done and placed his hand under the tented blankets to see if the desired perspiration had yet manifested itself. Later, when Rudolph's continuing moans again rose in pitch to screams as the pain from the hot mustard bath became unbearable, Dr. Mercier helped remove the tub, but kept the little patient cocooned in blankets some fifteen minutes longer. Then the two physicians dried him carefully and wrapped him in a single light blanket, so that Narciso could cradle him fondly in his arms, murmuring endearments, while Teresa flew to replace with dry linens the sheets his perspiration had soaked until even the moss-stuffed mattress felt damp.

"The sweat has come and that, as you know, is excellent," Dr. Mercier observed with obvious relief. "From now on it is merely a matter of giving him plenty of orange-leaf tea and Vichy water to drink, and tomorrow, perhaps, a mild dose of calomel. Let him have small pieces of ice to suck from time to time too. That will keep him from getting too thirsty, it will soothe his stomach, and it may save him from the painful experience of blisters or cupping. Be sure to keep a night glass by his bedside, of course, and save the contents till we can examine them."

He did his best further to reassure Teresa by urging her not to be unduly alarmed if the child's skin became yellow, almost orange-colored, for a time, or if his pulse rate became very slow. All promised to march well, so far! If only the *vómito prieto* did not come! For the rest, once their son had happily recovered from what gave every promise of being a benign attack, he would be an immune, who could walk unafraid through all the yellow-fever plagues of the future.

Teresa prayed, Dr. Mercier called twice a day, and Narciso spent at his son's bedside every moment he could spare from his rounds. Each morning he and Dr. Mercier would pour a bit of the night glass's cloudy fluid into test tubes, one of which Dr. Mercier held over the newly kindled flame of a spirit lamp while Narciso poured a few drops of acetic acid into the other.

"No albumen coagulates," Dr. Mercier observed with lively satisfaction, after the contents of his test tube had boiled briskly. "We should pay more attention to this, doctor, especially since Blair reported albuminuria in more than 500 fatal yellow-fever cases in Guiana."

"The cloudiness has all gone," Narciso reported, holding his test tube up to the light. "As for Blair, that's like all the talk about miasmata that has been accepted so complacently. None of us really knows anything about this disease."

"By the way, I asked Dr. Albers to be sure your home and its surroundings were disinfected thoroughly," Dr. Mercier went on. No such assurance was needed. The reek of carbolic acid and chlorine pervaded the entire neighborhood.

Neither albuminuria nor the ominous black vomit set in, and the small patient was not ushered out of the world by these or any other symptomatic heralds. After three days, the fever left him. He lay quietly abed then, in drained lassitude, while Teresa diligently spooned broths, barley water, orange-leaf tea, and custards into him. Dried leaves from the orange groves along the lower delta were a staple in almost every New Orleans household and grocery, for a decoction of these was held to be sovereign refreshment for invalids and convalescents.

Narciso continued to labor and to argue about prevention and causes, until cool weather brought surcease from the epidemic as October wore to its close. New Orleans was by no means the only sufferer during that autumn of 1867. Brownsville was just as hard hit, Narciso informed his wife, after receiving a letter from Dimas Barreda, welcoming him back to the Americas. Many of the Catalonian colony in Matamoros had succumbed to the plague. But he would remain in Louisiana, he assured her. Indeed as long as the epidemic raged, he was all but dragooned into continuing practice.

On the personal side, however, Narciso found nothing akin to friendliness among his colleagues. Existing rancor against collaborationists was now intensified by the descent upon Louisiana of a locust swarm of carpetbaggers. During this late autumn, a twelve-month before Republican extremists triumphantly elected Ulysses Grant to the Presidency, Andrew Johnson was already being harried and humiliated by every legislative device rapacity and implacable partisanship could bring to bear against him in Washington. Lincoln could have turned aside an onslaught of that sort with a pithy phrase or two; he had always succeeded in doing so before. Johnson lacked that gift of grace. Within ninety days he would be haled before the bar of the Senate on impeachment charges.

"Bless the President of these United States," prayed the Rev. Josiah Fisk before a carpetbag convention engaged in writing for Louisiana a new constitution dictated by those who demanded the South be treated as subjugated, not reunited, territory. "Bless the President of these United States. Enable him to pause in his career of vice and folly. May he cease from doing evil and learn to do right."

The new Constitution would disfranchise virtually the entire decent male citizenship of Louisiana by withholding the vote from all who did not sign a penitential acknowledgment that the "rebellion" and their individual share in it had been morally wrong.

A newly founded Republican daily, which would be kept alive by printing, as paid advertising at government expense, copies of bills introduced before the Congress in Washington, rejoiced: "It is certainly a great triumph for us to see proud planters, haughty chevaliers, humiliating themselves to the point of flattering their former slaves and crouching at their very feet."

Ten wretched years of such tragic excesses were to pass before a bloody pitched battle in Canal Street, and a bloodless but much more significant political barter in Washington were to release Louisiana

59

from occupation by Federal troops. It is therefore quite understandable that though Narciso was accepted professionally by fellow-practitioners in a season of critical emergency, he who had once made common cause with the Butlers was disdained as an individual. Other physicians would discuss with him the conflicting theories of how to combat Bronze John, but not the current play, the latest duel, the outrageous prices of inflation economy, or the iniquities of the rabble rout writing a new state Constitution in a shameful travesty of delegated assembly. Except in the field of medicine, he remained an Untouchable.

The epidemic of 1867 did not attain its peak of virulence until late autumn. Of the year's 3107 fever fatalities, 2709 occurred in September and October. And still physicians, sanitarians, and public officials were at loggerheads over every aspect of these almost annually recurrent visitations. Some held, with E. H. Barton, professor of medicine, president of the medical society, and chairman of a municipal sanitary commission, that turning up swamp soil and exposing its decaying "coffee grounds" to the air, released noxious vapors—miasmata —which in turn generated yellow-fever epidemics.

"Since 1796 to the present time," Barton declared unequivocally in an 1857 report, "there has been no great epidemic of yellow fever in this city without an extensive breaking up, disturbance, and exposure of the original soil of the country."*

Others insisted that the fever-producing agent, whatever it might be, was transmitted by fomites, a generic term applied to any porous substance, principally textiles, "those being the most dangerous which are the most porous." A Texas physician, Dr. J. S. West, reported in this same autumn of 1867 that a sack of coffee from stricken Corpus Christi had precipitated an inland yellow-fever epidemic in Liberty. He added that even when packed into other containers, "every family into whose house this coffee was introduced . . . was infected."

Still others clung to the theory advanced as early as 1815 by Dr. Jabez Heustis, a medical major with Andrew Jackson's forces at Chalmette: "A constitution unaccustomed to the climate is a predisposing cause, marsh miasmata the remote cause, and a fit of intoxication or exposure the exciting cause." However, Dr. Heustis also pointed out

---

* So firmly was this *ipse dixit* integrated into local folklore that the proposal in 1917, only a dozen years after New Orleans' last great yellow-fever epidemic, to dredge a ship canal from the Mississippi River to Lake Pontchartrain as a World War I project, evoked some near-hysterical protests on the ground that a fresh plague of yellow fever would be loosed upon the community by the exposure of virgin swamp muck. That was one reason the consulting engineer engaged by the city was General George W. Goethals, who had built the Panama Canal in an isthmian zone from which Bronze John had been successfully excluded.

that the "mosquitoes and other noxious insects were most numerous . . . where morbific miasmata are exhaled in greatest quantity. . . . It may therefore be considered that wherever those insects are most numerous, there also unwholesome exhalations prevail."

While physicians and sanitarians argued and debated, Bronze John continued to levy lethal tribute. New Orleans suffered annual epidemics from 1794 through 1803, when Louisiana became part of the United States. During the first sixty years of the century, the city passed through 48 major epidemics of the dread pestilence. In 1858, the year Narciso and Teresa came down with it, 4845 persons died of it in New Orleans alone; in 1853 Bronze John harvested a bumper crop of 7849 fatalities. And almost to the century's end, regardless of diaphoretics and disinfectants, only two sure safeguards against falling victim to yellow fever were acknowledged; flight from infested areas, which, in the days of darkest ignorance, was often prevented by shotgun quarantines, or recovery from a "benign" (meaning non-fatal) attack, which immunized the survivor for life against future infections.

In his conviction that filth and decay as such did not spontaneously generate yellow fever Narciso was by no means alone. Dr. Stanford E. Chaillé, later to serve as chairman of a government Yellow Fever Commission from the United States to Havana, with a brilliant young medical student from New Orleans, Rudolph Matas, as clerk, interpreter, and laboratory assistant, voiced the belief that "if infectiousness were a property resulting from filth and putrescent organic matter, the whole city was a laboratory for its generation, unsurpassed in magnitude and extent; and yet, over its entire length and breadth, the fever was confined to a narrow strip presenting an exception to the aspect of general immundicity." In fact, that epidemic appeared in, and was confined almost wholly to, a section of New Orleans which "presented an unexpectedly clean condition."

Nor were physicians the only ones to disagree among themselves as to the cause and prevention of such epidemics. Public authorities were equally at odds, especially in New Orleans, on how best to safeguard their cities. The first quarantine of inbound ships, established by Louisiana in 1820, was repealed after only four years of operation. Venice, proud mistress of the Adriatic, had set the quarantine pattern centuries earlier. Indeed, *quaránta* was the period of forty days during which inbound vessels were detained before being permitted to lighter either cargo or personnel into the Grand Canal.

In New Orleans, whose principal thoroughfare was and is Canal Street, the commercial community violently opposed any and all quarantine measures. The nation's largest maritime-and-inland-waterway junction was wholly dependent on its port not merely for prosperity but for survival, having no productive assets beyond a few handicraft enterprises like the making of fine furniture by François Seignouret. The export of cotton, tobacco, sugar, indigo, buffalo and beaver hides, the import of wines, textiles, lumber, and coffee from abroad, and such manufactured goods as nails, plows, glass, and similar products from the New England seaboard—it was on this economic pabulum that New Orleans had grown great.

Any interruption to its flow of trade by long quarantine halts in the river before a shipmaster received pratique to land and discharge cargo, hit the community squarely and painfully in its vulnerable moneybags. Consequently its nascent quarantine system was abolished four years after it was instituted, and Mayor Roffignac (who gained further renown by having a cocktail named after him) declared officially that "quarantine was not only useless but absolutely injurious to a city as exclusively commercial," and that "free and untrammeled trade . . . is a social necessity involving the question of subsistence or starvation."

Nonetheless, as epidemic thereafter trod on the heels of epidemic, the legislature appropriated funds in 1855 to build three new quarantine stations: one at the entrance to Lake Pontchartrain, one at the mouth of the Atchafalaya, and one in the Mississippi River, seventy-two miles downstream from New Orleans, at a point in the wilderness "where prevailing winds and tides would divert the effluvia and emanations of incoming ships away from New Orleans."

Detention of vessels for ten days at these stations is now known to have been futile in preventing yellow fever importation. This was definitely demonstrated in the case of the bark *Florence Peters* on which Mrs. Hooper had brought to New Orleans what became the epidemic of 1867. According to the official report of President S. A. Smith of the city Board of Health in that year the vessel "was stopped at quarantine for ten days [and] reported clean and healthy [after being] fumigated and released."

Quarantine was finally abolished for the second and last time under terrific pressure from the business interests, backed by an open letter from fourteen of the city's leading physicians, among them Dr. Chaillé and the same Dr. Edmond Souchon whom Narciso had met as a young medical student in Paris. As professor of surgery at what is now Tulane University he would soon instruct Rudolph Matas, who—looking still further ahead—would one day translate from the Spanish the first American publication of Carlos Finlay's epochal though modest report indicting the *Culex* mosquito as sole carrier of yellow fever to human beings.

Meanwhile others were already pulling and hauling at the outer fringes of the dragnet which would one day convict the mosquito under

Finlay's indictment. In 1858, Dr. Barton, some of whose findings have already been cited, made the declaration that "yellow fever is not personally communicable" and arises only where the foul conditions which "furnish its nativity" prevail. "New Orleans," he continued, "is one of the dirtiest and consequently one of the sickliest cities in the nation. Rain water [collected from roofs] should be filtered by passing through charcoal and the nidus of musquetoes [sic!] checked by having a float of wood on the cistern or [even by] placing small fish in the cisterns."

Dr. Joseph C. Nott, who had moved from South Carolina to Mobile, came closer to the bull's eye than any of the other early researchers.

"I propose to show," he wrote in 1836, "that yellow fever has inherent powers of propagation which accords in many respects with the peculiar habits and instincts of insects. . . . Persons often take yellow fever by coming to Mobile during the day, though the risk is certainly much greater at night. All attempts heretofore to account for the greater activity of morbific causes of yellow fever at night have failed, and in my humble opinion the facts may be much better explained by a reference to the habits of insects. The moth tribe and the night mosquitoes are familiar examples."*

Paralleling these acrimonious debates were equally inconclusive polemics on how to combat the plague once it appeared. Since no one yet knew who or what the enemy was, it is no matter for surprise that conjecture ran the gamut of conceivable and often contradictory possibilities.

Those who held the disease to be carried by fomites relied for defense against it largely on the reek produced by burning sulphur. In a confined space, such as the hold of a ship, this must unwittingly have accomplished a deal of good, since it did away with many a mosquito, quiescent and hidden in the darkness while poison sucked from the bloodstream of a patient in Havana or Veracruz was being incubated in its glands.

On the other hand, disinfecting a room in which a patient had died

* A notation for the it's-a-small-world department appears to be indicated at this point. Dr. Nott officiated as obstetrician at the birth of an Alabama male infant who was christened William Crawford Gorgas. As Surgeon-General of the United States, he first checked Walter Reed's Havana experiments in Cuba and then, using the knowledge thus gleaned, he eliminated mosquitoes from the Panama Canal Zone and so made possible the completion of that monumental structure. Like virtually every other adult dweller along the Gulf Coast, Dr. Gorgas was an immune, having come down with a benign attack of yellow fever while stationed at Brownsville as a newly fledged lieutenant in the army's Medical Corps. His attending physician on that occasion was another newly fledged medical graduate, loaned to Texas for the emergency by Louisiana: Rudolph Matas.

of yellow fever was about as potent in combating the spread of infection as wearing a dried spider in the shell of a hazelnut on a string about the throat. Mosquitoes which had drawn infected blood from the patient on the third day of his illness or thereabouts had long since hummed their way back into the open in search of water in which to deposit their eggs. But in those days even the corpses of Bronze John's victims were suspect as vectors. As late as 1879 it was urged that the bodies of those who had died of yellow fever be "thoroughly washed in a zinc solution of double strength, then wrapped in a sheet wet with the zinc solution and buried at once." If immediate interment were not possible, "the coffin should be filled with powdered charcoal [and] the casket containing the body should be packed in an outer tight box in which a second layer of powdered charcoal should be packed in such a manner as to surround it entirely."

Whether the sufferer died or recovered, the sickroom was disinfected. As reported by Dr. Alfred Perry, this was accomplished in 1867—as, for example, after seven-year-old Rudolph Matas could once more leave his bed—by closing the room tightly, stopping up the fireplaces, and burning two to four pounds of sulphur in the apartment, which was in addition well sprinkled with carbolic acid. Sulphate of iron was put into all the privies.

Carbolic acid came into general use during the 1850's. Literally tons of it were sloshed about the streets and gutters of New Orleans in yellow-fever seasons. Dr. F. B. Albers, sanitarian in charge of the municipal district in which the Matas family lived at the time of Rudolph's illness, reported that in this year "between Wednesday September 12th and Saturday 16th [1867] 10,000 gallons of carbolic acid [were] applied to filthy streets, unpaved yards, alleys, stagnant gutters, ditches, and manure heaps."

The extent to which disinfection of this sort was practiced may be gauged from another and later (1870) of Dr. Albers's annual reports, in which he stated:

"In every instance when a case of yellow fever took place, the house where it occurred, also its immediate neighborhood and premises were disinfected by setting free chlorine and sulphurous acid gas in the rooms where death had taken place. The gutters of the yard were sprinkled freely with copperas and carbolic acid, and carbolohydrochloride of iron used as a permanent disinfectant about the sinks, privies, and vaults. The streets and gutters of that portion of the district where the disease prevails were also disinfected by distributing five barrels of lime throughout the locality and following it up on the 15th day by distributing two barrels of carbolic acid on the same ground."

In the light of what has since been learned about yellow fever, it is obvious that while disinfection of the filth amid which Orleansians dwelt in the era of Rudolph Matas's boyhood must have promoted general hygiene, Dr. Albers could have checked the epidemic just as effectively by painting his class numerals on the sides of each house where the fever struck. He lived to acknowledge this himself, in effect, not because greater knowledge about the transmission of yellow fever had been gained but because he was honest enough to recognize and concede the futility of his lavish programs of disinfection.

In 1878, a year in which fever deaths in New Orleans totaled 4056, he reported that "the disease was unchecked by the cordon of carbolic acid and marched rapidly from district to district until every district in the town was invaded, and the infection was carried by steamboats and railroads far into the interior of the valley. The charmed spell of carbolic acid disinfection of gutters and streets was forever broken."

As the fever waned, Narciso found himself in an increasingly unhappy situation. Within and without the family circle he was made to feel the stigma of undesirability. Teresa reproached him day in and day out for having gambled away their security, thus forcing them to return to this alien place of fevers and stenches. She alternated this with spells of stony and forbidding silence, and it is difficult to imagine which phase Narciso found most difficult to endure.

His only escape from ostracism lay in the intermittent correspondence he kept up with his friends in the Brownsville-Matamoros area, especially with José San Román and Dimas Barreda. Since the fever situation was as bad along the Texas coast as in New Orleans, they had urged him to join them, assuring him of a warm welcome and abundant opportunities for professional advancement; but Rudolph's illness put aside any thought of leaving New Orleans.

Moreover the attitude of New Orleans toward him presented a challenge; not an adventurous one, to be sure, but a defiance to test a man's mettle, nonetheless. In time, he felt sure, he could overcome the hostility that currently held him beyond the pale. Despite the handicaps of Reconstruction carpetbaggery, New Orleans was growing, especially in the American *faubourg* above Canal Street.

Fortified by the support of Tomás Jorda, whose wealth was solid, and who would see to it that his sister and her family were never in want, and by the friendship of the aged and influential Francisco Sambola, Narciso might well have settled down to a rooted existence in New Orleans, with the purpose of literally forcing the community in time to accept him, if only as a returned prodigal. Moreover, his fiercely dynastic love for little Rudolph held family ties intact, even in the face of so unattractive a prospect as a workaday existence by the side of an elderly woman for whom he no longer harbored even casual affection, and whose attitude toward him alternated between unbroken scolding and unbroken silence.

Casting about for means to establish himself in active practice, he applied to Francisco Sambola, president of the Iberia Society, for appointment as that organization's physician. A benevolent fraternity for New Orleans' large Spanish-speaking colony, one of its charter provisions stipulated that the president must be a native of the Iberian peninsula.

In making his application, Narciso laid stress upon the fact that he too was Iberia born, and Sambola readily agreed to see what could be done. Narciso took this to be a virtual promise that the appointment and the wider field of practice to which it would inevitably lead were as good as his. He therefore besought Tomás Jorda's aid in purchasing a home, a project for which he needed little assistance financially, since most of the yellow-fever calls had been well paid. What he wanted was guidance in selecting a property which would be a sound investment. One such was found for him at 82 Circus (now South Rampart) Street. While not in the *Vieux Carré*, it was not far from its upper boundary and thus within easy reach of both the Latin and Anglo-Saxon sectors of the city.

However, while the cumbersome machinery for passing a notarial act of sale under the Napoleonic code ground its slow grist, another physician was appointed to the Iberia Society post Narciso had expected to fill. Sr. Sambola explained that the successful applicant, long a resident of New Orleans, had been in line for the appointment more than a year and could not well be passed over by reason of personal preference on the part of the society's president.

Narciso accepted the explanation with perfunctory expressions of thanks for the efforts exerted in his behalf but was more than ever convinced that local hostility had again blocked his endeavors to become an authentic part of the community. He might have decided to join the carpetbaggers in exploiting what was left of the South's wealthiest city, had he not received at this juncture still another letter from José San Román in Matamoros.

Its burden was that the San Román plantations stood in need of a resident physician. Now that his son had by the grace of God recovered from the fever, why should not Narciso return to friends who esteemed him of old and were eager to offer him the strong embrace of companionship? He might, if he wished, reside in Brownsville to establish United States citizenship while practicing both there and in Matamoros. His earnings as plantation doctor and the fees he would receive in private practice, which would come to him as it had in '62, promised ample provision for his family. . . .

One may be reasonably sure that it was this reference to his family and not the thought of greater earnings which decided him. Beyond question the thought had been in his mind that if New Orleans proved so unforgiving toward him, the hostility would carry over to include Rudolph, who must at all costs be spared the indignity of being held outcast once he reached the age of understanding. There would be no danger of this in Matamoros or Brownsville, where almost everyone had engaged in blockade running, so that no special odium attached to those who had dealt with both combatant sides.

Moreover, the West was not static. Fresh opportunities for adventure and fortune beckoned on every hand. The gold fields of California were just beginning to disgorge their fabled treasure. Everywhere fortune beckoned to men of decision. Not for nothing had that *yanqui* editor said, even before the war: "Go West, young man, and grow up with the country." What better springboard for the West could one possibly find than the San Román offer?

He told Teresa of his decision, directing her to remain with her brother until he sent for her and the child as soon as proper living accommodations could be arranged for them in Brownsville. Meanwhile, let the purchase of the house in Circus Street be consummated. In a rapidly growing city which soon or late would throw off the yoke of carpetbaggery, rents and the rocketing values of real property made the best depository for earnings accumulated during the 1867 epidemic, especially in view of the fact that a steady income now awaited him in Texas.

But it was to be an investment only. He was done with New Orleans. *Los Reyes* would leave their gifts for little Rudolph in Brownsville-Matamoros on Twelfth Night, and Teresa would find in the Catalan colony there an agreeable circle of friends. That much he could promise her. They would begin a new life with the new year.

They made the deadline, though by a scant margin. The transfer of title to the Circus Street house was not formalized by notarial act until December 26, by which time Narciso was already in Brownsville. On December 27 Teresa and Rudolph bade farewell to the city of which Dr. Chaillé, soon to be Rudolph's chief of mission, wrote that its lack of cleanliness "would be shocking to eyes accustomed to the filth of Constantinople or Cairo. Streets uncleaned for weeks together, two of our largest hotels pouring the contents of their privies into one of the main thoroughfares, with the ceaseless resources of Charity Hospital swelling the stifling current, gutters choking with filth or else emptying themselves by municipal authority into vacant lots. . . ."

Add to these physical details the overbearing exactions of carpet-baggery and implacable exclusion from communal existence even by those the carpetbaggers oppressed, and one can understand why both Narciso and Teresa felt no pang on leaving New Orleans. Rudolph, still weak from the blow Bronze John had dealt him, was about to acquire his ABCs in an English school under the tutelage of Miss Mary Butler, he would learn to engage in fisticuffs with other boys after the Anglo-American fashion, and he would soon experience authentic bereavement in the disruption of his home through the rift that separated his parents permanently.

CHAPTER VI

Only fragments of documented information remain today of Rudolph's boyhood in Brownsville and Matamoros. The Matas domestic situation was already approaching the point of no return through what, many years later, Rudolph conceded to be "the diluting effects of difference in age on the marital relationship." Narciso's reaction to this is textually spelled out in a letter to his son in 1880, when the possibility of Rudolph's setting up as a physician in Havana was being explored.

"Cuba is only a good place to speculate with marriage," Narciso wrote. "A young man he may found a rich girl to marry, but the man needs whole that fortune to keep such a woman and look out if you loose it. Now that I am speaking of marriage, bear in mind these advises from me; never marry too young . . . never marry a older woman than you, and one that she is not sufficiently intelligent to make you happy."

Nonetheless, efforts to rebuild, or at least shore up, the crumbling familial structure must have been undertaken when Rudolph and his mother joined Narciso in Brownsville during the first days of 1868. Perhaps prosperous Narciso, no longer a social pariah—in fact, already being looked up to as something of a community pillar on both sides of the Rio Grande—made a conscious effort to be an at least occasionally ardent lover despite his wife's spiritual withdrawal and obvious inability to attract him by physical charm.

In any case, Teresa conceived. On January 27, 1869, just a year after the family was reunited, Narciso delivered her of a girl infant in the house on Brownsville's Washington Street near Thirteenth, where he maintained both a family residence and a professional office-surgery. Teresa named the baby Elvira, and Narciso was enchanted by her chubbily Lilliputian prettiness. But this affection was nothing like the fiercely paternal pride and love with which he held his son near and dear. Moreover, thanks to Teresa's complete dominance over the daughter through all the formative years of her development, Elvira disliked her father almost from the first. In time, this dislike matured into the sort of cold hatred only a frustrated, self-centered, spinsterish disposition could engender.

Apart from the advent of his baby sister, other remembered highlights of this period include Narciso's gift to him of a zoetrope on his eighth birthday. These remarkable toys, for one of which the doctor had sent to Paris, were the offspring of an experimental apparatus designed by the great Belgian physicist, Joseph Antoine Plateau, who soon thereafter went totally blind as a result of staring open-eyed and unblinking at the sun to test a hypothesis on the nature of light.

Rudolph's zoetrope looked like the vertical rim of a lampshade, pierced by upright slits at regular intervals; about its inner surface, opposite each slit, was the picture of a horse in various running postures. When the "lampshade" revolved, anyone looking through the vertical slits saw the horse apparently gallop furiously along.

Ownership of such a treasure conferred enviable eminence in the Brownsville Public School where Rudolph, already fluent in French, Catalonian, and Spanish, first acquired a working knowledge of English. However, such eminence did not shield him from normal boyhood activities in the way of occasional fisticuffs, especially with one Irish boy—"rather a bully"—who challenged him to combat, whereupon "I pummeled him pretty well, being a stout little chap."

Another memorable event of this epoch was the arrival in Brownsville, late in 1869, of a cousin, Emilio Forto, a strapping youth of sixteen, whose mother, Ana, was Teresa's sister and had married Juan Forto in Gerona, emigrating with him to Cuba. He lived with his *tía* Teresa until some time after Elvira, nearly a year old, had been taken to Matamoros with due pomp and circumstance to be christened in the Church of the Immaculate Conception with Manuel de Liano and Lauriana Lareda as godparents. He remained in Brownsville when Narciso decided to move permanently to Matamoros.

This did not affect Elvira's status as a national of the United States, any more than did the fact that of her eighty years she passed less than eight in the land of her birth. Some sixty years later, Rudolph therefore found it possible, though difficult, to gain official permission for her departure from a Spain riven by civil war, for which she— a religiocentric scold, who found fault with everything and everyone—

gave him small thanks. She slipped back into Spain almost as soon as he returned to New York after leaving her in Paris.

During the first year of the family's residence in Matamoros Rudolph was entered in a parochial school directed by the Padre Periosat, a priest who did not wear clerical attire in public because of clamorous agitation against the Church at that era of Mexican revolutionary unrest. In this same year Rudolph also came down with typhoid fever, an experience permanently documented by the scars left at the back of his neck as a memento of his father's relentless application of a multiple-bladed artificial leech, followed by cupping.

Until his seventeenth birthday, when he entered the University of Louisiana's Medical College, his schooling was destined to remain a migratory, interrupted, sometime affair. Before he was well acclimated to the change from an English-speaking public school in Brownsville to a Spanish-speaking parochial school in Matamoros, he was forced into prolonged seclusion by the typhoid attack and the slow convalescence which followed. To his mother this was simply the last straw of an unbearable load of willful afflictions her husband had laid upon them. The moment Rudolph was well enough, she and the two children left, bag and baggage, to live with her brother Tomás in New Orleans.

They remained there nearly two years, until the spring of 1875. During this interlude, the boy attended a private school, recently founded by Colonel George Soulé, whose descendants still maintain it as a flourishing business college.

Since by then he spoke French and English with equal facility, it is likely he progressed well in a school which, like the community it served, was still largely bilingual. Among other studies, he attended classes in penmanship, as taught by a Mr. Montgomery, and in drawing, under the tutelage of an architect, Henry Whinry Carter, a plump, apple-cheeked little man with a bushy profusion of white beard and mustache which made him look—Dr. Matas recalled many years later —"like one of Walt Disney's dwarfs in Snow White."

Writing in 1925 to the one close friend he made among the students at Soulé's, William H. Hale, Dr. Matas made light of his scholastic standing there, recalling that "I chafed under the discipline of the pedagogic method and studied my lessons only sufficiently to keep at a respectable distance from the tail of my class." Narciso might have directed the boy's insatiable intellectual curiosity into channels of sound reading; but Narciso was in Brownsville, and Teresa had neither talent for nor interest in such things.

But in his joy at discovering facility in English, thirteen-year-old Rudolph began to read everything on which he could lay hands, aided and abetted by Billy Hale. "We were both passionately fond of reading, but rather gourmands than gourmets. . . . I loved tales of adventure . . . and narratives of heroic deeds . . . anything, whether fancy or fact that could thrill the primitive emotions and fire the imagination of the awakening juvenile mind. I had no wise mentor to guide the selection of the proper source of emotional gratification and the dime novel and detective stories which were cheap and within easy reach largely supplied the necessary pabulum."

Yet an approaching experience let him witness a bit of high and bloody adventure none of his dime novels could have outdone. The first Confederate metropolis to be captured by Union arms, New Orleans was likewise the last from which the onerous yoke of the carpetbaggers was lifted. The darkest decade of the city's tragic era was ushered in during 1868, when a new "constitution" disfranchised virtually all former Confederates. Thus an electorate composed almost wholly of former slackers and scalawags seated Henry Clay Warmoth as governor, with a freed slave, Oscar Dunn, as lieutenant-governor.

Taxes and the public debt were quintupled during the ensuing carnival of corruption, which finally sickened even a substantial segment of the carpetbag Republicans. This group of self-styled "Conservatives," spearheaded by Warmoth himself, made common cause with the Democrats in 1872 to elect John McEnery governor. But a Returning Board appointed by the "Radical" wing of incumbent Republicans, callously declared their candidate, William Pitt Kellogg, duly elected, with Pinkney Benton Steward Pinchback, a mulatto, as lieutenant-governor.

Warmoth, having supported Democrat McEnery, was promptly impeached by his fellow-Republicans. His lieutenant-governor, Dunn, had died of pneumonia the year before. In order to keep a *de facto* administration intact, the carpetbaggers' cash-and-carry legislature[*] then seated Pinchback as "acting governor," though he had not yet been inaugurated as lieutenant-governor, and his claim to even that office was based on nothing more substantial than a fraudulent Returning Board ukase. Nonetheless, he served as acting governor of Louisiana from December 9, 1872, until January 13, 1873, when Kellogg was inaugurated.

Pinchback was then "elected" to the United States Senate in 1873, by the same carpetbag legislature. However, this apparently gagged even the Grant administration's Congress, so that for three years the

---

[*] One member of the House of Representatives was absent on the occasion when a scandalous levee bill was enacted. The letter he wrote about this was later published. Over his signature he solicited from the Warmoth-appointed Levee Commission the same bribe paid to other members for their votes, on the ground that he would have voted for the bill had he been present at the time!

Senate refused to seat him. Immediately thereafter, in 1876, a pact was consummated, under the terms of which Louisiana's electoral votes gave Rutherford Hayes a tainted but final victory over Tilden for the Presidency of the United States, in return for which he agreed to withdraw occupation troops from New Orleans. Within a month of his inauguration he carried out his part of the bargain, and, without the protection of federal bayonets, carpetbaggery disintegrated, most of its leaders fleeing the state.

The reaction of Louisiana's reputable citizenry in the early 1870's to the looters' unending depredations and to the cynical tolerance with which the Grant regime in Washington connived at their partisans' continuing iniquities was not surprising. Underground resistance movements came into being under various names, but in New Orleans, the Returning Board's bald fraud made the situation so nearly intolerable that resistance was organized in the open, under the name of "White League," as the licit militia of a *de jure* state administration. Its members drilled in public and with no pretense at secrecy of purpose.

Meanwhile the carpetbaggers, entrenched in their fraudulently held but nonetheless *de facto* government, had already organized a quasi-military force called the Metropolitan Police, uniformed and fully armed, which by direction of the carpetbag legislature, "lawfully" superseded the municipal police force of New Orleans.

The White Leaguers promptly arranged for Northern sympathizers to supply them with arms. These were shipped on the steamer *Mississippi*, which docked at New Orleans on September 12, 1874.

However, the Kellogg organization got wind of what and where this shipment was, and promptly prepared to seize it. *De jure* Governor John McEnery was out of the state this day, conferring at Vicksburg with other Southern leaders on ways and means to restore order. Carpetbag mercenaries had already set up artillery pieces at the head of Canal Street, but the White Leaguers recklessly charged these cannon. At the cost of twenty-one killed, as against fifteen dead on the carpetbag side, they routed the Metropolitans who took refuge in Jackson Square. There the White Leaguers besieged them through the night until, the next morning, Kellogg surrendered the State House. Returning to New Orleans on the fifteenth, Governor McEnery was triumphantly inaugurated but held office for only four days.

Grant had promptly dispatched General Emory to New Orleans with orders to restore Kellogg to the office in which the Returning Board's fraud had placed him. In the face of a military ultimatum backed by federal occupation troops and such other forces as might be necessary, the White Leaguers withdrew, and efforts to have the legitimacy of their cause validated were shifted from the smoke-filled battlefield to smoke-filled rooms where the bargain with Hayes was finally consummated.*

Narciso would have understood more than enough of this politico-military point counterpoint to have kept his son at home, or at least away from Canal Street, on September 14. But Teresa, to whom talk of mass meetings, White Leagues, Metropolitans, *de jure* and *de facto* meant as little as had the war talk at Bonnet Carre in 1860 or at Paris in 1865, placidly sent Rudolph from the Jorda home to Soulé College, which at that time was on Camp Street, opposite the City Hotel. En route he passed within a block or so of the actual battleground.

Rudolph trudged dutifully to school that morning. If he noticed unusual activity on the roof of the squat, gray pile of a still unfinished Customhouse this made no impression on him. For one thing, the Gatling guns up there were so placed as to dominate the levee, and were therefore invisible from the street on the building's opposite side. He crossed 170-foot-wide Canal Street, quite unperturbed by a gathering storm of whose omen he had no inkling.

Great things were in store for him that day at Soulé's. Mr. Carter had pronounced one of his drawings good enough to be framed and had seen to it that this was done. The masterwork was ready to be taken home for prideful display; no wonder he chafed at the enforced wait before he could achieve this triumph. Having sweated out a near eternity by the time school was dismissed, he finally took his satchel of books under one arm, the framed picture under the other, and fared homeward. Then, just as he reached the corner of Canal Street, one short block from Soulé's, a man in uniform pelted past him, shouting: "Go away! Go away! Run! The shooting's about to start!"

Men carrying guns and swords, some uniformed, some not, hurried by him toward the river when the first cannon blast shook the ground beneath his feet. A fringe of black powder smoke and stabbing red

* Throughout the North and East, a deal of political capital was made out of the Battle of Canal Street, on whose ground a monument today carries the names of the twenty-one White Leaguers who fell there. For example, the New York *Tribune*, edited by Horace Greeley, whom Grant had defeated for the Presidency two years before, jeered that, by way of assisting Louisiana, Grant had "given it . . . Kellogg, Packard, Pinchback, and Poker Jack. He has filled its legislature with thieves, adventurers, barbers, bootblacks, bartenders, and confidence men. He has put its offices to the highest bidder . . . and brought business to such a pass that in some of the richest regions of the South nothing can be bought or sold except votes . . . and ungrateful Louisiana, after all this kindness, will not be quiet." There was even some talk that Ben Butler might be sent back to "restore order" to New Orleans; a local wag declared that, "Of all sad words of tongue or Penn, the saddest are these: we might have Ben." Other wits hastened to say reassuringly that since no silver spoons or other valuables remained in the twice-looted city, Butler would not trouble to return.

flame along the cornice of the Customhouse roof marked a ragged volley of musketry fire. In panic, Rudolph charged blindly across Canal Street. Midway he stumbled and fell headlong, when the sound of firing rose in pitch and volume as battle was joined in earnest. Glass and frame of his precious picture were shattered beyond redemption. Picking up his books, but abandoning his ruined work of art, he continued to run until he reached his uncle's home. By that time the battle itself was nearly over. All disorder had ended by morning. Then at last Teresa became cautious and would not let him return to school for days.

Perhaps that belated fright impelled her to return to her husband as soon as the Soulé school year ended. Quite possibly the parish priest to whom she made confession convinced her the path of piety was at her husband's side. One may assume Narciso was somewhat less than overjoyed by this turn of events, however rejoiced he might be by renewed companionship with the son upon whom he doted.

He discussed with the boy quite seriously the idea of taking up medicine as a career, held out to him the prospect of being sent back to New Orleans for professional schooling after his preparatory education had been completed, and retold the story of how his own career had been founded by working in the pharmacy of an uncle in Gerona. Rudolph, who had taken it for granted he would become a doctor some day, fell in eagerly with his father's proposals, one of which was that after school hours each evening he work at the *farmacia* of his friend, Vittorio Brayda.

He was entered that fall as a student of St. John's Collegiate Institute in Matamoros, under the headmastership of General Revueltas. Narciso let it be well understood that he expected the boy to carry off at least as many prizes as his father had won at the College of San Felipe Neri in Gerona. Meanwhile, Rudolph's extracurricular work at the Brayda drugstore would give him a thorough grounding in drugs and herbals; thus he would secure a tremendous advantage over most of his future classmates at the University of Louisiana. Narciso spoke from experience, he explained, having not only worked in a drugstore as a youth but having been graduated in pharmacy at the New Orleans School of Medicine while learning English and before beginning his medical courses.

Rudolph was also to study music and practice piano lessons faithfully. Such exercise of the fingers would later stand a surgeon in good stead, aside from which, cultural attainments were highly prized in the only circles where a physician could hope to establish a really remunerative practice.

Apparently Rudolph heeded all these paternal injunctions, though his attainments as a pianist were meager. "I was simply one among a small group of boys," he explained many decades later, "who played various instruments to amuse the girls, though naturally in a strictly chaperoned way."

But he read avidly the medical books in his father's library, and the pamphlets and other medical communications his father received. He also devoured his sire's complete set of the works of Eugène Sue, Emile Zola, and other novelists. Thanks to an amazing, phenomenally retentive memory, most of what he understood remained with him, whether the text was French, Spanish, or English.

In sum, it is of record that upon graduation he received prize copies of Jessup's *Botany*, Ganot's *Physics*, and Milne Edwards's *Natural History*, for leading his class in those subjects. Even in his father's estimation, this more than made up for any lack of virtuosity as a pianist, despite the best efforts of a gifted instructor, Sr. Krause, whose son, Luis, was Rudolph's chum and familiar.

A favorite among his instructors was a Sr. Kraskowski, a refugee from Czarist Russia, who taught philosophy. Required language studies included both French and Latin, most of the textbooks being French and Latin being the *sine qua non* of all higher education. Fr. Vigoreau taught both.

In this respect, the boy's familiarity with French, Spanish, and English put him well ahead of most of his fellows. He and his father conversed either in Spanish or French, as the mood of the moment struck them, though they wrote one another in English. His mother, of course, stonily insisted on retaining Catalan as the language of the household. She never spoke Spanish, unless forced to do so by the need for communicating with merchants or others who understood only that language.

Father Vigoreau's Latin instruction bore so immitigable a French accent that later Sr. Kraskowski, the philosophy teacher, replaced him. He had long been famous for almost interminable recitations from Caesar, Cicero, and Virgil, much of whose writings he knew by heart. The charm of these performances was, if anything, heightened by the Russian scholar's addiction to brown-paper cigarettes and the rankest of *puro* cigars.

Meanwhile, to Teresa's shuddering resentment, the country round about continued to seethe, like the Louisiana she had quitted, with the ferment of political unrest and armed revolt. Porfirio Díaz, ostensibly crusading against an attempt at dictatorship by Juárez's successor, Lerdo de Tejada, finally succeeded in winning the presidency for himself. Lerdo was safely exiled and Díaz would retain power for nearly forty years; but malcontents immediately organized counter-revolutions from Texas. Laredo, Matamoros, and Ciudad Juárez were natural targets for attack.

Writing a modest autobiographical paper in 1955 for inclusion in a volume on surgery, Dr. Matas noted that "many interesting episodes of this period of my life have already been printed, but I always enjoy the memory of my graduation. The (Reforma) theatre was crowded with students, graduates, their families and friends, faculty members, and city officials, presided over by General Revueltas. In the midst of an address which was being delivered by the principal orator of the occasion, a sudden noise was heard which was easily recognized as gunfire. When it continued, the audience became alarmed, people became restless and began to leave. At this moment General Revueltas stood up, calmly and quietly, and said: 'Ladies and gentlemen, you are unduly alarmed. There is no danger. What you hear is a military salute which I ordered to be fired in honor of the graduates and the students who are receiving prizes tonight.' His gracious words and calmness reassured the audience, the firing ceased, people returned to their seats, and the program went on without further interruption."

The next day it was learned that in reality a revolutionary attack on the city had been repulsed by the Federal garrison.

Rudolph spent some weeks after his graduation accompanying his father on professional calls and even assisting at surgery whenever this could be permitted. The rest of his free time he occupied by working at the Brayda drugstore. Money to send him through medical school was already set aside; no small sum, this, for though nominally part of the University of Louisiana, the Medical College maintained strict autonomy as a "proprietary" institution, whose instructors shared all tuition and other fees paid by students.

Only one obstacle remained to be overcome; a disagreement between his parents over where he was to live in New Orleans. Teresa insisted he should stay at the home of his uncle. Narciso flatly vetoed any such arrangement, declaring that Rudolph was now a man and must live like one, that he would be far too busy with didactic lectures, attendance at operations, hospital service, and night classes in dissection under a demonstrator of anatomy, to be fretted by the small amenities of being part of a household. He had, in fact, already written to Dr. A. C. Holt asking that friend to find a room in some boardinghouse near the medical school for Rudolph.

He had even tried to exert whatever political influence might be mustered to get for his son one of the coveted appointments as resident student at the Charity Hospital. But such plums were given out to those who stood high in favor with the powers, and that was one thing Narciso could not command. The whole system was bad, he raged.

Those appointments should go to the most deserving, as selected by competitive examinations, not to politicians' pets; especially when these politicians represented a newly restored faction to which anything that smacked however remotely of collaboration or carpetbaggery was anathema.

Late that August, Rudolph took ship at Port Isabel, voyaged across the northern Mexique gulf to Morgan City, there to entrain on the steamcars for his future domicile, a city that would shower him with honors and to which he would bring international renown, a New Orleans he was preparing to enter for the first time on his own and— he thought of the razor with which he meticulously scraped from cheeks and chin all but the still wispy mustache and imperial he affected in emulation of his sire—as a man.

CHAPTER VII

In 1877, as for many a decade theretofore and thereafter, any quasi-public building, be it post office, academy, state capitol, or whatever, was given the form of a colonnaded Greek temple. The Medical Department of the University of Louisiana was no exception. Its central structure, flanked by two lesser temples, occupied one entire side of the Common Street block between Baronne Street and what to this day is called University Place.

Either Dr. Holt or Uncle Tomás Jorda had secured lodgings in advance for Rudolph on Baronne Street, just around the corner from the college, opposite the church in which he had been baptized. He moved in at once with bag—a flashy affair of brightly flowered carpeting—and baggage—a box of books. Most important of all, he carried in a flat portmanteau two letters: one to Dr. Samuel Logan, professor of anatomy and clinical surgery, from Narciso's close personal and professional friend, Dr. Etienne Melou of Brownsville; the other from Ben Hibbard, manager of Brayda's Pharmacy, to John Walker Phillips, an executive of the I. L. Lyons Wholesale Drug Firm.

Putting up his few belongings after the landlady had been paid a month's rental in advance was a matter of minutes. Thereupon he made himself tidily presentable and called with some trepidation at Dr. Logan's office with his letter of introduction to the great man who would assist and advise him in mapping his course of study.

He had envisioned Dr. Logan as a sort of cloud-wrapped Olympian, and was surprised and delighted to find him both affable and gracious;

a man of middle age, florid complexion, clear bluish-gray eyes and reddish-brown hair, mustache, and goatee. He readily put Rudolph at his ease. The student-to-be was soon chattering away of his background, of his work at the Brayda pharmacy, of accompanying and assisting his father on professional calls during the preceding summer, even of Paris.* Dr. Logan gave every evidence of being favorably impressed, but there was little time for such red-letter interludes thereafter. The fixed collegiate curriculum accounted for almost more hours than were tolled off by the great clock which had been taken from the St. Louis Cathedral spire to be installed in the Charity Hospital façade.

First of all, he had to make a very formal call at the office of Tobias G. Richardson, Dean, to purchase tickets of admission to the lectures of each of his professors. On this score, Dr. Logan had warned him, as had Dr. Holt, to come cash in hand with the money in bills of large denomination.

"The Dean has only one assistant," Rudolph's preceptor cautioned him, "and it's neither right nor proper to waste the time of someone like Dr. Richardson in counting and recounting handfuls of dollar bills."

So Rudolph went to the offices of Gordon and Gomila† to change enough money into $50 and $20 bills to cover his tuition. Each lecture ticket cost $20, and eight of these were needed for the year's course. In addition, a $5.00 matriculation fee had to be paid directly to the University, $10 went to a demonstrator in anatomy for a special night course in dissection, and, by immemorial custom, tacitly recognized but ignored, an under-the-table payment of $10 had to find its way from nonresident students to the favored few Charity Hospital residents for the privilege of watching, and later assisting at, obstetric deliveries. Thus, without even allowing for textbooks, stationery, and

---

* Seventy-four years later, in 1951, when descendants of the Logan family presented a portrait of their distinguished forebear to Tulane University, Dr. Matas, though by then almost totally blind and deploring the fact that "my unfortunate visual defects prevent me at this moment from comparing (the features) as the artist has pictured them" with his early observations, spoke of Dr. Logan's "broad forehead, capped by light reddish hair, tending towards gray, covering a fine, rather thinly clad scalp and massive head. Though I was not then able to classify his skull into round or elongated, it seemed to me in later years when I knew more of anthropology, that his head corresponded to the type of 'roundheads' that were peculiar to his reputed Scotch ancestry. One thing was certain, that his head and features impressed even the casual observer as those of a man of superior intelligence and character."

† William Gordon and A. J. Gomila conducted a prosperous commission and brokerage firm at 100 Magazine Street. Narciso, once more bent upon amassing a fortune to replace the one lost in his Spanish railroad venture, was buying cotton in west Texas and shipping it to Messrs. Gordon and Gomila to be sold when the market was favorable. Thus he maintained an adequate credit balance on their books.

other such essentials, an initial cash outlay of approximately $200 had to be made by each student.

But after checking over the prospectus and ascertaining by diligent inquiry the personal data which transformed mere names on a printed list into flesh and blood individuals, Rudolph marveled that so much could have been acquired for so little. Dr. Logan he knew already; moreover, Dr. Melou, back in Brownsville, had sketched out a vivid thumbnail biography of his brilliant career. For the rest, the name of Dr. Tobias G. Richardson, Dean and professor of General and Clinical Surgery headed the roster; a veteran of the Confederate Army who had been cited and promoted for conspicuous gallantry under fire, a founder of the Louisiana State Medical Society, and president-elect of the American Medical Association. He was a giant even in his physical being, with thick shoulders and powerful hands, whose aura of virile force not even the dandified beard, parted in the middle after the day's foppish vogue, could veil.

Almost all the faculty members had seen service with the armies of the Confederacy. Samuel Merrifield Bemiss, first student to matriculate at the newly opened medical college of the University of New York in 1841, had practiced and taught in Louisville both before joining the Confederate Army, and after his discharge, when he became one of the first professors of Medicine (as distinguished from Surgery) in all the land.

Outstanding among the faculty's other Confederate heroes was Ernest S. Lewis, head of the Department of the Diseases of Women and Children. Lewis had sought to enlist with the opening of hostilities, but was persuaded by Dr. Warren Stone to complete his studies. Within a matter of months he was made acting house surgeon at Charity Hospital, being denied the full title only because he was but twenty-two years old.

After New Orleans was captured and Butler became military commandant over a subject city, Acting House Surgeon Lewis refused to receive Federal soldiers who were sick or wounded, though he admitted wounded or ailing Confederates. Butler promptly arrested Charity's entire Board of Administrators, but Dr. Lewis stubbornly maintained the stand that no Union troops would be received unless the occupation forces paid whatever additional physicians might be needed to treat them. Butler finally agreed. But when a Butler-appointed collaborationist Board of Administrators replaced the members who had been arrested, Lewis and two companions fled, slipping through the cordon of sentries that guarded the city, crossing the marshes to Lake Pontchartrain, and making their way to Mandeville on the far shore in a skiff for which they jury-rigged a sail.

They then traveled north by train and joined Bragg's army. Lewis was promptly commissioned and quickly won promotion for valor to the rank of Brigade Surgeon. He was finally made medical director for Wheeler's cavalry, serving thus with the Army of Tennessee to the war's weary end.

One faculty member who had not served with the Southern army was the same Edmond Souchon whom Rudolph's father had known in Paris as a stranded Louisiana medical student. He no longer affected the full, dark beard of his Paris days, but only a mustache. However, he still wore imported elastic-sided wooden-heeled French gaiters. When at last he returned to his native city in 1866, he bore a letter from Dr. Marion Sims to Dean Richardson and, with the latter as preceptor, he earned a medical degree from the University of Louisiana the following year. During the ensuing decade he became a living legend throughout the medical world by stealing most of a human body for science.

This specimen still holds a prominent place in the Surgeon-General's museum at Washington. The *genius loci* who put it there was to play a large share in shaping Rudolph Matas's future. William Banks, a Negro ship steward, had come to Charity in 1864, with a great, pulsing tumor at the base of his neck, just above the right shoulder. This was an aneurism of the subclavian artery, one of the large vessels leading from the aorta, which is the heart's principal arterial pipeline. The blood vessel had been damaged during a collision at sea, and the weakened wall, swollen by internal pressure, might rupture at any moment, an eventuality which, in such cases, was invariably and almost immediately fatal.

Aneurisms and amputations constituted the two major fields of surgical practice in that era. Principal causes of physical damage to artery walls were gunshot and stab wounds, or syphilis. Remedial surgery consisted in tying the damaged artery above—that is, on the heart side of—the weakened swelling. This rarely proved of lasting benefit. John Hunter in London was the first surgeon to make a substantial advance in lessening the omen of aneurismal ruptures. Instead of ligating the damaged vessel just on the heart side of the sac, he tied it at some distance higher up, where the arterial walls were still relatively sound and normal.

Meanwhile, in New Orleans, during the years when that city was sweating out the distempers of military occupation and carpetbaggery, Andrew W. Smyth, one of Butler's Republican appointees, became house surgeon at Charity, so that it was to him that the Negro ship steward, Banks, was brought on admission to the hospital. Smyth had been specially active in seeking new approaches to the treatment of aneurisms, one of his proposals being to plug the affected artery with a round lead ball large enough to act as a stopper. But when he saw Banks to all intents *in extremis,* he followed standard procedures and, taking a last-resort chance, became the first physician ever successfully to tie off the great innominate artery of which the subclavian is one major branch.

To the astonishment of all, Banks not only recovered, but returned to normal workaday life for ten years. During this interval, Edmond Souchon returned from Paris and in due time became Tobias Richardson's prosector; that is, he made the preliminary dissections Dr. Richardson would complete in classroom demonstrations.

His skill in this field was so widely recognized that by the time Rudolph Matas entered medical school Souchon had become demonstrator of anatomy, a post once held by Dr. Richardson himself during his younger days. Andrew Smyth also engaged him as prosector in the preparation of post-mortem studies at Charity Hospital. This was of special moment only in particularly noteworthy cases; but such a one was certainly the return of William Banks in 1874, a full decade after Smyth's daring and successful operation. Now he was back with another pulsating tumor at almost the same point, as large and as ominous as the original aneurism. This time even desperate measures proved unavailing, and Banks died within forty-eight hours after admission.

Smyth was understandably anxious to have the upper right section of Banks's body preserved to show that the original ligation, the first of its kind in all medical history, had been successful. Dr. Souchon therefore injected the decedent's blood vessels with cocoa butter and carmine and began swiftly to lay bare the vascular system in the affected area. The need for haste was vital. Though Banks had no surviving relatives, he belonged to a burial society whose officials were not minded to forgo renown as directors of so famous a funeral. They demanded that Banks's body be turned over to them instanter. As Dr. Souchon reported in a later monograph on "Original Contributions of Louisiana to Medical Science":

"I heard a great row in the waiting room of the dead-house. . . . I recognized the voice of Dr. Smyth clamoring over the others trying to pacify them again. He had a great influence over them, being himself a Republican. . . . I decided on a bold *coup d'état* to preserve the to-be-world-renowned specimen, so I quickly separated the interesting parts from the balance of the corpse, wrapped them in an old sack and pushed the package through a back window to an assistant keeper of the dead-house, telling him to carry it to my coupé which was standing in front of the hospital."

Dr. Souchon then clambered out through the same window but walked around the hospital in the opposite direction to throw off suspicion or pursuit, and finally took "the much coveted specimen from the carrier, placing it tenderly on the seat next to me." Then he clucked to his horse and set off "hugging closely my precious and ghastly companion."

The Burial Society officials raised a great to-do, but had perforce to practice their grandiloquent ritual over what remained of the late William Banks, whose other portion was sealed in a cask of alcohol and water which, in turn, was secreted in a building adjoining the Medical College.*

Souchon's exploit became a legend of medical education overnight and was repeated to the members of each incoming class of the University of Louisiana. Not only did it serve to stimulate scientific interest in the treatment of aneurisms; it was definitely a factor in crowding Dr. Souchon's extra-tuition night classes as demonstrator of anatomy. One of his most dedicated disciples was Rudolph Matas, who labored night after weekday night over one of the dissecting tables, each with its cadaver on which three or four students painstakingly worked under the watchful supervision of the dapper little perfectionist who ruled this grisly domain.

Walking from table to table, the wooden heels of his Paris gaiters clack-clacking on the cement floor, Dr. Souchon would pause here and there.

"Which nerve innervates this muscle?" he would ask, pointing. Gravely he listened to the student's hopeful reply. If this were correct, he would nod and move on. If not, he would say something like: "Between us, we will share a mark of 10, which is given for a perfect answer to this question. I will keep the 'one' and you can have the 'zero!'"

Rudolph retained his Baronne Street room less than a month and then moved to the establishment of a Mrs. Chapman, next door to Hawkins's bookstore on Carondelet Street at Lafayette. His first lodging was ideally near the college, to be sure; but it was also near the hubbub and revelry of boisterous Canal Street, which bordered the Tenderloin only a block away. The new lodgings, six blocks from the college, were in the more sedate "American" *faubourg* and only a few steps from the site of what had been his father's pharmacy on Lafayette (then Hevia) Street.

Here he could study undisturbed to prepare himself not merely for

---

* "I could ill afford to keep him in finer style," the Souchon narrative relates, and "having told [Dr. Richardson] what a drain this was on my shallow treasury" he and Dr. Groenvelt "arranged to have it sent to Washington where it now rests in peace and security in all its glory in a beautiful glass box with a fine crystal lid, bathed overhead in pure alcohol, the admiration of all who love subclavian aneurisms of the third portion."

the usual classroom and bedside quizzes, but to make ready for the first competitive tests on the basis of which medical students would thenceforth be selected for Charity Hospital residencies. This was a long step toward the redemption of that institution—temporarily, at least—from the sink of political logrolling into which it had been dragged by its collaborationist and carpetbag Boards of Administrators. During this fifteen-year era, residencies were parceled out as so much political pap for students whose families had been among the faithful.

Residencies were of almost inestimable advantage to their fortunate holders. For one thing, resident students were freed from classroom attendance, from what were known as didactic lectures, and from all periodic examinations except the so-called Green Room Finals, in which the entire faculty assembled at one end of a long table in a room with green calcimined walls and for hours mercilessly interrogated the degree candidate as he stood alone at the table's other end. Furthermore, residents received free board and lodging, such as it was, to say nothing of the cumshaw paid by nonresidents for the privilege of watching obstetric deliveries. And finally, no other medical students had so unparalleled an opportunity for bedside and amphitheater tutelage.

Francis Tillou Nicholls, a one-armed Confederate hero, became *de facto* as well as *de jure* governor. When President Hayes, validating the pledge of his supporters, withdrew Federal troops from New Orleans in 1877, Governor Nicholls replaced the carpetbag hospital administrators with carpetbag resistance stalwarts who, as a matter of course, were Democrats. These promptly dismissed Republican House Surgeon Andrew W. Smyth* from the Charity Hospital post he had held so many years and appointed Dr. George K. Pratt in his stead. One of Dr. Pratt's first formal announcements was to the effect that under his regime residencies would be given out solely on the basis of competitive examinations, open to all students of American birth. Not only that, but at the end of each year, residents would again have to compete with all other applicants if they wished to retain their prized positions throughout their three-year medical course.

Though he needed no added inducements to spur him on in his studies, Rudolph coveted one of these appointments on his own account. He was also by no means blind to the pride his father would feel if

* Having dickered himself into the White House, Mr. Hayes nonetheless kept his side of the bargain in spirit as well as in letter. He did not interfere with the dismissal of Dr. Smyth; neither did he abandon him. Instead, he appointed the famous surgeon to a nonmedical position as Director of the Mint at New Orleans, a capacity in which he served only a short time, before returning to his birthplace in Ireland for the remainder of his life.

"the doctor's dear little son" gained so signal a distinction. So he sealed himself off from everything except the confines of a small world bounded by the lecture halls, the hospital, his textbooks and lecture notes. Each morning he would hurry into Charity just as the big clock high on the façade began to boom the hour of eight. For the next two hours he and his fellows would make ward rounds with Dr. Bemiss or Dr. Logan, or they would attend operations in the big amphitheater, lost in admiration of the muscular speed with which the strong hands of Richardson wielded bistoury and saw in amputating a limb.

At ten o'clock the students sped from the hospital to attend lectures at the college until noon, when they might hasten to a nearby saloon for a glass of beer or wine with its concomitant of free lunch, or purchase a huge poor-boy sandwich from an old Negress who vended these meals-in-a-loaf from a wicker washbasket. Beginning at one that afternoon, and until three-thirty, there were anatomy lectures and demonstrations by Dr. Logan, with young A. B. Miles as prosector and chief of clinic, or by Dean Richardson, with Edmond Souchon as demonstrator. Chemistry lectures by Dr. Joseph Jones followed, or discussions of materia medica and therapeutics by Dr. John B. Elliott, or the crusading homilies of Stanford Emerson Chaillé, preaching the new doctrine of preventive medicine:

"Disease fosters immorality . . . public health is a nation's greatest wealth . . . no one of the four branches of state medicine involves the public welfare to so enormous an extent as preventive medicine . . . while yellow fever is not personally contagious, it *is* communicable, and unknown conditions favor the growth of the poison . . . in my classes you must give heed to three professors boiled into one: the professor of hygiene, of physiology, and of pathologic anatomy."

Each night, after a hastily gobbled, dreadful twenty-cent table d'hôte dinner, the hours from seven till nearly ten sped by while Rudolph was engrossed in dissections of cadavers—an upper extremity on one, the abdomen and genitalia on another; and always ready to praise, to rebuke, to help, was that relentless perfectionist, Dr. Souchon, clacking from table to table on wooden-heeled gaiters. Then back to his quiet room at Mrs. Chapman's, to read and memorize by lamplight until the printed or written words began to blur before overstrained eyes; and so, stumbling and bone-weary to bed for brief slumber before arising at dawn, or even earlier, and returning to his books till the moment when it was necessary to dash out to Charity once more, arriving on the stroke of eight to make rounds with Dr. Bemiss, perhaps, and to listen as the great man spoke, standing beside a hospital bed, his frock-coated professional dignity accentuated by the full, square-cut beard and the fastidiously trained mustache which blended into it at the sides.

"Gentlemen, attend me closely, if you please. This patient has now been in the hospital three days, and he has had a chill on the first and third days of his stay here. Not only is his temperature very high at these times, but there has been a marked variation between his morning and evening temperature readings. He is, as you will observe, a well-built, muscular white male, and if you examine his abdomen you will note the presence of some peculiar spots. You will also see on closer examination that his liver is slightly enlarged. So is his spleen. We must therefore determine whether we are dealing here with typho-malaria* or with one of the remittent or intermittent fevers. We note further that his urine is scanty, his tongue dry, and that it is obvious he has recently been losing considerable weight. Knowing all this, what should we do to aid this patient? Probably the best line of treatment would be frequent spongings and a course of quinine while we observe the further progress of the malady. . . . I want you each to palpate the patient's abdomen, to take his pulse and note its character, and not to overlook such other factors as the marked dryness of his skin. . . ."

Or, if the students were making rounds with Rudolph's preceptor, Dr. Logan, they would follow him into a ward whose nature became obvious the instant they were enveloped in the sweetish-foul odor of cotton-bale dressings saturated with purulent discharges from wounds or from the stumps left by amputation; "laudable pus," it was called, on the assumption that in time it would favor the healing granulation of tissue. Sisters of Charity glided quietly about, engrossed with their nursing missions. Convalescent male patients, many of them acting as orderlies, sometimes paused to listen. Perhaps the first major halt would be at a bed where it was evident both to sight and smell that abundant pus was present and anything but laudable.

"This patient, gentlemen," Dr. Logan might explain, "suffered a leg fracture about ten days ago. The story is that he fell from the deck of a ship into the hold, while the vessel was being unloaded at dockside. Our first examination after he was brought in showed that he was unable to move his foot from the unnatural position in which it was angulated. We would therefore have recognized this at once for a fracture, even if a broken end of the fibula had not been sticking out through a break in the skin. The patient was immediately given chloroform, and under anesthesia the deformity was reduced, the wound was washed with

---

* Typhoid fever was not generally recognized in Louisiana as a specific entity, a condition brought about by one particular bacillus, until circa 1894.

soap and water, and a carbolized dressing applied, after which splints were put in place. You notice, however, that not only is there a good deal of pus but that the wound edges do not look healthy. The foot is still badly swollen and discolored. The toes are blue. In other words, there is evidence of interference with circulation, and it is likely that to save his life we will have to amputate. In fact, if he does not show any improvement by tomorrow morning, we will take off the leg, amputating just below the knee to avoid any spread of this infection. . . ."

Laboratory sessions, tests for sugar or albumen in urine, the use of the microscope, bright dyes to bring out the presence of micro-organisms in smears, the coin-piled arrangement of blood corpuscles, basic instruction in chemistry, meals snatched on the run and not enough hours in the day to encompass all that had to be acquired before a fresh avalanche of essential information came thundering down upon the students next day. Now and then a brief pause to scratch out a hasty letter to his father, with a meticulous accounting for all expenditures: five cents for a stuffed crab as a midnight meal, fifteen cents for a container of shoe polish, fifty-five cents for the laundress, six cents for a notebook and pencil. No day of rest on Sundays, no visit for a big meal with Uncle Tomás or the Sambolas, though all urged their hospitality upon him. No time even to glance at newspapers —L'Abeille, the Picayune, the Democrat, the Times, or even that innovation in Southern journalism, an afternoon newspaper, the Item. Yet one of its early staff members, Lafcadio Hearn, was to play quite a role in Rudolph Matas's dawning medical career.

When the carpetbag regime disintegrated in April of 1877, its newspaper organ, The Republican, immediately followed suit. Eleven printers and writers thus thrown out of work banded together that June to found a co-operative daily. Lacking funds with which to pay for telegraphic "advices," they filled its columns with local items, gathered during the morning and published that afternoon. The product was therefore christened "The Daily City Item." A few months later a starveling out-of-work scribbler from Cincinnati applied to the co-operators for employment and served for three years—at $10 a week —as associate editor. His name: Lafcadio Hearn. A wordy genius whose swollen rhetoric of Godey's Lady's Book vintage could sometimes make the ridiculous sublime, but just as often made the sublime ridiculous, he nonetheless conferred upon the fledgling Item a savor which gained it immediate community acceptance.

He and Matas did not meet until nearly three years later. For the moment, such things as newspapers, theaters, New Orleans' flamboyant Tenderloin, the bull-baiting rings across the river in Algiers, the ever more stylized gaiety of Mardi Gras with its masquerades and pageantry, the steamcars to such resort centers as Milneburg and Carrollton, the sculling races on Bayou St. John, and such posh restaurants as Antoine's, Maylie & Esparbé's, or Tranchina's, with their leisurely twelve-course succession of superb dishes, the race tracks, and other diversions, simply did not exist for Rudolph Matas, whose conscious being was wholly absorbed in attaining the goal he had chosen: appointment to a residency at Charity Hospital.

Unfortunately, a casual remark by Dr. Holt all but shattered his faith in himself and his future, though it was meant to be reassuring. His father's old friend halted Rudolph one day in one of the hospital corridors to say that a technicality had been invoked against the young man's application for a residency on the ground that he was not a native, and therefore not a citizen, of the United States, since he was registered at the University from Matamoros, in Mexico. However, Dr. Holt added, he and Dr. F. C. Boyer convinced the examiners that Rudolph was not merely a native of the United States but of Louisiana, and therefore met every stipulation of the law under which Charity Hospital was state maintained. A copy of his baptismal certificate from the Jesuits' Church, just around the corner from the College, had clinched the matter.

Instead of being heartened by this intelligence, Rudolph was deeply troubled. He interpreted it as meaning that some members of the hospital staff were looking for pretexts on which to deny him the precious opportunity he sought. Beset by these doubts, he wrote to his father, along with a penny-by-penny accounting for December disbursements, that despite his unceasing work, he was far from confident of receiving the desired appointment; in fact, he had reason to believe efforts were under way to bar him from even taking the examinations, which were now set for the first week in March. Narciso's reply obviously sought to lift his son out of his depression. Under date of February 2, 1878, he wrote:

"My dear son Rodolfo:

I have just on hand your favor last with your current account for the month of December and I have nothing to say about it as you could not live more economical. I notice that you have not gone at the theatre yet as I recommended to you for your distraction and lesure. I hope if you feel like going you will not stop to the consideration of expending a few dollars more. I told you also to hire a piano for cultivating and conserving the music. But as you say you will not have time to spaire for it I let it to your own discration.

It is good to be a good boy and studious but you must have your time for your rest otherwise you will be sick and you'll loose more by it.

You must have certain time for your studies and no more. If you can't do all this year you will do it next, as everything requires time and you will injure your health if you overpower yourself. I am glade that Mr. Adolphe Marks has been kind to you. But I regret to know that he has not been able to give the recommendation to the Director of the Hospital that I expected. Never the less don't get discourage and if you can't get in the Hospital this year you will go in next and if you could not go at all I think I will be able to pay your expenses until you finish your studies.

I am very sorry to know the poor condition of our compatriot who occupies our house. But we can not help it. We must try to get some rent out of the unlucky houses. I wish somebody would set fire to them, so to have nothing to do with it no more. If I have a chance to sell them even with great lost, I will do it as I have no hopes for any improvement in value of the property.

If you have no money you will call at Mr. Gordon & Gomila for it.

I have but very little news to tell you since my last. My professional business not very brisk as there is not much sickness at present.

I have only 2 cases of neumonia, one is well the other is not yet out of danger. I have Mrs. Sander's babe with lubular neumonia from the effects of measles. The child run two months without any treatment until septic symtoms come on and at my first examination I give the alarm and I told them that the child's condition was so bad that I could not undertake his treatment without having first a consultation which was accorded, and Dr. Combe was call by the family and aprooved completely my diagnostic pronostic and treatment the child although much neglected by the careless of the mother he is doing better and I have hopes to save him.

The mother of Rosita Chapa your Comadre died very sudenly a few days ago. I was call the previous day she died and I found her suffering from Cupilairy Bronchitis and much depression of general system on account of moral effects and lost of appetite for last two months.

I make her go to bed and I put her under the stimulants and Dovers powder. She had no sleep. 5 grains Dover every four hours. But to the astonishment of all after the second powder she died and not body noticed until two hours afterwards.

I was send for it and found that she died from a syncope of the heart as there was nothing else to cause the death. She was pale and the pupils very dilateted.

As the death acurded sometime after the powder I beg the family to investigage the case by other Physicians, so that nobody had any bad opinion about it. She took 5 grains at 4 o'clock and 5 at 8 o'clock at night. that all.

Although that there is not bad feelings about it the circumstances are very regretable as not the family nor myself expected such a suden accident. That shows how cautious a physician must be and how he can lose his reputation in spite of doing his duty.

I always expect to have some trouble in collecting Madraso's bill and so has been the case. He refuses to pay but will make him pay one way or the other.

We propose to have a meeting in a few days with object to establish a medical society for the purpose of regulating our tarif and protect our interes and the dignity of the Profession.

Elvira has received the stereoscope and the pictures and seems to feel very much please with it.

Give my best regards to your Uncle Thomas and to all our friends, Victor Buell, Mich. and all friends here send you their sweet rememberances including the best wishes of your father for your success and health sending to you his heart and love.

N. H. y Matas

P.D. Mrs. Levy will leave to morrow for New Orleans please go to see her and the babies."

When March came in like a metaphysical lion, bringing with it the competitive examination, this was little more than an interlude in the relentless, unceasing grind of study. Rudolph was back at his round of didactic lectures, bedside demonstrations, dissections, laboratory tasks, and night-long study periods when the announcement was made that his name headed the list of those passing the test. Duplicate copies were posted on the bulletin boards of college and hospital. For a time he found it difficult to grasp the full import of the fact that he had not only passed but was ranked first in the standings. Not until Dr. Holt reminded him he would now be unable to go home for the vacation months, since residency was a year-round appointment, did he even remember to send his family a telegram with the great tidings. A joyous reply from Narciso arrived by the next mail boat. Like all his father's letters, it was addressed to "Master Rodolfo Matas," but unlike others this was an almost undecipherable pencil scrawl. It read:
"My dear Son:

Without any of yours to answer I take the pen today to give you my most heartey congratulations about the fine success of your examination.

I was expecting by last mail a letter from you giving us the accounts of your trial and the feeling anxiety you had before knowing the result.

Now thank God you must feel happy and I am glad that you may rest from your hard work and fatigue. You deserve this success for your good aplication in your studies and I was quite sure of it. Taking all things in consideration you have accomplished a great result and showes what you are capable of accomplishing hereafter. It is your first serious trial and I know it will leave an impression on your mind for ever. I can hardly describe to you how happy feeled when I received your telegram. Doctor Melou was with me and he was the first who read it I went all around and I showed to my friends who all congratulated me for such happy news. Florida was home and that day we all celebrated the event with splendid dinner. After dinner I came back to Brownsville and I send the answer to your dispatch which to be more sure I addressed to the care of your Uncle Thomas.

We are awaiting with anxiety your letter in which I expect you'll give us full accounts.

Nothing has transpired since my last letter which be worth while to reffer.

I therefore take leave of you till next mail hoping you feel happy and enjoy always good health.

I think your mother is writing to you and I shall leave to her care to describe the sensation she and Elvira received from your telegram.

Your father who loves you dearly, Dr. N. H. y Matas.

Excuse me for writing with pencil I am in a patient's hous and I could not get any other convinience to write. It is 12 o'clock and the mail start to morrow morning early."

By the time this letter reached New Orleans "Master Rodolfo Matas" had already moved into the residents' dormitory at Charity Hospital. The roommate assigned to share his quarters was a young man from Mobile, James Pepper by name, a shy, reserved youth who was almost as deeply absorbed by and in his studies as Rudolph. The two young men took an instant liking to one another but had little time to develop their acquaintance into enduring friendship, for this was the summer of 1878. The steamer *Emily B. Souder* had docked at Erato Street on May 23 from Havana, and the worst yellow-fever epidemic the United States was ever to know had already begun.

CHAPTER VIII

The breach between Narciso and Teresa Matas became absolute during their son's second year as medical student. No one now recalls what incident played the traditional role of last straw. In all likelihood Narciso, who had just turned forty, looked afield for solace from his wife's chill nagging. Temperamentally, he was still the romanticist he had always been, but nothing about the bitter fifty-year-old woman at his side could kindle or respond to ardors engendered by one glimpse of "the beautiful young lady with long black hair" who had passed through a room in San Felíu two decades earlier. Teresa's voluble charges of promiscuous infidelity were no doubt overdrawn but not baseless.

The irreparable rift which parted his parents proved to be less of an emotional upheaval for Rudolph than might have been anticipated. For one thing, his mother and sister arrived from Brownsville with all personal belongings while New Orleans was setting off what became the most virulent yellow-fever epidemic in the nation's annals.

As it began its savage sweep inland from the Mississippi River's mouth ultimately to devastate no less than 132 city-size communities, some of them as far north as Illinois, Rudolph worked practically around the clock. The alternation of night and day lost all meaning for him, as it did for every physician, near-physician, hospital employee, nursing sister, sanitarian, and sickroom attendant. He did help install Teresa in the vacant one of his father's two "unlucky" houses at 82 Circus Street; and a few days thereafter he assisted in the enrollment of Elvira at the Sacred Heart Convent School. But he simply did not have time for family chit-chat or his mother's monotonous tirades about her husband.

At the hospital, new patients were being admitted by the hundred, day after stifling, oppressive day, as the deaths of those admitted earlier made room for newcomers. The dreadful cry of "Bring out yo' day-yud!" echoed alike through squalid slum and gilded garden district.

Inasmuch as even yet no one knew just what the cause of yellow fever might be or how contagion was transmitted, the source of epidemics was all too often undiscoverable. Not so with the scourge of 1878, which was accurately pin-pointed at the New Orleans wharf where the steamer *Emily B. Souder* docked on May 23 from Havana, with two ailing ship's officers aboard, a purser named Clark and an engineer named Elliott. Going ashore that same day, they came down almost at once with unmistakable cases of yellow fever, and thus vectored an epidemic in which 15,934 of more than 75,000 cases would die.

Even prior to that date of omen, Rudolph's time had been fully occupied with his new duties as resident. Among the chiefs from whom he learned most, three surgeons stand out: Samuel Logan, Tobias Richardson, and Moritz Schuppert, a German-born stormy petrel of surgery under whose direction he took a humble but ever memorable part in the first major operation carried out in New Orleans under the principles of antiseptic surgery, newly given to the world by Lister.

Schuppert had no direct connection with the medical department of the University of Louisiana; on the other hand, setting aside personal feelings toward him as an individual, he was widely recognized as one of the city's most brilliant surgeons. A native of the old cathedral town of Marburg on the placid little Lahn river, he had been the darling of a wealthy father who provided for him the finest medical education available. He came to New Orleans in 1853 and served with such distinction during the yellow-fever epidemic of that year that he was invited to become a permanent member of the visiting surgical staff at Charity.

In 1859 he and Samuel Choppin, later head of the city health board, founded New Orleans' first Orthopaedic Institute at 179 Carondelet Street, where Schuppert performed an apparently fabulous number of operations and, according to an obituary tribute in the *New Orleans Medical and Surgical Journal*, became "especially skillful in the treatment of deformities." The same source speaks of him as a man of "strong prejudices, bitter hates, deep-rooted convictions which . . . like Luther, he dared maintain against the world."

One of these convictions was complete acceptance of Lister's newly enunciated theory of antiseptic surgery. Up to that time the only recognized defense against postoperative infection was operative speed: wash the limb to be amputated well with soap and water, semiliquid green soap for preference; use heavy knives to sever the flesh swiftly, tie off the blood vessels, rasp through the bone as hastily as possible with a great butcher-type saw, put in a continuous suture of waxed silk or linen thread, clap on a huge "cotton-bale" dressing of ordinary, unsterile lint, finish the job with all dispatch, and hope that only "laudable pus" will exude from the raw tissues before they granulate and heal.

From almost the very moment when Lister published his epochal findings, passionate controversies raged between standpat adherents of traditional speed surgery and converts to the Listerian techniques. As usual, these disputes generated more heat than light. Writing in 1878 for the A.M.A. *Journal*, Dr. B. A. Watson quoted Assistant Surgeon-General of the United States, A. C. Girard, to the effect that, during a visit to England, "it happened my first intercourse was with some of the most decided and renowned opponents of the system . . . and [I] received therefore the glowing accounts of Lister's disciples with an incredulous ear [but] I became convinced that if it is not the only proper wound treatment, it is the safest one and renders conservative surgery possible beyond what had ever been believed."

In 1876, Moritz Schuppert, newly returned from a summer abroad with his two physician sons, declared with characteristic truculence that "amongst the many improvements I met with, nothing surprised me more than the results obtained by the so-called antiseptic method of Lister, and having seen its wonderful and astonishing results, I do not hesitate to proclaim it one of the most important improvements in modern surgery, and I stand today fully committed to it."

By 1878 Dr. Schuppert had already used Lister's methods on a recorded 173 operations, but it happened that none of these involved abdominal surgery. It must be borne in mind that during the 1870's —indeed, until well into the 1890's—an abdominal operation was rare to a degree it is difficult for this day and age to comprehend. Charity Hospital records show just one such operation in 1878, and only one other during the year that followed. Surgery was then almost wholly confined to amputations, fracture corrections, ligation of aneurisms, obstetric emergencies, and the removal of external tumors.

But, though Dr. Schuppert found no opportunity to apply the Listerian method to abdominal cases, he did make converts in great numbers. One of these, Dr. William Carson, was chief of the surgical section at Charity to which young Resident Matas was assigned. Thus when, in 1878, a case of ovarian tumor, which clearly called for last-resort abdominal surgery turned up, Dr. Carson decided to use the technique exemplified in orthopedic operations by Dr. Schuppert. He also asked the latter to supervise all preparatory steps and stand by as adviser and consultant during the actual operation. In addition, he requested Dr. Schuppert's two sons, Charles and William, to assist him, since they had frequently assisted their father with whom, three years earlier, they had toured European hospitals and medical schools.

The patient in this instance was a white woman, well past middle age; recording his recollections of the case half a century later,* Rudolph Matas described her massive tumor as being "of a size now (1940) never seen, but common enough when tumors grew unmolested in a patient living in the rural districts like trees of a primeval forest which have never known the aggression of the sawyer or the lumberjack."

The day was hot, even for New Orleans; the humidity of that operating amphitheater must have been almost unendurable, since every table was draped in a freshly laundered sheet wrung out in a 5 per cent carbolic acid solution; the freshly scrubbed instruments were still glistening and wet with the same solution; nurses, surgeons, and assisting residents were clad in freshly laundered gowns, these and the clothing beneath them being the only textiles in the room not soaked with the Listerian disinfectant. All hands of physicians and nurses had been scrubbed first with green soap and then with 5 per cent carbolic acid, a steam atomizer maintained a continuous spray of the same sort of solution over the field of operation during actual surgery, and two residents, one of whom was Rudolph, stood on stepladders holding up spread cotton bedsheets which had been drenched with it.

The patient was prepared by having her abdomen plastered with green soap and then scrubbed; a freshly laundered linen towel wrung out in alcohol was then laid over the operating field to keep it from contact with air until Dr. Carson, with the elder Dr. Schuppert seated on a stool beside him, made the initial cut. The abdominal opening had to be very wide to enable the younger Schupperts as the operation progressed to wipe out the cavity with large marine sponges soaked in 5 per cent carbolic acid solution.

For those accustomed to the traditional school of swiftest possible surgery, the operation seemed endless. Moreover, a number of unlooked-for difficulties served to prolong it. Small tears in the intestinal walls had to be sutured as they developed in freeing the enormous tumor from other tissues with which it had become involved. The

* "Surgical Operations Fifty Years Ago," *American Journal of Surgery* (New York), vol. 51, 1941.

moist and stifling heat of the chamber made it necessary for one nurse to do nothing but wipe the foreheads of Drs. Carson and Schuppert with cloths wrung out in ice water.

Rudolph stood patiently on his ladder through it all, observing Carson's surgery with constantly rising doubts. What effect would this prolonged spraying and sponging with carbolic acid have on the patient's kidneys? Moreover, what price disinfection and gowning and all the other precautions if an ever-growing host of onlookers, none of whom were gowned or scrubbed, was permitted to crowd elbow to jostling elbow into the small operating room to observe the new technique?

Final stages of the operation had to be hastened on the traditional pattern of speed, after all, because the elderly patient began to show alarming symptoms of approaching collapse. Yet for two days she appeared to rally from her ordeal and actually gave promise of recovery. On the third day, however, nephritis set in, her kidney function slowed and finally failed altogether. This was followed, on the sixth day after the operation, by death. Naturally enough, that set off a renewed fury of polemics.

Another operation that same year also left its impress indelibly on Rudolph's remarkable memory, despite the competition of crowded hours. He and a fellow resident, Charles S. Mercier, son of the Armand who had treated him during his siege of yellow fever, were summoned to assist Tobias Richardson in an operation to be performed in a room of the St. Charles Hotel. This establishment still claims distinction on the ground that it was and is the first hotel, as differentiated from an inn, to be opened in the United States. Though twice gutted by fire, it was rebuilt on the site it occupied at its dedication in 1836 and continues to occupy today.

Dr. Richardson's patient was Mrs. Lucinda Davis Stamps, only surviving sister of former President Jefferson Davis of the Confederate States of America. He was to operate on her for the removal of a breast cancer. His two assistants carried instruments, anesthetics, dressings, and all else that might be needful, in towel-wrapped packets. Mr. Davis, who would be the guest of Judge and Mrs. Charles E. Fenner at their Garden District home, as he customarily was in those days during visits to New Orleans, accompanied his sister when the physicians arrived but left as soon as preparations for surgery were under way. The patient was given a hypodermic injection of morphine while seated on the divan of the ornate suite the hotel had put at Mr. Davis's disposal and then anesthetized with chloroform dripped onto an open cone. Dr. Richardson still enshrined the Confederate cause as something sacred. To him the unconscious woman somehow symbolized the Cause. He bent over her, lifted her in his great arms, and carried her ever so gently to the bed which had been divested of everything but tightly stretched fresh sheets. Bending to place her there, he kissed her forehead in all reverence . . . but at that instant the Southern idealist made way for a coldly unemotional surgeon, and the operation began. It was completed with the swift precision that Richardson not only preached and practiced but demanded of his disciples. Within the fortnight Jefferson Davis took his sister to Beauvoir to complete her convalescence.

Lesser incidents likewise served in their own peculiar fashion to exalt the Jovians on the faculty in Rudolph's eyes; for example, the morning when Dr. Logan, with Rudolph to assist him, was about to remove a tumor from the back of a male patient before a crowded amphitheater of students. Just as the surgeon bent over the table where the patient lay prone, a paper pellet struck him squarely where the hair of his domed head was thinnest. He laid down the instrument a nurse had placed in his palm, straightened his shoulders, looked coldly about the suddenly hushed amphitheater, and said, "The one who did that is an arrant coward." For still another breathless moment no one stirred. Dr. Logan stared ramrod-straight at his students and made no move to begin the operation.

Finally, one hapless member of the class shamefacedly confessed himself the culprit, but added that no disrespect had been intended, only faulty marksmanship being to blame. Another student had dozed off, and the pellet was meant merely to rouse him from his slumbers. Unsmiling, Dr. Logan nodded and began to operate.

There had been another electric moment during a major amputation by Dr. Richardson. Reaching for the heavy bone saw, he suddenly waved the proffered instrument aside, stared at the patient, then seized a scalpel and made a vertical slit in the man's throat, just beneath the Adam's apple. Through the opening thus made, he thrust one end of a rubber drainage tube into the man's windpipe. "Cannula!" he said, crisply, holding out his hand without taking his eyes from the patient. Rudolph searched through the bright objects on the instrument tray until he found the desired metal tube, which Dr. Richardson deftly substituted for the rubber one he had used as an emergency measure.

"It didn't occur to you to let me know our patient had stopped breathing, did it?" he asked the now terrified anesthetist caustically. Then he turned to the students and other onlookers. "If, during an operation, the blood that follows the scalpel suddenly begins to look dark, almost black, instead of bright red, check at once to see whether or not your patient is still breathing just in case your anesthetist"— with a withering glance at that unfortunate—"may have gone to sleep himself. This man's lips were already blue. If I were to hazard a conjecture, it would be that a clot of mucus, which frequently forms during chloroform anesthesia, settled in his throat. Bronchorrhea, it is called." He picked up the heavy saw and swiftly completed the amputation.

No matter how pressed by work, Rudolph took out time at least once a month to write to his father briefly, inclosing an invariably scrupulous accounting of every penny he had spent out of the allowance Narciso made him. His father always replied promptly and asked how Elvira was getting along, but never inquired after Teresa. Elvira, incidentally, was becoming an insufferable little prig, who sniffed disdainfully whenever her brother, who adored her, snatched time from his duties for a hasty visit to 82 Circus Street and told her that her father had sent her a kiss.

Visits of this sort were necessarily few and far between. When the ominous rise in the number of daily yellow-fever admissions that summer first was noted, this had been hopefully ascribed to customary increased summer incidence. But such optimism was short-lived, and the physicians who, two years earlier, had given their professional imprimatur to the demand for relaxing quarantine detention of inbound vessels in favor of simple fumigation, were beginning to wish they had not signed the published document that stated categorically: "It has been clearly proved that quarantine does not protect this city from Yellow Fever." Among the signers had been Bemiss, Chaillé, Souchon, Lewis, Logan, Richardson, Schuppert.

Now Dr. Joseph Jones, head of the State Board of Health, remarked anent the two ships' officers who had gone ashore from the *Emily B. Souder* within twenty-four hours after the vessel had been merely fumigated instead of detained at quarantine: "It is but reasonable to conclude that if a definite period of detention for vessels from infected ports had been enforced by the Board of Health at the Miss. River quarantine station, cases of Yellow Fever could not have passed unobserved."

Nonetheless, Dr. Matas himself was to write, as late as 1935, that "only those of us who have survived the horrors of the great epidemic of 1878, with its 5000 dead in New Orleans alone, can realize the terror and apprehension in which we lived in fear of other visitations, not only the fear of the disease, but restrictions and trammels put on commerce by the rigid quarantine, often of the shotgun variety, that forbade all communication by land or water with the metropolis and other suspected places."

Men, women, and children were dying by the hundreds before the eyes of helpless physicians; and one fourth of all those who came down with the terrible infection, whatever its cause might be, were fated to die of the Black Vomit. At the Medical College of the University of Louisiana, Dr. Sam Bemiss shared—and impressed upon his students—the belief that in the dissemination of yellow fever "atmospheric air is the usual medium through which the infection is received into the human system through the respiratory passages," and this belief in the *contagium virum* theory of yellow-fever transmission was stoutly supported by Dr. Chaillé in his lectures on pathology.

Dr. Albers, the municipal sanitarian who had so valiantly disinfected the neighborhood of the Matas residence when little Rudolph lay ill there in 1867, insisted that "the yellow fever germ or poison is probably not generated in the human system nor transmitted from one person to another in any way . . . it is an organic poison, the resultant of the decomposition of the excretions and secretions of the human body, accumulated and confined in ill-ventilated habitations . . . and moving along the ground, not influenced greatly by winds, or it would spread more rapidly." And so he continued to deluge gutters, privies, back yards, streets, and vacant lots with carbolic acid. And still the disease spread from district to district that summer of 1878 until every district of New Orleans was invaded, and the infection "was carried by steamboats and railroads far into the interior of the valley" where, as along the Gulf Coast, one out of every four who felt the first agonizing head pains and the onset of chills, collapsed and died after the *vómito prieto* manifested itself three to five days later.

"The fever is caused by something that has the power of propagation and is therefore alive, it is a germ that reproduces itself in human blood. . . . It is killed by cold, and that is why the epidemics invariably stop with the first touch of winter weather. . . . It can't be a germ, for the malady is not personally contagious. . . . The spirillum in the blood of all patients suffering from relapsing fevers. . . ."

The arguments raged to and fro, and still among slums and rich, garden-surrounded mansions, carters raised the harrowing cry of "Bring out your dead!"

The Howard Society did what it could to supply medicine, nursing aid, and other relief to the fever's victims. But physicians who battled the epidemic also had to amputate gangrenous limbs; women had to be tended in childbed; colds and indigestion had to be treated. Private practitioners, hospital staff members, and even the young residents were actually grateful for the sight of a patient who was not merely part of a statistical group of which one fourth was doomed to dreadful death no matter what aid medical science might seek to render them.

Though they shared the same room at the hospital, Rudolph and James Pepper saw very little of one another. Both worked until they could work no longer, then slept in utter exhaustion until dragged back to duty by the moment's inexorable need.

As weary days became stagnating months, incessant toil began to levy a tribute of fatigue among the younger physicians. Rudolph was less susceptible to such disruptions of normal existence than were most of his classmates. Though not a celibate in a community whose mass-morality code was notoriously lax, he had been too greatly absorbed in his studies and had seen too much in the hospital's free clinics of the price venereal distempers exacted for casual indulgence to qualify as anything of a libertine. Hence the unremitting demands of hospital service in that fearful summer deprived him of time he would otherwise have devoted to his books and his laboratory, especially as regards the taking and interpretation of photomicrographs, which was then a relatively new field of biological inquiry.

Rudolph's roommate, James Pepper, developed a sort of fixation that he was destined to die of yellow fever during this siege. Nothing Rudolph could say would dispel these forebodings, though he fetched from the orderly storehouse of his memory all known arguments showing that yellow fever was not directly communicable from person to person.

"One of the remarkable things that has been established is this"—he pointed out time and again—"doctors and nurses who are in almost unbroken contact with fever patients rarely come down with it. One might think that intimate association with those who have the sickness protects one against contagion."

But Pepper took scant encouragement from such reminders, pointing out that it was all very well for Rudolph to talk, since he was an immune. So Rudolph took another tack, arguing that in any case his friend Pepper was no worse off in New Orleans than he would be at home; by that time Mobile was as heavily hit by the epidemic as was New Orleans.

Meanwhile, casualty lists, printed daily, lengthened into column after column of agate type, and this meant a corresponding fourfold increase in the number of those stricken with the yellow contagion. Each newspaper's issue was seized avidly as it came off the press; only thus could one learn which friends or acquaintances had died during the preceding twenty-four hours.

Then came a midmorning coffee pause when Rudolph halted abruptly to cast a searching glance at his roommate. Without doubt the conversation followed what had become almost a standardized pattern in that calamitous season of dread.

"What's the trouble? Are you feeling bad?"

"Just a headache. Some of this swill they've been feeding us residents must have disagreed with me. It's nothing."

"Why? Your stomach feel upset?"

"Some."

"Better take it easy, Jim. You look like you'd been out on the town. Why don't you stay in bed till you feel better? I could tell Dr. Pratt. . . ."

"Don't you tell anybody anything, Rudy. Anyway, the nausea's gone. It was just something I ate. I've felt worse than this many and many a time."

But the next morning his eyes were bloodshot and the pain in his temples, back, and legs had become outright agony. His teeth chattered, and his shoulders shook convulsively in a hard chill. Dr. Pratt isolated him in his room since his roommate was an immune, shook his head at the cloudy coagulate forming in a specimen of the young man's urine as the flame of a spirit lamp heated the test tube. The next morning Pepper was jaundiced and delirious and began to retch with the black vomit. During the night he died. The body could not be dispatched to Mobile at that time, so a burial service of sorts was held in New Orleans. Rudolph sent the Pepper family Jim's watch, ring, and other valuables, and tried to tell himself that this death was only one of thousands which blighted other homes each grievous, steamy day; but even in his letter to his father he could not be quite matter-of-fact and professional in relating what had happened. Here, for the first time, he had felt the warmth of adult friendship. Now he suddenly found himself in unaccustomed solitude.

Then came a day in September when his faith in the immunity conferred by benign attacks of yellow fever was rudely shaken. He himself fell suddenly and violently ill of a fever which his teacher, Dr. Bemiss, declared to be yellow fever. Yet he recovered rapidly and boasted to his fellows that he was the only one among them who had twice won the title of "immune."

Not long thereafter he suddenly realized one early morning that the air was cool. The number of hospital admissions had perceptibly decreased. There were moments when one could relax restfully from the ardors of the day. Finally there was a full week when not a single new yellow-fever patient was brought to the hospital. Once more the city bestirred itself. Wharves were piled high with cotton bales brought by each incoming river steamboat and loaded by singing screwmen, the aristocrats of New Orleans' work-along-shore men's guilds, into ocean packets bound for Liverpool, Boston, and Yokohama.

Dr. Chaillé stopped him in one of the hospital wards one day and asked him to come to his office that afternoon.

"George M. Sternberg, one of the Army surgeons in Washington," he began, "has been saying right along that the facts relating to the spread of anthrax and relapsing fevers, and what little we do know for sure about the pathology of yellow fever, make it probable—he's very hopeful about this—that if we go to some endemic focus of the disease with a properly financed and equipped expedition we might be able to demonstrate what organism in the blood is responsible for it. He wasn't able to get anyone of any consequence interested in it till this year, when yellow fever spread to a lot of communities that had never known it before. They were brave about it as long as it was just something that happened to others, but now they all demanded action. So Congress organized a National Board of Health; incidentally, a good friend of your father's, who graduated from the same medical school a year or so after he did, Dr. Jimmy Dupree, helped a lot to get that movement organized. He is a member of the legislature, had the fever himself this year, is public health officer of Baton Rouge, and so on. Anyway, the first thing the new National Board of Health did was appoint a commission to go down to Havana next year and make a real study of yellow fever, right where it's at home. I've been asked to be chairman."

Rudolph congratulated the great man warmly, and said something to the effect that this was a signal honor not merely for Dr. Chaillé, but for the whole medical school.

"We're going to need an assistant to act as clerk and laboratory technician, someone who is immune and who speaks Spanish, so that he can also double as interpreter," Chaillé interrupted, smiling. "I have nominated you. Brush up all you can on preparing celloidin sections of tissues for microscopic examination, staining blood smears, collecting blood samples, taking care of laboratory animals, and so on and so forth. We'll leave in July, probably, shortly after the end of the school year, most likely from New York."

CHAPTER IX

They went pitching down to the Pearl of the Antilles that summer aboard the good ship *City of Washington* with their microscopes, their cameras, their laboratory animals, and also, since they were a government group, reams of printed forms. En route they discussed organization of the task ahead, eschewed shuffleboard, beanbag tournaments, and other shipboard diversions, and only now and then, after they had surged into warm Gulf Stream waters, did they pause to watch the flying fish as these skimmed from one long-backed comber to the next.

For Rudolph and Dr. Chaillé, the trip was merely a continuation of the sea voyage which had brought them from New Orleans to New York, where they organized the mission in due form, with Dr. Chaillé as chairman and Dr. Sternberg as secretary. Other organizational work was done on shipboard, under instructions from Dr. James L. Cabell, president of the new National Board of Health, of which body the commission was officially an agency and to which it would report its findings.

In a number of respects their project was unique. For one thing it was the first scientific mission ever sponsored by the United States to seek protection for "the lives and health, and therewith the wealth and property, of its *human* inhabitants from disease." There had been expeditions to study fungus parasites and other diseases affecting livestock and agricultural crops—wheat rust, cotton wilt, potato blight and hog cholera. But never before had such a group been set up governmentally to find a defense against an epidemic which struck down only human victims.

Nor had any such expedition ever been more lavishly equipped. Two main lines of investigation were to be undertaken. The first was to determine, if possible, the "pathological anatomy" of yellow fever, along with the nature and history of its cause or causes. This field was allotted to Dr. Sternberg and Dr. Juan Guiteras of Philadelphia, a native of Matanzas in Cuba. Dr. Chaillé and Colonel T. S. Hardee, a sanitary engineer who would join the mission in Havana, were to study the actual field conditions there as regards hygienic precautions and determine what bearing this might have on the endemicity of yellow fever. Why should this ancient city—San Cristóbal de la Habana—be the focal point from which every traceable yellow-fever epidemic had been transmitted to the United States?

In fitting out the mission, expense had been all but disregarded. Dr. Sternberg was an advanced investigator of what was still a relatively new field in those days, the microscope hunt for subvisible living organisms in diseased tissues or body fluids. So Karl Zeiss, in Jena, at that time the world's foremost lens maker, had been commissioned to grind and assemble the two finest microscope objectives ever produced, oil-immersion magnifiers, one of which would enlarge an object by 1450 diameters. In addition, photographic equipment had been devised to make a permanent record of such magnified views.

Only three years earlier an obscure German country physician named Robert Koch, had furnished experimental proof of the relation between *Bacillus anthracis* and the deadly disease it caused. Working with homemade materials in the back room of his surgery at Wollstein, carrying forward what Louis Pasteur had discovered only a decade or so before, he had succeeded in inoculating rats unfailingly with fatal attacks of anthrax.

The Pasteur Institute would not even be founded until 1886, though in Glasgow the great Lord Lister had recently developed Pasteur's discoveries of what caused fermentation in milk, wine, and ale into his still-controversial system of antisepsis. And throughout the scientific world, scientists were seeking other bacilli which could be convicted as causative factors in disease. Small wonder Sternberg's hopes of solving the mystery of yellow fever in this fashion were so high.

"I was familiar with the most approved method of mounting and staining micro-organisms," he reported, "[and] . . . not only did I feel that I was equipped for the recognition of any micro-organism which might prove to be present in the blood, but I was prepared to photograph it, and thus to show to others what I might see in the blood drawn from yellow-fever patients."

Indeed, his assignment appeared much simpler than that to be undertaken by Dr. Chaillé, as the latter pointed out during the uninterrupted round of shipboard conferences which engrossed them even at their meals during the four-day journey. "Did you ever try to assemble statistics from nonexistent hospital records?" he would ask ironically. "Local health boards are supposed to gather them for us, but even the government hospitals publish no reports and seem to keep no records beyond those of the immediate present; at least no records of any value to the sanitarian."

Actually all they knew was this: while the New Orleans from which they set out had undergone 21 major assaults of yellow fever during the preceding twenty-eight years, the Havana that was their goal suffered yellow fever endemically twelve months out of every year. From November to April the rate of incidence slackened, rising ominously to epidemic heights from then until fall. Among the population every native adult was an immune, because no one lived any length of time in Havana without dying of yellow fever or becoming armored against it for life by surviving a "benign" attack.

According to statistics subsequently assembled, the civilian death rate was 45.83. The death rate of U.S. soldiers during the Spanish-American War was 67.94; after the famous mosquito campaign of Gorgas in 1901–2, it dropped to 7.

But this still lay far in the future when the Chaillé mission was received with official honors at Havana on July 7, 1879, and escorted to the San Carlos Hotel, the entire top floor of which had been set aside for their laboratories, offices, and living quarters, while a special section of the flat roof was equipped to house their laboratory animals —dogs, cats, rabbits, guinea pigs, chickens, pigeons, geese, and monkeys. The Governor and Captain-General of Cuba, don Ramón Blanco, marqués of Peña Plata, was plainly under instructions from the highest authority to do all in his power by way of assisting the *yanqui* mission, for the Crown desired particularly at this juncture to impress the *norteamericanos* with Madrid's eagerness to co-operate.

Alfonso XII, barely past twenty-one, had finally come to the throne three years earlier and was earnestly seeking to restore orderly government to the shambles his mother had made of Spanish administration before her expulsion. He had managed to patch the home government and was anxious to avert the loss of his empire's only remaining colonies in the western hemisphere, Cuba and Puerto Rico. Less than a year before the Chaillé Commission reached Havana, an inconclusive struggle for Cuban independence—the so-called Ten Years' War—had been terminated by an equally inconclusive peace through the Convention of El Zanjón, in which Alfonso made a number of concessions to the Cuban Separatists.

As always under such circumstances, Spain's well-armed soldiers could and did win every battle. But they could never win the war, since Separatist guerillas simply melted into the jungle when they were routed. They could not be pursued one by one, and soon regrouped elsewhere. Over the years this had drained Spain's already anemic national treasury. It had also threatened to bring on intervention by the United States, which had pointedly refused to join other powers in guaranteeing Cuba's possession to Madrid.

Alfonso's concessions to the Separatists momentarily eased the ferment of his colonial rule but brought on still greater disaffection at home. Naturally, the termination of the Ten Years' War was reported as an unconditional victory. According to the invariable pattern of reaction to the end of an overseas conflict, an immediate clamor was raised by the families of expeditionary soldiers to "bring the boys back home." And it was at this juncture that yellow fever which, for ten years, had caused horrifying mortality among the nonimmune Peninsular troops, struck its most vicious blow. The year was 1878. Spanish soldiers died by entire companies on the transports that were bringing them home, in their staging areas, in military hospitals.

Foreign policy considerations aside, it was therefore no wonder that Madrid's attitude was, in effect: "If the *yanquis* can do something about the *vómito negro*, let them have anything and everything they want in the way of facilities."

Thus an official delegation, a military guard of honor, and an auxiliary commission of Cuban physicians, scientists, and sanitarians met the arriving Chaillé mission at the quai, under the guns of Castillo de los Tres Reyes del Morro. In addition, a delegation of Forto kinsfolk, headed by young sublieutenant Juan, was on hand to welcome Rudolph. Cousin Emilio, at Brownsville, to whom Narciso had proudly communicated the news of Rudolph's appointment, had notified the entire *gente* of their distinquished young relative's prospective arrival. Since even the least of these scientific missioners was a notable, they made much of him throughout the three months of his stay.

To the auxiliary commission Captain-General Blanco had appointed Director Parenas of the Royal Military Hospital, Drs. J. G. Lebredo, F. Zayas, Felipe Rodriques, and Abraham Moroján (a recent graduate of the University of Pennsylvania), a Dr. Canada, and the corresponding secretary of the Cuban Academy of Medicine, a tall, angular, stoop-shouldered physician, peering nearsightedly through gold-rimmed spectacles, Carlos Juan Finlay. Shepherded by Consul-General H. C. Hall and Dr. Daniel M. Burgess, U.S. sanitary inspector of the port, they paid a formal call on the captain-general in the *sala capitular* and found him the soul of co-operative urbanity.

All Havana laid itself out to extend hospitality to the visitors from the United States. Lavish entertainments, both official and unofficial in character, were the order of the day and night, especially the latter, though Dr. Chaillé had announced at the outset that every evening but Thursday, from seven-thirty to nine, the members would be at home to callers in their G.H.Q. on the top floor of the San Carlos. In Rudolph's case, the Forto tribe was anxious to lionize their kinsman, to show him off at the theater, at dinners in their homes in the Cerro, at social functions of all sorts.

The two boys, young army officers, regarded it as a matter of course that they were to take Rudolph out on the town, making the grand tour of palatial barrooms, gambling casinos, and, equally as a matter of course, the brothels, circuses, and peep shows along Progreso Street. Rudolph, it must be confessed, had small taste for this carbon-copy-of-Paris night life. Essentially, there was no difference between Progreso Street in Havana and Customhouse Street in New Orleans. Moreover, a crowded schedule left him little time and less energy for casual venery, and, finally, he was more interested in occupying free hours with Carlos Finlay, as they could converse with equal facility in English, Spanish, or French. It was natural that despite the difference in their ages—Finlay was approaching forty-six and Rudolph would not be nineteen for another two months—they should find one another congenial.

As for young Matas's schedule, his small zoo on the roof had to be maintained scrupulously, along with copious records of when which animals were inoculated with how much blood from what yellow-fever victims. This was in itself a laborious and ultimately fruitless chore. The distinction between urban yellow fever, which attacks only humans, and sylvan yellow fever, whose prevalence in certain jungle animals is a matter of concern among sanitarians to this day, had not yet been recognized.

In addition to his more immediate duties, this teen-age missioner suddenly found himself caught up in a new enthusiasm: beriberi. He knew next to nothing about it, when he discovered to his surprise that it was at that time widely diffused throughout Cuba and had a high fatality index among Negroes and Chinese. He encountered only one case but seized every opportunity to discuss it with a world authority, Dr. Serafino Gallardo, one of whose lectures he was fortunate enough to attend.

"I devoted my leisure moments," he recalled later, "to the collection of what data I could find pertaining to its prevalence in Cuba and

America generally, in order that some day I might if possible interest some of my confreres in this subject . . . if it be only through its very novelty."

The Forto boys shook their heads in bewilderment over this young and obviously virile cousin, who yet preferred the company of Dr. Finlay or Dr. Gallardo to that of girl entertainers in one of the world's gayest cities. Incidentally, Rudolph's schedule included many other duties. He had also to make numerous visits to military hospitals, where the fever was at its worst, since nonimmune youths from Spain were concentrated there. He had to collect blood samples from the newly dead and the dying, keeping the identity of each with the meticulous accuracy with which he still kept the accounts of his penny-by-penny personal disbursements. This identification had to be maintained through all stages of the scrutiny to which the samples were subjected. Sternberg and Guiteras made individual smears of them on glass slides, stained them, peered at them through the powerful oil-immersion objective of their microscope hour after sweating hour, and photographed them, seeking spirilla, or rods, or chains, or other patterns such as Koch and Pasteur had showed so clearly in the blood of sufferers from other maladies.

Tissue specimens had to be taken from the skin, muscles, and internal organs of those who had died of the Black Vomit. These had to be passed through graduated concentrations of alcohol for complete infiltration with celloidin, mounted in a microtome submerged in alcohol, and sliced to a thinness measurable only in fractional thousandths of an inch; then the slices were affixed to glass slides and stained for microscopic study of the cell structure to see what changes, if any, Bronze John had wrought.

Reports had to be dispatched weekly to the National Board of Health, Dr. James L. Cabell, president, in Washington. The fact that there was nothing of substance to report, made the task no less onerous for the authors of these documents.

It must also be conceded that in many respects, living conditions were anything but pleasant. Water was scarce throughout the capital; even for household use it had to be purchased from itinerant vendors, since all wells in the porous coral rock upon which the city was built were incredibly contaminated by the seepage of nearly four centuries of excreta from densely packed humanity. The law of supply and demand being what it will always be, water was so expensive that Rudolph and the other members of the mission paid approximately 30 cents to have one shirt washed; 30 cents "oro," not "plata," U.S. pennies being worth two Cuban coppers.

"The insanitary evils resulting from this general insufficiency of water in a tropical climate," the mission's final report was to chronicle rather plaintively, "are much greater than would ensue farther north. When bathing becomes difficult . . . it is not strange that an unusually large portion of the people are offensive to the smell."

Dr. Daniel Burgess, sanitary and quarantine inspector for the United States and local aide to the Chaillé Commission, had lived in Havana since 1866, and reported to Congress that "heaps of excrement, garbage, and dead animals, putrefying in the tropical sun, are common. . . . The universal household receptacle for human excrement and household slops is merely an excavation in the rear of the house. The effluvia therefrom pervade the houses, and the fluid contents saturate the soil and the soft, porous coral rock. . . . Thus Havana may be said to be built over a privy."

Dr. Lebredo, member of the Cuban auxiliary commission, remarked wryly at a meeting at which the sanitary situation was discussed: "To one who asked an inhabitant of the Pontine marshes how life was there possible, the answer was given that 'We do not live here, we die here!' So might we, who dwell in Havana and other parts of Cuba, reply to that question."

Those were the surroundings amid which, for three months, the Chaillé Commission sought to establish some point of reference in solving the mystery of yellow fever. The incredible lack of sanitation was bad; but, as in New Orleans, Havana's few clean and well-kept residential sections were plagued by yellow fever at a rate similar to that in the foulest of slums.

Again, yellow fever was obviously a nautical disease, since ports were invariably the focal points from which the infection was vectored, and ships the principal agency by which it was transmitted. Yet the fever never appeared spontaneously in ships which had not first stopped at some infected port, notably Havana or Veracruz. Again, with abattoirs, forts, military hospitals, soap factories, and the gas works all emptying their sewage and refuse into Havana harbor, the water there, "though examined carefully and repeatedly by Dr. Sternberg, failed to present evidence of special putridity."

Similarly, every other avenue of investigation turned out to be a cul-de-sac. For example, the "poison of yellow fever" *must* be a living organism, since it incontestably propagated and reproduced itself. Yet nowhere—not in the foul harbor water, not in the blood or tissues of yellow-fever patients or corpses, could the highest power of the microscope show any identifiable agent that could be charged as causative factor of the epidemics.

And so it all came to nothing. The hours spent amid the dead and the dying in military hospitals, the countless sessions around the conference table, the "visiting office hours" each night except Thursdays at the San Carlos, the search among reeking cesspools, the long, stiflingly hot nights when Sternberg, Guiteras, Mancel, and Matas hunched over microscopes, fussily adjusted their camera, ran less-than-paper-thin sections of flesh from yellow fever corpses through brilliant dyes, photographed them as magnified, or cleaned the cages of rabbits, guinea pigs, monkeys, and geese.

Some long-standing fallacies about what caused yellow fever were demolished; a number of fruitless avenues of investigation were definitely sealed off as blind alleys. But in late September, when the great Yellow Fever Commission sailed from Havana for New Orleans to compile a voluminous final report, its members took away with them not one jot more about yellow fever than they had brought with them three months earlier.

They had confirmed to some extent what was already accepted widely in regard to the spread of these epidemics, namely, that yellow fever could be contracted only in infected localities; in other localities it could not be transmitted even by patients dying of the malady. Residents of Mexico City, visiting sea-level Veracruz in fever time, might and probably would contract the disease. But even if they came down with it after returning to the mile-high altitude of the capital, they never communicated it to others.

The Commission was also able to negate definitely the belief that in yellow-fever patients the blood is "completely disorganized." The falsity of this was shown by photomicrographs of blood taken from dying fever patients, the pictures clearly revealing that "both the red and white corpuscles retained their normal appearance."

But no micro-organisms could be made visible in that blood! Rudolph Matas had collected in all 98 samples from 41 incontestable cases of yellow fever among the soldier patients in the military hospital of San Ambrosia. At a magnification of 1450 diameters (which means the total area of each corpuscle was nearly two million times as great on the photograph as in life), 105 negatives were made "which show satisfactorily everything demonstrable by microscope. . . . It is doubtful whether any objective has ever been made capable of showing more than is revealed by this magnificent lens [i.e., the specially made 1/18-inch objective]. With the power used, organisms much smaller than those described as existing in the blood of charbon or relapsing fever would be clearly defined. If there is any organism in the blood of yellow fever demonstrable by the highest powers of the microscope, as at present perfected, the photomicrographs taken in Havana should show it. No such organism is shown in any preparation photographed immediately after collection."

RUDOLPH MATAS

In short, what Koch had done with anthrax, Pasteur with hog cholera and milk, and others were demonstrating with charbon and various fevers, the Chaillé Commission had not been able to do with yellow fever. Its final report, made in 1880 and published by the government printing office the following year, frankly confessed its failure to advance the knowledge of any substantial facet of the yellow-fever problem.

"The members, neither of the National Board of Health nor of its Commission indulged in any illusory hopes," the document conceded. "It is believed that while this report is destitute of the record of any wonderful discovery, it none the less will tend to correct many errors, to strengthen some truths, and to suggest some special researches."

Its general conclusions were brief. Summarized, the Chaillé Commission found that yellow fever was neither inoculable nor personally contagious; that ships, steamboats, and railroad cars were the chief disseminators of the fever's poison," which in turn "spreads, multiplies, and is endowed with the functions of reproduction which is limited to living organisms." The doctrine that yellow fever originates spontaneously on ships was, as previously noted, rejected as unproved. As for the failure of Drs. Sternberg and Guiteras, together with their assistants Matas and Mancel, to demonstrate any living organism in more than 100 microscopic studies or photomicrographs, "a belief in the existence of living organisms, invisible to the highest powers obtainable by the microscope, is just as logical as is the universal belief in extra-microscopic atoms and molecules."

That was all; and one is bound to admit it was thin stuff for a scientific mission which had brought together the best-trained available scientists and had given them everything they could possibly ask in the way of equipment and assistance, under the authority and backing of two governments. Certain it is that Drs. Chaillé and Sternberg, along with their fellows, were those most keenly disappointed. Yet, could they have realized it, the photomicrograph prints made by the Mancel-Matas laboratory team from Sternberg's negatives were destined within the year to become the first basic step in the conquest of yellow fever.

The man who used those photomicrographs as a springboard from which to vault to the solution of a deadly mystery, may have reached the right answer for the wrong reason and from a fallacious premise. His logic may have been as faulty as the speculation which led Aristotle to declare the human brain to be nothing but a cool organ which properly refrigerated blood for the heart.

Yet within less than two years of the Commission's departure from Havana, one of their Cuban auxiliaries publicly declared, on the basis

113

of experiments undertaken after a close study of their photomicrographs, that the dread disease was spread by the "sting" of the female *Culex* mosquito. But he merely urged that his "suspicions," though fully borne out by the few simple experiments he had conducted, be subjected to intensive and controlled experimental tests. . . . And practically no one in the United States or Havana or elsewhere would pay the least attention to him!

He was the son of a French mother and a Scottish physician of Camaguey, who named him Carlos Juan at his birth in December 1833. The elder Dr. Finlay spared nothing in affording his first-born the best education the times afforded, sending him to private schools in Havre and Rouen, with a year in London, before entering him in Jefferson Medical College at Philadelphia, where he received his M.D. degree at twenty-two. Even then, Carlos was not yet willing or ready to settle down to the routine of amputations, obstetrics, cupping, and 150 golden prescriptions. For ten years more he traveled through North, Central, and South America, France, Germany, Austria, and Britain, making a particular study of epidemic diseases, since these, more than any other ailment, harried his homeland.

He returned to Havana immediately after the close of the Civil War in the United States, married a girl from Trinidad, and became a general practitioner in the best tradition of the times. His work was painstaking, rather than impressive; yet his treatise on "The Atmospheric Alkalinity of Havana" in relation to the incidence of yellow fever and other epidemics attracted enough attention so that he was appointed to the auxiliary yellow-fever commission by Governor Blanco in 1879. It must be remembered that though at this time yellow fever was still regarded widely as being telluric in origin—that is to say, springing from soil conditions—Dr. Bemiss in New Orleans had committed himself to the *contagium virum* belief, in which he was supported by Dr. Chaillé, that the epidemics were atmospherically borne and entered the human system through respiratory passages.

Though Carlos Finlay was nearly thirty years older than Rudolph Matas, the oddly assorted pair were strongly drawn to one another from the first—the dapper, short, slim Matas, black hair *en brosse* after the fashion affected by his father, mustache and imperial fastidiously groomed; Carlos Finlay, on the other hand, was tall, inclined to be gangling of figure, his domed head beginning to show through thinning hair above a luxurious mustache which merged into no less luxurious mutton chops at the base of each cheek, his large-boned stature accentuated by the traditional frock coat of medical practitioners in that era.

Something in the nature of each undeniably struck a spark in the other. Both were confirmed skeptics, eternally on the lookout beyond traditional acceptance for something tangible, something capable of laboratory proof, on which to build scientific advances. As the farewell gift which Rudolph knew his much older friend would prize, he left him a set of prints of the photomicrographs he had helped Mancel to make of Sternberg's magnificent negatives.

Like the United States members of the Chaillé mission, Finlay harbored no illusions about what that body had achieved in the way of tangible results. Yet he studied and restudied those photomicrographs, time and again. Over and over he compared what they showed with what he could see in fresh sections and fresh blood smears. The longer he studied them the more firmly convinced he was that the very thing that had disappointed Sternberg so keenly—failure to show any change or abnormality in the blood of dying yellow-fever victims even under the highest possible magnification—was supremely significant.

"What more especially elicited my attention," Finlay wrote in his first modest publication, which Rudolph Matas translated for the *New Orleans Medical and Surgical Journal*, "was the fact demonstrated in these photographs that the red blood corpuscles were discharged entire in the hemorrhages . . . [which] take place without any apparent rupture of the blood vessels."

Yet hemorrhages did take place. The blood in the stomach of dying victims, acted on by acids, constituted the "black" vomit that presaged fatal termination.

"This symptom (hemorrhage) being the most salient clinical feature of the disease," the Finlay report went on, "surely pointed to the vascular endothelium (the inner lining of the blood vessels) as the site of its principal lesion."

In other words, as Dr. Gilberto Cepero of Havana related the story after decades had passed, Finlay argued that yellow fever was an "eruptive affection," like measles and chicken pox; but instead of erupting outwardly through the skin surface, the eruption apparently turned inwards, through the walls of the smallest blood vessels desquamating their lining. The infectious matter of such maladies was always to be found in the erupted lesions. Measles and chicken pox, bearing these on the outer body surface, were thus directly contagious from person to person. Yellow-fever patients, on the other hand, bore the seeds of epidemic proliferation along the innermost walls of their smallest blood vessels. Hence (Finlay reasoned), it followed that some bloodsucking insect must draw out the "inoculable material" and finally transfer it to the blood vessels of another and healthy individual who, if not immune, promptly contracted the disease.

"All the requisite conditions for the transportation of the inoculating virus," Finlay pointed out in the Matas translation, "are admirably combined in the mosquito, the sting of which it would be almost impossible for us to imitate with the comparatively rude and coarse instruments which could be manufactured by our most dexterous artisans."

To test this hypothesis he imprisoned female mosquitoes in glass jars, let them feed from a yellow-fever patient, and after a period of incubation, permitted the same mosquito to "bury its lancets," impregnated with the virulent particles," in an unacclimated human volunteer. In almost every instance, this procedure was followed in the non-immune subject by a "benign" attack of yellow fever.

"My only wish in presenting this communication," he wrote, in making public his findings, "is that note be taken of my observations, and that the truth of my suspicions and conceptions be left to the decisive evidence furnished by direct experimentation."

The paper in question was delivered in Washington, before an International Convention of Hygiene in February 1881. It was ignored by all. Then, after further experiments, he delivered it in amplified form in August of that same year before the Academy of Sciences in Havana, under the title: "The Mosquito Hypothetically Considered as the Transmitter of Yellow Fever." Far from being accorded a warmer welcome and a more attentive hearing by his compatriots, they were so little impressed that the paper was tabled without discussion. Sixty years later, at elaborate ceremonies marking the 108th anniversary of Finlay's birth as Pan-American Health Day, Dr. Cepero was to write:

"[Finlay's] words evoked no echo beyond that of the chamber itself. . . . He sought to convince with his theory his contemporaries who witnessed with dread the Dantesque spectacle of looking on helplessly as the insatiable yellow monster destroyed thousands of human lives. And this happened, as Guiteras has said, 'not through his fault, but ours, who did not understand him.' Only one friend and convert, who practiced medicine in the stricken city of New Orleans, showed confidence in the Mosquito Maniac (*El Loco de los Mosquitos*). Dr. Rudolph Matas had the courage to transcribe the Finlay article in the renowned *New Orleans Medical and Surgical Journal* in February 1882; appearing in the same number of this review, a work by Dr. Henry Stone attributes Yellow Fever to electrical changes brought about by telegraph lines. . . ."

Two decades of fever epidemics were to pass before any one in authority finally decided to put the Mosquito Maniac's theory to the definitive test. And ever since that time the Cubans, who were the first to scoff at *El Loco de los Mosquitos,* have sought—and not always successfully—to counteract the impression that the discoverer of the mosquito's role in disseminating yellow fever was a North American named Walter Reed.

But after his mad hypothesis had been proved up to the hilt, Carlos Juan Finlay was no longer without honor in his own country. He was made Chief Public Health Officer of Cuba in 1902, a post in which he served for eight years. And in 1941, a portly, retired, but still world-renowned surgeon, Rudolph Matas by name, was called to Havana so that the president of the republic, Fulgencio Batista, might confer upon him the first award of the Finlay Medal, as the world's first, foremost, and most consistent *Mantenedor del Finlayismo*—Defender of Finlay-ism.

CHAPTER X

Rudolph Matas became a Doctor of Medicine at noon on March 19, 1880, though he would not be twenty-one years old for another eighteen months. The stately ceremony was modified in his case by the introduction of an element not ordinarily part of an elaborate ritual that brought together some of the nation's greatest medical authorities.

Narciso did not come to New Orleans to glory in his son's memorable welcome into the ranks of licensed and practicing physicians. He would have given the eyes out of his head to do so but sacrificed that supreme moment of paternal pride lest the obvious breach between himself and Teresa, publicly observed, cloud Rudolph's triumph. Even *in absentia* he was one of the architects of that triumph, however, whereas Teresa and Elvira were merely passive spectators.

For months Narciso had followed every incident of his son's final student year, not only through the boy's letters, which faithfully detailed all his activities, but from reports by acquaintances who traveled between Brownsville-Matamoros and New Orleans, such as Nina Sherwood, daughter of the Gomila family whose patriarch was Narciso's broker.

The final year of his training course was Rudolph's busiest. His work as resident would have been more than enough in itself to keep him fully occupied. Nonetheless he must now prepare, in addition, for the ordeal of his Green Room orals, after two years of not attending didactic lectures by the very faculty members who would quiz him relentlessly before deciding whether or not to admit him to their inner circle of medical practice.

However, his fantastically retentive memory stood him in excellent stead. He read not only textbooks and copies of lecture notes obtained from other students by loan, purchase, or by barter for the privilege of attending an obstetric delivery; he also devoured any medical publication on which he could lay hands, especially the foreign-language pamphlets which came to Dr. Bemiss, publisher-owner of the *New Orleans Medical and Surgical Journal.*

By January Narciso began a series of clamorous demands for the exact date of the college's prospective graduation exercises, an item of information no one was as yet in a position to supply. In his letters he also made increasingly petulant inquiries about Elvira, who seems to have broken off all correspondence with her father at this time. But Rudolph determinedly closed his mind to all such distractions, gulped coffee for breakfast, and, at other mealtimes, with an open book beside his plate, ate whatever was put at the residents' table.

Ignoring what was there set before him assuredly involved no hardship. The hospital administrators had too Herculean a task on their hands in this year to lavish much attention on the residents' cuisine. The old building's dilapidation had gone so far during nearly two decades of military occupation and carpetbag rule, that much of the bedding was worn out, while here and there the soft brick of the walls was crumbling perilously. Governor Nicholls's newly installed appointees did what they could to remedy the worst ravages of neglect. They demolished the foul and fetid privies and replaced them with what passed for sanitary brick structures, they bought new hospital cots of black walnut, and—wonder upon wonder!—they connected New Orleans' only public hospital by telephone with the rest of the community.

Utterly oblivious to what went on aside from his work and study, Rudolph had not so much as an inkling that early in March Mr. Gomila had delivered personally to Dr. Chaillé some packages and a letter Mrs. Sherwood had just brought from Brownsville. These had been entrusted to her nearly a month earlier by Narciso, who wrote that they included "the following articles, viz: one ivory handled cane—one diamond finger ring—one gold watch and chain and one letter addressed to Rodolfo—all of which I wish you to retain in your possession until the day of the distribution of diplomas, on which occasion I wish you to present them in my name to my son Rodolfo, if possible at the same moment his diploma is handed to him and in the presence of the large assemblage of people who will probably witness the act. I wish to take him completely by surprise and hope you will not let him into the secret before hand. It is a small reward for a son whose merits and good deportment and exemplairy life are familiar to all, and by which he has won the simpathies and respect of his companions and professors, and the pride and idolatry of his father . . . Hoping you will grant me the favor I have asked of you and join me in giving a nice surprise and many congratulations to my Son (whom you also like so well) on the occasion of his admission to the high and responsable position of a new member of the medical profession."

Narciso must have beggared himself in purchasing the gold watch and chain, the ivory-handled cane and the diamond finger ring with which to launch his son on what would be nearly seventy years of active medical practice. He confessed as much to Rudolph later, when he bewailed his inability to send him to Paris for a year's postgraduate study. The letter which accompanied the gifts addressed his darling for the first time not as "Master Rodolfo Matas" but as "Doct. Rodolfo Matas, Graduating Hall, N. O."; and he explained that while it was impossible for him to be "contributing with my presence to increase your pleasure and happiness for the glories won to day," he nonetheless thanked Dr. Chaillé for assisting him in preparing an agreeable surprise by "delivering to you this letter with a few presents." He continued:

"Please accept them, My dear Son, not alone as a token of the love and admiration of your father, but also as a reward of merit for your good deportment during the prosecution of your studies and your exemplary life while a student. . . . Receive many hearty congratulations for your final success from your father who loves you dearly.

"N. H. y Matas M.D."

Rudolph received another letter from his father a few days after graduation, though this had been written and dispatched before the great event. It was a reply to the young man's jubilant telegram announcing his conquest of the Green Room finals, and shows how very deeply Narciso was moved by this fulfillment of all his dynastic hopes and aspirations.

"Although I will not be present," he wrote, "my heart and soul will be with you and I would pay a thousand dollars if I could wittness without been seen the affects of your unexpected surprise.

"Let me thank God my dear son for his goodness in saving your life hearing my prayers which addressed to him from the bottom of my heart and for having let you accomplish your studies so well and so satisfactory and for keeping you such a good boy and such a good son to be the comfort and the pride of your father. Joy to day my dear son and feel yourself the happiness and contentness with which my heart is full to day for your success.

"I intent to celebrate this day in my house in Matos [Matamoros] and give a dinner to your friends here in commemoracion of your graduation day if my occupations allow me to do it. O how I would like to see in the list of your graduates the name of Joseph Peper. Poor parents. I imagine how I would feel myself now if at that time you had been like him the victim. Oh I shever all over, only to think of that and thank God a thousand times for this kindness. . . .

"Tell me how Elvira was happy when she seen the pretty things I sent to you. Did she like that nice ring of yours? Tell her that her papa likes her as well as you and she will have also her things sent to her the day she finishes her education if she is a good girl and loves her papa dearly like you do."

But in the next letter to Rudolph, Narciso included a plaintive paragraph in which he said of his daughter that "I like to know how she don't write to me anymore? I pourposely did not answer her last letter a few months ago, except through you, because I want to find out whether she will write to me again or not. I think she is trying to punish me for that fault and although she might feel hurt I do not think that she is acting right by following such strict etiquet with her papa . . . it looks to me like she is enterely lost to me and that she can live just as well without my love. Poor thing. She does not know what she is doing now and she can not appreciate how much I love her. It is not her fault but the fault of better advises. God Bless her and forgive her like I forgive all her unresponsable faults give her a sweet kiss for me and tell her that her papa loves her dearly."

The foregoing letter was written on March 28, nine days after a stately academic procession marched at noon from the Medical College along Baronne Street, past Rudolph's onetime lodgings, and across Canal Street to the arcade of the Grand Opera House.

In the lead walked Dean Richardson, with President Randall Hunt of the University of Louisiana at his side. Though technically part of the University, the Medical College never failed to make a public show of autonomy. Hence the University's president, who would hand the graduates their diplomas but would first receive these parchments from Dean Richardson, was an invited "guest" at the ceremonies, as were other notables from far and near. Among these was Dr. Samuel D. Gross of Philadelphia, a founder of the American Surgical Association and the American Medical Association. He and his son Haller had traveled two and a half days by train from Philadelphia via Louisville to attend the ceremonies. Dr. Richardson had been one of Dr. Gross's favorite pupils. But the latter was merely another visiting notable at the graduation exercises, the commencement orator being James B. Eustis, one time member of the United States Senate. One of Dr. Gross's fellow guests, incidentally, was Dr. George M. Sternberg, of Washington, under whose supervision Rudolph had labored in Havana the year before.

Protocol was meticulously followed in seating these bigwigs, the governor, the mayor, the clergy—and the graduates, of course—on the big Opera House stage, with the Thirteenth Infantry Band in the orchestra pit, and the boxes crowded with relatives, friends, and thrill-seeking spectators who had come to gape at a for-free performance. The custom of wearing academic gowns with hoods lined with the bright colors of various universities had not yet come into vogue at New Orleans; faculty members and other dignitaries all wore conventional frock coats. But lack of academic color was more than compensated for by the floral tributes with which the graduates were literally overwhelmed.

According to an obviously entranced scribe, recording current events for the *New Orleans Medical and Surgical Journal,* the orchestra struck up the strains of Lang's *Flower Song* while "a committee of students commenced the arduous task of carrying to the stage the floral tributes of the newly made doctors: bouquets, baskets of flowers, crowns and in fact every conceivable emblem almost, wrought in the most delicate of roses, violets and exotics. Such was the prodigality of the lady friends of the graduates, the stage was almost carpeted with Spring blossoms and some of the gentlemen were almost knee deep in the fragrant blooms. . . . As each happy graduate received these tokens of kindly feeling and well wishes the house applauded to the echo."

Rudolph received his meed of such tributes from the Jorda, Sambola, and Gomila families. But his real moment of triumph came later. Dr. Benjamin M. Palmer, organizer of the First Presbyterian Church and one of the Confederacy's secessionist leaders, and Bishop John N. Gallaher offered prayers, President Hunt introduced Senator Eustis, the topic of whose commencement address was the controversial and still very touchy subject of "Commercial Intercourse Between Communities and States During Epidemics." Thereafter Dr. Richardson presented the graduates, calling them up one at a time to receive their diplomas. At the conclusion of this ceremony, he asked Dr. Chaillé to take over. The latter called out Rudolph Matas to receive not only his father's gifts but in addition a glowing personal encomium on behalf of the faculty. Then he invited Dr. Gross to say a few words informally. This address, though unscheduled, became the most memorable feature of the occasion.

For one thing, Dr. Gross paid high tribute to the memory of two departed New Orleans physicians and the living presence of a third member of the city's medical faculty. The first two were Dr. Warren

Stone, a founder of the college whose forty-sixth class was thus being graduated, and Dr. Charles A. Luzenberg, who had been Dr. Gross's instructor and demonstrator in anatomy at Philadelphia's Jefferson College in 1826. The third was his friend, former pupil, and present host, Dean Richardson. He recalled among other things that Dr. Luzenberg had invited him to join the faculty of the new Medical College of Louisiana.

Rudolph Matas's attention was not too sharply focused on this address, since it was delivered after he had received not only his father's "nice surprise," but Dr. Chaillé's remarkable encomium as the class's best student. Yet nearly sixty years later, in 1937, when called on without prior notice to give a convention of the American Surgical Association in New York his impressions of Dr. Gross, he did so quite extemporaneously and with a wealth of detail that is almost beyond belief.

As "perhaps the only one here present who can claim to have heard the voice of the great founder" of the Association, Dr. Matas described how "Dr. Gross spoke at the commencement exercises of the Medical School. This was in 1880, and I was one of the graduating class to whom he addressed his remarks. Well do I remember his venerable figure; tall, erect, and remarkably well proportioned, stately despite the burden of his 75 years, speaking without notes in a deliberate, resonant but well-modulated voice . . . He spoke of [Warren] Stone as a man whose heart was as big as that of an ox, from which poured a constant stream of human sympathy and endless charity. . . . In life the best loved citizen of New Orleans, and after death his loss deplored by a whole population as a public calamity. . . . These reminiscent remarks I fear only serve to confirm the President's reminder of my antiquity as the oldest living president of the American Surgical Association, and perhaps justify the vanity of age which still finds enjoyment in the recognition of self in the pictures of historic events long forgotten by younger contemporaries."

Since Dr. Matas's memory remained so sharp after the lapse of more than half a century, one is bound to regret all the more keenly that the letter he addressed to his father on March 24, 1880, in which he detailed what took place at the graduation, was not preserved. All that remains is a transcript of his father's reply, written in Matamoros ten days after the great event, addressed to "Mr. Rodolfo Matas, M.D.," and covering nearly a dozen closely written pages.

"I read with the greatest joy," he wrote, "the contents of your valuable letter of the 24th. . . . Glory. Glory to you, my dear son, and I thank God for your success and for your merits. . . . Your letter is a long one but I feel so interested in it that I read it over and over 3 or 4 times. Besides, I participated its contents to all our friends who have feeled the greatest admiration for you. All the newspapers of Brownsville and Matos have made some kind remarks about you and I inclose and addresse to you the principal ones you can judge by this all the sympaties you have in this place and how proud I feel of it. I see by your letter that Dr. Chaillé had another mission besides mine which is one of the most flatering to you and to me in fact to honor you before your companions and before the public audience in the name of the Faculty in such absolute and remarkable terms as he did, stating that you have been the best student in capacity and good behavior, is realy very flatering and I hope you will thank him and the Faculty very cordialy for me for their kindness."

Narciso then offered reams of advice on planning for the immediate future. Obviously Rudolph had suggested the possibility of opening an office on Canal Street and also remodeling one of the "unlucky" Circus Street houses along rather lavish lines. At any rate Narciso replied, on this score:

"I think an office in Canal Street or in its near abouts would cost too much for a biginer. Now according the plans that have been presented to you; I do not consider it very advisible and would be very hard for me at the present conditions of my financial resources."

He confessed quite frankly that ordinarily he would have sent Rudolph forthwith to Paris for a year of further study, but in this respect again money was too hard come by in these troublous days along the border. Washington would serve to bring his son into contact with the nation's great ones, it was true; but setting up for medical practice in Washington would be feasible only if he could receive employment with the National Health Board or some other such body, to defray necessary expenses. Joining the Army or Navy was to be eschewed by all means, since this offered so limited a career and would lose Rudolph the field of practice he had already established in New Orleans. Cuba was only good for someone who wanted to speculate with a rich marriage; moreover, political conditions there were more unsettled even than along the Mexican border.

As for the Canal Street office, that should be considered only if he could associate himself with "Doct Logan or some other prominent physician to assist him as secretary adjutant to his office and allow to put your name in his door." However: "If you think that your plan is the best, and there is no way to avoid the expense of the 400 dollars I am willing to make any sacrifice for you even to hire the money if I have non. Since the beginning of the present year I am doing nothing and I can not collect hardly any bills. Here we have 4 new physicians and the competence and business are so bad that I am affraid I shall have to mouve from this place, if the conditions do not change soon. Dr. Melou is doing nothing and he is very much despaired like me. In fact I do not know of any physician who does much work now in this place. I do not beleave however that it is because the people is too poor to call a physician. I have an important affair in my mind which I shall submit to your consideration in some other occasion when you be definatly setled in your profession."

Narciso was thus obviously not the only member of the family to feel the pinch of a money shortage at this time. Rudolph had an ivory-headed cane, a diamond finger ring, and a gold watch and chain, but no instruments and no money with which to supply himself with all the hundred and one items of equipment among the minimum essentials a surgeon must have. It becomes evident that he sent word to his father by friends, asking that whatever instruments Narciso could spare be sent him as a sort of surgical seedbed. The postscript to the foregoing letter reads:

"To day I payed a visit to Mr. and Mrs. Carson and I was delited to hear your triumphal event from their friendly and entusiastic lips. The instruments I could send to you are no account, and you can buy those that you need and draw against your uncle. I shall send to you the geography and some other books as soon as I shall have an opportunity of some acquitence going to New Orleans. Please tell me in your next letter how much rent you get from the corner house. I understand that business have improved considerable and property like rents must go high——"

It was when Rudolph asked Uncle Tomás for permission to draw on him for the cost of basic surgical equipment that the latter gave him his graduation present: appointment to the post of physician of the Sociedad Unión Española de Beneficencia. This was the very post that had been denied Narciso thirteen years previously, whereupon that hot-tempered venturer renounced New Orleans for Brownsville-Matamoros. Tomás Jorda had succeeded the late Francisco Sambola as president of the society, whose member families were assessed $2.00 annually for each individual in the household to defray the cost of medical service. With this income as nucleus Rudolph could afford to buy not only the instruments and other items of equipment he needed. He could also afford to transform part of one of the unlucky houses at 82 Circus Street into a reception-examination-consultation suite.

Almost overnight finances ceased to be a problem for him. Though Rudolph was only a little more than twenty-one years old, Dr. Arthur de Roaldes put him on Charity Hospital's visiting staff and explained to the resident medical students who were assigned to his service that they were singularly favored.

126

Finally, Rudolph was formally associated with the *New Orleans Medical and Surgical Journal* when Dr. Bemiss sold it to a group of local physicians. He had been translating and abstracting foreign-language papers for Dr. Bemiss during most of the preceding year. Now he became part owner and associate editor, the new publisher being Dr. Lucian F. Salomon, with Drs. Frederick Loeber and D. C. Holliday as associates.

Moreover, the publicity attendant upon his connection with the Chaillé Commission to Havana less than a year before, the announcement of his appointment as physician to the Spanish Benevolent Society, and the word-of-mouth reports of the encomiums publicly bestowed upon him on graduation combined to build with unusual rapidity the nucleus of what was destined to become one of the finest and most remunerative medical practices in the professional annals of New Orleans.

His mother kept house for him and Elvira, a moody and withdrawn adolescent approaching the close of the formal schooling open to young ladies of that era. But he had little of what is commonly understood by the term "home life." Assuredly he did not share the cold disdain with which Teresa and Elvira regarded his father, and it is equally certain they could offer him neither adequate companionship nor intellectual stimulation. Fortunately his practice now took up most of his time; whatever free hours remained he devoted to the reading of professional publications at the office of the *New Orleans Medical and Surgical Journal*.

The one bond that still linked him closely to his mother and sister was that of their religion. Within the year that tie slackened away. It was first loosened during the long, hot nights of confinement to a hospital barge moored at the foot of the bluffs atop which Vicksburg's half-starved, cave-huddled defenders had surrendered to Grant in 1863.

CHAPTER XI

Rudolph Matas's first twelvemonth of practice was highlighted by another yellow-fever epidemic and by the inception of the one great, consuming and apparently hopeless love affair of his life.

The revelation came to him between clock ticks in one of the Charity Hospital's public wards on a steamy morning of late spring. In the open gutters, sided by heavy cypress planks, the hot season had already launched a fermentation which spread the iridescence of decay over all standing water. Rudolph was not yet opulent enough to set up a horse and buggy; indeed, he still lacked much of the equipment he meant to acquire before permitting himself anything in the nature of a luxury. So he was grateful, not only for the shadowed coolness but for the clean-scrubbed hospital smell that greeted him as he entered the main building where young Chassaignac, his intern, awaited him.

As they crossed the tessellated vestibule, with its checkerboard floor of black-and-white marble flags, Chassaignac began a rapid summary of pending cases, laying special emphasis on a newly admitted patient in the ground floor men's ward that was their first scheduled stop.

" . . . not the sort of person you'd expect to find in a charity bed, Doctor," young Chassaignac was saying. "For that matter, not the kind of family you'd expect to find there either. His wife and daughter are with him; ladies of culture and background."

"Tell me about him, first. What seems to be the trouble?"

"Some sort of dysentery, I suppose. At any rate, a dreadful, chronic diarrhea that's pulled him down—he must have been a muscular man in his day!—but this sickness has pulled him down to nothing. No temperature, pulse and respiration both normal."

By this time they had entered the ward, with its two rows of narrow, black walnut beds, each with a tester from which the grayish folds of a tucked-back mosquito-bar depended. They paused at one of these.

"Captain Goslee, Doctor," Chassaignac murmured in the professional low tone he cultivated for ward rounds. "Mrs. Goslee and her daughter."

Fumbling out his hunting-case gold graduation watch, Rudolph looked up absently from the bed, where the features and appearance of the patient had claimed first interest. His casual glance met the fathomless pools of a girl's dark eyes and locked there. Never again throughout his life would he look upon any other woman with ardor, yet it was all over by the time he had finished withdrawing his watch and had snapped its lid open.

"Please ask the ladies to wait in the hall until I can make an examination," he said to Chassaignac. Turning to one of the Sisters of Charity who constituted the hospital's nursing staff, he asked that screens be placed around the patient's bed. The nurse moved away to comply. The wide, starched wings of her snowy coronet wavered above the dull blue of her robe, and the beads of the rosary at her girdle clashed as she walked.

Later, after he had palpated the patient's shrunken abdomen, listened to his breathing, peered into his gaping mouth, and otherwise completed his examination, he shook his head.

"I'm afraid there isn't much we can do here," he said ruefully to Chassaignac. "How old did you say he is? Fifty-nine? And he's never been in the tropics? Certainly there's no palpable mass in the abdomen, and yet I have a feeling we'd find a cancer there if we could look. For the present, all we can do is try to check the diarrhea with powdered bismuth and chalk every three hours and laudanum morning and night."

He walked out into the hall where Mrs. Goslee and her daughter were waiting.

"You are the patient's wife, aren't you?" he asked, addressing the smaller of the two women.

"I am Mrs. Goslee, yes, and this is our daughter, Adrienne—that is to say, Mrs. Landry."

The world collapsed in fragments about young Dr. Matas, but outwardly he gave no sign. "Mrs. Landry," he murmured, without raising his eyes from the nod of acknowledgment he had directed toward her before turning once more to her mother. "I'm sorry to have to tell you we've got a very sick man in there. . . . It's too early, of course, to speak with certainty, but I assure you we'll do what we can for him. For one thing, we can make things easier, at least. And within a few days we hope to have him strong enough so that we can send him home to you, where he'll get more individual attention and be in more cheerful surroundings. You and—and—Mrs. Landry can minister to his wants perfectly well, and I shall be glad to call at the house to keep an eye on the patient's progress. . . ."

Bit by bit, the story of the Goslee's tragedy was pieced into a coherent whole. Mrs. Goslee—her first name: Ermance-Marie—was the daughter of Professor Charles Edmond Marc, who had taught French, literature, and Latin at the DeLord Institute for many years, at Mme. Fornaris's Overseas Institute and at other select private schools. It was from him that Adrienne had learned to read so beautifully and to speak not merely the Creole patois of New Orleans but the classic French of the Paris where her grandfather had studied as a youth.

Professor Marc had looked with favor upon the suit of the handsome, dashing Kentuckian, Thomas R. B. Goslee, for the hand of Ermance-Marie. Tom Goslee was not merely dashing of appearance; he had become a hero among both the Union and Confederate sympathizers in captured New Orleans when he daringly ran the entire Mississippi River blockade in '63, from Morganza south with the Confederate gunboat *Webb*. Flying a Union flag, he passed Donaldsonville and Baton Rouge by night. At New Orleans, where the levee was literally swarming with small Union warships, he waited until he was opposite Algiers Point and then, in full view of all, defiantly lowered the Stars and Stripes and raised the Stars and Bars.

A fast Union gunboat immediately set out in pursuit. When he saw he was being overhauled, Tom Goslee beached the *Webb*, set fire to her, and escaped into the swamps with all ship's papers and other valuables and without losing a man of his crew.* After the war he returned to the river as a pilot, until he was able to finance the purchase of his own packet. He was also a musician of parts; the excellence of his ship's orchestra, maintained to furnish music for arrival and departure at important stopping points, was known from St. Louis to the Gulf. It was an open secret that no instrumentalist who found himself

* The foregoing is taken from an obituary printed on June 21, 1881, in the Evansville (Ind.) *Courier*, Captain Goslee being a native of Evansville. However, Charles L. Dufour—writer, historian, member of the Tulane University faculty, and founder of the Civil War Round Table of New Orleans—declares categorically that either there were two such incidents and two ships named *Webb*, or the Evansville account is wholly incorrect. He cites the official Naval reports in which no officer by the name of Goslee is listed among those aboard the *Webb* at the time she made her spectacular dash, which took place in 1865.

stranded anywhere along the river need fret about free loading it home, if one of Captain Tom Goslee's vessels was anywhere about.

This well-favored gallant wooed and won petite Ermance-Marie. They were a devoted couple, and the union prospered in every material way. Ermance-Marie bore her husband one daughter, and then six sons. The girl, Adrienne, was Gran'pere Marc's special darling. He taught her French, Spanish, and even a smattering of Latin. But best of all, he introduced her to the treasures of French and English classical literature and would listen in delight when she read to him.

All had gone well until steamboating declined, as railroads absorbed more and more of the nation's freight traffic. Professor Marc died in 1875, and the next five years were especially hard for the Goslee brood. Not only did the Captain's income dwindle, but his health gave way; in time he became a chronic invalid. Adrienne married Arthur Landry in 1879. He was a reasonably prosperous liquor dealer and did what he could to help, but even he could not take on the entire support of his parents-in-law and six brothers-in-law. Gradually all the family possessions had to be sacrificed. Even Professor Marc's magnificent library was sold piecemeal to Goldthwaite's Bookshop to provide funds for the traditional economy diet of Creole New Orleans: red beans and rice.

Rudolph was scrupulous in making professional calls at the Goslee home at Orleans and St. Claude Streets, but did not see Adrienne again until June 12, when he signed Captain Goslee's death certificate. Even then, however, he could not rid himself of her image. By day and by night the thought of her buxom beauty, of the shadowed, fathomless eyes beneath hair darker than black walnut, haunted him. It followed him to Vicksburg in August, when he was appointed inspector of river traffic there.

This assignment was an outgrowth of the 1881 yellow-fever season. Though not as severe as the dreadful scourge of 1878, memories of that plague's balefully swift inland penetration along the Mississippi River system were still sharp; they prompted the two-year-old National Board of Health to institute a rigid inspection service for all river traffic.

To be sure, no one knew one whit more about yellow fever than had been known half a century earlier. Dr. Joseph Jones, for example, president of the State Board of Health, was still staunch in the conviction that lack of sanitation gave rise to such scourges. In his memoirs he noted for 1881 that "New Orleans has no system of sewers, the excrement of 200,000 inhabitants and strangers who constantly crowd our streets must be moved by hard manual labor. . . . It is horrible to contemplate the effect of hoarding this vast accumulation of human filth in this damp, hot, semi-tropical climate." He likewise laid heavy emphasis on "the affectionate proximity" of milk rooms and privies in most of the city's dairies.

For many years quarantine and fumigation had been imposed intermittently at or below New Orleans on inbound ocean vessels, without perceptibly affecting either the incidence of the virulence of yellow-fever epidemics. Nonetheless, memories of the contagion's rapid inland march three years earlier prompted the National Board of Health to decree that river packets, towboats, and barges plying the Mississippi and its tributaries would no longer be permitted to clear from New Orleans for upriver ports without certificates of freedom from fever cases among passengers and crew and from obviously insanitary conditions of hold and cargo, issued after presumably thorough inspection. All too often, however, unscrupulous steamboat-men would leave New Orleans without notifying the inspectors of their imminent departure or would pick up additional barge tows surreptitiously a short distance upstream, after receiving clearance certificates before casting off from the crowded levee.

Inspection stations were therefore established at Vicksburg and at Memphis; however, the inspection system contributed nothing useful toward the prevention or even checking of yellow fever. Looking back from the vantage point of the late twentieth century, one can sense fully the tragic impact of the fact that 1881 was the year in which an international congress of sanitarians remained completely indifferent to the suggestion of Carlos Finlay that the "*Culex* mosquito be considered hypothetically as the sole carrier of yellow fever."

Under such circumstances, it can hardly be considered too remarkable that at Vicksburg the incidence of epidemic fevers was far higher among health-board inspectors than among the population in general. For one thing, they were restricted to the waterfront's low ground and prohibited from passing back and forth to the town site on relatively high ground atop the east-bank bluffs. Confined to the humid, mosquito-swarming lowland, in close proximity to such fever patients as were detained on the hospital barges, it is small wonder the new Health Board's inspectors—northern Republicans, naturally—were rapidly expended. No less than six of them succeeded one another in swift succession during the first two months of the 1881 fever season, a new one being dispatched to the post as his predecessor succumbed, which was usually after little more than a fortnight of local service. Collins took over the Vicksburg station when it was opened on the 18th of May, fell ill, and had to be relieved by Winn on June 7. Winn was prostrated on June 28, and relieved by Ashe, who was already coming down with a malarial chill when he reached Vicksburg, and resigned as soon as a successor could relieve him.

This was Dunlop, on temporary assignment which shifted him from duty at his regular post in Memphis where the district superintendent, Dr. W. F. Reilly, filled in for him after frantically asking that an immune, well salted to all local fevers, be sent to Vicksburg from New Orleans without regard for political affiliation or previous connection with the Confederacy's military or civilian regime. On that basis Rudolph Matas was appointed and moved in on August 24. A harried Federal government blandly disregarded the fact that he would not be twenty-one until three weeks after his appointment went into effect; this ineligibility factor was ignored not merely because the new appointee was an immune but because he was specially qualified by service in Havana with the Board's own Yellow Fever Commission under Chaillé and Sternberg two summers before.

One can still almost hear the sigh of relief with which the Board's 1881 report set down at this point the notation that at Vicksburg "no further changes were made during the remainder of the season."

It is difficult to imagine the stifling, hemmed-in loneliness of the months Rudolph passed at his Vicksburg post. The city proper had not yet truly begun to rally from the pitiless siege to which it had been subjected in 1862–63. With the possible exception of Atlanta, no Confederate metropolis suffered more physical damage from enemy action; no other was reduced to a rat-and-mule meat diet before its final capitulation.

In addition, ten years after hostilities ceased, the Mississippi River abruptly cut across the narrow neck of the great meandering loop which passed at the foot of Vicksburg's tall bluffs. Quite possibly the ditch Grant's command dug across this neck of land during the winter of 1862–63, though not successful in diverting the river's main stream from Vicksburg at the time, was the proximate cause of the cutoff which, in 1876, relegated one of the Mississippi's most important ports to "Centennial Lake," a semistagnant backwater, leading in characteristic oxbow form upstream from the new channel.

In that backwater at the foot of the bluffs which shut him off from breezes, Rudolph Matas sweltered through his twenty-first birthday and through all the stifling, mosquito-whining nights that followed. He was isolated by his assignment from his family and from other natural human companionship; and by her prior marriage from the only woman he would ever love. "She possessed me completely," he confided diffidently later, "from the moment I first saw her. I realized that in a single instant I had found and lost the one woman who could have made my life complete!" Finally, the irreconcilable breach between his parents sealed him off from contact with his father, that vivacious rolling stone who nonetheless was the only kinsman in whose company Rudolph could find the intellectual stimulation he prized so highly, just as Adrienne was the only woman who could have given him emotional release. And both were utterly lost to him. What was it his father had said in that long letter of advice he wrote after his son's graduation? "Never marry a older woman than you, nor one that she is not sufficiently inteligent to make you happy."

Ah, but Adrienne did have intelligence to complement her beauty. A gifted musician, one who spoke French, Spanish and English with the same fluent facility with which Rudolph himself had mastered them, a girl familiar with the classics—and the wife of another man, the mother of another man's child! He must forget about her at all costs. Even if she might feel for him the unquenchable yearning which possessed him at the mere thought of her, even if she left her husband, she would be a *divorced* woman. The Church would never sanction his marriage to such a one. He must accept the hopelessness of his passion as a doom that had been laid upon him. His mother, though living apart from her husband was still Narciso's wife. She would cast Rudolph out of her life too, if he entered such a union, since the Church would regard a divorcée as still the wife of another.

Rudolph had always been and still was a dutiful son, to whom his mother represented something sacred which would be violated if he permitted himself so much as one unfilial thought. Nonetheless he could now understand how tragically Teresa must have failed his father's need, his brilliant intellectuality, his romantic craving for the fulfillment of his passions. Now that he knew what emotional possession really meant, he saw with shattering clarity, not merely the constriction of his mother's mental horizon but the utter impossibility of ardent or even companionable relations between his parents.

Living in the isolation his duties imposed upon him, he sought refuge in the great box of books he had brought with him from New Orleans. As he wrote many years later to a classmate of his Soulé days, William T. Hale of New York: *"No hay mal que por bien no venga!"*— a Spanish variant of "It's an ill wind that blows no good." Among other things, Dr. Matas reminded him of their wide and indiscriminate reading as boys:

"While this may have been unfortunate in some ways, the capacity to enjoy one's own company or rather the capacity to live in perfect contentment in the company of the silent but fascinating authors whom we invited to our inner sanctuary and who exacted no favors in return, is indeed some compensation for the loss of that polyvalency that makes the hail-fellow-well-met. . . . I always feel sorry for the unfortunates who hate their company. . . . They are indeed to be pitied who can find no solace in their own thoughts or in the realms of the imagination when this has been fed by a rich and varied literature. . . . Your passionate love of reading and of books suggests that we both found greater enjoyment from the written than from the spoken word."

Thus, through sweltering night after sweltering night, solitary but never lonesome, with the turbid water gurgling as it sucked against the blunt bows of the hospital barges, he read till the dawn. Then, in the brief interlude of comparative coolness just before daybreak, he would retire within the grimed netting of his mosquito bar and sleep till the coming day's round of duty summoned him anew.

Two of his books he read time and again. Pondering their content, he turned away from formal religious observance. "My faiths became attenuated in that summer," he confessed many years later. "I almost became an agnostic." Thenceforth he referred to himself as "a hereditary Catholic, one who clings to the ethics but not the dogmas of formal religion."

The volume whose influence upon him was most profound along these lines was John William Draper's *History of the Conflict Between Religion and Science,* which had evoked widespread discussion ever since its publication in 1874. Draper, who later collaborated with "Cump" Sherman on a history of the Civil War, was a native of England. He emigrated to the United States during the early thirties, was graduated in medicine from the University of Pennsylvania but turned to the teaching of chemistry and physics at New York University, where ultimately he was made the head of its College of Medicine. Primarily, however, he was still a physicist and achieved some astonishing results in the field of spectrum analysis by his pioneer researches. In connection with his researches into the nature of light, he made, among other things, the first satisfactory photographic portrait of a human countenance.

His was the many sided, brilliant type of mind, to whose articulate expression a youthful searcher after knowledge, keeping a solitary vigil through the long, fever-ridden nights, could be expected to respond. "For a time thereafter," Dr. Matas later recalled, "the more I became a physician, the less religious I was."

The second writer whose work he read over and over made a deep impression on his future thinking in another respect. This was Alexander Bain, a Scotsman, who became professor of logic and philosophy at the University of London, where he was the first preceptor to introduce into his lectures on these subjects the study of psychology. *Mental and Moral Science* and *The Relation of Mind and Body* were the titles of books through which he established himself as for that time the foremost advocate, as well as one of the first, of medical recognition of the links relating physiology and psychology. It was from this beginning that the young physician continued to "find solace in the realm of his own thoughts" about his profession, and devoted to it an "imagination . . . fed by a rich and varied literature."

In any case, the Rudolph Matas who returned to private practice at New Orleans—and to the distaff side of his family—in November of 1881, was not the Rudolph Matas to whom Teresa had said farewell three months before. The comparative stranger who came back to 82 South Rampart* Street was now alienated from the family group, not merely by professional interests and duties but by a new outlook on one of the fundamentals of his mother's existence. Physically the home was cheerfully familiar, and the young doctor still thrilled to see the sign suspended above its entryway: "Dr. Rodolfo Matas, Physician and Surgeon." Affixed to the door was the well-scrubbed school slate, with slate pencil dangling on a string, for the use of those patients desiring to leave a message for the doctor. Living quarters for his mother, sister, and himself were on the second floor. But he was doubly grateful now for the fact that in his office, with its roll-top desk, small cabinet of gleaming instruments, framed medical diploma on the wall, and leather-upholstered couch which did duty as examining table, he was safe from intrusion.

This individual isolation was increasingly important, now that he was unable to accept the rigid, pietistic thought patterns Teresa still prescribed for a son from whom she expected unquestioning obedience. He realized all too well he could never discuss with her what she had neither the wit nor the natural inclination to view as a divergence of opinion. To her, Rudolph's nascent rationalism would simply have been heresy and sacrilege, punishable as such both here and hereafter.

As a matter of course the passage of time softened all harsh outlines in his memories of both parents; the silent, unsmiling mother whose only interest seemed to be hatred of her husband and inflexible compliance with all formal observances of her faith; the paradoxically brilliant father who could "become a Yankee overnight" for profit and could later divorce his wife without hesitation in order to remarry, but who beggared himself to give his idolized son a moment of unalloyed triumph.

Thus Rudolph wrote to Mr. Hale in 1925 that, though his father, a

* Originally Circus Street on the upstream side of Canal Street and Rampart Street on the other, the name was unified by council action, though part of the upstream extension of the same thoroughfare became Danneel Street in 1910, which ran through a quiet residential area whose householders did not want to be known as living on a street one part of which, far downtown, was famous for its wicked gaieties.

man of "very good literary tastes," was not near enough to guide his son's boyhood reading, "my mother was with me, and the purity of her example, her deeply rooted religious convictions and stern adherence to the fundamentals of a clean, honest and decent life saved me from perils that would otherwise have beset my path."

However, it must be conceded that an unbridgeable chasm yawns between a septuagenarian's mellowed reminiscences of his dawning teen-age and the realities of a young physician's outlook on the world about him. As surely as he later conceded the "attenuation" of his adherence to dogma in 1882, the ties between himself and his mother slackened very sensibly in that year; the first of many, many years, moreover, in which he acknowledged himself utterly "possessed" by a love no less overpowering because he recognized it as hopeless. Perhaps it was just as well, all things considered, that formal appointment as editorial associate of the *New Orleans Medical and Surgical Journal* came to him at this juncture, for the new duties, to which he devoted every moment he could spare from his practice, took up what might otherwise have been free time.

Founded in 1844 as the first Southern periodical of its kind, the *New Orleans Medical and Surgical Journal* necessarily suspended publication during the Civil War. It was resurrected by Stanford Chaillé in 1866; in the following year Tobias Richardson and Samuel Bemiss were among those who joined its editorial staff.

At the close of 1881, negotiations were already under way for the purchase of the *Journal* by a group of younger physicians. Meanwhile, Rudolph Matas, newly returned from Vicksburg, received a reprint of Carlos Finlay's still almost wholly ignored paper on the mosquito as possible transmitter of yellow fever, together with a letter from its patient author. Young Dr. Matas was enthralled by the clarity of Finlay's unassuming statement and no little thrilled by the realization that the photomicrographs he had helped to make in 1879 had laid the foundation for Finlay's reasoning. He was equally impressed by the modesty with which the Cuban presented his findings and conclusions merely as something that might prove worthy of more conclusive experimental definition.*

* Two years later, Dr. Matas was still tub-thumping for Carlos Finlay's hypothesis. In an editorial published by the *New Orleans Medical and Surgical Journal* in October 1883, on the morphology of blood in yellow fever he wrote: "We really believe that the condition of the blood in yellow fever as presented by [Dr. Finlay] is the existing one, and we are supported in our belief by the remarkably clear and to us *conclusive* evidence furnished by the integrity of the blood corpuscles in . . . the microphotographs of the Havana Yellow Fever Commission. . . . Whoever has examined these beautiful specimens of photographic art cannot fail to be impressed with the final character of the evidence they furnish."

He promptly prepared for his colleagues an English summary of what Finlay had advanced as a hitherto untried hypothesis and sought to interest them in carrying the work forward. But he found himself baffled by the same bastions of casual indifference or willful opposition which Finlay himself had earlier encountered, an attitude which would delay the conquest of yellow fever by more than two decades. Unable to do anything further along these lines, Rudolph almost reverently translated Finlay's brief treatise into English for publication in the *Journal,* which consistently gave space to all serious discussions of yellow fever. The Matas translation was published two months later, in February 1882, just at the time when formal transfer of *Journal* ownership was to be consummated. After a brief interregnum, Rudolph Matas became the new editor.

Announcement of the change was validated by a permanent masthead which read: "Communications relating to medicine invited from every source. Matters of more than ordinary moment are occurring daily to country physicians, brief reports of which this Journal will be glad to get. In sending such communications address Dr. Rudolph Matas. Matters pertaining to business should be addressed to Dr. L. F. Salomon."

Even at this late day, and to laymen, the appointment of a physician who, as the Creole idiom of South Louisiana puts it "had just made twenty-one," to the editorship of so important a publication bears eloquent witness to the regard in which he and his attainments were held. As a matter of fact, half a century later, in the course of an article published in this same journal under the title of "One Hundred Years of Medical Journalism," he still confessed that he was more than a little overwhelmed by it all himself.

"It was with great humility and hesitation," he wrote, "that I accepted the invitation to succeed so able a man [as the former editor]. But the situation was looked upon as an emergency, as the other members of the group, who were my seniors, were carrying heavy obligations too important to divert them by the exacting duties of the editorial chair. I finally consented to remain, with my friend Dr. L. F. Salomon, Secretary-Treasurer of the group, to continue in charge of the business management. I had begun to work with considerable vim and enthusiasm, when an unexpected and imperative business called me to the Far West, where I was detained until the fall of 1883."

That unexpected but categorical imperative began with the incidence of another yellow-fever epidemic in the summer of 1882. It spread with frightening rapidity along the Gulf Coast westward to Brownsville-Matamoros and across the Rio Grande into Mexico, exacting a far heavier toll among Mexicans than among other elements of the population. As usual, all civil authorities in the affected areas at first insisted that most of the fatalities were due to malaria, that no epidemic existed, and that such undeniable yellow-fever deaths as might occur were "sporadic." But the time came when physicians and other authorities of the twin cities of Brownsville and Matamoros confessed themselves unable to cope with the situation.

Narciso was not among them, having but recently taken two important steps in deciding his future. The economic conditions of which he had complained to his son after the latter's graduation in 1880 had steadily worsened. Matamoros was impoverished by revolutions. The large plantations were no longer productive. A man of spirit must seek new fields of endeavor or admit failure. Where else should he look for them but in that dazzling Golconda, the West?

Almost certainly he envisioned California as his goal, but something —to this day no one knows or remembers what—halted his westward march at Tucson. Perhaps a local physician persuaded him to stay; perhaps an enthusiastic chance-met promoter convinced him that here, in the burgeoning territory of Arizona where new mines were being discovered daily, a fortune awaited him. Perhaps he met here for the first time Mrs. Louisa Mallett Aphold,* the lady who was to become his second wife, and found himself irresistibly drawn to remain at her side. Perhaps successful treatment of a casually encountered invalid moved a segment of the pioneer population to urge him to make his home among them. At any rate, for the rest of his active life, he resided in Tucson.

Hence it was not Narciso who appealed to the national health authorities at Washington and New Orleans for assistance in battling the Brownsville-Matamoros plague; nor was it he who asked specifically that Dr. Rodolfo Matas be sent to aid the stricken communities. It was the Nestor among local physicians, Dr. Melou, who recalled that the protégé in whose behalf he had interceded with the faculty of the University of Louisiana five years before had served as resident in New Orleans' great Charity Hospital during the appalling epidemic of 1878, had labored in Havana with the Chaillé Commission in '79, had served as a government inspector at Vicksburg the previous autumn. In the name of the councils of the two municipalities, would it be possible to send him back to assist the afflicted home of his boyhood?

Infected areas on each side of the border were already isolated by

* Mrs. Aphold was a native of Brownsville, and Teresa had left Narciso four years previous to his departure from Matamoros. It is much more likely, therefore, that he and Mrs. Aphold met while he was still practicing and lonely in Brownsville, and that he sent for her after he had secured a divorce from Teresa through the territorial court of Arizona in 1883.

an armed, nonintercourse quarantine; drugs and other supplies were exhausted. Even the army's medical officer at Fort Brown, who had braved court-martial to succor the civilian population in this hour of disaster, was coming down with yellow fever. He was a newly commissioned lieutenant named William Crawford Gorgas.

And so, in the foul and fetid quarantine of a yellow-fever epidemic along the Rio Grande, chance brought together Rudolph Matas and William Gorgas, who, when experimentation finally proved Finlay's hypothesis wholly correct, cleared first Havana, then Cuba, and finally Panama of the Black Vomit by applying the selfsame principles Finlay had tentatively advanced twenty years before.

CHAPTER XII

Through the years, at various times and places, Dr. Matas himself gave so many contradictory and conflicting versions of why and, for that matter, when, he was "called to the far west" in the early 1880's, that it is difficult to separate provable fact from special pleading designed to gloss over, a fact he wanted very much to ignore. In recalling almost bashfully his acceptance at age twenty-one of a renowned medical journal's editorship, he said in so many words:

"I had begun to work (in 1882) with considerable vim and enthusiasm, when an unexpected and imperative business called me to the far west where I remained until the fall of 1883."

Yet one of his medical papers, published in 1884, another article written sixty years later for *El Excelsior* of Mexico (March 20, 1943), and numerous other statements, letters, and publications make it not only abundantly clear but certain that he did not remain in the far West for a year but returned to New Orleans in November 1882 and left again during the summer of 1883, at the close of his school year's teaching activities, for a brief visit to Tucson.

Why this huggermugger of dates and motives? Were these merely lapses of a memory which in other respects was capable of virtually total recall? Certainly not. With a filial devotion toward both parents that excluded anything but hallowed images of father and mother, he did everything in his power to soften and if possible to conceal the facts attendant upon his parents' parting. One must bear in mind particularly the circumstance that the rift was climaxed when, in the district court of

143

Pima County, territory of Arizona, Narciso brought a divorce suit against his wife on the technical ground of desertion, after writing her a stilted letter demanding that she rejoin him, a letter which her brother answered for her in the negative. In those days a heavy taint of obloquy attached to any divorce action per se. Small wonder then that in no scrap of even his most private and personal correspondence did Rudolph let slip so much as a hint of this one. The only surviving record of Teresa's altered marital status remains on the acts of sale transferring the title of the two "unlucky houses" on South Rampart Street to her; there, and on the deeds effecting her disposal of these properties when she returned to Spain in 1886, she is formally described as "divorced wife of Dr. N. H. y Matas."

Seeking to conceal these facts, and trying manfully to make it appear that his comings and goings at this time were merely on imperative business affairs, it is scarcely a matter for surprise that Rudolph became tangled in his semifictional web. Thus we find him recording in one place that he was absent from New Orleans for more than a year at this time; in another—a letter he wrote to Dr. F. I. Nixon, of San Antonio, in 1939—that he was called to Brownsville-Matamoros for emergency service in an epidemic during 1881, and that in 1882 he was "on my way with a sick relative to Arizona"; elsewhere that he served the lower Rio Grande valley as relief physician in 1882 and returned to New Orleans that same November. The truth is that he was simply trying to conceal even from himself an interlude during which he wrote what he later described regretfully as "a lot of very sassy letters to my dear papa."

It might be as well to point out that Rudolph and his father were by no means the only practitioners exchanging "very sassy" communication at this time. Dr. Chaillé, New Orleans supervisor for the National Board of Health, and Dr. Joseph Jones, President of the Louisiana State Board, were having at one another over the latter's actions in respect to quarantine.

The epidemic that was to become so virulent along the Rio Grande began in New Orleans, where it remained mild. At least, the first cases appeared there; in all likelihood the Brownsville-Matamoros vector was a separate importation. In any case the tragic aspect of such debates as the Chaillé-Jones controversy was that both parties to the feud were so devastatingly wrong. Sanitarians, physicians, and others, though completely in the dark as to the cause, nature, and transmission of yellow fever, still determinedly ignored Carlos Finlay's modest hypothesis.

The controversy began in New Orleans. Governor McEnery had issued his annual quarantine proclamation, leaving the State Board of

Yellow Fever Commission of National Board of Health, sent to Havana, Cuba (1879). Seated, from left to right: Mr. Hardee, an engineer, H. C. Hall, U.S. consul to Havana, Dr. Stanford E. Chaillé, chairman of the Commission, Dr. D. M. Burgess, sanitary and quarantine inspector. Standing, from left to right: Mr. Henry Mancel, photographer, Mr. Rudolph Matas, clerk, Dr. George Sternberg, secretary, and Dr. J. Guiteras.

Dr. Rudolph Matas (1884-85).

Portrait of Adrienne Goslee (1887). This portrait appeared in
Harper's magazine as "A Creole Belle."

Professor Rudolph Matas (1903).

Mrs. Rudolph Matas (1900).

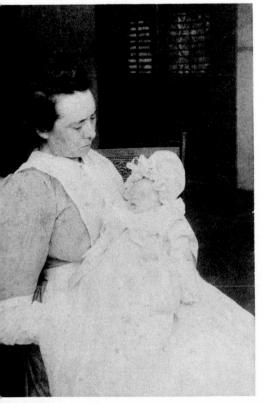

Photo of stillborn child of Dr. and Mrs. Matas (March 13, 1902).

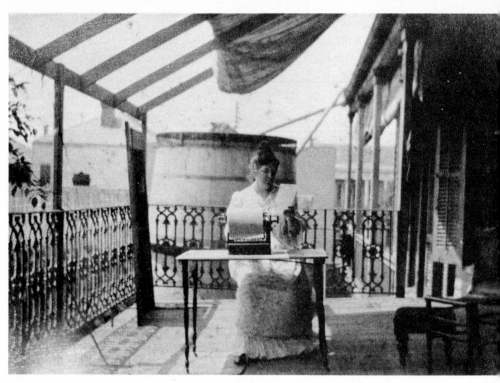

Mrs. Matas at typewriter (1903). For many years Mrs. Matas did all of the typing for Dr. Matas.

Dr. Matas on Mount Mitchell, North Carolina (September 1903).

jor Rudolph Matas, director of spe-
course in surgery of fractures and
er emergencies, established at Tu-
e University by order of the Sur-
n-General (1917-18).

Matas, president of the American
llege of Surgeons (1925).

Presentation of annivers
volume by Dr. Isidore Co
chairman of committee, to
Matas, commemorating
seventieth birthday (Dece
ber 17, 1931).

Portrait of Dr. Matas
Thomas C. Corner. Port
made for American Colleg
Surgeons, presidential gro

Health to implement it. That body was, as always, under terrific pressure from the business and transportation interests to exempt this or that Caribbean or Gulf port from prohibition against entry of its vessels into New Orleans. Yielding to these pressures, the State Board issued a curious pronouncement early in June, to the effect that "the port of Veracruz, *which is known to be at present perfectly healthy*, shall be exempt from the effect of this [i.e., the governor's] proclamation until the further date of July 1."

As the National Health Board's supervisor of federal inspectors for the area, Dr. Chaillé lodged an immediate and very caustic protest against the Board's action, and more particularly against the queer reasons the Board had advanced for taking such a step. Calling barbed attention to "the superlative strength of the words 'known' and 'perfectly,'" he denied that the State Board could have such "knowledge," if only by reason of the fact that Veracruz, like Havana, was never "perfectly" free from yellow fever at any season of the year.

In this respect Dr. Chaillé's position was fully substantiated by subsequent developments. Early the following year Dr. Juan Guiteras, who had served with him on the 1879 Yellow Fever Commission to Havana, compiled a tabulation according to which fifty-eight Veracruz cases of yellow fever had been admitted during 1882 to the hospital of San Sebastian alone. Thereupon Dr. Chaillé renewed his polemic of the year before, pointing out that San Sebastian admitted only adult males, and that if proportional incidence of the fever among women and children were taken into account, the tally must have been triple the figure cited by Guiteras for a period during which the State Board "knew" Veracruz to be "perfectly" healthy.

In this he was powerfully supported by a Dr. Mainagra, an Orleanian stationed at Veracruz on the staff of the United States Marine Hospital service, who cited data showing that more yellow-fever fatalities had occurred at Veracruz during June than in any other one month of 1882, though as always some deaths from this cause had occurred in every month of the twelve.

In time, therefore, it became completely obvious that Louisiana's State Health Board had taken an untenable stand in 1882, by clearing vessels from Veracruz for New Orleans without restriction during the very month when the Mexican port was suffering its worst yellow-fever incidence of the year, on the ground that it was then "known to be perfectly healthy." At the time, however, unwilling to lose face by retreating from a publicly announced stand, the Board not only refused to put Veracruz back under quarantine, but issued an additional exemption to another Latin American port, this being Colon in Panama. Thus the *Ile Marthe* from Colon landed at New Orleans on June 12.

Its stone ballast was discharged in a thickly populated section of the waterfront and was immediately used for the repair of nearby streets. By coincidence, the first and only yellow-fever cases to occur in New Orleans that month were reported in dwellings—as Dr. Chaillé was quick to point out—"within a stone's throw of this ballast."

Dr. Jones retorted that Colon was not infected and "hence the ballast could not be." Thereafter argument raged not about whether stone from an infected port *could* transmit yellow fever, but whether this particular rubble had done so. Meanwhile other vessels from Veracruz were churning northward across the Gulf to Mobile and New Orleans, and along the Mexique coast to Tampico, to the mouth of the Rio Grande and thence by river to Brownsville and Matamoros. There the infection detonated upstream and outward along both banks with a ferocity no other epidemic in this region had ever before shown. Its swift deadliness threw both Tamaulipas and Texas into a state of near panic.

Brownsville was immediately quarantined by executive order of Governor Oran Roberts. Then the Surgeon-General of the Marine Hospital Service at Washington ordered a cordon of mounted shotgun guards thrown from Laredo to Corpus Christi, thus sealing off from all communication by land an almost equilateral triangle at the southernmost tip of Texas; the Gulf, the Rio Grande, and the line of guards formed its three sides.

"The heroic, unconquerable city of Matamoros," wrote Dr. Matas many years later, "could no longer claim this title . . . for the Ogre of the Antilles, yellow fever, had taken possession . . . and strolled through the streets, prostrating a great part of its inhabitants and covering many others with the heavy shroud of death. The epidemic spread to the entire Rio Grande valley with monstrous rapidity . . . attacking the Mexican populace with dreadful malignancy and fatality."

Two years earlier Narciso had written to his son that physicians found themselves unable to earn a competence amid the Brownsville area's economic depression, and that those who remained did so only in the hope of surviving until better and more prosperous times returned. But now only Dr. Melou, an immune, remained active. The others were themselves down with fever, and the supply of medicines was exhausted. At Fort Brown, most of whose garrison had been evacuated for an isolation camp as soon as the epidemic had been clearly recognized, every military physician was prostrated; only Dr. Melou, civilian contract surgeon to this military post, ministered to the garrison as best he could.

But without medicines he confessed himself helpless, and telegraphed the National Board of Health at Washington for assistance, asking on behalf and in the name of the city council of Brownsville that young Dr. Matas be sent to Brownsville as special assistant to the municipal health authorities.

So Rudolph Matas, accompanied by Dr. Mark J. Lehman, was sent west by Dr. Chaillé, and reached Galveston via branch-line train from Houston on September 7, bringing with him a large supply of drugs and disinfectants. He and Lehman purchased as much more such matériel as they could find in Galveston, amassing some 400 cases in all. Since land communication between other sections of Texas and the afflicted region had been cut by quarantine, these supplies were loaded into the revenue cutter *McLain*, which was to take the physicians ashore at, but not into, Brownsville. As they were on the point of casting off, a minor tropical storm swept inland from the Gulf, and they remained in port. September 12 marked the birthday on which Rudolph became twenty-two years old. He celebrated it by waiting impatiently aboard the *McLain* for calm to be restored to the storm-tossed Gulf. When at length they did reach their goal, they and their supplies were lightered ashore.

At Brownsville-Matamoros, and later at Mier, where not a house or hut was without its fever victim, Dr. Matas undertook a radical departure from traditional yellow-fever therapy.

"Apparently all the known medical and home treatments had been of no avail," he explained in a memoir written in 1943, "and it was useless to continue with the same tactics, especially since in many cases the treatments were not only useless, but even homicidal. Therefore we abandoned all the bloodletting, the taking of calomel, the blisterings, the purgatives and emetics that had remained as Roman relics of the doctrines of Rasori and Broussais. In effect, all nauseous and repugnant medication was forbidden in my practice. There remained only the Hippocratic principle of *primum non nocere*."

It is fair to assume that of all the patients Rudolph treated in this season of disaster, one was more grateful than the other for his abolition of "all nauseous and repugnant medication." This would have been First Lieutenant Gorgas. Alabama born, he had received his medical education in New York. The Rio Grande epidemic marked his first contact with the "ogre of the Antilles." Fortunately the attack was benign, and under young Dr. Matas's sit-tight therapy, he did not fall victim to accepted medication. But unfortunately the selfsame Dr. Matas who was both florid and fluent in reporting so many recollections of that siege, has given us in "Personal Experiences and Reflections on Yellow Fever"* only a very sketchy summary under the heading of "WILLIAM C. GORGAS, BROWNSVILLE, 1882." Here it is:

"I am also glad to recall that it was during the epidemic at Brownsville, Texas, in 1882, that I first met Dr. William Crawford Gorgas, then Lieutenant, M.C., U.S.A., who had been assigned to that post immediately after his graduation at the Army Medical School. He had never been in contact with yellow fever and it was not long after his arrival that he was stricken with a severe attack of the prevailing [yellow] fever. It was during this illness that I called on him as relief physician and assistant to a mutual friend, Dr. Melou, the contract surgeon of the post. As the outcome of this bedside acquaintance a friendly relation was established which he remembered to the end of his glorious career. There were beautiful traits in his character which gave charm to his personality; but it was yet too early to foresee the path which, twenty years later, was to lead him to the pinnacle of fame as the 'conqueror of yellow fever' in Cuba and Panama by his mastery of the principles and practice of sanitation by mosquito eradication."

That is absolutely and tragically all. Young Dr. Matas was still fired with the zeal of recent conversion and ever eager to talk shop to one whom he could edify and instruct—yet not a written or printed line remains to show us how destiny was shaped as he initiated William Gorgas into the lore of yellow fever. In his memoirs Rudolph set down that when the epidemic had finally given way to the attrition of cool weather "I again said farewell, taking on my return to the United States the treasure of a therapeutic experience of immeasurable value. I also took with me the great wealth of blessings from a multitude of grateful patients, which has served to sustain me as a comforting tonic . . . since the day that I tenderly took my leave from the good people who wept at my parting with all the grief felt when an irreparable loss is sustained."†

* *New Orleans Medical and Surgical Journal,* July, 1943, pp. 10–13

† Lieutenant Gorgas (later General) was the son Captain Josiah Gorgas, Commandant of Mt. Vernon Arsenal in Alabama, and Amelia Gayle, daughter of Alabama's then governor. He was an "Army brat," as his father was shifted from one post to another, until the outbreak of the Civil War. Then Captain Gorgas resigned his Union commission to become, by appointment of President Davis, ordnance chief of the Confederate forces. After the war he became president of the University of the South, at Sewanee, where William was graduated in 1875. The youth was eager to become a career officer in the army; but his father, a former Confederate general, was unable to get him appointed to West Point, not even by appealing to his own onetime fellow-West Pointer, President Grant. William then took up medicine, but only as a possible avenue of entry into the Army, studying at Bellevue in New York. By this time his father had become president of the University of Alabama, where his mother remained as librarian after her husband's death.

But he recorded nothing of conversations between himself and William C. Gorgas, though such conversations must have taken place. The two men had so much in common that shop talk would have been inevitable. Gorgas had received his M.D. degree while Rudolph was in Havana. He was commissioned a first lieutenant in the Medical Corps the year Rudolph was graduated. He had been treating yellow-fever patients almost from the very moment of his arrival at Fort Brown; in fact he had been placed under technical arrest for diso-bedience of orders when he assisted Dr. Melou in dissecting the cadaver of a soldier who had died of yellow fever. In his therapy he had followed the traditional routine of purgation and diaphoresis; yet when he contracted the disease, his physician jettisoned all such treatments as "homicidal." Moreover, this physician, though six years younger by the calendar, was of precisely the same age, medically. He had been a member of the famous Havana Commission. . . .

Why, it is simply unthinkable that two such men, who later became fast friends, should not have talked shop. A constitutional zealot like Rudolph Matas, crusading against the "homicidal" therapy his elders still venerated, the lone convert to Carlos Finlay's mosquito hypothesis, could no more have resisted the opportunity to share with a contem-porary his knowledge and his philosophy than, by a mere impulse of volition, he could have resisted the opportunity to breathe.

There was also a romantic phase to this meeting. When the first cases of what was to become the virulent epidemic of 1882 made their appearance in Brownsville, the commandant of Fort Brown, Colonel William J. Lyster, ordered most of his detachment moved to an isolated camp some two miles downstream. This camp was quarantined against the post, and the post was rigidly quarantined against Brownsville. Colonel and Mrs. Lyster and her sister, Marie Doughty, remained at the fort. When Lieutenant Gorgas reported for duty, he was assigned to remain there too. He was also ordered on no account to visit any of the isolation wards where military yellow-fever patients were confined. As already related, he disregarded this order, and the act very nearly cost him his commission. One of the factors that saved him was that despite all precautions in quarantining the post, Miss Doughty contracted an unusually severe case of yellow fever, and Lieutenant Gorgas was the only physician available to minister to her needs.

Within the week, however, he too became one of Bronze John's casualties. Young Dr. Matas had reached the scene by this time, and was taken by Dr. Melou on his rounds. Thus he attended not only the Lieutenant Gorgas who was sick, but the Miss Doughty who was convalescing and who, two years later, became Mrs. William C. Gorgas.

In sum, while the conclusion is inevitable that long conversations between two young men linked by so many personal and professional ties of mutual interest did take place, not a syllable has been preserved in the writings of either Matas or Gorgas, nor in those of Mrs. Gorgas, who penned her illustrious husband's biography. No black-on-white record remains beyond Rudolph Matas's casual observation that: "As the outcome of this bedside acquaintance, a friendly relation was established which he remembered to the end of his glorious career."

Just as the Rio Grande epidemic began to slacken, Rudolph shared another brief encounter in Matamoros; brief and bitter. On his return from Mier, when he and Dr. Lehman began to envision the day of their homecoming as something in the foreseeably early furture, he met his father. Narciso's friends among the San Román and Bareda *gente* on the Matamoros side of the river had written him in Tucson, appealing for assistance in battling the plague that so cruelly beset his former home. A knight-errant type could not turn a deaf ear to such a plea, though this mission of mercy and a similar one the following year to Hermosillo in the state of Sonora mark the only two occasions on which Narciso left Tucson until his final journey to New Orleans in 1904.

The meeting must have been equally and painfully embarrassing to both father and son. Rudolph knew his father had filed divorce proceedings that Spring, and in an aching way he understood that Narciso's temperament could not and would not indefinitely brook either a monastically solitary or a furtively amorous existence. Yet the interchange that followed a formal, stilted embrace of greeting must have been bitter on both sides. Assuredly the "sassy letters" rankled.

Narciso, one feels, would have requested his son to "tell your mother I shall marry Mrs. Aphold this summer. Rudolph might have retorted that his devout mother would recognize neither the divorce nor the marriage, and at some time during the discussion, Narciso would have offered to settle both the Rampart Street houses on her, adding caustically that, given her choice of ownership of this valuable real estate, or a return to his bed and board she, who no longer cared anything for him, she who had taught Elvira to look down upon and hate her papa, would unhesitatingly express a preference for ownership of the houses.

Rudolph was no doubt torn by conflicting emotions. After all, his father was still a legendary sort of hero, a gay and tender companion, a wise and skilled physician by whose precept and example he had enormously widened his own horizons, a devoted parent whose sacrifices had given his son a crowded hour of unalloyed triumph. On the other hand, young Dr. Matas, just turned twenty-two, was inclined to be priggish, especially according to the mores of a New Orleans which flaunted licentiousness as an officially recognized way of life. How many harlots and their patrons had he not treated for various venereal diseases at Charity Hospital? How many of his friends and acquaintances kept mistresses?

The filial side of Rudolph wistfully longed to embrace his sire in affection and in gratitude for all he owed him. But his alter ego was outraged by the very notion of a divorce suit that named his mother as defendant.

Narciso too was prey to the pushes and pulls of conflicting impulses. The adoring father wanted to fling his arm about the shoulders of this brilliant young son in whom he saw himself so magnificently fulfilled. But Narciso the swashbuckler, who had run the Union blockade with cotton for Liverpool and who at forty-five was still eager to push beyond frontiers in quest of treasure, that Narciso would no doubt have relished the opportunity to hammer some of the self-righteousness out of the young Pharisee he had begotten.

In all likelihood, then, this was their only meeting, and the parting note on which it closed must have left each with a desolate and wistful sense of having lost an irreplaceable part of himself, of emptiness, of a yearning to undo what had occurred despite a realization that this was impossible.

Hence, it was with a heavy heart that Rudolph accepted the praise and the acclaim that greeted him and Dr. Lehman on their return to New Orleans in November. He had to tell both his mother and her brother that, while Narciso would remarry as soon as the divorce had become effective through the issuance of a final decree at Tucson, the two houses on Rampart Street would be deeded to Teresa for her very own. Under the community property provisions of the Napoleonic code on which Louisiana's system of laws was based, half of everything either she or Narciso had acquired after their marriage belonged to her. But as "master of the community," Narciso could legally have sold the houses to some one else. Half the proceeds of such a sale would belong to Teresa, of course, but she would have been effectively evicted from her home.

In order to comply with the complexities attendant upon the transfer of ownership of real property, Rudolph and his Brownsville cousin, Emilio Forto, left for Tucson some time after Narciso notified them of his return to Arizona. They were en route from Laredo when Forto came down with a violently acute attack of "perityphlitis," a condition known as appendicitis today. Rudolph took his cousin from the train at San Antonio and rushed him to Santa Rosa Infirmary, where a Dr.

Cupples assumed full charge of the case and, "under hot fomentations, opium, starvation diet and absolute rest, the patient improved and recovered within a week without apparent suppuration. Curiously enough, the patient lived more than forty years without a recurrence, dying of what we now would call coronary disease."

The foregoing is taken from a letter to a San Antonio physician who sought information about Dr. Cupples. However, the incident at the time heavily underscored a theory young Dr. Matas had been laboring in his medical discussions and which he was preparing to commit to paper in the *Journal*. In the diagnosis of appendicitis, then known as iliac phlegmon or perityphlitis, operative procedure, necessarily involving the perilous laporotomy, was not employed save as a very last resort, after suppuration—the rupture of the appendix—had occurred. By that time surgery was too late, and the drainage it was designed to achieve too little.

Rudolph Matas had already decided to explore the possibilities of surgery as a desirable early treatment, to be undertaken as soon as diagnosis was positive, not merely as a last, desperate resort after all else had failed.

Meanwhile, the week or more during which Cousin Emilio was bedfast passed pleasantly enough, once anxiety as to his recovery was allayed. Rudolph actually reveled in watching Dr. Cupples display in operating on other patients an amazing swiftness of skilled surgical procedure, developed in an era when anesthesia was relatively new, antisepsis was still vigorously debated, and asepsis had not yet been envisioned as a remote possibility.

For the rest, he found San Antonio's tranquil, almost somnolent atmosphere delightful. He visited the ancient mission whose caretakers boasted that "Thermopylae had its messenger of defeat, the Alamo had none," and tried to envision the grimy, scrubby-jowled band which faced the end without hope but without fear and thus achieved immortality. He rambled along the minuscule river, a mere meandering thread of silver compared to the Mississippi's turbid yellow width, and noticed the absence of the *huisache* trees so abundant along the lower Rio Grande valley.

However, he was glad when Cousin Emilio, having survived the opium, the starvation, and the hot fomentations, was once more able to travel. What they had to do would at best be unpleasant; the sooner it was over, the better. Cousin Emilio would handle all the details. Rudolph need appear for no longer than it would take to hand his father a silver dollar and then sign his name to some documents. In the office of the clerk of the Pima County Court this was done, with no word exchanged between Rudolph and his father. Narciso, acting for the community, agreed to sell the "unlucky houses" at 82 and 84 South Rampart Street to his son, Rodolfo, for $1.00, which Rudolph silently paid him in the presence of the clerk and the office staff. The transfer of title was not completed until sometime in June, when the decree of divorce sundering Narciso Matas and his wife, as of April 3, 1882, was made final.

Then the signed and attested deed to the houses was mailed to Rudolph, who deposited the papers formally in the notarial archives of Orleans Parish, before Charles J. Theard, Notary, on July 30, thus validating his ownership. The next day, July 31, he sold the property to his mother for $1.00, with all the pompous circumlocutions prescribed for such rituals in the Code Napoléon. By that time Narciso and Mrs. Aphold were married and had settled in Tucson.

Rudolph plunged with even more singlemindedness than heretofore into his professional labors. In addition to his general practice and his calls as physician of the Spanish Benevolent Society, he was chief of clinic and prosector for Dr. Souchon and assisted the demonstrator of anatomy, Dr. A. B. Miles. Whatever free time remained, he devoted to editorial tasks for the *New Orleans Medical and Surgical Journal* in the modest office he shared with Lucian Salomon at 32 Baronne Street.

They were working there until late one night, when Charles Whitney, *Times-Democrat* city editor, entered. Since Dr. Salomon was his family physician, and Whitney worked mostly by night, he was a frequent visitor. On this occasion Rudolph broke into the conversation.

"I've been meaning to ask you, Mr. Whitney, who writes those translations, weird sketches, and fantasies for your paper," he said, "especially those on your editorial page on Sundays. I've meant to find out about this from you time and again, but I am always so interested in whatever else you're discussing that it slips my mind till you're gone. I enjoy those wonderful writings ever so much. Who does them?"

"A queer little chap, very shy, very self-conscious, with only one working eye, which is maybe why he's so self-conscious. Would you like me to bring him around some evening?"

"I would, indeed."

"It's as good as done, then. His name's almost as odd as he is: Lafcadio Hearn."

CHAPTER XIII

When Rudolph returned from Tucson in the summer of 1883, he was in a state of emotional shock. Earlier that year, he had delivered Adrienne of a second child, Lucian, born after she and her husband had been legally separated. By every principle his mother had inculcated in him, any marriage between himself and the woman he loved —a divorcée—was unthinkable.

Yet hard on the heels of this heart-tearing realization he found himself compelled to live with the fact that not only were his parents divorced, not only had his father remarried in a union the Church would not sanction or even recognize, but his mother had surrendered a supposedly sacred principle for material gain by submitting for a cash consideration to what she had theretofore defined as sacrilege.

Inasmuch as this served to nourish and strengthen his still tenuous skepticism in matters of dogma, the rational materialism to which it gave rise made the contacts between him and Lafcadio Hearn a far more significant mingling of personalities destined to influence one another than would otherwise have been the case.

True to his promise, City Editor Whitney of the *Times-Democrat* finally dragooned Hearn into accompanying him to 82 South Rampart Street one night. This had taken quite a bit of doing, for Hearn's withdrawal from social contacts was little short of pathological. It emanated primarily from an overmastering sense of inferiority. In a land where most men are tall, Hearn's stature barely kept him from being classed as a dwarf. His optical deformities gave him a cast of countenance from which little children instinctively shrank and some-times fled. At school in England a chance blow from a knot at the end of a rope had destroyed the sight of his left eye, leaving its surface covered with milky white scar tissue, while his right eye bulged outward grotesquely. He was so nearsighted that, as Dr. Matas related years afterward: "When reading, he looked as though he were rubbing his nose along the printed page."

Quirks of personality still further isolated him from friendships and other normal human contacts. Intolerably ill at ease among what would ordinarily be considered his own kind, he deliberately sought compan-ionship with dwellers of the abyss who could not possibly look down upon anyone. Thus, in Cincinnati, before coming to New Orleans, he married a wanton Negress, mother of a miscellany of illegitimate children, and lived with her in a shantytown hutch. When he decided subsequently to journey downriver he needed no legal rigmarole to sever his matrimonial bonds. Under Ohio law his marriage to a Negress had never been valid. He had long since tired of her, as he did of every new enthusiasm and, finding himself free to leave, he left.

New Orleans enchanted him at the outset. He sent back reams of copy to the Cincinnati *Commercial,* each dispatch, like each of his early letters to his friend H. E. Krehbiel, a rhapsody of lyric prose about New Orleans' siren spell. Yet when he left the city some years later for the West Indies, via New York, he wrote Dr. Matas from that great metropolis: "This, dear friend, is the world you should be in. You are too grand a thinker to remain in what is undeniably an old-fashioned provincial town."

A week or so after that, having landed in Martinique, he wrote: "I have come to the startling conclusion that civilization is a cold and vapid humbug; the tropics are the only living part of this dying planet. . . . This is altogether divine." A short time later, in another of the twenty-two letters Dr. Matas received from Hearn: "Martinique is simply heaven on earth . . . as for the climate, it is divine . . . and I have begun to hate all that is energetic, swift, rapid in thought or action . . . it is enough to live here: no, it is too much!—it is more than any ordinary human being deserves to enjoy. . . . Couldn't I induce you to abandon the beastly civilization of the U.S. and live somewhere down here forevermore, where every one is honest, good natured and courteous and where everything is divine?"

That was on July 30, 1887. In September of that same year he wrote that "the thermometer tells atrocious lies" about "the most damnable heat" and likened the climate to "a New Orleans August day just before a shower—perpetuated into years and centuries of heat. . . . At

2 or 2:30 P.M., if you try to write your head feels as if a heated feather pillow had been stuffed into your skull."

Then, in October, preparing for a brief trip to New York: "Northern air will do me good, though I do not like the idea of living in it. But after this stupid, brutal, never-varying heat you steam North . . . and the first grand whiff of cold air comes like the advent of a Ghost—Lord, how one's brain suddenly clears and thrills into working order. It is like a new soul breathed into your being through the nostrils after the Creator's fashion of animating his Adam of clay."

He left at last for Japan where, among men of stature as short as his own he felt at ease, as among small women, so that he no longer needed to seek security and a sense of superiority among Negro strumpets in New Orleans bagnios or among the amoral "milattes" of the West Indian tropics. He married a Japanese woman, became a pillar of society, and a university schoolman; but death overtook him while he was moving heaven and earth to gain readmission to the United States for himself and for his darling, his first-born son.

Ever hagridden by delusions of persecution, he formed new friendships of almost frantic intensity and then abrogated them in bitterness, one and all. Even his apparently deep friendship with Rudolph Matas was doomed to wither on the vine since, after leaving the United States for the Orient, Hearn never again wrote him so much as a syllable, while Rudolph sedulously preserved and held in inviolable confidence the twenty-two letters he did receive during Hearn's stay in the Antilles. Half a century later he gave a few carefully culled excerpts to George Gould of Philadelphia, rigidly censored lest anything that might betray a professional confidence or show Hearn in an unfavorable light become a matter of public knowledge.

Something in the abnormally sensitized stuff of Hearn's being must have instantly detected the sympathy and understanding that animated the young physician, nearly ten years his junior, to whom Whitney introduced him that December night in 1883. At the moment, Hearn happened to be in quest of information about early Arabic medical practice and practitioners; he therefore asked young Matas where such references might most readily be found. The reply made Hearn blink in astonishment. As he wrote George Gould at Philadelphia a few weeks later:

"My friend is very young but already somewhat eminent for some years at our University, and will ultimately, I am sure, turn out a great name in American medicine. He is a Spaniard, Rodolfo Matas. I first felt quite curious about him after having visited him to obtain certain materials for a fantastic anatomical dream sketch and asked where I could find some good information regarding the lives and legends of the great Arabian physicians. When he ran off a long string of names, giving the specialties of each man, and criticizing his work, I was considerably surprised and even a little skeptical, until I got hold of Leclerc and Sprengel and found the facts there as given me by word of mouth."

The material in question appeared in sketches originally printed in the Sunday *Times-Democrat:* "Strange Leaves from Strange Literature," and "The First Muezzin, Bilal." Hearn's style at that time was florid to a degree almost beyond modern comprehension. It spread to those with whom he and his writings became a matter of cult rather than culture. After he and Dr. Matas met, the latter began to show unmistakable signs of that ornate verbosity that ultimately made him the despair of program chairmen whose time limitations were compressed into fixed schedules, and of publishers who could never make him understand that the type metal they used was not compressible, and the steel forms into which it was locked were not elastic.

Small wonder, then, that Rudolph Matas, worshiping at Hearn's shrine, phrased his otherwise sober psychosomatic analysis of the latter in such words as: "His mind towered like a cloud-capping mountain on one side, while on others it was not only undeveloped, it was a cavity!"

Leona Queyrouze, one of the relatively few women of culture with whom Hearn came into contact in New Orleans was so moved by three letters he wrote her about some of her "poetry" as published in New Orleans newspapers that she wrote of him: "Happy is the man who has not drained the last drop of the sparkling philter from the fragile crystal cup held brimful to his ardent lips."

Yet in other respects Rudolph Matas's appraisal of Hearn became objective enough as year followed year into Gould's "ruined centuries." His verdict: "[Hearn] would bitterly denounce his enemies in language that was frightful to listen to, inventing unheard-of tortures for those he deemed plotters against him. Yet in reality he was gentle and tender-hearted as a woman, and as passionately affectionate . . . but there was an almost feminine jealousy in his nature, too."

Certainly no one had a better opportunity to observe the man than Dr. Matas. For almost four years they were as nearly inseparable as the divergence of their respective callings permitted. They had come to New Orleans in the same year, 1877; Rudolph as a medical student, Hearn as a starveling penny-a-liner who thought to support himself by writing communications for the Cincinnati *Commercial.* The editors of that distinguished journal did indeed want some factual dispatches from New Orleans about the Hayes-Tilden electoral *quid pro quo,* climaxed by the withdrawal of federal occupation troops within a month of Hayes's inauguration. Instead, Hearn bombarded them with lush panegyrics about the French Market, the bayous, and what not. His first earnings from this source he spent in exchanging his heavy Northern garb for more suitable attire. A broad-brimmed plantation hat replaced a railroad engineer cap with bill pulled low over his milkily fixed left eye. In time he also sheared and scraped away his curly beard, leaving only the brown mustache. But his magniloquence remained as high-flown and discursive as when first he debarked at the Canal Street levee.

Unwilling to pay good money for reading matter of little or no interest to its Cincinnati circulation, the *Commercial* set him adrift. How he subsisted for the ensuing few months has always been something of a mystery. But he cast up at length as ten-dollar-a-week "associate editor" on the yearling *Item*. For his ten weekly dollars Hearn abstracted into English the French "exchanges" from Louisiana's country parishes, wrote editorials, reviewed books, drew cartoons, composed what were known as "Fantastics," and translated the works of Zola, Loti, and other French writers whose novels were in the public domain, there being as yet no international copyright convention.

Two years later, in 1880, having failed as proprietor of a restaurant where every dish was priced at a nickel, he sought to recoup his losses and eke out his *Item* wage by writing an occasional Sunday feature for the *Democrat*, a morning newspaper. When that daily was amalgamated with another into the *Times-Democrat* in December 1881, he left the *Item* and became a permanent member of the *Times-Democrat* staff at the lordly salary of thirty dollars a week. For this sum he wrote, in addition to his daily stint, most of the text for a Sunday editorial page. In 1884, shortly after he and Rudolph Matas had met, he also became associated with the Cotton Centennial Exposition, which began that year. Here he literally haunted the Japanese exhibit, becoming very friendly with Dr. Jokichi Takome and Ichizo Hattori, its managers. Time after time he gave Rudolph glowing reports of the daintiness and elfin quality of the décor, of the Oriental folklore he had absorbed, of their flower arrangement rituals. This was his latest and at the moment most consuming enthusiasm. Rudolph had been talking about a trip to Europe they must make together one of these days. Instead, Hearn now insisted, they must journey to Japan, and the sooner the better. Had Rudolph seen or heard about the water hyacinths and the loveliness of their lavender blossom-spikes? Could he envision what it would be like to see acres and acres of such transcendental beauty?

Rudolph did not respond as warmly as would have been the case a year earlier, for he had not yet recovered fully from the emotional disturbance caused by the death of his uncle Tomás. A bachelor, Jorda had been living with the Matas family at 82 South Rampart. For more than a year, his health had been deteriorating ever more markedly. Naturally, Rudolph had known all too well what was portended by the swelling about the ankles and the retention by those tissues of the imprint of a probing finger in the peculiarly shiny skin surface. Moreover, the fifty-four-year-old Jorda was considered in those days to be a man of advanced years. The inked notation on the death certificate Rudolph signed read: "chronic Bright's Disease." Teresa and Elvira went heavily, almost opaquely, veiled in black thereafter when they appeared in public and were zealous in decorating the tomb in St. Louis Cemetery with chrysanthemums on Toussaint (All Saints'). Jorda's will had bequeathed to his sister the entire fortune he had amassed as agent in Louisiana for the Royal Havana Lottery. The house seemed strangely empty and forlorn without the presence of another man.

The remarkable esteem in which Rudolph was held by the lay community of New Orleans throughout his adult life was already making itself evident. It was the custom until the latter 1920's to publish elegiac "poetry" in the classified columns of all daily newspapers. Hack rhymesters secured cumshaw by furnishing such verses to those who could afford proper tributes to departed members of the family; the less well-to-do simply substituted desired names in form doggerels furnished as part of the mortuary service by undertakers, or as lagniappe by the want-ad clerks of the papers.

But a week after Jorda's death on May 18, there appeared in the *Times-Democrat* a rhymed tribute not to the departed, but "To Dr. R. Matas on the Demise of his Beloved Uncle, Thomas Jorda." It was signed by the initials "M.B., Jr." Two of its quatrains read:

> Your wondrous art, your gentle, soothing skill,
> Your tireless watching and your deep-read lore,
> Were given in vain—Heaven willed it so—
> And your beloved was borne beyond the shore.

> To you hereafter will the blessings go,
> Like sweet shower of thanks upon your head,
> For duty done, for all that makes men true,
> Your memory'll live, although we mourn the dead.

Three even more significant tributes were paid him at this stage of his career by professional colleagues. The twenty-three-year-old prodigy was chosen to deliver the principal address at the annual meeting of the parish Medical Society that spring. In September, when the Medical College became part of the Tulane University of Louisiana and instituted a Department of Pathology, Dr. Matas was chosen to deliver the oration presenting to the new department a portrait of Dr. H. D. Schmidt, long Charity Hospital's pathologist. And finally, in the following spring, when Dr. A. B. Miles resigned his position as Tulane's demonstrator of anatomy in order to become head resident at Charity, the Medical College faculty elected Rudolph Matas to succeed him. He was nominated by Edmond Souchon; others who voted for him were Drs. Richardson, Chaillé, and Lewis. But Dr. Joseph Jones, then at the bitter climax of his controversy with Dr. Chaillé over quarantine enforcement, voted for Dr. George B. Lawrason of West Feliciana parish in order to avoid voting with Dr. Chaillé about anything. He had also voted against Dr. Chaillé to succeed Tobias Richardson, retiring dean of the Medical School, and against the appointment of Dr. Augustus McShane as Dr. Matas's assistant.

The first thing Rudolph did on receiving the appointment was to surrender his post as physician of the Spanish Benevolent Society of which his late uncle Tomás had been president. For one thing, the fees paid by those taking his anatomy course would amount to substantially more than he received from the Society, though only ten hours a week were thus taken up for twenty-six weeks, as against a year-round spate of office consultations and house calls demanded by his Society practice.* For another, "clients wanted me to continue [the Society practice] but I explained to them I could not continue to make house visits. If they wanted to come to my office as private patients, I would be willing to see them. A great many of them did so. . . . I developed a very nice clinic in the office at 82 South Rampart."

Finally, the new arrangement left him more time for two major avocations. One of these was the nocturnal rambles with Hearn and the talk that occupied the two friends on such excursions; the other a fury of dissections, not merely in the dank, stone-floored chamber over which he now presided as demonstrator of anatomy but also in the dead house at Charity Hospital, where he availed himself of every opportunity to perform a necropsy. Ever since his cousin Emilio Forto had been brought to death's very door by perityphlitis in San Antonio, Rudolph had read, studied, and discussed with others everything

---

* In the summer of 1886, while in Spain, he wrote for the *Journal* a report on Iberian medical practice and education, in which he noted that "I could devote a good deal of space and perhaps much more of your time by comparing the emoluments of practice in our country with those obtaining in Spain. It will suffice to state that a practitioner in [Barcelona] and in Spain is not insulted by being offered a peseta, or 20 cents, for a visit *a domicile*. This is almost as cheap, though not quite so low, as the pay given by some of our benevolent societies in New Orleans."

known about or bearing upon this commonest of frequently fatal abdominal maladies.

"Typhlitis" is any inflammation of the caecum, the blind terminus of the large bowel from which the appendix depends; "iliac phlegmon" was the term given to any abscess in the iliac (i.e., lower) area of the body cavity. In that era one of the standing assumptions of medical practice was that, unlike the rest of the intestines, the inner (as distinguished from rectal) end of the large bowel was not within the peritoneum but, like the kidneys, between the peritoneum and the muscles sheathing the lower part of the back. If that were true, an abscess here would not rupture into the main abdominal cavity and produce peritonitis; it would "suppurate" into the space between the peritoneum and the muscle layers just beneath the skin of the back, and could be drained through a surgical incision without performing the dreaded "laparotomy"; that is to say, without surgical exposure of the abdomen's interior. Even as late as 1900 not many surgeons were bold enough to undertake a laparotomy except as a straw-clutching last resort.

And now, in defiance of all established shibboleths and credos, young Rudolph Matas—a medical stripling of twenty-four—began to insist that the caecum and the appendix were intra-peritoneal organs; in other words, that they were wholly enclosed within the peritoneum and not outside of it. All his dissections of cadavers proved it, he reported. Waiting until an abscess burst into the peritoneal cavity, he explained to Hearn during one of their walks, was simply waiting until the horse had been stolen before even attempting to do something constructive about the stable door. Hearn listened attentively, goggling the while at his slim and, by comparison tall, young companion, as the latter, seeking more to clarify ideas to himself than to instruct, lectured about typhlitis and phlegmon and drew diagrams beneath the gas street lamps in the dust of unpaved roadways with the ferrule of his ivory-headed cane. Except when the weather was too foul to permit it, they wandered aimlessly about the quiet and vaguely gaslit streets of the upstream *faubourg* above Canal Street, a region somnolent, almost deserted, a ghost town compared to the raucous gaiety of the Tenderloin below Canal and behind Basin Street.

Each week night, Rudolph would teach from seven to nine as he had once studied under the sharp eyes of dapper Edmond Souchon, who even yet affected wooden-heeled, elastic-sided French gaiters. At nine, Hearn would be waiting outside the college entrance in Common Street, or Rudolph would go to Mrs. Courtney's Gasquet Street boardinghouse. There he would find his comrade seated at a plain wooden table upon which a flat leather valise had been laid. On this valise's upper side Hearn put the paper on which he wrote, an arrangement which brought the sheets within six inches of his protruding, myopic eye as he scrawled, scratched, erased, rewrote, and labored over some opus for the *Times-Democrat*'s editorial page.

Having met at one rendezvous or the other, the two friends would then roam about lonely thoroughfares in a section which at this hour was deserted by all who sought either domestic privacy or public wassail. Sometimes Hearn did most of the talking "as we were released from the world of fact in order to enter a realm of fantasy in which his fertile brain was given free rein. His literary projects were then passed in review and his fantastic stories were then extemporized, rehearsed and given form as our footsteps echoed on the silent street . . . and I, listening, enjoyed in silence the gradual unfolding of his story as he told it in a gentle, flowing word stream which culminated in a climax with vividness and descriptive power that was uncanny in its fascinating and realistic effect."

At other times it would be Rudolph who did the talking, hotly defending Finlay's hypothesis and explaining why, regardless of the skepticism of his elders, he espoused it, just as he believed implicitly in Hearn's future literary fame; or perhaps he would describe his latest dissection of a "subject" that morning at the Charity Hospital Dead House and add that "I am coming to the definite conclusion that where the appendix is seriously diseased the safest plan would be to remove it at once, just as gynecologists would not hesitate to remove an ovary that endangered its possessor." Then there might be an occasion when Rudolph, brimming with enthusiastic admiration, would speak of Dr. W. S. Halsted of New York: "There's a pioneer for you! A man who is not afraid to experiment with something new. He has been working with cocaine anesthesia; a local anesthetic, you know, trying it out on himself and his assistants. A month or so ago he decided to try a major operation on a patient's arm, a delicate operation on the plexus of nerves that go from the spinal cord on each side to the two arms. . . . Well, he insisted on doing this under Listerian antisepsis, but the dominating and domineering majority of the Bellevue Hospital doctors wouldn't let him use Listerian methods in the main amphitheater. Know what he did? He built a tent on the hospital grounds, fitted it out as an operating room, and by injecting the roots of the nerves deadened them so that he could free them a little at a time from adhesions that were giving the patient no end of trouble. Halsted! One of these days I'm going to meet that man just so I can tell him what a wonderful doctor he is; wonderful person, too. If Finlay had more of his drive and boldness. . . ."

Frequently they walked to the home on Claiborne Avenue near

Girod Street to which the Goslees had moved from the more select below-Canal-Street residential area where they had lived before the captain's death. Hearn could not be induced to visit this house by day because on one such occasion little Lucian and one of the other children had fled from him in headlong terror, appalled by his Cyclopean deformities. But he admired Adrienne devotedly, and, indeed, secured from her many of the recipes he is supposed to have contributed to a volume on the Creole cuisine, though his authorship of this treatise, as in the case of the Centennial Exposition guidebook also attributed to him, has never been established.

Occasionally they finished their stroll at 82 South Rampart Street, where Hearn would continue to talk while Rudolph dripped coffee for a midnight snack. But it was not often Hearn could be induced to go beyond Rudolph's office-consultation room, for Teresa and Elvira not only made no effort to mask their complete disapproval of him but went out of their way to emphasize it.

Sometimes they met Jimmy O'Connor at Staub's bookstore. Jimmy had served the nascent *Item* as newsboy when Hearn first joined that shaky venture's staff. Now, a self-taught stenographer of parts, he was reading law, having financed his education by hawking newspapers about the gaming houses and sporting saloons of the Rue Royale and along the edge of the Tenderloin, where tips were generous. Often, when they encountered O'Connor, Hearn suggested an expedition to one or another of the Negro brothels and, when the other two declined to companion him, gave out paeans in praise of "statuesque gold-bronze goddesses," and finally cursed them root and branch as unbelievers, abandoning them for a debauch in some incredibly foul dive which his flawed vision enabled him to transform imaginatively into a haven among the Hesperides. Myopic and monocular, he was incapable of seeing anything in sharp outline; his visual perception consisted of nearly abstract splashes of rich colors. When the spell was on him, any female form was that of a divinity.

"It was amusing," Mrs. Marion Baker recalled of him later, "to hear him ascribe youth and beauty to persons who possessed neither, but as the illusion was a pleasant one, it would have been a pity to dispel it."

Hearn's excesses apparently did not leave him scatheless. For almost half a century Dr. Matas withheld from publication the letters he received after his friend left New Orleans, on the supposed ground that the association between them had been personal and "professional." It is a matter of record that he did treat his friend on several occasions when the latter suffered bouts of breakbone (dengue) fever, or a touch of malaria. Hearn acknowledged that Matas's advice had greatly improved the use he could make of his one good eye. That he must have suffered other disorders which put the relationship between him and Dr. Matas on a still more confidentially professional basis seems clear from such passages as the following, in a letter which Hearn wrote to his friend from New York, en route to the West Indies:

"I have observed one of your prophylactic injunctions so far;—I have been strictly chaste . . . the splendid beauty I have seen here—that magnificent girlhood which makes desire seem almost sacrilegious, or at all events spiritualizes it into romance—will render it very easy for me to avoid any curiosity regarding the bronze beauty of the tropical half-breed women who are the only foci (I suppose) of the fearful creations you have described."

But a few weeks later he wrote from Barbados: "It's all very well to speak of the sy . . . coccus* and the other; but I'd like to see *you* live from one of these purple ports to another in a condition of compulsory laziness, and in view of all tantalizing things, and continue to neglect the Apples of Paradise."

And again: "As, under a perpendicular sun, I wandered down the narrow, curious yellow painted streets of Martinique, I looked about me; and lo! the fear of the g——coccus wholly passed away . . . in a little while I ceased to be in the street; under the guidance of a half naked mulatto I had found my way into the upper chamber of a queer building, overlooking a court full of cabbage palms and breadfruit trees; —there was a girl there—the tallest and most generally appetizing possible to conceive—a Martinique octoroon. I thought once or twice of salutary advice; but only in such a dreamy way as when one has swallowed a heavy dose of opium. . . ."

Such correspondence still lay two years in the future, however, when for a period of months bridging the winter of 1885 with the spring of 1886 they talked of a new tale Hearn was gestating, a tale based upon the historic episode of an 1856 hurricane which wiped out the Trade Winds Hotel on Ile Derniere, a resort spot on the Gulf Coast. Only a barely discernible sandspit remained of Last Island thirty years after the great storm, but in its day it had been Louisiana's most fashionable summer resort among wealthy city and plantation aristocrats. Hearn envisioned a situation in which the small daughter of one such family might be rescued from the storm's fury by a Spanish fisherman who lived along the coast, while her parents, returning to the exclusive Creole section of the old Esplanade in New Orleans believed her lost; and of the meeting between the girl and her father

* These and similar substitutions for letters are Hearn's excisions.

years later, neither aware of the other's identity, just as the father was dying of yellow fever.

Night after night, Hearn cross-examined Rudolph exhaustively about all the things he needed in fashioning this tragic tale. For one thing, he knew no Spanish. "What," he would ask, "is the expression a Spanish father might use in greeting the little daughter who runs out to meet him as he returns to his cottage at eventide?" "How would a woman, kneeling beside a deathbed, say in Spanish: 'O merciful Jesus, have pity on him!'?" "What are the morbid symptoms of the terminal stages of yellow fever?" And Rudolph would reply in great detail, especially where medical matters were involved, such as, "Would there be much pain if an invalid were dying of consumption instead of yellow fever?"

In order to spare his eye, which he felt had been vastly benefited by the therapy Rudolph had prescribed and for which total abstinence from candle-lit scribbling was a *sine qua non*, Hearn did all his writing during daylight hours. Aside from his journalistic efforts, he still had much writing to do. The newspaper pieces, by his own admission, were done "for to make the pot boil." But now he was additionally engaged in writing a series of Creole sketches of New Orleans for *Harper's* magazine, a welcome and well-paid opportunity which had come his way by a curiously roundabout route.

In the New Orleans of Hearn's time, George W. Cable was still the leading literary figure. The cordial intensity with which the Creoles later came to hate him, in the belief that his efforts to transcribe their quaint nuances of phraseology and pronunciation spitefully lampooned their culture and their way of life, did not affect the sale of his books in more profitable Northern markets. Moreover, Cable had as fine a talent for alienating friends as had Hearn. Mark Twain, an early Cable enthusiast, invited him to make a joint lecture tour. In the course of this journeying, Cable's Pharisaic piety (he once refused to travel even as far as from Manhattan to Brooklyn by ferryboat on the Sabbath) infuriated Clemens, who wrote their lecture agency that Cable's attitude was enough to make him—Mark Twain—hunt up "new and troublesome" means to dishonor the Sabbath by way of protest.

Cable and Hearn became friends of a sort in 1878, when the latter first joined the *Item* staff. Both were enthralled by the jungle beat and counterbeat of "gombo" songs, whose music Cable could transcribe. Hearn had never learned how to do this but he did have a fine ear for the words and so offered to assist Cable in making a collection of the mocking chants in which former slaves made fun of fictional white overlords during Sunday fetes in Congo Square. Yet the entente went into a rapid decline; the two partners were barely on bowing terms when J. O. Davidson, a staff artist in the employ of *Harper's Weekly*, came to New Orleans with a proposal for Cable to write text for a series of sketches and etchings Davidson had been assigned to make there.*

Cable demurred on the ground of his connection with Scribners and the Century Company, but he introduced Davidson to Hearn, with the recommendation that the latter be commissioned to write the desired textual matter. Thus began the steady though frequently stormy alliance between Hearn and *Harper's*, a liaison that endured until long after he had become a Japanese citizen, teaching English in a succession of district schools and universities.

During this, his second year as demonstrator of anatomy, Rudolph strove consciously to overwhelm in a flood of work the gnawing sense of discontent that ever more insistently claimed him. Most of it stemmed from increasing tension in the relations between himself and his mother. Since Tomás Jorda's death Teresa and Elvira, lacking any other outlet for their arbitrary possessiveness, concentrated all of it on Rudolph, of whose every interest beyond the immediate sphere of their familial influence they were passionately jealous. The two most readily available targets for their fulminations were Rudolph's closest friends, Adrienne and Lafcadio.

At Hearn's urging, Davidson had drawn a charming portrait of Adrienne for anonymous reproduction under the title of "A Creole Belle," as illustration for one of Hearn's descriptive passages about the Creole City.† Apparently this set the capstone on the arch of suspicion and dislike Teresa and her daughter were erecting against both of Rudolph's friends, but especially against Adrienne, who was now re-garded—and spoken of—by mother and daughter as an adventuress intent upon snaring an innocent youth in the toils of her godless charm. Rudolph had continued to call at the Goslee home, of course; on one occasion he had set Lucian's collarbone, fractured in a rough-and-tumble playtime mishap. He found in Adrienne's presence both a boon and an affliction. Certainly her nearness gave him moments of surcease from his mother's shrill and unremitting curtain lectures. Having no other focus for her passion to possess those about her, Teresa demanded blind filial obedience from her son in all things, as though he were still a child, subject to her every command. Rudolph, on the other

---

* The idea that *Harper's* was trying to get Cable away from Scribners, and for that reason had sent Davidson to New Orleans to tempt him, probably originated with Cable; also the notion that he and Davidson "got Hearn between us on a sofa and made him promise to write for *Harper's*." For one thing, Hearn would have received with open arms any proposition that promised a reasonably secure degree of support if he left newspaper work.

† A reproduction of this sketch was not used until the January 1887 number of *Harper's*, where it appeared as the magazine's frontispiece.

hand, a man of consequence in the community, recognized all too clearly his mother's mental and ethical limitations.

Adrienne's quiet charm, her obviously genuine liking for him, her wit, her familiarity with the classics of both French and English literature, her talent for music, her gracious acceptance of "Leocadio" for what he was—all these afforded a cherished retreat from the shrewish authoritarianism of both his mother and sister. On the other hand, the harsh realization that as long as Adrienne's divorced husband lived, Rudolph and the woman who became dearer to him with each passing day could not marry, threatened to rend him afresh each time he found refuge in her presence from a household that had long since ceased to be a home. So he did his best to drug himself with the anodyne of work. Until far into the night he read, made notes, and scribbled. If he woke at two, he would rise, drip a pot of fresh coffee, and study or write until time to set out on hospital rounds or house calls.

There was always more to be done, fortunately, than could be crowded into even a twenty-hour working day. Merely the abstracts, book reviews, and translations he made for the *Journal* could have provided full-time employment. For example, in 1886 Carlos Finlay, still patiently seeking to buttress his derided mosquito hypothesis, experimentally inoculated a number of nonimmunes with yellow fever by letting infected mosquitoes sting them. He thus added a number of significant corollaries to his theory. One was that, to carry infection, the transmitting mosquito must draw blood from a fever patient on the third to sixth day of his illness. Before or after that period, no contagion was acquired or carried. Another was that an infected mosquito, if allowed to sting an immune before stinging a nonimmune, a much milder attack of yellow fever was sustained by the latter than would otherwise be the case. Similarly, if the mosquito was allowed to draw blood twice from yellow-fever patients before sheathing its lancet in the tissues of a nonimmune, an extraordinarily severe attack of fever followed.

Finally, having read and digested everything that had ever been written or reported about perityphlitis or iliac phlegmon in the literature of medicine, past and present, Rudolph prepared a monumental paper on the subject, categorically defining the caecum and appendix as intraperitoneal organs, crediting Frederick Treves of London with being the first to enunciate this view of the iliac region's anatomy, and urging immediate operation once a positive diagnosis of imminent rupture could be made. But he also warned against laparotomies undertaken simply because one or two extraordinarily gifted surgeons had the skill which promised for such bold surgery a reasonable assurance of success, or because "laparotomy is now the fashion."*

Even so, in the frantic rush to get this copy in hand without cutting its length (Rudolph Matas never did learn the meaning of a copy deadline or space limitation) he found later that his researches had not gone far enough; the Da Costa edition of Gray's *Anatomy* credited him with statements and conclusions quoted from his treatise on iliac phlegmon, but he had to publish a later article admitting that Bardeleben in Germany had anticipated Treves's work by a good twenty-five years.

Before he got the last of his copy into the printer's hand, Rudolph was practically beside himself. Early in 1886 his mother determined that by leaving New Orleans she would end, once and for all, the association between her son and the two friends she most disliked. It seems not even remotely to have occurred to her at any time that Rudolph could have or exercise any choice in the matter of accompanying her. The ostensible reason for their departure was to return her brother's mortal remains to San Felíu de Guixols; but her real motive was revealed unmistakably in a moment of sudden tension when Teresa announced she would sell both her Rampart Street houses. Rudolph's reaction to this must have been an immediate inquiry concerning what was to become of him if both these houses were disposed of. . . . After all, he had just been elected president of the New Orleans Medical and Surgical Society and he had "developed a very nice clinic at 82 South Rampart," which was not only his mother's legal property but his personal and professional residence as well. One is bound to conclude that in this very fact Teresa at last found an opportunity to accomplish what her husband had so long denied her. It was, she undoubtedly explained, quite simple and sensible; they would all three return to the Costa Brava to live in the land that had given her birth, a land they should never have left, and where they would yet be dwelling in peace and plenty had it not been for her husband's plunge, against her express advice and wishes, into railroad speculations that robbed them of their entire fortune. Rudolph could practice in Gerona or in Barcelona. His teaching? What teaching or what nothing? As for his friends. . . . If he meant that hideous one-eyed madman, he was better off with an ocean between him and such friends; and as for others she could name. . . . Well! When the time came Rudolph would marry

* The word "appendicitis" was coined and first used by Reginald Fitz of Boston in 1886, the year in which Matas's two-part serial on iliac phlegmon was published in the *New Orleans Medical and Surgical Journal* (vol. 14); and the first deliberate appendectomy successfully carried out was performed by Thomas G. Morton, of Philadelphia, in the following year, on April 27, 1887.

one of the girls from his own station in life and his own people. . . .

When her son made plain his resolve to remain in, or at least to return to, New Orleans and to resume his classes, practice, and editorial duties as soon as he had seen his mother and sister safely settled in San Felíu, Teresa reminded him that he would have to come back to America without her; that the Rampart Street houses were her property and hers alone, and that he would therefore face the future without so much as a roof over his head. Obviously this carried no weight with Rudolph, since his earning capacity and income were both substantial and his position in New Orleans was securely established.

Yet it was a trying time. Above all else, at the moment, he missed Hearn's companionship; but "Leocadio" was on Grand Isle, living at Krantz's Hotel and working on "our" Chita as he called his novelette of Ile Derniere. Since this was now merely a deserted sandspit, the only comparable site and source of authentic local color was Grand Isle, which boasted two resort hotels, a Coast Guard station, and a small conglomerate population of fishermen and cucumber farmers. Many of these claimed descent from the smugglers of Jean Lafitte's band, which had occupied a stronghold on Grand Terre Island, on the opposite shore of Barataria Pass.

Here Hearn bathed in the rolling surf and watched advancing and retreating surges design a tracery in the sand which made the beach look "like a shuddering brown skin." Here he watched threshers dance on piles of pink, sun-dried shrimp to rid the rubbery meats of their brittle, glassy shells. Here he wrote, rewrote, tore up, and fashioned anew the romance which ultimately brought him fame and fortune; a firstling he dedicated to Rudolph Matas as "our" *Chita.**

That bedeviled young man found parting, though sorrowful, anything but sweet. Endless niggling details attended the sale of Teresa's two houses, and curiously enough the buyers, Jean Jane and his wife, Eliza Tribout Jane, each purchased one of the houses with the stipulation that neither should become community property. Teresa cleared $7300 cash on this transaction. Together with the $5000 paid her by Narciso not to contest his divorce and the very sizable estate bequeathed her by Jorda, she was now independently wealthy.

Meanwhile the cumbersome legal machinery to permit opening

* This dedication was withdrawn from the flyleaf in all but the first printing of *Chita* in book form. *Harper's* received numerous inquiries about this omission and explained vaguely that such things were sometimes necessitated by considerations of format in determining how many blank pages could be included in a book's make-up. In all likelihood Hearn himself directed the original dedication's omission for the future. At least, this coincided in point of time with the abrupt cessation of correspondence from him to Matas.

the aboveground vault in which Tomás Jorda's coffin had been sealed *à perpétuité* and to permit the withdrawal of this casket and its shipment to Spain had been set in motion. Fortunately, Rudolph's position with the health and quarantine authorities was now such that some of the otherwise endless red tape could be stripped away to facilitate matters. But it was a harried, lonesome, and altogether dreadful time for the young surgeon nonetheless, and left him tragically little opportunity to exchange farewells with Adrienne. These were by now, however, mostly assurances and reassurances that, regardless of what his mother might think, say, or do, he would return to the New Orleans with which his entire future was now identified. Underscoring this resolution, he made arrangements to buy a three-story house at 72 South Rampart Street, just a block distant from the home his mother had sold. His instruments, his office furniture, his books, and the like were moved to the new address by arrangement with the owner-occupant, John Baptiste Lavigne, who had agreed to this at the time he accepted earnest money with a memorandum of the contract to sell.

In case of sudden need—for, after all, who could say what might happen?—Adrienne was to communicate with Lafcadio. Rudolph had written him explicit directions on what to do in given eventualities and had put at his disposal certain sums on which he could draw. He had also left with her mother an emergency fund, just in case. Finally, Adrienne was to harbor no smallest doubt on one score: he, Rudolph, would be back in New Orleans before the new Tulane scholastic year began. In token of this promise, here was a phial of her favorite Piver perfume; he would bring her more of it, and in more beautiful containers, from Paris, where it was made.

And so they parted, these two who were so strongly drawn to one another and yet forever debarred from union. The ship that bore the crated casket of Tomás Jorda had already proceeded downstream. Rudolph, Teresa, and Elvira boarded the Shenandoah Valley train at the foot of Canal Street, a scant stone's throw from the spot where the White League fought its bloody battle against carpetbaggery on an almost forgotten September afternoon when he was a panic-stricken schoolboy. They left New Orleans on Saturday noon, June 26. Their tickets, he was careful to note in his journal, cost $34 each, and they would not reach New York until 1 P.M. three full days later, on June 29.

CHAPTER XIV

The three-day railroad trek from New Orleans to New York must have been a fairly severe ordeal; primitive transport accommodations restricted Rudolph's freedom of movement so that he was constantly in company with his mother and sister. Teresa exulted openly over her success in bringing about, at long last, the family's return to San Felíu and at the same time severing Rudolph from Adrienne, all through a single, well-thought-out coup. Elvira, whose eyes held a secretive glint of triumph as well, said little.

Rudolph withdrew into himself as much as possible, realizing the real battle with his mother was yet to come. He was well aware that she now saw herself as head of the clan, and as such assumed she could forbid her son to leave her, regardless of what his wishes might be. There would be a scene when she found out how wholly erroneous this assumption was. Meanwhile he would concentrate on the wonders to be seen during their first visit to fabled New York. Though they would be there less than two full days, he planned to crowd as much as possible into this interval, leaving professional matters and the greatly anticipated personal meeting with Dr. Halsted, as well as contacts with other medical notables, for a more extended and leisurely stay during the return voyage that fall, when he would have no wishes other than his own to consult or consider.

As always, he kept a meticulous account of expenditures, his ledger being a notebook, small enough to fit easily into a vest pocket. It had been given to him two years earlier by the William F. Kidder Co., of

New York, makers of Hydroleine, "the only pancreatized oil on the market." From the pencil scrawls between its leatherette covers, it is quite obvious that Teresa permitted her son to defray all costs of the journey while she kept her letter of credit intact; also that Rudolph watched his pennies sedulously. His original plan for their Atlantic crossing had contemplated a stateroom on the White Star Line's *Britannia;* this routing would follow the track of his first European journey of 1863 from New York to Liverpool and thence to Paris. But a *Britannia* stateroom for three would cost $240 and would entail an additional expenditure of $21.95 per person for passage from Liverpool to Dover, Calais, and Paris; whereas the Hamburg-American liner *Lessing* offered passage at $67 each, or $201 in all for through transportation from New York to Paris, via Plymouth and Cherbourg. Naturally, the Matas reservations were made for accommodations on the *Lessing.*

Travel, he discovered, brought in its train a host of unlooked-for expenditures. Breakfast at Philadelphia for himself, mother, and sister, on the final lap of their three-day rail journey to New York, cost $1.35 for three, and the cabman who drove them from the station in New York later that morning to the Sinclair House charged $2.00 for the trip. The afternoon's sightseeing that first day in New York was anything but lavish; they rode across Brooklyn Bridge on the cable cars for a total of 15 cents, and that night's dinner at Martinelli's cost $3.75, or, as Rudolph carefully noted in parentheses, "(1.25 each)." Wednesday morning's tour was likewise thrifty: 30 cents for three cups of coffee by way of breakfast, 15 cents for streetcar fare to Central Park, and $1.40 for lunch for three. The afternoon's fling made up for earlier frugality, however. It included a carriage tour through Central Park to cover ground they had been unable to traverse on foot and to take them past the Vanderbilt and Jay Gould residences, with a stop at St. Patrick's Cathedral. With dinner at the Sinclair House, this added a staggering $9.75 to the day's disbursements, to which it became necessary to append $5.75 more for their hotel bill, $1.50 for their baggage, $2.00 for a hack to the Hoboken pier from which the *Lessing* would pull out at 4:30 A.M., a dollar for porterage, two more for rental of a deck chair, and an item of $1.35 for "literature," which included a copy of the current issue of *Harper's.*

Rudolph retired at ten-thirty, but was awakened by the stir and bustle of departure. "Thus far excellent," he noted in his journal the next day. "Sea blue and tranquil and smooth as a mirror. Took 15 minims of a solution of cocain 2 grains to ounce as was feeling symptoms of nautopathy. Read *Harper's Magazine* and Andrew Lang's *Mark of Cain.* Very fascinating book." That was Thursday, the first full day at sea. Saturday, on the other hand, "woke late and felt well—gave 25 cents extra to steward, stewardesses $1.00 (50¢ a piece). This is necessary to propitiate these mercenary people." Fourth of July fell on Sunday, so there was no celebration until the following day, which saw the presentation of an "excellent entertainment at 8:30 in honor of July 4th (25¢)."

Another adventure into the social amenities of transatlantic travel may or may not have exacted additional but unspecified contributions. Two pages of the Hydroleine notebook bear in tabular pencil notations the names and values of all poker hands, set down in their proper order. No amount in monetary figures appears with them. Obviously, therefore, any thirst for knowledge in this particular field which Rudolph might have felt was soon quenched, if indeed it was not satisfied by purely academic researches into the comparative worth of poker permutations. In any case, he made no confession even to himself of sums lost to those generously offering to initiate him into the great American pastime with which this was obviously his first contact.

And so the journey wore on, tediously, because "most of the officers and men on board speak very poor English. This is a very disagreeable feature of the trip." Even the ship's surgeon spoke but little French and no English whatever; Gustave Simonson, a New Yorker, professing to be a medical graduate en route to study in Berlin, "is evidently a better chess player than a physician." On the ninth day out from New York they paused at Plymouth, then crossed the Channel to the mole whose ancient cannons still "guard" the harbor of Cherbourg, and here the Matas party debarked after Rudolph "gave servants $5" and noted the outlay of an additional $2.65 for sundries. His fluent French stood him in good stead during the routinely passionate and high-pitched argument with voluble *douaniers;* after the payment of 7.50 fr. in customs duties on soap and similar belongings, they came at last to an old stone inn, where an equally aged-seeming crone lighted two candles from one already burning in a niche at the foot of a stone stairway and thus led them to their respective bedchambers.

The huge immobile four-posters felt disturbingly unfamiliar after nine nights in cramped and tossing berths aboard ship, but morning found them rested, refreshed, and aboard the boat train rumbling through a pleasant countryside of "beautifully cultivated farms" with fruit trees espaliered along sunlit walls where "houses all look new and very calcareous." The hotel bill at Cherbourg, not included in the passage money, had come to francs 30.50, lunch at Caen had cost 5 francs each, and another franc seems to have been squandered for "fruit and sundries" along the way. However they did reach Paris through the Gare du Nord at last, and, once settled for a week's stay,

Teresa even went so far as to spend some of her own funds. At least the notation "Matas money" appears beside entries of 151.30 fr. paid Au Bon Marché for "goods"; 9 fr. for a copy of Baedeker, 5.50 fr. for a telegram, 8 fr. for a pocketbook, 42 fr. for hats, and 20.75 fr. for a "Duster's bill"—whatever that may have been.

But it was still Rudolph who paid for fiacres at the rate of 25 fr. for a full day, and settled such items as 4 fr. for a bath for mother and sister (3.50 fr. for a bath for himself); ten works by an author whose penciled name is undecipherable, but whose paper-backed romances retailed at 60 centimes each, plus a whopping 2.75 fr., or 55 cents, for a *Traité de Beauté*—presumably the title of a book of sorts—and 9 fr. for three tickets to the Hippodrome. At a Sunday concert on the Champs-Elysées, the day after their arrival in Paris, Rudolph was charged 5 fr. for three water ices; that is to say, the equivalent of a dollar for three dabs of sherbert. He was so profoundly outraged by this that he entered in his Hydroleine notebook the smoldering notation: "At concert in Champs-Elysées, for ices and theft, 5.00."

They left Paris from the Gare d'Orléans on July 16, following station by station the journey Rudolph and his parents had made in 1865 after Narciso's certification in ophthalmology. Nightfall saw them at Limoges, where they transferred to a *coupé-lit*, in which the arm rests of the benches on each of the compartment's sides could be lifted to let passengers stretch out and, if possible, sleep; but they kept this luxury *"jusqu' à Toulouse."*

Toward the close of the next day's forenoon they detrained at Barcelona, from which, relatively speaking, it was but a step to San Felíu de Guixols—half a world away from Tucson, where Narciso lived in loneliness that summer as a twofold grass widower. The "young lady with long black hair" he had married thirty years before was once more in her birthplace, an embittered woman of sixty, clutching the fortune for which she had agreed not to contest his divorce; Louise, whom he had married after that divorce, was in Los Angeles, where she was delivered of a daughter, Irene, youngest and last of Narciso's get.

Almost as soon as his mother and sister were safely installed with relatives at San Felíu, Rudolph left for Barcelona to study hospital administration and local systems of medical education. He did not return before leaving on his homeward journey. Toward the end of July he received his first news from Louisiana—a long letter from Hearn who was back at Grand Isle for a month's stay and was apparently writing little beyond random notes on the characteristic locale. As a matter of fact, a year later, in March 1887, a hastily scribbled note from his Gasquet Street address, conceded that *Chita* was even then no more than half completed. After asking for Spanish equivalents of "phrases of compassion—short and quick—uttered in a moment of awful excitement," the letter went on:

"Half my sketch is done; the other half, alas!—is still a chaos of notes, perfected pages, outlines, ideas in embryo—all tangled up; a half suggested thing, like a *subject* partially dissected."

As a matter of record, *Chita* was not completed until yet another year had passed; indeed, Hearn, then in the West Indies, was still making revisions after the first edition was on the book dealers' shelves.

Rudolph Matas put in at least a month in Barcelona, while his mother and sister remained in San Felíu de Guixols, though they visited him in the capital from time to time. At least, he was still there when Hearn's letter, mailed in Grand Isle on July 8, was delivered to him. The transit to New Orleans, New York, and so to Spain could not possibly have taken less than sixteen or seventeen days if all connections had been clock perfect. But if Rudolph hoped to find in this missive news of the one person who was first and oftenest in his thoughts, he was foredoomed to disappointment. Hearn clearly feared his letter might fall into Teresa's hands, in which case Rudolph would never see it unless it was innocent of any mention of the woman she now recognized as a rival for her son's loyalties, just as another temptress had bereft her of her husband. So he confined himself to rhapsodies about Grand Isle, writing, "Did I know for certain you would get this letter, I might try to make it a little more interesting, but I feel so much in doubt as to you ever receiving it that I fear to waste my sweetness.

"I am writing you from Krantz's Hotel, Grand Isle, on a wild, windy, dark day, beside the roar of a thousand breakers. It rains diluvially. Moreover I am sick, with all those colics, cramps, headaches which accompany a thorough change of habit and diet, preparatory to building up the system anew. My first swim made every muscle as sore as if I had been beaten with a stick; but at the end of the first week I hope to be as brown as a seal and as hard as a piece of wood. I am going to remain here a month. Meanwhile I have separated myself entirely from my beloved books, being determined to devote myself wholly to literary work, not to literary *pleasure*. The present conditions are favorable, as there are few guests, perhaps a dozen; but outside of human guests I have plenty of delightful natural visitors; tree-frogs that sing in my room, mud-daubers building their nests above my bed, while birds pipe on my roof, and occasionally a harmless garter snake peers at them with his beautiful topaz eyes. At half past four I rise to bathe and to view the birth of the morning—the advent of the light—the blossoming of the vast and Mystical Rose of Sunrise. Seabirds follow me out, and fly low over me, with their sinister little sharp cries; and I feel at intervals weird little touches, as of phantom hands—the bodies of tiny fish touching my own.

"So I wait for the poet's pentecost—the inspiration of nature, the descent of the Tongues of Fire. And I think they will come, when the wild skies brighten, and the sun of the Mexican Gulf reappears for his worshippers—with hymns of wind and sea, and the prayers of birds. When one becomes bathed in this azure and gold air—saturated with the perfumes of the sea, he can't help writing *something*. And he cannot help feeling a new sense of being. The soul of the Sea mingles with his own, is breathed into him, the spirit that moveth over the deep is the Creator indeed, vivifying, illuminating, strengthening. I really feel this Religion—the sense of awe that comes on one in some great silent temple. You would feel it too under this eternal vault of blue, when the weird old Sea is touching the keys of his mighty organ.

"I trust you will have enjoyed your trip by the time these few pages reach far-off Barcelona. I received your postal—which amused me exceedingly with its pithy criticism of Mategazza. Glad that book is not with me in Grand Isle!!! I am not yet well acclimated, but each day I feel more and more the truth of the Greek fancy that a certain delicious goddess was born of the creamy seafoam. Was—yes! and is!—she is being eternally reborn therefrom! And I am to stay here a whole month! Think of it! I must be even as the disciples of Sakya-Mouni.

"Now I shall say, 'Go with God!' You will have my thoughts wherever you are, and my earnest wishes will supplement all of yours. Give my sincere regards to Mrs. and to Miss Matas who, I trust, have enjoyed the voyage."

The letter's closing sentence, like its opening one, indicates that Hearn was giving full weight to the possibility his words might fall under the eyes of Teresa, whose cordial dislike of him he reciprocated. If there was further correspondence between him and Rudolph that summer, no documentary evidence of it remains. In view of the zealous care with which Dr. Matas preserved every scrap Hearn is known to have addressed to him, this points to the strong likelihood that only one exchange of letters took place; also, that Rudolph must have begun his journey home shortly after receiving this Grand Isle communication. In any case, Rudolph's creative-writing energies were fully occupied in reporting on Spanish medical practice and education in Barcelona and Madrid and in sending back an exhaustive holograph on his findings by mid-August for publication in the *New Orleans Medical and Surgical Journal*.

Among other noteworthy features he emphasized that Iberian physicians fell into two classes: those who were merely graduates of an accredited college, had passed the equivalent of what New Orleans knew as the Green Room Finals, and were therefore entitled to practice as licentiates; but they were not permitted to use the title "Doctor" until they had written and defended a thesis before a board of medical examiners.

"The examination hall, or 'Green Room' as our students would call it," he wrote, "is a somber apartment well calculated to test the moral courage of the aspirants. The examinations are open to the public and the student is exposed to the gaze of his fellow students and friends, who sit in long rows of antique chairs. . . . Professors still cling to the long academical gowns and mantles. It would make an American feel as if he were about to be tried by a Council of Grand Inquisitors preparatory to the delights of an *auto de fe.*"

By this time the summer was running out, and the climax of conflict between himself and his mother could no longer be postponed. In all probability Rudolph wrote her from Barcelona that he would leave for the United States on a given date, and she came from San Felíu to order him to remain. No details of how the silver cord was severed are to be found. One reference vaguely mentions that Teresa introduced her son that summer to a family among whose members was a highly eligible daughter "with whom I might have become infatuated." But the explosion of a bomb in a Granada theater killed a number of spectators, among them this girl whom Teresa presumably hoped to see first as her son's *novia* and ultimately as her daughter-in-law. It is difficult—indeed, impossible—to say how much of this matchmaking-bombing episode is apocryphal. . . . Approaching his ninetieth birthday, Dr. Matas sought to enshrine, on his own account rather than for others, the memory-images of both his parents. In doing so, he endeavored, among other things, to destroy by fire all letters or other documents pertaining to what he called "family matters." It was by the sheerest chance that a few letters—those written by Narciso at the time of Rudolph's graduation, for example—and such things as the Hydroleine notebook survived this holocaust.

Unfortunately, the penny-by-penny account of his return journey did not escape. Beyond doubt he kept such a record at the time; the habit of itemizing expenditures, begun during his student days to account to his father for disbursement of his allowance, remained with him for life. As president of the International Surgical Society, nearing eighty, he still set down apologetically that he had given a ten-cent tip at a lunch counter near Charing Cross in London, but only because the service had been so very excellent that he felt moved to reward the waitress with a larger-than-ordinary gratuity.

In short, he must have kept a journal of his return-trip disbursements in Madrid, Paris, and finally in New York. Thus it is simply beyond belief that he made no notation of the circumstances under which he and his mother parted, presumably forever. Yet all that is known with certainty is that he saw her only once more, and then—a decade later —under circumstances of extreme bitterness when Teresa, grasping, made him pay through the nose to be left in peace, just as once she had made Narciso buy from her an agreement not to contest his territorial divorce in the courts of Arizona. Not only did he destroy all records of this last encounter; he went out of his way to deny, at least by implication, that it had ever taken place.

But it did take place, in 1896, and though Teresa lived a dozen years after that final meeting, she and Rudolph never saw one another again. Perhaps it was this prolonged absence that enabled him in his later years to speak so often of the simple piety and devotion with which both his parents reared him to follow the path of righteousness and faith. Yet because of the very nature of the one brief encounter in which Teresa and her son met for the last time, we are bound to assume that the parting between them a decade earlier in Barcelona must have been both stormy and harsh. Teresa had counted on her matriarchal authority to keep Rudolph at her side and away from Adrienne. When her twenty-six-year-old physician son bluntly refused to "obey," one may imagine the outburst with which she cast him off and perhaps the secretive glance of veiled triumph with which Elvira took in the scene that made her Teresa's sole remaining family treasure.

Thus it was as a quasi-orphan, one who had broken relations with his father some years before and was newly excommunicated by his mother, that Rudolph journeyed to Madrid, where he entrained for Paris. There, in a mood in which eager anticipation of what the future had to offer overcame any lingering trace of regret over past bereavements, he strolled the boulevards and sought out the world-famous establishment of L. T. Piver, from which the druggists of New Orleans imported that community's favorite perfumes. At this point one is bound to feel a very special twinge of sorrow that no written memoranda of the return journey survived the years. What sort of notation did the man who had been so deeply outraged by a 5 fr. charge for three water ices make when he lavished who knows how many francs on small bottles of Florayme and Azurea perfumes, on cut rock-crystal atomizers, and on ornate flasks of Nelori cologne? These gifts for Adrienne, and a pierced sandalwood fan for Mrs. Goslee, were packed with affectionate care before he left Paris for Hamburg and Cuxhaven, and so once more to debarkation in sight of the dingy waterfront tenement-hives of Hoboken and across the Hudson river to New York.

He had allowed himself time to meet William Stewart Halsted before moving on to New Orleans. But that intrepid pioneer of local anesthesia, who had set up his operating room in a tent when Bellevue Hospital's conservative staff denied him permission to operate under Listerian techniques within that institution's portals, was not to be found. Only later did Dr. Matas learn the background of one of the most dramatic episodes in the history of American medicine.

Halsted had set out to prove that in certain operations involving nerve trunks localized cocaine anesthesia was preferable to general anesthesia by chloroform or ether. He had performed his spectacular tent operation on the nerve plexus running from the spine to the arm; but this was not until long after he and his assistant, Richard J. Hall, had tested cocaine anesthesia upon one another. They had served as their own guinea pigs—until both were utterly enslaved by cocaine addiction. Halsted's brilliant career was thereby threatened with extinction at the very moment when Johns Hopkins University invited him to become professor of surgery on the same faculty on which William Osler had already accepted the chair of clinical medicine.

Evaluating his situation with pitiless objectivity, Halsted had himself committed to a sanitarium in Providence, Rhode Island, for a year, in 1885, before coming to Johns Hopkins; even after he joined the Baltimore university's faculty, he returned voluntarily to hospitalization in Providence for an additional period of months. In this way he succeeded in throwing off the shackles of addiction, renewed a great career, and achieved honors and recognition. His original contributions to the advancement of his profession range from such matters as introducing the use of rubber gloves in operative practice to devising a technique for removal of the breast in cases of cancer. Richard Hall, his assistant, was less fortunate. In the course of unavailing efforts to break the hold of narcotic addiction, he died.

At the time of Rudolph's return to New York, Halsted was in Providence. With only a scant interval remaining before the opening of medical instruction would necessitate his presence in New Orleans, he took train to Washington where he visited George Sternberg, his former superior of the Cuban mission, now deputy Surgeon-General of the Army.

He hastened his departure because it was necessary to set up an entire household in New Orleans, not merely a new office with slate and pencil dangling on strings beside the front door of 72 South Rampart Street. The details had been fully worked out in his mind before ever he left Barcelona; he had written Adrienne from abroad what he had in mind when first he arranged to purchase a house of three floors, a residence far larger than a single young man needed. Adrienne and her mother were admittedly finding it no easy task to support a brood of eight boys for whose wants they must somehow provide. Rudolph needed and would have to engage a housekeeper in any case, one who would live on the premises to take calls when the doctor was out. To be sure, if Adrienne accepted such a position, tongues would wag, shoulders would shrug, and eyebrows would lift. However, if not merely Adrienne but her mother, her six brothers, and her two sons also lived there no Dame Ashfield could possibly be moved to demand: "What will Mrs. Grundy say?" Rudolph would have his surgery, consultation rooms, and living quarters on the first floor, Adrienne and the Goslees would live on the second and third. Under such an almost ideal arrangement he would not be left to the irresponsible mercies of unsupervised servants, he would be free to devote his time and energies to professional work, and the Goslee ménage, being assured of an adequate and comfortably appointed home, would be released from the constant fret of financial worry. Could any conceivable arrangement be better all around?

Thrust into the cloudy background of his thoughts, the obvious answer to that question was sternly suppressed, and though Rudolph chafed at the frustrating unattainability of one so dear and now so near, at least the three-story residence at 72 South Rampart became more of a sanctuary than he had ever found as an adult in the home his mother dominated. Lafcadio, now a frequent visitor in the house where he was made to feel welcome, tended to scoff at the scruples which kept Rudolph and Adrienne from marriage, or at any rate from union; but he did this gently, sensing intuitively how troubled these two friends must be. From Adrienne, meanwhile, he received recipes and Creole proverbs for his Sunday page and for magazine articles; from Rudolph he siphoned the medical and Spanish material he needed for *Chita*.

And so the two friends, Matas and Hearn, approached the year in which both scored their first notable professional triumphs although, oddly enough, neither was to grasp the full import of his achievement until years had passed, and they had long since lost touch with one another.

CHAPTER XV

Having severed all filial ties without hope of finding compensating bonds in matrimony, Rudolph sought to deaden the Tantalus pangs of his beloved's nearness in the narcosis of fatigue. The relentless fury with which he now drove himself to multiply his labors left him scarcely a free minute.

Almost every night he returned to his home so late, and so aching with physical weariness, that not even Adrienne's solicitous welcome could dispel the druglike effects of overwork. In addition to the phenomenally growing private practice which now claimed much of his time, he had to devote a major portion of each morning to Charity Hospital service as visiting physician; he had to fulfill his editorial duties at the *Journal* and his nightly three-hour stint as demonstrator of anatomy; he had to take care of a multiplicity of details imposed by his presidency of the New Orleans Medical and Surgical Association. Moreover, that same autumn he helped to organize a group calling itself the New Orleans Pathologic Society, with Dr. H. D. Schmidt, the revered pathologist of Charity Hospital, as perpetual president. The members were all interns and ex-interns whom Dr. Schmidt had trained in microscopy and they met each week at his home.

The unrelenting intensity with which Rudolph labored drew protests even from Lafcadio.

"I know what vultures are tearing at your bowels," he would say, "and I have told you what abysmal folly it is to let them continue to prey on you. But at this rate you are plunging headlong toward a nervous or physical breakdown—or both."

August McShane, Rudolph's assistant demonstrator at Tulane, also urged him to ease the violent pace of his work but, like Hearn, he talked to the wind. Fortunately New Orleans was free from yellow fever that year. Not a single death from this cause was reported during 1886. But an outbreak of "fever"—specific nature not disclosed in the beginning—did occur at Biloxi, just beyond Lake Pontchartrain in Mississippi. By midmonth its prevalence had increased to such an extent that public health authorities of New Orleans and Louisiana declared a flat quarantine against their Gulf Coast neighbor. A committee from the *New Orleans Medical and Surgical Journal,* headed by Dr. Matas, sought to investigate the Biloxi situation, map the epidemic's incidence case by case, and if possible discover where and how it had been vectored.

But President Holt of the State Board of Health, still feuding with Dr. Chaillé and the municipal authorities, declared that inasmuch as by this time some physicians in nearby Bay St. Louis had officially pronounced the epidemic one of yellow fever, any investigator who went from New Orleans (or any other Louisiana point) to Biloxi would not be permitted to return until the quarantine was lifted.

Even so, the alarm was enough to send off on hasty journeys those Orleanians who could afford to travel; the more fortunate to the cool of the Great Smokies or to the New England seaside; the less wealthy to nearby inland points beyond range of infection. Those who perforce remained at home summoned their physician or hastened to his office at the first sign of malaise. Thus the waiting room at 72 South Rampart was crowded during office hours; the slate beside the door was usually covered with scrawled messages by the time Rudolph returned from hospital rounds and house calls.

The medical department of Tulane University opened its preliminary courses, one of which was Demonstration in Anatomy, on October 18. Prior to that date, Rudolph had been busily reactivating the New Orleans Medical and Surgical Society after its passive estivation during the summer term. At the year's final meeting, when Dr. Henry Dixon Bruns was elected to succeed him, his idolized chief, Dr. Souchon (who, a year later, would succeed Dr. Bruns as president) delivered a paper on "Chronic Spasm of the Membranous Urethra Treated by Perineal Section." One of the cases he cited bared another of the tragic dramas in which so many of that era's medical men were involved.

A young New Orleans practitioner had long been treated by various of his colleagues for urethral spasticity, without securing the least relief from his agony. "I would occasionally meet the poor doctor,"

Souchon reported, "and he would tell me about his sufferings which were plainly visible in his face and in his manner, as were also the effects of the morphine he had taken to relieve his pains. . . . I placed myself at his disposal either to operate or assist any one he would select to perform the operation . . . but [he] could not make up his mind. Finally, however, he decided, and with the kind and valuable assistance of Dr. F. W. Parham, of Dr. E. S. Lewis, and of Dr. R. Matas, the operation was performed. . . . I saw him lately, and from the account he gives of himself, I find that his bladder troubles are over, but he is still a slave to morphine."

Edmond Souchon was a rock-ribbed conservative, who did not take kindly to innovations. Until he retired in 1907, to devote the remaining seventeen years of his life to the treasured medical museum he had founded at Tulane, he continued to exemplify the old school of swift surgery, with his son, Marion Sims Souchon, as principal assistant. In amputations he would use a large knife, ivory handled, instead of the small bladed modern scalpel, and a heavy saw, like a butcher's, for cutting through bone, instead of the Gigli "saw" of braided wire. He disapproved his protégé's tendency to jettison the accepted shibboleths of their profession, particularly his advocacy of Carlos Finlay's revolutionary doctrines of yellow-fever transmission, which ran counter to all the accepted beliefs of men like Chaillé, Sternberg, Gorgas, and other recognized authorities.

None the less, the icon-smashing young Rudolph Matas was still espousing Finlay's hypothesis. Two Latin-American physicians, Dr. Domingo Freire of Rio de Janeiro, and Dr. M. Carmone y Valle of Mexico, had each just published books in which they claimed to have isolated the yellow-fever "germ." Freire called his the *Cryptococcus xanthogenicus*, and said he had discovered it in yellow-fever blood under 750-diameter magnification. Carmone called his organism *Peronospora lutea*.

In relatively restrained scientific words, young Dr. Matas hooted at these claims and at the demands of President Joseph Holt of the State Board of Health, that a Federal commission be dispatched forthwith to investigate them. He pointed out it was all but inconceivable that the lesser magnifications used by Freire and Carmone could show what the 1400-diameter magnification used by the 1879 commission had failed to reveal either to those on the ground or later to Dr. Schmidt, a microscopist who "perhaps had had more experience in the examination of the blood and tissue of yellow-fever cases than any other living pathologist." He added:

"We have examined the claims of Dr. Freire and Carmone (having procured copies of their complete works) with candor and coolness, and find them upon their own showing, so utterly devoid of all scientific value, that we regard it as both foolish and extravagant to expend upon their investigation one single cent of money."

Not long after his return from Europe, a copy of Finlay's latest paper had come to hand; another modest and self-effacing report on further experimentation with fever inoculation through mosquitoes. This time the report covered no less than twenty-four human volunteers who had permitted themselves to be stung by mosquitoes which had previously drawn blood from the veins of yellow-fever sufferers. This paper, published in full by the *American Journal of Medical Sciences,* was abstracted by Rudolph for the *New Orleans Journal* of November 1886:

"[Finlay] selected the day mosquito," he wrote in part, "the culex mosquito, apparently the same little gray pest that is so familiar to the inhabitants of this city. . . . The doctor had been 'able to prove that the sting often retains spores of microscopical fungi'. . . . A mosquito was captured while in the act of stinging by inverting an empty phial or test tube over it. . . . After a few hours the mosquito was taken to a yellow-fever case and allowed to competely gorge itself. . . . After it had digested its previous supply of blood, it was allowed to sting an individual liable to yellow fever. . . . In all, 24 persons were inoculated . . . one died of a malignant form of yellow fever . . . [and] two either left the country or were otherwise lost sight of. 'Six of these inoculations were followed within the ordinary limits of yellow-fever incubation by . . . the exact counterpart of mild attacks of yellow fever . . . proved by subsequent immunity. Eleven inoculations, though not followed by any morbid manifestations, appear to have likewise conferred immunity. Finally in four instances . . . at the end of several months, a mild attack of yellow fever was observed. . . .'

"The doctor concludes . . . that 'this disease is incapable of propagation wherever tropical mosquitoes do not or are not likely to exist, ceasing to be epidemic at the same limits of temperature and altitude which are incompatible with the functional activity of these insects; while, on the other hand, it spreads rapidly wherever they abound.' "

In Biloxi the fever epidemic waned, as always, with the onset of cool weather. On Toussaint—All Saints' Day, which is still a legal holiday in Louisiana—flower-laden pilgrims visited the cemeteries of the southern parishes; and in the piney woods north of Lake Pontchartrain they rimmed every grave with golden-flickering candles at nightfall and crossed two evergreen boughs within the glowing rectangle.

A gay and rackety Noel was planned, with firecrackers, Roman candles, bonfires, and lavish gifts of perfume for Adrienne. But the party fell flat, for Hearn neither put in an appearance nor did he explain his failure to do so, and Rudolph was called to the hospital on some sort of emergency.

Hearn was now beginning to absent himself more and more from 72 South Rampart. When Rudolph first came back to New Orleans from abroad, he and Lafcadio resumed their companionable routine as naturally as if there had been no summer's interruption. Lafcadio would call for his friend at the offices of the *Journal* or the Charity dead house when he finished his work at the *Times-Democrat* about ten at night; or later in the year, in Common Street* outside the Medical School building where Rudolph conducted his nightly anatomical demonstrations. Hearn and Matas would then roam about the streets in the old warm fellowship.

By the time they ended their nocturnal rambles at 72 South Rampart, Adrienne would have a supper spread for them: a savory coupling of ham-flavored red beans and snowy rice, or perhaps a huge tureen of *fruits-de-mer* gumbo, thickened with *filé* made by Choctaw squaws at Lacombe by pounding dried sassafras leaves to powder. Sometimes young McShane accompanied the two friends, saying little and listening worshipfully to every word the great men uttered.

Hearn was complaining in ever-mounting bitterness against the editorial heads of the *Times-Democrat* in this period. The situation there was becoming intolerable, he declared. The idea that he, Lafcadio Hearn, could be told by dullards who possessed no talent beyond a flair for making money how and what to write was nothing short of revolting. Nearly two years later this corrosive bitterness still rankled. In April 1888 he wrote Rudolph from St. Pierre in Martinique:

"I never hear any news from N.O., so that your letters are a great revelation as well as pleasure. In fact, I don't want it known where I am or what I am doing, especially by the T-D people; it will be time enough when I succeed . . .

". . . Even now, while I have had some bad luck, I have the satisfaction of being my own master, and of being out of sight and hearing of a great number of shitasses whom I was obliged to say 'Goodday' to in N.O. No: I will never set foot in N.O. any more—rather die."

In short, Hearn was already minded in 1887 to break away from what he regarded as serfdom, and the sooner the better. But such outbursts were usually followed by disappearances, during which he confined

---

* Beyond the upper limits of the original walled city of New Orleans—the *Vieux Carré*—a grassy common was provided where the residents of the built-up municipality could graze domestic animals. The upper edge of this common became and remained Common Street.

himself to his lodgings. He would work night and day without intermission; or perhaps he would vanish from sight for a wild fling among the Negro brothels of the district beyond Customhouse Street. Then he would reappear in a subdued, chastened mood, and be lectured by Rudolph, who offered to take him to the hospital where he could see for himself some of the more appalling examples of luetic decay and other venereal afflictions. Properly contrite, he would promise to abstain from further excesses.

He might have continued to alternate thus between two poles-apart extremes of mores, and he might have remained in New Orleans, had he not met Leona Queyrouze in January of 1887. In the presence of such cultured women as those with whom, from time to time, he had come into contact in the past—Mrs. Baker, Elizabeth Bisland, Adrienne Landry—Hearn was never wholly at ease. He could not divest himself of consciousness of his almost dwarfish stature and of his ocular deformity. Only in the presence of such obvious social inferiors as the crib-house prostitutes was the burden eased.

Leona Queyrouze was still young when she and Hearn met—twenty-six years old, very small of stature, not particularly well endowed even in the charm that is inherent in girlhood. To judge by later photographs, she must have been rather mousy in appearance. Yet it has been said that her arms, toughened by constant practice with the foils while fencing with her brother, were astonishingly muscular.

By all contemporary accounts, she was a very remarkable young woman, who had been educated in the classics by Hyacinth Loiseau and in music by the mother of chess master Paul Morphy. In a Victorian era when the word "feminist" was widely used as an epithet, she was the first Louisiana woman to deliver a public address, speaking on "Tolerance" at l'Athénée Louisianaise. And she wrote poetry—at least the lines scanned and rhymed—in ornate French periods, and they were published in the daily journal of M. Placide Canonge, the Gallic thunderer of *L'Abeille de la Nouvelle Orléans*. These outgivings were signed with the pen name of "Constant Beauvais."

Leona knew Hearn's "Vendor of Wisdom," M. Garcin, very well indeed. His daughter had been one of her schoolgirl intimates. When she decided to meet Hearn, she took up the project with M. Garcin, but the latter told her it would be futile to arrange such an encounter; Hearn would simply avoid it. However, he added slyly, Hearn had sent word he was coming to the bookstore that Sunday morning, so. . . .

So Leona, the modernist, the little flouter of conventions, took the initiative by introducing herself to Hearn, who could hardly break into flight when cornered in one of the dim and dusty aisles of M. Garcin's establishment. She asked permission to send him the manuscript of a blank-verse epic on which she was at work and requested that he criticize it. This was agreed to. Moreover, Hearn seems to have taken the little lady at her word; he told her the opus was merely prose broken up into short lines, and not even very good prose. He did this in a long letter, penned in his myopic, almost illegible script.

In all she received only four letters and a note of five scrawled lines from Hearn during their brief acquaintance, but he called often at the house. No doubt the Queyrouze table was lavishly and excellently supplied. Leona's father was a wealthy wine merchant. And it was during this interval that Hearn all but wholly absented himself from the Matas home while he maintained his first and only personal contact with the old Creole *haute monde* that still looked down its aristocratic nose at the "Kaintock" element of New Orleans' melting-pot population.

That Leona was possessed by a romantic infatuation for the still-unsung genius she saw in Lafcadio Hearn is not to be doubted. Almost half a century later, in 1933, when she was a septuagenarian widow, Mme. Pierre Marie Etienne Barel, she published (at her own expense) a volume printed in Tokyo under the nostalgically yearning title of *The Idyl: My Personal Reminiscences of Lafcadio Hearn*. In it her story of the relations between them is set forth in florid phraseology, and all five of the letters he wrote her are reproduced in facsimile.

Even after a lapse of half a hundred years, she could still write of him: "He was an admirable human radio, marvellously adapted to receive and transmit divine vibrations." And again: "His mind was a crucible in which precious thoughts were melted together in a wonderful metal to be cast into the sacred mould of inspiration."

During the three or four months of Hearn's companionship with "Medea," Rudolph and Adrienne saw very little of the man and wisely made no effort to seek him out. Incidentally, it may well have been in the Queyrouze home that the idea of making Martinique the next anchorage of his wanderyears had its inception. In her book Leona, rather naïvely for a widow in her seventies, relates fully how Hearn quizzed one of her maids, a 55-year-old octoroon native of Martinique. "Tell me about your beautiful country and La Soufrière and Mont Pelée," she quotes Hearn as demanding of her servant. "You know, I am going there sometime, before long."

"Toward the latter part of February," she confides to the pages of *The Idyl*, "a tiny fleecy cloud came up over the serene tide of our friendship, threatening to dim its luminous transparency." Never seek to discover what or who was luminously transparent, for it will next be mentioned as "a limpid current." All of it boiled down to this: instead of bringing a copy of Spencer's *First Principles* to her by hand, he sent it by post and "stayed away several days without sending me a note."

At length Leona—hurt, bewildered, and patently unskilled in this sort of fencing—wrote to him. The letter was a thank-you note for the book and added that some Creole phrases for which he had asked were ready; since he had not called in person, she was mailing these to him, together with a sonnet and an invitation to an informal musicale. He replied by letter: he had been hard at work, trying to "stenograph the conversation of sundry shadowy fishermen," and "had used the little notes you gave me to good purpose—the Creole phrases." Then, without further preamble, but in all likelihood as a reference to some prior conversation, he continued: "Medea, the beautiful witch-maiden, heard of a certain shepherd who kept bees which manufactured a particular sort of honey. She sent for him to come and tell her about the bees. He went for that purpose; but Medea sang him songs, and looked at him; and entangled all the web of his thought, and made his head feel as if many hives of bees were in it—so that he was never able to tell her anything about the honey. It was her own fault that she never became a bee-keeper."

The letter was dated March 27. "Swift as an arrow," related Leona in *The Idyl*, "from my heart and brain surged and flashed forth the sonnet 'Réponse,' 'Answer,' published under my nom de plume in the Sunday edition of L'Abeille, two days after, March 29, 1887. It bore no dedication and he alone would understand." She reprinted it in full, both in its original French version and in a subsequent English translation—a curious mélange of petaled verbiage to the general effect that where blessings fell aforetime the flowers of hate now grew.

This brought an immediate reply from Hearn. The very next day he sent a note explaining that "only just now (Monday morning) did I read the decidedly weird, *Réponse*. But my Medea was not so sinister. She was the beautiful Colchian girl of Kingsley's Heroes . . . I shall never attempt any more allegorical epistles—because, as in the subtle fingers of a Japanese magician, the papered story may become either a *papillon* or a *phalène*. Your Medea is much too weird. Of course, she is but a Shadow; yet the Shadow is so fantastic that one hesitates to look toward that which casts it. . . .

"Charles Dudley Warner is in town, to remain for a month, I believe. My work is progressing—soon I shall be able to cry 'Finis!' Meanwhile, believe me very truly the same.

"Lafcadio Hearn."

Abstention from allegorical epistles did not put an end to the idyl, however. Shortly after dispatching the foregoing note Hearn called at the Rue St. Louis with an autographed and inscribed copy of his new book: *Some Chinese Ghosts*—and "the light white cloud had floated away from the limpid current of our friendship." A few days later, when *Chita* was supposedly finished (but was not), he called again with a large envelope which enclosed a photograph of himself. "This is not intended for the family album," he said. "It is to remind Medea sometimes of Aristaeus the Honey-Maker." He had written to *Harper's*, suggesting he be commissioned to do a series of West Indian sketches, and the suggestion had been accepted. This, then, was how he announced his approaching departure.

They never saw one another again. Leona, no longer a Medea, married Pierre Barel and her Aristaeus married a woman of Japan, where *The Idyl*, rejected by publishers in the United States, finally saw the light of print after a son of Jean Garcin arranged for its publication by the Hokuseido Press of Tokyo long after Hearn's death. The volume was "Respectfully dedicated to Dr. Rudolph Matas, the illustrious friend and admirer of Lafcadio Hearn in the dark days."

No one can now say with certainty that this girl's obvious worship triggered Hearn's precipitate departure from New Orleans in the early days of June 1887. He would have left in any case, soon or late, his temperament being one that brooked none of the restraints of static sojourn. If not his innate restlessness, his growing discontent with his *Times-Democrat* superiors, his passion for new horizons, or his interest in Japan would have driven him forth. Yet in the first letter he addressed to Rudolph from New York (July 1) he closed with this paragraph:

"Sorry you did not meet Miss Q. . . . Would so much have liked to know your idea of her. I am not *sceptical* now; but do not know what to do. I fear to write to her. All fire and nerves and scintillation; a tropical being in mind and physique—and I could never be to her what I should like to be. I wish I had a chance to chat with you about her.

"I am so crowded now with preliminaries of getting off, that I feel I cannot write good letters. Shall do when I get down South. Meantime, remember me in your letters to your mother and sister, as kindly as you can, and give my regards to all whom you know care for them, and believe me always your best friend.

> "With love,
> "Lafcadio Hearn.

"I am 27 now. Drank champagne on the 27th to celebrate it. Ghosts of dead birthdays trooped in—looking glum. The bright-faced ones must be off in the Future somewhere."

Obviously, Hearn's four months of truancy had opened no apparent breach in the association between him and his "best friend." Rudolph continued to busy himself with an overload of work throughout a summer when, blessedly, once again no yellow-fever deaths occurred in New Orleans, though controversies over quarantine and over the cause of such epidemics continued to rage. The Matas paper on the appendix as an intra-abdominal organ was finding ever-wider acceptance, but Rudolph was off on a new quest now: an intestinal suture which would reduce the appalling mortality rate for such surgery from its statistical level of nearly 50 per cent.

Physicians were still chary of laparotomies. The elective opening of an abdomen was something to be undertaken only in the direst of emergencies, and as a last, desperate resort. But abdominal injuries were grimly frequent in a community like New Orleans, a seaport where gunshot wounds and knife slashes as the result of barroom or waterfront brawls were the rule rather than the exception. Punctured or lacerated intestines had to be repaired at once, if humanly possible. Heretofore surgeons employed for such emergencies what were known as the Lembert suture and the so-called "shoemaker stitch" of Stanhope Bishop, and only about half the patients survived their injuries, the remedial surgery, or both.

The first investigator to come up with a reasonably promising solution was one of the foremost surgeons of his day, Dr. Nicholas Senn, a Milwaukee practitioner who became professor of surgery at Chicago's Rush Medical College. In a paper read before the Ninth International Medical Congress at Washington in September of 1887, Dr. Senn reported gratifyingly favorable results from the use of small decalcified bone plates to support the stitches with which bypass openings from one part of the intestine to another were secured.

These plates were cut from thigh and shin bones of slaughtered beef cattle and were then placed in dilute muriatic acid until their lime component was dissolved, leaving the balance pliable and gristly, so that in due course they disintegrated. A central opening was then cut out of each such decalcified plate, after which four small holes were pierced in its rim, one at each of what might be called the cardinal compass points. A suture, complete with needle, was threaded through each of these small holes and securely fastened there.

In cases where the intestine was blocked by injury or disease, it was necessary to make an "anastomosis"; that is to say, a loop of intestine from just above the blocked passage would be joined to one from below it. After a lateral opening had been made in each, Dr. Senn would pass one of his prethreaded plates through each, attaching it firmly to the inner intestinal wall with the four sutures with which it had been supplied at the time of its manufacture. Thus re-enforced and sewed together, face to face, the tissue walls round the openings would be pressed against each other. By the time they knitted into union, the decalcified plates that had re-enforced them would have been digested and absorbed, leaving an unobstructed passageway. The mortality percentage after such procedures was only about a third as great as that which followed unaided intestinal sutures.

Dr. Matas read the Senn paper, when it was published in the *Annals,* with steadily mounting enthusiasm. His eagerness infected one of his associates, Dr. Paul Michinard, with whom he began to experiment in making decalcified bone plates by the Senn method. Just as twenty-five years earlier his father had persuaded the butchers at Les Halles in Paris to save for him the eyes of slaughtered sheep and cattle, so Rudolph now visited the Treme and French Markets from time to time, seeking gifts of shin and thigh bones and even shoulder blades from butchered calves; for New Orleans was—and still is—a community which consumes far more veal than beef. If at such times his enthusiasm was momentarily shadowed by the thought that no small son, trudging by his side, might one day be brought to share the mystique of surgery, as he, Rudolph, had learned from his father to identify *la cornée* and *la pupille,* he undoubtedly put the thought swiftly aside, for his loyalty and devotion to even an unattainable Adrienne never faltered.

He and Paul Michinard first practiced with their homemade plates of the Senn pattern on cadavers at the Charity Hospital dead house. Having mastered the basic techniques, they next operated on laboratory dogs, but here they encountered disheartening failures at the outset of their experimental work. Despite the firmness with which their aided sutures held two intestinal surfaces in juxtaposition, these would frequently fail to knit.

It was Dr. Matas who suggested that perhaps if they scarified the two surfaces lightly before bringing them together, a better union could be effected. This did indeed prove to be the case.

But they were still not satisfied with their craftsmanship, that winter of 1887–88, and did not use the Senn method on human patients, though the number of abdominal gunshot and stab-wound cases coming to their respective Charity Hospital services was undiminished, and their private practices included the usual quota of gastro-intestinal maladies. Nonetheless the new field of research absorbed whatever free time Rudolph might have been able to devote to social and even professional contacts. For example, he had undertaken to deliver a paper before the Louisiana State Medical Society's convention in Alexandria under the title of "A Method of Localizing Cerebral Centers." But this opus was read by title only, convention minutes noting that:

"A letter was received from Dr. Matas regretting his inability to be present, as also to finish his paper in time for the meeting. On motion of Dr. Bruns, Dr. Matas was given time to finish his article and forward it to the publication committee."

Complete candor compels the admission that in all human probability the delay was not due wholly to an overcrowded work schedule. Throughout his long life, Rudolph Matas never finished a piece of writing within the compass of the space allotted to it by editors or by the deadline set for delivery of the finished manuscript. In every convention he ever addressed, he was the despair of program chairmen who had carefully apportioned a given length of time to each speaker. As additional and suddenly recalled data came to mind from the inexhaustible trove of his memory, he would talk on and on and on, utterly oblivious of this encroachment of the time of those scheduled to follow him.

When he made his truly classic contribution on vascular surgery to the encyclopedic compilation edited by William W. Keen, of Philadelphia's Jefferson College, his section of the work had been scheduled originally for Volume I, which was published in 1906. He finally sent in the manuscript barely in time for inclusion in Volume V, which was published in 1909!

So far as Adrienne was concerned, he saw her briefly in the mornings when, like any other proper New Orleans housekeeper, she brought "first drippings"—a demitasse of strong, chicory-blackened, dripped coffee—to his bedside. She also acted as his receptionist during afternoon office hours. Even when she did not wait up for his very late homecomings after some unusually long day's labor, he always found a tray of substantial food, the whole covered by a snowy napkin, waiting on a convenient table.

Adrienne also saw to it that his apartment was meticulously swept and furbished and that everything was put in order; everything, that is, except the big desk at which he wrote. This she was under stern injunction never to touch, no matter what unstable mountain ranges of pamphlets, reprints, books, papers, manuscripts, letters, notes, and other such accumulations towered there.

In turn, he would leave gifts of Piver perfume for her to find from time to time, or copies of the latest sheet music. The ebony square piano on which she had first learned to play was one of the very few possessions to which Adrienne had been able to cling despite the pinch of adversity that followed her gentle and scholarly grandfather's death. Thus Rudolph had easily fallen into the habit of making an excursion to Werlein's music house in Canal Street every so often. This was the oldest and largest establishment of its kind in the South, selling not merely all manner of musical instruments, "finger exercizes for the piano-forte," and the like, but publishing original compositions as well.*

* Werlein's, now nearing its 140th anniversary in a career interrupted only temporarily by the Civil War, was the original publisher of "Dixie."

Here he would buy the newest songs popularized at various music halls, and bring them to a delighted Adrienne, who leavened her effusive thanks with a tart reminder that apparently he no longer cared to hear her play, as in the days when he and Lafcadio would return together for leisurely visits at unearthly hours when proper individuals—which assuredly included neither him nor Lafcadio—were asleep.

She knew, of course, that the two men still maintained a voluminous correspondence. Hearn had taken ship from New York for the West Indies in July and had voyaged to Barbados, Trinidad, Demerara and Martinique, from each of which he sent chatty letters. He returned briefly to New York but went back almost at once to pass the ensuing winter in and about St. Pierre.

"Mr. Alden,"* he wrote, "thinks I can make a little fortune and live where I please . . . living here is so cheap—about $25 a month. . . . I have excellent opportunities for making character studies, and am going to write only stories for the moment. If these succeed, I shall try studies of Coolie life in Guiana and Trinidad. . . . My new story is already under weigh; the proofs of our† 'Chita' will come to me by the next N.Y. mail. . . . 'Chita' will appear entire in a single number of Harper's Magazine (Lippincott style), before being put into book form."

He appended the following postscript to still another letter:

"Aftermath—

"By the way, I am making my heroine die of consumption in New York City. Could you not, when you write again, tell me a few of the more poetical and agonizing pathological facts of death from consumption?—mental and physical: spasms and pains?

"I am studying locally the pathology of snake bite—diplopia, forking, and tremulous duplication of objects—for another story. But I expect that the phenomena of death by consumption of a Creole girl in New York would offer some peculiarities.

"Siempre su querido amigo
"Leocadio.

"Next week I will have a chance to write you about the morals here—some oddities."

At about the time this letter was received, early in the fall, when the

---

* The editor of Harper's.

† Hearn's use of "our" in connection with this and other references to Chita at this stage is particularly noteworthy, because of the deletion of his dedication of the volume to Rudolph Matas from all but the first edition of his novelette in book form.

summer's heat invariably reaches its peak of intensity in New Orleans, Rudolph's excessive overwork finally caught up with him, and he succumbed to exhaustion. But he had inherited his father's toughness of fiber. Under the enforced rest, prescribed sternly by Dr. Souchon and hopefully by August McShane and Paul Michinard, convalescence was swift. He enjoyed the relaxed exemption from responsibilities and at this time either developed or revealed a heretofore latent passion for mystery novels, trashy and otherwise, that was to remain with him to the end of his conscious life.

He also cleared the voluminous professional and personal correspondence that had been accumulating in staggering piles on his desk, dictating to Adrienne who turned over housekeeping and marketing tasks to her mother, that she might have all her time free for nursing duty. The comfort of her presence, the beauty of her voice when reading aloud to him, and her devotion as an amanuensis enabled Rudolph to adjust not merely with acceptance, but with a certain degree of enjoyment, to the role of invalid.

From Morne-Rouge in Martinique, Lafcadio wrote in December: "I always feared you would overwork yourself; and your letter has confirmed that fear. You are young and splendidly strong; but take care of the head, dear friend—and the nervous system; another would have broken down under what you have been doing; and I think the men more careless about themselves [than any other] are conscientious physicians. I know what mental overwork is by experience; but you are so strong that I trust you will pull through all right. Could you not take a vacation in the tropics? It does not rain all the time, you know, in the rainy season here: only an hour a day or so; and here in the mountains the coolness is like that of a clear spring day.

"More anon. I send you also a pretty chef-d'oeuvre of a Martinique Creole. Love to you.

"Siempre su amiguito Q.B.S.M."

By now, the wild magic with which Hearn could endow a descriptive phrase was emerging from the ornately over-adjectived "fine writing" of his journalistic adolescence. Otherwise, however, his unabashed and uninhibited mode of life remained what it had always been; it may even have engendered in his continent *fidus Achates* a touch of wistful envy. One can picture Rudolph, returning late at night to 72 South Rampart, a neighborhood plainly on the downgrade, which yet calls him back after the long day's tasks, the nights of instruction, and the endlessly repetitious research surgery on cadavers, as he reads one of Lafcadio's letters aloud to Adrienne, carefully omitting any lapses into starkly Anglo-Saxon phrasing.

For example, there was that letter from Morne-Rouge, the one whose closing paragraph urged Rudolph to be less prodigal in the expenditure of his strength. It was headed "Personal Always." But, as Hearn well knew, that did not exclude Adrienne. Its salutation was *Queridissimo Amigo* (dearest friend) and it continued:

"I know you are beginning to think—well, to think I am ungrateful, especially since my delay in answering your last kind letter. The truth is I have not had one day's rest till now; I have been engaged on a novelette of Martinique life, or rather a study—which has just been finished and sent away—170 pp. It deals with the impressions of the North on a tropical nature. Meanwhile 'Chita' is to appear before the W. In. sketches—that is, in the Magazine. I have much more to do here —enough to keep me here for six months; and then I go South again. Martinique will always be my headquarters. I would like to live here always, if conditions were as they are in the English islands; but there are terrible possibilities involved by the present social situation. I have not written as yet to any one else in N.O.; it seems to me as if I would like to forget all my life there, with the exception of our walks and talks. I don't know whether I should be pleased to read anything the N.O. papers say.* I would rather have one line from you than 60 columns of notices.

"Enclosed you will find two typical Coolie heads I had posed and photo. for me. (Any photos I send you do not allow to leave your hands; they may be duplicates of material purchased by the Harpers.) I think the sinister one is totally Dravidian; the other from Central or Northern India; the photos give no conception of the eye, which is exceptionally brilliant. I had to surrender some nudes at N.Y.; but can replace them when I get South, and add to them. The prettiest, how-ever, I had sent one of them on my first trip to P. Baker—a young Coolie girl at Trinidad.

"Ethnologists would be puzzled here. All the ordinary statements accepted as to negro physiology and anatomy are wonderfully contradicted by nature here. Prognathism is rare; the heel does *not* protrude; the foot is *not* flat, but perfectly arched—the calves are admirably developed. To see one of the tall black girls employed in coaling vessels or carrying heavy burthens over the mountains is to see the animation of an antique bronze—only the face and hair are African. You cannot help admiring them; and they will laugh and say: 'Yo ouli bien fe yonne ti milatt avec on.' More than once I should have liked to take them at their word. You cannot quite realize, without living here

* In the letter to which this is a reply, Rudolph had apparently offered to send Hearn some of the New Orleans papers, or at least clippings from them, to keep him in touch with news of the community of which for ten years he was a part.

awhile, the oddly natural character of this life. A young mulatto brings his baby for me to look at; as pretty as a ripe sapote it is. 'Why, Lucius, I didn't know you were married!' 'Moin pa maie; mais ca pa empeche moin ni zenfan; moin ni tois zenfans.' The absence of the marriage restriction makes you confident about approaching a girl to ask the fatal question. And here in a place of pilgrimage (Morne-Rouge: 2500 feet above the sea) where all the hills are covered with shrines and crosses, my landlady tells me it is the custom for gentlemen, *when* they want a girl, to bring her in by the back door instead of the front entrance. That is the only difference! But I have my *doudoux* in town, and do not care to seek fresh fields . . .

". . . You must not trouble yourself about the *consumption* matter: I have done the work in a better way—treating only the ghostly, not the physical side of death, which is more revolting.

"If you go to New York, you *must not* fail to call on Mr. Alden. I have not told him anything about you but what is strictly true, and what I know—you will not be sorry to meet him. He loves to chat with a *thinker;* and in the New York atmosphere men have acquired a capacity for putting the thought of a whole year into a phrase. Really, you have no business to live in New Orleans. You ought to be in New England or New York. Even Philadelphia, I imagine, must be dull. I hope to go to Cayenne later on, where there are costumes most fantastic and beautiful. Those Venezuelan regions are all strange. The dead trees burn with a cold light; as you walk, the mold flames under your feet.

"I cannot thank you enough for your trouble about the books; but with a friend the formality of thanks means so little. You know how I feel about it. In his last Mr. Alden said he was sending you the $7.50—so I trust you have received it by this time. And whatever I can get for you, either here or elsewhere in the South, let me know. I shall be travelling in queer places—unless I travel to darkness eternal—for years to come. . . ."

By the time this letter reached Rudolph, Christmas had come and gone, and with it the Tulane holidays which had given him and Michinard welcome leisure to practice intestinal sutures. Once or twice during the holidays he had taken Adrienne to Spanish Fort or West End for a festive meal at one of the famed lake-shore restaurants. However, he was always careful to have several members of the family— her sons or her brothers or her mother—accompany them.

Adrienne was no longer the slim girl with whom he had first fallen head over heels in love. She was putting on weight very perceptibly. Slim silhouettes, calorie counting, and dietetic reducing fads were still undreamed of as a way of normal life. But the plump-and-growing-plumper Adrienne, who kept his home and made possible the incredible hours of work he could crowd into each day, was no less dear to him than the slender girl with enormous dark eyes he had first glimpsed across her father's hospital bed when she was the wife of another man. If their relationship lacked the raptures of shared consummation, they did have much of the serene and solid contentment of untroubled domesticity.

Adrienne's older son, Arthur, was of a retiring and studious bent, living a withdrawn existence, even as a lad. He had long since decided that at the earliest moment he would study dentistry. The younger brother, Lucian, was stocky, sturdy, boyishly belligerent in his relations with his playmates. He too was doing well at school. That Christmas Rudolph had given Adrienne, in addition to cut crystal containers of perfumes, a diamond brooch whose central stone was taken from the finger ring his father had sent him as a graduation gift, a ring he had never worn since he and his sire parted in such bitterness at Tucson years earlier.

The winter hunting season and the holidays brought to the accident ward at Charity Hospital the usual grist of tetanus cases from infected firecracker burns, the victims of shooting and stabbing brawls in the dives of "The District," and those wounded in hunting accidents. One of the latter, a brawny twenty-six-year-old Negro plantation hand from St. Mary Parish, Manuel Harris by name, was admitted to Charity Hospital on March 30, 1888. Two months earlier, while hunting rabbits with a group of fellow workers, he had been accidentally wounded, the entire fine-shot charge of a muzzle-loader lodging in and about his left shoulder blade and the back of his left upper arm. Such mishaps were common with the old percussion-cap-and-hammer shotguns, the hammer being dragged back by a branch or a fence wire, and then snapping into place with force enough to discharge the piece.

Many of the small pellets had lodged just beneath the skin and were safely encysted there at the time of Harris's admission to the hospital. One, however, had passed into the fleshy inner side of his left upper arm, injuring the main artery in its passage. This made itself evident when, a fortnight after the accident, by which time Harris was congratulating himself on complete recovery, he noticed a swelling on the inner surface of his arm, midway between armpit and elbow. The swelling steadily increased in size and in tenderness to the touch. Of late it had begun to pulsate. So much of the patient's history was taken down by Henry Scherck, the intern on Dr. Matas's service.

Then, attended by a retinue of students, Dr. Matas himself entered the ward and thereby crossed a threshold beyond which lay professional immortality.

CHAPTER XVI

An operation through which Rudolph Matas saved the arm and the life of Manuel Harris ultimately won him world-wide renown as "the father of modern vascular surgery." Yet twelve years elapsed before this magnificent tour de force was undertaken for a second time and became "the Matas operation." It was performed in the first instance as an act of necessity. Dr. Matas no more planned it in advance than Manuel Harris planned to be shot accidentally or than the Negro boy who was hired to beat the marine sponges used in the operating room decided that the time was ripe for a turning point in medical history.

Such a boy did indeed play a mute, inglorious role in the first Matas operation. In that era surgery still depended on natural sponges to dry and clean the operative field. Dr. Robert T. Morris's volume *How We Treat Wounds Today* was published in 1886 by Putnam's; in 1888 it was still the last word in handbooks of surgical practice. It directed that for ordinary operating-room purposes reef sponges be bought by the pound; that they be soaked first in potassium permanganate and then in weak hydrochloric acid and sodium hyposulphite; after this they were to be dried thoroughly and, as final step, a boy was hired to beat them free of sand with a mallet. "At the operation," Dr. Morris suggested, "a few of the sponges are removed from their jar, squeezed and thrown into a bowl of 1:2000 bichloride solution. . . . They do not cost much and the surgeon can throw them away after employing them once."

Up to this time, the only operation of election (as distinguished from and opposed to "operation of necessity") performed to cure or relieve aneurisms, was the Hunterian ligation or, as Rudolph was careful to call it in the presence of his venerated chief, Dr. Souchon, the ligature of Anel. Over this difference in nomenclature, an implacable and passionate controversy raged between British and French physicians. The latter insisted that John Hunter had done nothing more in 1785 than to shift the position of the aneurismal ligation a trifle farther above the sac, the operation remaining essentially the same as when Anel originated it in 1710.

Edmond Souchon, an ingrained, die-hard conservative, had absorbed with his mother's milk a meed of the Anglophobia which inspired his forebears to perpetuate Bossuet's cry of *"Perfide Albion!"* His medical training had been acquired in France under the great Velpeau.* Let others, then, prate of Hunterian ligatures; to him it remained the operation of Anel, and in his *cher maître's* hearing, Rudolph strove to echo him, as a loyal disciple should.

Meanwhile his own still younger disciples followed him across the threshold of a Charity Hospital ward, over the splintery, pallid-scrubbed wooden floor and to the bed where Henry Scherck had just completed his case notes on the history of Manuel Harris, c., m., 26, St. Mary Parish, La. The other resident students assigned to the Matas service watched their bearded young professor admiringly; youths like Randall Hunt, grandson of the university president from whom Rudolph had received his diploma eight years earlier; Oliver Pothier, Felix Larue, Albert Rocquet, John Thomas Delaney and Hardy Black. Rudolph checked his intern's notes, felt the pulsation in the viciously distended swelling on the patient's arm, applied his stethoscope to the taut surface and listened to the ominous, purring murmur beneath it. He dug his right thumb expertly down upon the spot under which the uninjured upper portion of the brachial artery ran; the swelling promptly ceased to pulsate and shrank until the sufferer's left arm was only a little larger than the right.

"Diagnosis," he wrote later, "is, plainly, traumatic aneurism of the brachial artery"; and he added: "In view of the readiness with which circulation in the tumor was controlled by pressure, the Esmarch was applied." The Esmarch was a bandage of sheet rubber. It was used

* In the latter 1840's Velpeau wrote a textbook on surgery in which he inveighed against all who spoke of the Hunterian ligation as "The New Method, the Method of Desault and Hunter." All of these, he insisted "are inappropriate phrases which ought to give place to the title 'The Method of Anel', its true inventor. . . . Is it for having applied the ligature at three inches above the point selected by Desault that Hunter merits the title of inventor of this affair?"

principally to wrap tightly about the outer extremity of a limb on which a tourniquet was to be placed, so that the veins in the area on the far side of the tourniquet should not become engorged with blood, their relatively thin walls being much more readily squeezed shut than the thick, muscular walls of an artery.

In this instance, however, Dr. Matas used the Esmarch itself as a tourniquet, winding the rubber strips tightly about the arm above the tumor ". . . but this had to be removed ten minutes after application, owing to the intolerable pain. . . . The patient protested so emphatically against this method of treatment (Reid's method) that it was not repeated."

Calling his intern and the resident students about him in one of the anterooms, the young physician paced up and down with short, impatient steps, holding an audible one-man consultation with himself, as was his habit whenever confronted by the need for making a critical decision. He was neither asking advice nor lecturing; he was simply bringing the tumbled profusion of data from remembered reading, nearly eight years of active professional experience, and his brilliantly projected imagination into orderly array, so that each might play its part in saving a life. Now and then he unclasped his hands and passed one of them over his smoothly tended, raven-black beard and mustache, no longer the wispy imperial of his Havana days, but a heavy, virile Vandyke.

". . . So we are confronted with a situation which demands positive and immediate action if we are to save this man's life," the high-pitched voice went on, as the pacing was resumed. Head bowed, bearded chin almost touching the breast, it was as if he were talking to the tips of his gleaming shoes. These, by the way, were another instance of his almost worshipful acceptance of Dr. Souchon's example. Rudolph Matas wore gaiters, as did his chief. "Well, we must inquire of ourselves now what resources can we summon to aid this man? What can the past teach us? I shall ask you to consider, gentlemen, that our first preceptor in this instance was Antyllus, perhaps the greatest surgeon of all time when we recall that he lived about 300 A.D., somewhere in Greece. He was the first physician to lay out a method for the treatment of aneurisms—by surgery, that is. He probably had a lot of it to do, for in the time of Valens—one of the Roman emperors of Greece in that century—or perhaps the first Theodosius, there was much fighting with the Visigoths, so of course there were many spearwounds of the arms and legs, much like the traumatic aneurism of the arm with which we must deal in this patient. My, my, my . . . after all these centuries the same problems remain to be solved!"

The students listened in rapt attention. They knew from experience that a profile of Western civilization, as exemplified by medical progress, from the days of Rome's Eastern Empire to what we know now as the gaslit era might follow before a definite conclusion as to the treatment of Manuel Harris was reached.

"Well, then, gentlemen," continued their youthful preceptor reflectively, "the method of Antyllus was to lay open the wound, bare the injured artery, tie it off above and below the aneurismal sac, and then open the sac itself. Usually a clot of blood filled it, once the circulation was cut off. So Antyllus would open the sac, empty it of its clot, pack it with myrrh, close the wound and let it heal by granulation —if suppuration from infection or gangrene from the shutting off of circulation from the extremities did not set in. Think of it! For a thousand years that was the only treatment for battle injuries of this nature, when the longbow and the arquebus supplemented the lance, and gunpowder followed, and. . . . Finally in 1710 Dominique Anel devised a ligature to tie off the artery immediately above the tumor on the theory that this would relieve it of internal pressure so that it would collapse, while collateral branches of the vascular tree carried blood to the extremities previously supplied by the ligated artery. Sometimes they did even more, they carried blood right back to the aneurism, and when that happened the only remaining course was amputation of the limb above the tumor."

He paused in his speech and in his pacing, looked thoughtfully up at the ceiling, shook his head, and clucked sympathetically.

"In fact, there were and still are those who think amputation is the only safe and sure solution where an aneurism occurs in the extremities. In the event gangrene sets in, the limb would have to be sacrificed anyway. However, about a hundred years ago, John Hunter, in England, reasoned that since the arterial walls of the vessel adjoining the aneurism must be weak from either injury or disease—for aneurisms are the result only of trauma or of syphilis—the proper thing to do was to locate the ligature far enough above the swelling to make sure the artery wall was still healthy and intact at the point of ligation. That is still our principal recourse. That was what Andrew Smyth did in the historic instance in which, in this very hospital, he became the first man to ligate the innominate artery and effect a cure. To be sure, the cure was temporary, since the tumor returned after about ten years. Think of it, ten years! My, my, my!"

He looked from one of his listeners to the other, until he had come full circle, as if inquiring whether each had followed the discourse to this point. Shaking his head, he walked to the window from which he could stare out at a grassy courtyard where convalescents sprawled at ease in the warm sunlight of March.

"So what are the possible courses of treatment we must consider?" he asked, without turning, as if addressing the question to himself. "First, a direct tourniquet which is strong enough to compress the vessel until such time as the aneurism collapses and closes without surgery. But this appears to be out of the question. When we tried the Esmarch, we found that the pain of such compression was past human endurance. To be sure, we *could* try digital compression. I could assign you gentlemen to take turns sitting beside this patient, with your fingers compressing the brachial artery above the pulsing tumor, in one-hour watches. We could, if necessary or if indicated, keep this up for days. That was another of the methods by which medicine sought to cure aneurisms in the old, old days."

Abruptly his manner became more decisive, his address more forceful.

"But we have a better way of graduated compression," he said. "The Massachusetts General Hospital has recently perfected a device that can be adjusted to slacken the pulsations in the tumor and thereby weaken the radial pulsation too, of course, by degrees. Perhaps we can avoid surgery by using this apparatus; for surgery, we must concede, always involves a possibility of losing the arm. After all, this young Negro—a splendid physical specimen—is a plantation laborer whose livelihood depends on his muscles. He needs two good arms."

On this note the "consultation" came to a close, the compressor was applied, and was kept on the artery all day and all night. Under Henry Scherck's supervision the pressure was alternately tightened and relaxed, in accordance with the patient's need for periodic relief from the excruciating pain of compression. And it was all to no purpose. Whenever the compressor was removed, from time to time, Dr. Matas noted that "the tumor pulsates most vigorously and the arm measures now fifteen inches in circumference."

Yet the treatment was continued for nearly twenty days. In addition to the compressor which encircled the limb just beneath the armpit, the forearm was flexed tightly back and tied into position against the upper arm, the entire flexed member being then rigidly tied to the head with a well-adjusted bandage to hold it flexed on the shoulder, but—

"The patient, who is anxious to get well," Dr. Matas set down in the running account he kept of the case, "and is willing to do all in his power to facilitate a cure, has stood with fortitude the ordeal imposed upon him, though an occasional hypodermic of morphia has been required to help him, especially at night-time . . . [and] the tumor has not been in the least affected by the therapeutic measures thus far instituted. It pulsates more vigorously than ever . . . and the sac is apparently becoming much thinner on the inner aspect of the arm, where it threatens to rupture."

Since rupture meant almost certain and almost immediate death, Dr. Matas performed the Hunter, or if Dr. Souchon were in earshot, the Anel, ligation on April 23, and "immediately after ligation the pulsation and all the active phenomena in the aneurism were arrested. The tumor became hard, the radial pulse imperceptible. The arm shrank one and a half inches at the maximum circumference of the tumor."

Unfortunately, however, the shrinkage stopped right there. A week after the operation, when the dressing was removed, the incision showed itself to be healing "by first intention"; no pulsation was noticed, but also no further shrinkage. Two days later, on May 2——

"In examining the case, my attention was directed to a slight localized pulsation in the tumor, by one of the students in attendance. This pulsation became more marked the next day and progressively continued until it was almost as pronounced, and the tumor as painful, as when the patient was first seen."

Here was a fine kettle of fish. "Naturally," he muttered testily to himself as much as to the students and to his intern when they had withdrawn from the ward to the anteroom for another one-man consultation, "naturally, the simplest and surest way to solve this problem, is as Alexander did away with the knot by which Gordius had fastened the pole of his wagon to the yoke, defying anyone to untie it. Alexander slashed through it with his sword. By this I mean that we could amputate and thus avert all further danger to the patient from this aneurism. But that would still leave a strong young man with his earning power so reduced for life that in effect he would henceforth be dependent on others."

He clasped his glossy black Vandyke with his right hand, as though milking it. "The only possible way in which that swelling and that pulsation could have recurred in so short a time," he continued, "is for another, smaller artery, a collateral branch of the vascular tree, to be opening into the brachial artery below the tumor, letting the blood flow back into it. My, my . . . we'll simply have to place another ligation on the distal side of our aneurism, at the bend of the elbow, gentlemen, and if *that* fails to halt the pulsation, we'll go back to Antyllus and empty the sac, or, if necessary, dissect it right out of the man's arm. Mr. Scherck, will you be good enough to see that the patient is prepared and in the operating room promptly at seven tomorrow morning?"

In the 1880's, many operators still "dressed" for surgery simply by taking off their coats and rolling up their shirt sleeves. Some even kept a special frock coat, spattered with blood and otherwise maculated by use, to be worn during operations. But Rudolph Matas was advanced enough to wear a clean, white short-sleeved smock while operating, though he modestly retired to a private room before donning this freshly laundered garment, lest the nursing sisters be embarrassed by having him shamelessly remove his coat and roll up his shirt sleeves before their very eyes. Then he returned to the amphitheater, where the patient already lay on the table. Other physicians and medical students occupied all the tiered seats, many of them with opera glasses which they kept trained on the operation. Intern Scherck was already dripping chloroform on the cotton-padded wire mesh cone he held over the Negro's mouth and nose, while the more muscular of the residents stood by to restrain the patient's involuntary struggles against surrendering to unconsciousness. Just before the operation began, Dr. Souchon appeared at the amphitheater door, from which vantage point he watched the subsequent proceedings with close attention.

Dr. Matas dipped his hands into a special vessel, filled with 1:2000 bichloride solution, on a stand of its own beside the operating table. To the end of his career, just such a vessel was kept on just such a stand whenever he operated; the less reverent among his students and interns, and even among the nurses, referred to it as "the font of Matas's holy water." Later on, he rinsed gloved hands in this vessel, but rubber gloves were not introduced into normal surgical practice until 1896, some years after W. S. Halsted of Baltimore, who was to become one of Rudolph Matas's most intimate personal and professional friends, had devised them for the benefit of his nurse (whom he later married), who was allergic to bichloride solutions. In 1888, however, surgeons still worked barehanded.

Dr. Matas checked the patient's respiration and pulse. The flow of talk which would continue until the operation was completed had already begun.

"Some of you may have wondered," he was saying, "why chloroform should be the anesthetic of election in the South, whereas ether has so many advantages over it that it has become almost universally the anesthetic of election in the hospitals of the North. This is because, here in the South, most homes and other establishments are lighted by oil lamps, which have open flames. Well, then—ether is much more inflammable, in fact explosively so, than chloroform. My, my, my, we do seem to be ready to proceed, do we not?"

Having dipped his hands once more into his font, Dr. Matas took a scalpel and made a short, neat incision on the inner side of the arm, near the bend of the elbow, carefully separated and retracted muscle fibers, and finally exposed the brachial artery below the no-longer-pulsing tumor from which a tourniquet had shut off all circulation. He tied a ligature of Kocher's catgut tightly about the vessel, talking all the while. Still talking, he walked to one of the far sides of the operating stage to announce that if a collateral artery was supplying blood to the aneurism from below, this second ligation most certainly would check the dangerous pulsations, even if the aneurism, in which by this time a clot might have formed, did not shrink immediately as it had when the ligation above the tumor had been tied.

Not once did he stop talking while he worked; talking about aneurisms in general, about special cases, or about surgical techniques and their development, drawing upon the seemingly inexhaustible storehouse of his memory. Sometimes he mumbled into the perfumed beard of which he was inordinately vain. Sometimes he addressed one or another of the resident students by name, sometimes he lectured to the entire group in the amphitheater in his high, thin voice, gesturing vigorously with wet and glistening freshly dipped hands, and talking, talking, talking without interruption.

"I don't need to read journals or textbooks," one of his students, Hermann B. Gessner, once observed. "I just attend all of Matas's operations and listen. Sooner or later I'll hear it all from him."

He would most certainly have heard a great deal on this day when, after the second ligation, the tumor pulsed as vigorously as before. Returning to the operating table, Dr. Matas automatically dipped his hands into his font, washed one over the other, and peered angrily at the taut distention of the Negro's left arm.

"Con-*fusion!*" he burst out. "Our ligature this morning has not had the slightest perceptible effect on either the pulsation or the size of the aneurism. Not the slightest! There's nothing left now but to try to extirpate the whole thing by dissecting it out of the arm in its entirety. Put the Esmarch above it—tightly, now, we'll have to shut off the circulation before we start, or else, when we cut into the aneurism to remove it, the same thing might happen that happened to Smyth's patient during the second operation. He tried to stop the hemorrhage with a packing of bird shot inside the wound, but the blood burst out again and the patient died in a matter of minutes, as Dr. Souchon could tell us in greater detail, for he assisted Smyth in this memorable operation and later preserved the specimen which is now in the Surgeon-General's museum in Washington. My, my, we wouldn't want anything of that sort to happen to us or to our patient, eh? Well, then, is everything in readiness?"

He rinsed his hands and picked a scalpel from the sheeted instrument table.

"No half measures, now," he continued, as he set to work with swift and beautiful exactness. "We'll incise the skin—so!—from our primitive incision of ten days ago, when we ligated the artery above the aneurism, and from there all the way down to the one we made a few moments ago when we ligated the brachial below it, at the elbow—and without the desired result. My, my, my—I've got into this now, and we'll have to make a rapid but close dissection if we hope to extirpate the sac."

He did not stop to walk about the arena now; the swiftly moving hands kept pace with his words in admirable precision. Then suddenly he did stop, with an explosive "con-*fusion!*" Both ends of the sac were exposed by this time; so was its upper and inner surface, still distended, but not pulsing since the Esmarch had shut off circulation. Dr. Matas shook his bowed head from side to side as he peered into the gaping opening at the spindle-shaped tumor it revealed.

"I ask you, gentlemen, to take note of the intimate association of the remainder of this sac with the deeper structure of the arm, with the nerve plexus and the muscles, especially the biceps and the brachialis anticus," he said. "We must take into account that this very intimate adhesion of the sac walls to the surrounding tissues involves great risk of injuring the median and ulnar nerves which, as you can see, are actually incorporated in the sac walls, so that if we persist in trying to dissect out the sac, we will almost surely leave this man with a paralyzed, completely useless left arm. My, my, my! We might just as well amputate the arm as leave him in such a situation. We can't possibly do that in good conscience as long as any other recourse remains."

He paused thoughtfully, discarded the scalpel with which he had been gesturing to emphasize the various points he sought to impress upon his students.

"We must now consider," he continued more thoughtfully, "whether there *is* another alternative. We have tried the Hun"—here he shot a covert glance toward the doorway where Dr. Souchon stood—"we have tried the operation of Anel and have failed. In the hope of extirpating the aneurism we started to dissect out the sac, but for the considerations enumerated, such as the possible paralysis or loss of the arm, we have abandoned that. Is there another expedient? Are we justified in trying the method of Antyllus: opening the sac, turning out the clot, packing it with *charpie* or gauze, and letting it heal by granulation? In my opinion, we are more than justified, for if the most unfavorable possible outcome should follow, we are no worse off than now. So——"

With finicking, exquisite precision, the scalpel slid along the length of the spindle-shaped sac at each edge of its exposed portion, so that an elliptical piece of its surprisingly tough wall could be lifted out. The hard clot which filled it was next removed, and the cavity thus laid bare was irrigated with Laplace's solution. A Greek of whom nothing is known, not even the city in which he lived nor whether he was of noble or proletarian lineage nor whether he was married and passed on the qualities of his mind to begotten sons nor what gods he worshiped—nothing but the fact that he was one of the greatest physicians of all time—had done this same thing 1500 years before. No one else is definitely known to have attempted it for nearly two centuries when young Dr. Matas decided to revert to ancient lore on the chance, at least, of keeping a Negro from going back to his workaday world with a useless arm or the stump of one.

The Esmarch kept the opening free of blood. Irrigation and the painstakingly careful sweep of well-beaten pieces of reef sponge now revealed why neither of the two ligatures, one above the tumor and one immediately below it, had arrested the swelling or stopped the pulsation. The bearded surgeon rinsed his hands, and looked up with something like exultation.

"There's our culprit!" he exclaimed. "Look at it! In addition to the openings at the top and the bottom where the big artery entered and left the aneurism, there's one in the deepest part of the sac's floor. So now we will pass a rubber catheter into the upper opening—you'll observe it admits the gum catheter quite easily and lets it pass up into the artery as far as—— Ah! It has stopped at the point where we applied the ligature ten days ago. That assures us that our ligation is tight, and the circulation is blocked at that point. Now we'll insert this other gum catheter into the distal opening, which likewise admits it easily, but only to the point where we ligated the artery within the past few minutes. . . . Now for this small opening in the floor of the sac. You will notice it is too small to admit any of our catheters but it is still large enough to keep this tumor distended with pulsing blood, distended and thinning until sometime—almost any minute, indeed—it will burst and the man will die. Con-*fusion!* We simply must do something about that opening. It is obviously the mouth of a vessel which we cannot reach to ligate, because it is under the point where that nerve plexus is incorporated right into the wall of the sac itself. Oh, con-*fusion*, con-*fusion*, con-*fusion!*"

He dipped his hands into his font, wrung them, clasped them, mumbling and muttering, with occasional staccato bursts of "My, my, my!" He walked to the rim of the theater, stared testily at the wall, then turned abruptly and, hurrying back to the table, once more peered into the open incision.

"There is one more venture we might undertake," he began, "even though, so far as I know, it has never been done successfully in a case of this sort. Perhaps it has never even been tried. But as I look at this open sac with its walls infolding now that the pressure has been relieved, it seems to me there is no great distinction, surgically, between what we have here and the several intestinal orifices Dr. Michinard and I have been suturing all this past winter in laboratory dogs. In the one case we have had to appose serosa to serosa; that is to say, inner lining to inner lining. In this instance the inner arterial lining, the intima, is continuous in the sac, so if we bring the lips of these orifices together, we can expect the surfaces to unite in precisely the way as the coats of the bowel unite when sutured. If they unite, there can be no further flow of blood into the tumor, and hemostasis will have been achieved."

The students nodded and leaned forward to watch. The onlookers in the amphitheater craned for better views.

"So we will see if what I have learned in suturing the intestines of dogs and the practice I have acquired will serve us here. Have we any fine—I mean very, very fine catgut? None? My, my, my! We shall have to see what we can do with silk. Our smallest needle please."

Clucking and talking as he worked, the opening in the floor of the sac was sealed with four interrupted—that is, separate and individual—sutures. Not a droplet of blood seeped into the sac through this opening when, after that, the Esmarch was relaxed, but——

"I was considerably surprised," Dr. Matas recorded with rather natural chagrin in his first report of the operation, "to notice a decided flow of blood from the other two orifices, notwithstanding the fact that the vessels with which they communicated had been apparently controlled by previous ligatures."

Hastily tightening the Esmarch again, he glared at the blood welling from the end openings of vessels, each of which had been twice ligated, rinsed his hands, irrigated the sac, and sponged it dry.

"My, my. I'm afraid we can come to only one conclusion now, gentlemen," he declared resentfully. Glancing toward the door he saw that Dr. Souchon was still watching the procedure. This was not too reassuring. He knew how his professor felt about the "Anel method." But there was nothing for it now, except to continue: "In other words, there must be some important lateral branches which communicate with the brachial artery between the points of ligation and the aneurism. Even if we could ligate every one of these branches, which appears out of the question, we would risk closing off all circulation from the forearm and the fingers, which would then become gangrened. Well, then. We have sutured the lips of the small opening in the floor of the sac as we would a cut intestine, so we will now sew up the lips of these larger openings too, intima to intima. Some fine sublimated silk, if you please. . . . And so. . . . And *now* we relax the Esmarch again and we shall see whether complete hemostasis has been achieved."

They drew together in almost breathless suspense as the tourniquet's constriction was eased, little by little, until as the field remained dry, the elastic band was removed altogether. "The openings were sealed," Dr. Matas wrote later "and not a drop of blood entered the aneurismal sac henceforth." The rest of the procedure was routine. As he wiped the perspiration from his forehead and eyes with the hem of his white gown, he directed his assistants to pack the wound with sublimated gauze and close it. The patient made a fantastically rapid and permanent recovery, being discharged on May 21, fifteen days after the operation, "completely cured, and with only a linear cicatrix to indicate the site of the aneurism."

Seventeen years later, in an address delivered before the Medical Association of Alabama, Dr. Matas provided the following addendum to the inscription on a major milestone of surgical history: "Nearly ten years after the operation, in 1898, I again accidentally saw this patient. He was perfectly well and engaged in very laborious work on a plantation. The radial pulse had returned, and nothing but a long scar in the arm indicated the site of the former aneurism."

And yet for twelve inexplicable years, Rudolph Matas could not "muster sufficient courage"—the words are his own*—to repeat this operation, whose results had proved so wholly beneficent.

The twelve-year hiatus remains unexplained to this day by anything but Dr. Matas's own casual and vague comment, half a century later, that "I could not muster sufficient courage to battle against tradition." Some facts, all of them well established, have a direct bearing on this enigma; but conclusions based on these facts are necessarily extrapolations.

The first fact: Rudolph Matas did not make his report on this epochal modification of revived Antyllian procedure in the *New Orleans Medical and Surgical Journal*, where his reports on appendicitis (iliac phlegmon), his pioneering use of local anesthesia, his description of intestinal sutures, and virtually all his other surgical reports were published at the time. He sent it instead to the *Medical News*, of Philadelphia, to which he had never before submitted a professional article, although it was edited by Lafcadio Hearn's friend, George

* "Personal Experiences in Vascular Surgery," *Annals of Surgery*, vol. 112, Nov. 1940, pp. 802–36.

Gould. This journal published "'Traumatic Aneurism of the Left Brachial Artery,' by Rudolph Matas, M.D., Visiting Surgeon Charity Hospital, Etc., New Orleans, La." on October 27, 1888.

His departure from custom in this respect may or may not have been significant. Certainly the *Medical News* of Philadelphia enjoyed a wider distribution than did the *New Orleans Medical and Surgical Journal*. Philadelphia was still the nation's medical capital, though such rivals as New York, Baltimore, and Boston were beginning to shoulder it from primacy. Hence the Philadelphia publication could assure for the Matas paper on the first intra-sacular suture for curing an aneurism a substantially wider readership—except among Rudolph Matas's immediate circle of colleagues in New Orleans.

We also know that in making his confession of inability to muster enough courage to battle tradition, Rudolph Matas said in 1906: "A long interval elapsed between this and the next case [of suture within the aneurismal sac] which occurred in my practice. . . . Several opportunities had presented themselves for the application of the suture method . . . in the interval between 1888 and 1900, but I had not mustered enough courage to battle with tradition." However, he added a codicil to this statement, as if citing extenuating circumstances for an admitted error: ". . . enough courage to battle with tradition, which had imbued me, as it did almost every operator, with the fear of the dangers of atheroma and secondary hemorrhage in suturing injured arteries."

As a collateral fact which may bear on this unsolved enigma, we also know that prior to 1888 Rudolph Matas had on several occasions editorially proclaimed his acceptance and endorsement of the Finlay hypothesis of yellow-fever transmission through the *Culex* mosquito, and that in 1941 the Cuban government conferred on him the Order of Carlos Finlay and the title of Primer Finlayista, as the sole *Mantenedor del Finlayismo* in the years when Finlay first published his doctrine. Yet from 1888 to 1900, when the so-called Reed experiment and its practical application by Gorgas gave full validity to Finlay's theory, Rudolph Matas published not so much as one syllable in support of the great Cuban epidemiologist.

Perhaps it is mere coincidence; but it is nonetheless a fact that Rudolph Matas was silenced by someone—himself, perhaps—or something during the same dozen years from 1888 to 1900 about the achievement which ultimately made him world-famous and about the long battle which made Carlos Finlay immortal.

Let us consider yet another indisputable fact. The two principal demi-gods in young Rudolph Matas's professional pantheon were Edmond Souchon and Stanford Chaillé. Both were conservatives. Chaillé was one of the last to accept the idea that mosquitoes transmitted yellow fever. Up to the time this was proved beyond all possibility of doubt, he clung to his conviction that fomites were the principal and perhaps only carriers of the contagion. Yet compared to Edmond Souchon, Chaillé was an indulgent liberal. It was said of Dr. Souchon, not by way of hyperbole but as a fact, that he was so set in his ways he would leave the breakfast table without eating if, on arrival, he found his oatmeal spoon on the wrong side of the coffee spoon.

Surely no great stretch of the imagination is required to picture this adherent of the old school, in which his outlook had been formed by Velpeau, testily warning his protégé against recklessly going counter to all accepted professional concepts. Perhaps Dr. Souchon did not put his disapproval into words. Perhaps it was manifest only in his attitude. But one is left in no doubt as to his feelings. As late as 1895, reporting on 115 cases of subclavian aneurism, Dr. Souchon wrote categorically: "The efforts of such experimenters as Lister, Wyeth, Senn, Ballance and Edmonds have established *beyond doubt* that the proper course for the future is to ligate the artery aseptically with absorbable ligatures without rupturing the coats of the artery. *All surgeons are now of the same mind,* except Halsted, who prefers extirpation."

This was written and published seven years after Dr. Matas's first intrasacular suture. If "all" surgeons but Halsted were of the same mind, certainly Dr. Souchon meant that his favorite pupil, Matas, was of this mind too. He does not even mention sutures as a possible treatment.

Still, no one can prove that he impressed this view on Rudolph with such earnestness and emphasis as to deprive him for a dozen years of the courage to battle medical traditions which he never hesitated, before or afterward, to challenge. That he finally did break free from whatever restraint had been laid upon him is now a matter of official record, not merely in the medical and surgical statistics of countless hospitals, clinics, and universities, but in the tributes that are still being paid to the "Matas operation" during the seven decades since it saved the life and the arm of Manuel Harris.

Nowhere was the Matas achievement more vividly set forth than at Radcliffe Infirmary, Oxford, England, in 1915, at a time when wounded British soldiers were streaming back from the bitter battlefields of France. The speaker on this occasion was Sir William Osler of Canada, Philadelphia, Baltimore, Britain, and all the world. He said:

"Antyllus, 'so blindly has oblivion scattered her poppies,'—to quote Sir Thomas Browne again—that not a fact of his life is known; yet through the mists of eighteen centuries he looms large as one of the most daring and accomplished surgeons of all times, and we may say, the creator of the surgery of the arteries . . . Within the next year there will be greater opportunities for vascular surgery than have ever before been offered. The results of the last wars should be carefully studied by our surgeons, and may I refer the younger army surgeons to the section on aneurism in Keen's *Surgery*, by that modern Antyllus, my old and valued friend, Rudolph Matas of New Orleans?"

CHAPTER XVII

No one today knows what one word or deed terminated the friendship
between Rudolph Matas and Lafcadio Hearn. The latter took umbrage
at some real or fancied slight at the hands of everyone else with whom
he had ever been linked in friendship. It would therefore seem reasonable to assume that he flew into characteristically unbridled fury over
something Rudolph wrote him; and though no copies of the Matas
letters were preserved, it is plain from the context of one of Hearn's
replies that, during the late autumn or early winter of 1887, something
Rudolph had written concerning Page Baker triggered one of these
towering rages.

Early that September Hearn was still signing his frequent letters to
Rudolph with such subscripts as *Su amiguito siempre y siempre* (your
friend always and always) and passing on such intimate items as:
"I have been for four months without a cent of money [and] . . .
worst of all, there is no inspiration in the tropics—no poetry, no psy-
chological life, no aspiration, no self-sacrifice, no human effort. . . . I
still prefer one year of Martinique to a thousand years of New York."

A fortnight later, at which time Hearn was briefly in New York, he
was still referring to *Chita* as "our" novel. "Dear friend Matas," he
wrote. "I am going back to the Tropics—probably for many years. My
venture has been more successful than I ever hoped;* and I find myself

* This refers to an agreement by editor Alden to commission Hearn to write a
series of West Indian sketches for *Harper's* magazine. Among other things, *Harper's*
furnished him with a camera and paid him a substantial advance.

able to abandon journalism with all its pettiness, cowardices, and self-ishnesses, forever. I am able hereafter to devote myself to what you always said was my *forte:* the study of tropical Nature—God's Nature—violent, splendid, nude and pure—I never hoped for such fortune. It has come unasked. I am almost afraid to think it is true. I am afraid to be happy!

"I go back in a few days—with a splendid camera, and photographic apparatus. My pen sketches appear before our novel—very soon—fully illustrated. You will like them."

In this same letter he also urged: "You must write me whenever you feel like it: we must never lose sight of each other. Do not think it a *duty* or a *constraint*—only write when you are moved to do so. . . . Good-bye for a little, and believe me always devotedly and sincerely —Lafcadio Hearn." A one-line postscript reads: "I have made arrangements about our 'Chita'."

The Morne-Rouge letter with the assurance that "I would rather have one line from you than 60 columns of notices," was dated December 5. Of New Orleans he wrote at that time: "It seems to me as if I would like to forget all my life there, with the exception of our walks and talks." This was the letter Hearn signed with the Spanish phrase "Ever your friend who kisses your hand"—and for nearly five months he did not write Rudolph so much as another line!

What happened was this: by mere chance, Page Baker was in New York at the time Hearn was making the arrangement with Alden that sent him back to Martinique. Returning to New Orleans and learning there of Hearn's brief sojourn in New York, Baker expressed extreme displeasure over the fact that the man he had gone to such lengths to befriend had not troubled to seek him out. Apparently Rudolph made some mention of this in his answer to the Morne-Rouge letter. He received no reply. Knowing all too well the intemperate outbursts which even the most trivial provocation evoked in his friend, he was deeply distressed by this silence.

During the relatively rare occasions when he and Adrienne found time to chat of something other than the household or the office, they must have discussed this situation at length. In any case, she did persuade him to write again, and at last, not more than a day or two after Manuel Harris was discharged as cured, Rudolph received a lengthy letter, one of the only two communications Lafcadio was to send him all that year.

"Dear Friend: Loving you too much to have even ever an unkind thought of you," Hearn wrote, "I could not have mistaken the motive of your letter so as to have been angry; but I was indeed much worried by it, as the circumstances referred to involved some extremely disagreeable recollections which I am trying to forget, in order to be able to do anything here. And I felt as if a sort of occult malevolence were pursuing after me even here . . . I wrote one letter to New Orleans, since I heard from you—that was many months ago though I cannot tell when it was received; for the mails are all irregular now. I owed that to Mrs. Courtney since October last. . . ."

He went on to explain that the island of Martinique had been under rigid quarantine because of a smallpox epidemic which left the entire surviving population of St. Pierre disfigured. As for himself, "I got one of those old slow cold painful fevers which laugh at quinine; and spent six weeks on my back." He added that "the only reason I did not see Page in New York was simply because I did not receive his address until I reached Martinique . . . He will probably not believe this but you will, and that is all I care about . . . Page's extraordinary readiness to believe that I did this and that, and did not want to see him in N.Y. is quite characteristic. He was always willing to believe any (here follows the conventionalized sketch of a chamber pot)* who told him that what I wrote was scandalous or untrue or offensive to Jesus-C & Co. If he likes to believe I did not want to see him—he can go to perdition."

"I keep house!" he continued. "It is the only earthly way of living comfortably here. No one thinks it scandalous, even if your house-keeper is young and pretty, and have a baby suspiciously like you. Fine folks come to visit you all the same; it is the custom! With me, however, there is no romance in the business as you might have suspected: I have just a good, plain, sensible little housekeeper who is really a *bonne*, and that's all! You see, I could never do literary work, and have any nonsense going on in the house. You believe all this—don't you? Of course you do! . . . .

"Best love to you and never think unkindly of me.

"By the way, 'Chita' is out—and I *hope* will appear in book shape; but much will depend on how it takes. The Tribune gave it a shabby paragraph of sarcasm.

"Su amiguito,
"Leocadio Hearn.

"—I'm going to go on right ahead in what I think a true literary principle; and I am sure I'll win, if I can keep well for a couple of years more."

Before Rudolph could answer this letter he received another, which,

* Hearn's drawing of a chamber pot carries a footnote at the bottom of the sheet to the effect that "they have a different shape in Martinique, where they afford the only means of defecating in comfort—since there are no W.C.'s Height 1 ft. 6 inches to 2 feet."

except for the final sentence, was as impersonal as a crop report, beginning: "I find there will not be a mail steamer for days: I have a chance to send you a few notes on the country. . . . Guidebookish paragraphs of description close with: "I will write about other things later on." Don't show my letters to anybody. Goodbye with love, Leocadio." On the margin appear the words: "It is by no means improbable that I may be able to take a European trip with you before many seasons pass."

The whole tone of the letter is as artificial as if Hearn had written: "so I thought I would take pen in hand and drop you a line." And he did not "write about other things later on." More than a year was to elapse before he sent, from Philadelphia, another and final letter; a year during most of which he dawdled fruitlessly while "keeping house" in the West Indies.

During that same year Rudolph's work schedule became heavier and ever yet more heavy, not merely because, as heretofore, he sought in physical fatigue an anodyne for the emotional distempers that harried him but because he was possessed by the eternally new wonders of his daily rounds. Night after night, from seven to ten, he and August McShane supervised their large class as demonstrators of anatomy. One night a week they met, at the close of their labors, in the home of Dr. H. D. Schmidt at 290 Canal Street—now the very heart of New Orleans' business section.

A chronic sufferer from one of the more malevolent forms of arthritis, Schmidt was regarded by many as the leading pathologist, microscopist, histologist, and biological laboratory technician in the United States. Though at all times confined to a wheel chair, it delighted him, as a onetime apprentice to a maker of scientific instruments in his native city of Marburg, to demonstrate the artistry with which he could sharpen a scalpel or a microtome's sectioning knife.

McShane's attitude toward Rudolph Matas had been one of frank hero worship from the outset of their association. He had followed his preceptor quite naturally into the circle that informally called itself a Pathological Society with Dr. Schmidt as perpetual president. He followed him likewise into the editorial orbit of the *New Orleans Medical and Surgical Journal,* where his passion for work and his accomplishments as a linguist made him a more than welcome addition to the staff. Henry Dickson Bruns, presiding editor at this time, Frederick W. Parham and George B. Lawrason, both of whom were faithful and industrious in writing reviews of current publications for the *Journal,* were also members of this group; and, in addition, Rudolph Matas was Dr. Schmidt's personal physician in his interminable siege of *arthritis deformans.*

Rudolph also took McShane with him into the faculty of a newly formed New Orleans Polyclinic, out of whose curriculum the Tulane University's Graduate School of Medicine was to evolve. It was organized originally in response to an urgent demand.

The final third of the nineteenth century witnessed the most dramatic and abrupt change in all medical history. Koch, Pasteur, and others were overturning the entire earlier concept of medicine; the relation of "germs" to disease was for the first time clearly recognized. Lister's "new" antiseptic methods were already being superseded by asepsis. In this dawning era, when three- and even four-year courses of instruction barely allowed time enough for the adequate initiation of neophytes into all the new fields a physician's practice covered, Tulane University's College of Medicine was recognized as one of the nation's foremost centers of medical training. Indeed, Dr. Chaillé, successor to the ailing Dr. Richardson as dean, pointed out in his first commencement address that students from other medical schools were literally streaming to New Orleans for their final year's instruction, seeking the highly prized Tulane degree, at that time far better known than that of a young school of medicine at Johns Hopkins in Baltimore.

Older physicians, many of whom had been in active practice for twenty years or more, were the product of two short terms of didactic lectures, anatomical demonstrations, bedside instruction, and operating room observation. As the 1880's drew to a close, such doctors felt ever more keenly the lack of any real, first-hand knowledge concerning modern discoveries and the newly developed technologies of their profession. Obviously they could not re-enter school to go through a four-year course from the beginning. To meet this situation a number of New Orleans' outstanding younger physicians—De Roaldes, Parham, Archinard, Chassaignac, Lawrason, Bruns, Blanc, J. H. Bemiss, Matas, and McShane—established what they called a New Orleans Polyclinic. It offered to those who might desire to take advantage of such opportunities, refresher courses in medical fields with which matriculants were already familiar and instruction in the many new techniques developed in various research centers throughout the world.

Beginning with the autumn of 1888, Dr. Matas lectured in the Polyclinic for an hour each on Tuesday and Saturday mornings and demonstrated surgical procedures on cadavers for an hour each on Wednesday and Friday afternoons, using the amphitheater and the dead house at Charity Hospital as lecture hall and laboratory. The Polyclinic was so well attended from the very outset that by 1890 it had acquired a building of its own.

While McShane was the colleague to whom Rudolph felt himself most strongly drawn, it would be inaccurate to infer that the latter filled the vacuum Hearn's sulky defection had left. After all, McShane was a normal, hard-working, intensely studious devotee of his profession, identifying himself with this devotion just as did his idol, Rudolph Matas. Far from being given to excesses like Hearn's periodic and furious flings into debauchery, McShane was a teetotaler. Surely McShane was a more faithful friend, and more loyal, than Leocadio had ever shown himself to be. But in that busy season when 1888 became 1889, and success assured the permanence of the new Polyclinic, the long night walks with McShane lacked the stimulating savor the rambles with Hearn had provided in such full measure.

Matas and McShane talked shop, of course—"we were thoroughly in love with our work." And there was much to engage their minds, apart from purely medical matters about this case or that, this student or the other, or even "the young mulatto boy brought to my service on July 6, 1888, for the relief of a traumatic aneurism of the vertebral artery, resulting from a gunshot wound of the upper part of the neck." This had led to prolonged discussion. In the first place, no case of this sort had been admitted to Charity Hospital in nearly 25 years; not since "the memorable operation by Smyth in 1864." In the second place, the injury was cured by a real Antyllian operation; not by an internal suture like that performed on Manuel Harris two months earlier, but by the physical extirpation of the sac.

The young patient had suffered his wound in a Fourth of July accident from a pistol supposedly loaded only with blanks; at admission to the hospital, his condition was already critical. Having located the aneurism, Dr. Matas ordered him put to bed, with a three-pound weight held tightly over the pulsing tumor by an elastic bandage. Four days of this treatment, however, failed to modify the ominous pulsations.

Rudolph's next step was an effort to plug the vessel from within by seeking to promote clotting electrically. "Two long electrolytic needles connected with the negative pole of a galvanic battery were introduced as deeply as possible into the softest part of the tumor, and the current furnished by twelve cells applied."

The battery coils snarled thinly as moment followed moment for an hour, during which Dr. Matas spoke steadily of aneurisms and their treatment, including the Moore-Corradi method to which he was then resorting "although we really have no means of knowing whether the electric current has anything whatever to do with the clotting when this occurs. It could very easily be merely the result of introducing fine wires which act as a mesh, much as cob-webs do when applied by tradition to stop the bleeding of a surface cut." When it was obvious no clot was about to form in the aneurism then under treatment, the battery was disconnected, the long elecrolytic needles were withdrawn, and Dr. Matas announced his decision to operate forthwith. "Forty years ago," he said, "Warren Stone, one of the fathers of genuine medical practice in Louisiana, treated a case of this sort by opening the sac and plugging the wounded artery with *charpie* lint. We are admittedly clutching at a straw in resorting to this now. But in the nineteen cases of which we have a record when this expedient was tried, five recovered, whereas when we dealt with primary bleeding from nonaneurismal injuries of this same vertebral artery, only two out of twenty-two recovered. So we have that much of a percentage differential in our favor."

On July 12, then, the patient was wheeled into the operating room, the tumorous, pulsing sac on the back of his neck and at the base of his skull "was incised and the sac extirpated, and the bleeding points plugged with small aseptic sponges over which a thick packing of iodoform gauze was applied . . . and the whole firmly held in place by an elastic woven bandage wound over the forehead and neck. . . . Three weeks later the patient was discharged from the hospital entirely well."

But there were matters of greater moment than the vagaries of individual case histories to be discussed in the long McShane-Matas talks, notably the growing agitation for a workable and effective medical practice law. As matters then stood, anyone could practice medicine in Louisiana (as in most other states and territories) simply by registering as a physician with the clerk of the parish or county in which he resided. In some cases a diploma was required; any diploma, whether it had been conferred by a reputable college after four years of medical education or purchased over the counter at a print shop.

Efforts to reform this condition by the enactment of regulatory legislation was very vigorously opposed not merely by leeches, nostrum peddlers, and other quacks, but particularly by graduates of the Hahnemann School of Medicine, the homeopaths who held with the founder of their cult that any ailment can be cured by drugs which produce in the human body reactions similar to the symptoms of the patient's disease. The feeling between homeopaths and allopaths was extremely bitter, the former charging that efforts to create a State Board by which all medical practitioners must be licensed was merely a thinly disguised artifice to deny homeopaths the right to practice in Louisiana.

Another fruitful topic of discussion during these rambles was the long polemic waged that year by the *New Orleans Medical and Surgical Journal* against the Louisiana State Medical Society as then constituted. This was launched by an editorial, published in the June issue of 1888, whose opening salvo concerned the state Society's recently adjourned annual meeting in Monroe. It read in part:

"We gather from the official minutes of the recording secretary . . . that the meeting was characterized by the same indifference, idleness, and slipshod irresponsibility that have for years made the Medical Society of Louisiana a disgrace instead of a pride to the profession of the State . . . a meeting (of the state society) is the straggling together in some locality of a dozen or so of languid, inconsequent unprepared medical men. . . . It is known that the Society has accomplished nothing in the way of medical legislation . . . although the Legislature just elected is so constituted as to offer us greater advantages than have been presented for many years. . . . The Louisiana State Medical Society should either undergo a great awakening or be abandoned—cleared away as a useless time consumer and cumberer of earth."

This set the tone of other equally forthright strictures directed against "Society practice" by physicians who accepted annual retainers from fraternal organizations at rates which depressed the general level of medical earnings in the area; against the Charity Hospital Board's summary dismissal of Dr. Parham as Assistant House Surgeon at Charity in order to put Dr. J. D. Bloom into this position.

That September, Rudolph journeyed to Washington for the annual Congress of American Physicians and Surgeons. While there, he became a charter member of a relatively short-lived American Association of Anatomists as well. He also went shopping for perfumes, cologne, and sheet music for Adrienne, and for some more sedate sort of gift for Mrs. Goslee. But the high moment of the Washington Congress came for him when Nicholas Senn demonstrated clinically on a human cadaver the use of his decalcified bone plates in suturing severed intestines.

"When I read the paper he delivered last year," Rudolph told Michinard on his return, "I did not realize the full import of what that man had done, or what an extraordinary development he had laid the foundation for. You mark my words well: since Senn's actual demonstrations at Washington, the next few months are going to show an increased resort to abdominal surgery that is without parallel!"

This prediction was fully verified, not merely in New Orleans but throughout the world. For the time being, however, Matas and Michinard continued to practice on laboratory dogs and to perfect themselves in the making of decalcified bone plates, although these were now being offered for sale by a St. Louis supply house. The price was $2.00 a pair, and that, it must be conceded, was very much of a deterrent to Rudolph Matas, who thriftily continued to secure without charge the leg bones of slaughtered cattle at various butchers' stalls in nearby public markets.

However, research of necessity had to be relegated to whatever hours could be spared from the more immediate and pressing demands on a popular young physician's time, portions of which were also claimed by editorial, professorial, and medical duties. The heavy case load Rudolph Matas carried at Charity Hospital alone included two major "firsts" that autumn of 1888: the first thyroidectomy for a malignancy reported in the history of New Orleans, and the first attempt to relieve acute anemia by the intravenous infusion of saline solutions. Moreover the first writing for which he was to receive pay was completed during this same year: a chapter on dengue, or breakbone fever, for a Cyclopedia of the Diseases of Children published by the J. B. Lippincott Co. He was paid $54.37.

The volume of other copy he also turned out at this season was nothing short of prodigious. Three major contributions by him on important surgical developments appeared in the *New Orleans Medical and Surgical Journal* for the year, as did also his classic paper on intrasacular suture of aneurisms in the *Medical News* of Philadelphia. One reports in detail the extirpation of a thyroid tumor from the neck of James Lines, a bearded Negro laborer. Apparently the young surgeon rushed it into print without waiting to read it before some medical society, in order to have the facts on record while the patient was still alive. In many respects the incident was one of the most dramatic ever enacted at the old Charity Hospital's amphitheater.

Lines was admitted on September 26, 1888. A medical student named Borde, the resident on Dr. Matas's service, took the first case history on it, noting that a swelling "a little smaller than a mandarin orange" had first become noticeable at the base of Lines's neck about six months before, but had caused neither pain nor inconvenience until the early days of September, when difficulty in swallowing and later in breathing began to manifest itself.

Before a retinue of assistants, residents, and Polyclinic students, Dr. Matas held his inevitable one-man consultation. What is our diagnosis? What are the surgical indications, if any? We know, first of all, that this tumor is solid and not cystic, that it was of rapid growth, since it reached its present proportions in six months, and in view of the fact that the man is sixty-five years old, we know it appeared late in life. . . .

"This last consideration would eliminate such diagnoses as goiter, inflammatory enlargements, and, for that matter, all or practically all benign growths," he went on, checking the various possibilities off, finger by finger. "That leaves us the problem of differentiating between sarcoma and carcinoma. Of course, we could wait to see whether there will be a secondary enlargement of the lymphatics, and precociously presented further respiratory difficulties. But when that stage is reached in any sad and difficult case of this sort, though the diagnosis is made easily enough, *cui bono?* From an operative standpoint the diagnosis is by that time a superfluous luxury, which at best will bid the prudent surgeon to limit himself to the task of palliation and keep him from undertaking a useless if not fatal operation."

All this while, of course, he was pacing back and forth, stroking his beard, clasping and unclasping his hands behind his back.

"What is the most urgent symptom our patient complains of?" he asked, continuing. "It is difficulty in breathing. Several factors are involved in such dyspnea. One is the direct pressure on the larynx of this rapidly enlarging growth, which flattens a normally round tube into an ever narrowing scabbard. Another might well be infiltration of the growth into the larynx. Hence a tracheotomy must soon be performed in any event. Shall we also try to extirpate the tumor? The growth appears to be distinctly encapsulated, the patient's general condition is good, so that, despite the known fatality of thyroidectomies, we will a least begin by ligating the four thyroid arteries and, after that, if it appears that conditions are favorable, we can follow this by complete extirpation of the gland."

The patient was taken to the amphitheater on October 11. Charity Hospital records indicated that no other thyroidectomy had ever been performed there.* Consequently students, physicians in attendance at the Polyclinic, and whatever other surgeons could find time to be present crowded the tiered seating rows, notebooks and opera glasses in hand, when Henry Scherck began to drip chloroform onto his gauze-lined cone, with intern Sabatier and resident student Borde standing by as principal assistants.

Dr. Matas, as always, kept up a running fire of talk from beginning to end, punctuating his remarks on the history of thyroid diseases with staccato interjections of "My, my, my!" and an occasional explosive "Con-*fusion!*" while from time to time he rinsed his hands in the "Matas font" beside the operating table. At the very outset he called attention to the fact that the patient's difficulty in breathing—dyspnea—seemed markedly heightened by the air of excitement that surrounded the procedure and by his natural fear of the impending ordeal.

"We confront a critical situation here," he commented while waiting for anesthesia to become surgically total. "At any moment a trache-

* Six months later, the detailed report Dr. Matas published about the case noted that "out of a total of 75,697 indoor patients treated at Charity Hospital in the decade 1878–88, only one case of thyroid disease, excluding the present case in 1888, has been reported. Furthermore, the operation of thyroidectomy is not mentioned in any of these reports, and it is almost certain this is the first instance of its performance in our institution, if not in our city."

otomy* may have to be performed, if the patient's difficulty in breathing should become so great as to threaten his life. Oh my, yes, indeed. And if we wait until this moment of crisis is upon us, he may succumb to a too hasty attempt at the performance of a tracheotomy, since there will not be time, perhaps, to observe all the precautions so vital a procedure demands. I am therefore going to clear the trachea now—at once—even before anesthesia is complete, exposing it here above the sternum, so that all will be in readiness for an immediate emergency tracheotomy should this be necessary."

Borde and Sabatier held the still-conscious patient while Dr. Matas drew his scalpel steadily downward in a straight line from throat to breast-bone. Talking without interruption he retracted skin, divided muscles, and worked the handle of his scalpel gently to separate loose connective tissue from the major blood vessels.

"My, my, my," he marveled, shaking his head. "Just see how far to the right and back toward the vertebral column the enlargement of the thyroid gland has pushed the trachea . . . and the way the trachea has been flattened into a scabbard. . . . What we must consider, however, is that the operation, though one of the most formidable in surgery, is one with whose technique we in this part of the world are not familiar by practice because goitrous conditions are so rarely encountered here. However, it has been thoroughly perfected by the great continental masters in Europe, where they are called on so frequently to perform it—Kocher, Billroth, Mikulicz, Lücke,—— Oh, con-*fusion*! Just see what we have here! The trachea is crossed by a large, pulsating blood vessel above it. Probably this is a right carotid, originating anomalously. . . . My, my, my! The presence of this vessel in the small area the displacement of the trachea has left accessible reduces the space available for introducing a cannula to less than half an inch. You see here the dreadful danger that would have attended a hasty tracheotomy in this instance, were an emergency to arise. Braun and Rotter report that of fifty thyroidectomies performed for malignancies, thirty died within a matter of hours or days, classifying excessive hemorrhage as the most frequent cause of death with suffocation next. Here we might well have had both suffocation and excessive hemorrhage, had we not discovered by advance preparation that in the very area in which the first incision for a hurried tracheotomy would normally be made, an anomalous artery. . . . My, my, my!"

Thereafter the painstaking and infinitely careful dissection of the malignant thyroid growth went forward until, as Dr. Matas later

---

* An incision into the windpipe, through which a metal tube can be inserted to bypass whatever obstruction makes normal breathing difficult or perhaps even impossible.

described it in his paper, "for some reason, perhaps increased compression of the trachea due to manipulation . . . the patient suddenly began to gasp for breath, the veins in the wound became turgid, the lips cyanotic, the pulse weak, irregular, almost imperceptible at the wrist; in short, the patient was about to die from apnea. There was not time for delay. The trachea was immediately opened below the tumor, and a large cannula inserted into the windpipe. The relief was instantaneous. The cyanosis . . . disappeared, and the patient at once dropped into an easy and calm attitude. . . . The chloroform had been completely stopped on the appearance of the threatening symptoms, and we now decided to complete the operation without the anesthetic."

In this fashion surgery proceeded to its termination, the entire tumor was excised, the operative field irrigated and closed with silk and silver sutures. Despite the ordeal he bore so manfully for an hour and twenty minutes, the patient actually sat up on the table for the final dressing and was sent back to his ward in a wheel chair.

But Dr. Matas, watching Lines's progress from day to day—indeed, almost from hour to hour—became increasingly dubious. "The stridor of his in-breathing is greatly improved," he noted, "but its persistence leads me to fear that mischief is yet brewing within the larynx, even though the tumor showed no sign of penetration beyond its capsule." So a second operation was performed on November 27, nearly seven weeks after the first one; exploration revealed a granular mass of tissue in the larynx, almost closing it to the passage of air. Much of this growth was removed, and the patient was still alive six months later, but, reported Dr. Matas: "It is not probable that [he] will survive many weeks longer, as the disease shows a manifest tendency to encroach deeper into the trachea."

The case attracted wide interest among physicians and educators; its details were reported in various sections of the South by those physicians who returned to their practices after attending the first Polyclinic session. With ever-increasing frequency, Rudolph, though not yet thirty, was asked to address medical gatherings, a trend which reached what might justly be called a brilliant climax in 1893, when he was invited by the Postgraduate Medical School of Chicago to address their Columbian Quadricentennial Congress with famous surgeons from all the world in attendance, on any subject of his choosing.

Much more significant for the future progress of medicine, yet evocative of far less contemporary interest, was Dr. Matas's pioneering —incidentally, unsuccessful—use of intravenous infusions of normal salt solution in cases where great loss of blood had brought sufferers to the point of collapse. For one thing, the first recorded trial of this sort occurred in midsummer, when neither the Polyclinic nor the medical school was in session. For another, intravenous saline infusions had been used during early cholera outbreaks in New Orleans and, according to a subsequent Matas article, "a dim indication is also met here and there of the direct and indirect transfusion of blood in surgical practice." Nonetheless, "it is, I believe, historically correct to state that no attempt prior to July 1888 had been made to infuse intravenously a saline solution for the relief of acute anemia."

The case was that of a twenty-six-year-old south Louisiana farmer (indentified in subsequent reports only by the initials "R.C.") who, when eleven years old, had fallen out of a tree so that the sharp, jagged point of a pine stump was driven about four inches into the inner portion of his thigh. The wound healed and apparently gave no hint of trouble for a dozen years. Then a small tumor appeared at the site of the old injury and during the next three years became larger and ever more troublesome.

Surgery disclosed that the great swelling was not a tumor but a cavernous growth, whose spaces were filled with venous blood and serous fluids, a great deal of which was lost when an incision was made. Moreover, the growth was so thoroughly involved with the skin above it and the sheath of the thigh bone within, that it was impossible to dissect it out. As an emergency measure, the leg was amputated.

Because the patient had been thin, undernourished, and careworn from anxiety to begin with, Dr. Matas was deeply troubled, and revisited the hospital late that afternoon before going home. He found his patient prostrated and ordered him warmed with blankets and hot stupes. He lifted the limp wrist and peered down at the gold watch his father had sent him with such fond pride only eight years before. So shallow, thready, and intermittent was the prostrated sufferer's pulse that it could not be counted. Dropping the nerveless arm, Dr. Matas applied his palm to the patient's forehead and found that, despite the blankets and stupes, it was still chill and clammy to the touch.

Bending low to catch the sense of a murmur, as he saw the man's lips move, Rudolph heard something about a fire that was burning him, and "a great burning thirst." Thirst, of course. It was difficult even to estimate the amount of fluid lost through rupture of the cavernous growth and through the operation that followed, though Dr. Laplace, his assistant, had been swift and efficient in tying off the blood vessels as these were severed. If only some of that fluid could be restored!

It came to him then, out of some odds-and-ends compartment of his phenomenal memory, that in earlier cholera cases, saline infusions had been given intravenously, and on the spur of that recollection he ordered two pints of distilled water, with a dram of common salt dissolved in each pint, to be brought at once. While this was being prepared he slid the point of a large hypodermic needle skillfully into a vein on the inner side of the patient's right arm. The slow seep of the solution had hardly begun to make its way into the impoverished blood vessels when the man sighed in obvious relaxation and relief. In bayou French he exclaimed that a delightful coolness was spreading through him. Picking up the patient's wrist once more, Dr. Matas felt the pulse readily, slowed down to not much above normal and much more resistant to the light pressure of his fingertips.

"Give him nourishment through the night," he directed. "Beef tea, mainly, and a little brandy in warm milk. I'll stop in first thing in the morning."

But by the next morning prostration had reasserted itself, and, though a second infusion was provided, its beneficent effects, though real enough, were transitory. They lasted only about fifteen minutes, after which the patient once more relapsed into a stupor in which, during the night, he died.

To his residents and interns Dr. Matas stressed a rationalization of what had taken place, pointing out that the patient had long been in a state of extreme nervous tension, which, taken in conjunction with the shock of a prolonged operation and loss of blood, led to fatal termination. However, it was to be remembered that the saline infusions had afforded him even in these extreme circumstances prompt and decided relief, that without them he would have died thirty-six hours earlier than he did, and that in any case his last hours had been made infinitely more comfortable.

And so the year of the first "Matas Operation," the year of pioneer researches with saline intravenous infusions, the first full year of instructing very much senior physicians at the new Polyclinic, the year of the first thyroidectomy ever performed in New Orleans to extirpate a malignancy, neared its end. By all the portents Rudolph Matas should have been a supremely contented young man, justly proud of the success he had achieved and the recognition he had won among those whose opinions he prized most highly. But this was far from being the case. The nebulous frustrations of his Platonic relation to Adrienne became a sense of something akin to actual bereavement, though he sorrowed not for a possession lost but for what was both unfulfilled and to all seeming, unfulfillable.

This sense of desolation was sharpened in October, when he received word that his father's friend, Dr. Etienne Melou, the same Dr. Melou whom he had assisted in battling the yellow-fever epidemic at Fort Brown in 1882, had died suddenly at his Brownsville home, though only fifty-five years old. It was through Dr. Melou that he had been receiving occasional news of his father at Tucson, where, apparently, Narciso was forever on the point of becoming enormously rich through streetcar franchises or mining strikes and continuing to finance these ventures by practicing medicine. Dr. Melou's death thus severed one of the very few slender threads which yet remained of the familial weft of Rudolph's being.

The poignancy of his desire for genuine family life, something which union with Adrienne might have provided, had not abated, either with the passage of time or with the continuity of her presence. On the contrary, it was intensified with each new day when he did not dull his conscious being to the point of exhaustion by unremitting work.*
And now the only other person for whom he harbored a deep affection, Lafcadio Hearn, was somewhere in Martinique, sulkily letting resentment over a mild rebuke continue to fester and rankle. Months had passed since Rudolph's reply to the letter Hearn wrote him in July, stating that "I will write about other things later on." And then, one afternoon, an unrelated circumstance temporarily blotted out all vapors by sending him full cry along a new research trail.

While subscribing unreservedly to Dr. Senn's principle of the "aided stitch" in intestinal sutures, Matas and 'Michinard were nonetheless aware of certain flaws inherent in putting this principle into practice. One of these, for example, was that if the bone plate was not completely decalcified, it would not be fully digested; the stony residue, remaining in the intestine, might conceivably cause still another blockage. The Senn plates had to be made long in advance and did not always fit the size needed at the critical moment, which might involve the small intestine of an infant or the large bowel of a fully grown man. Often enough, in their practice operations, Michinard and Matas had speculated upon the possibility of making an adjustable aid for the work.

Late one afternoon Dr. Matas walked from the hospital to Werlein's, with nothing more serious in mind than the purchase of one or two new ballads as a sort of peace offering for Adrienne, who had been urging him vainly to come home at least for meals, instead of sending out for a poor-boy sandwich and washing it down with coffee. When he reached the big music store, it chanced that all clerks were busied with earlier customers, so that Rudolph rather idly walked from one counter or display case to another, admiring the craftsmanship with which an

* A typewritten scrap of paper found among Dr. Matas's documents bears the notation that a Eugene Arthur Landry had been killed in a pistol duel at Marksville, seat of the parish of Avoyelles. From the context it is clear that every effort was made to ascertain whether this might have been the Arthur Landry from whom Adrienne had been separated.

accordion's keyboard had been inlaid with mother-of-pearl, or perhaps speculating on the motives that might have prompted a Belgian named Adolphe Sax to invent a metal clarinet called a saxophone. Suddenly he stiffened as he looked at a card to which a circular winding of what resembled very thick catgut was fastened.

"What are those?" he asked the clerk who came at length to wait upon him.

"Drum snares," replied the latter. "They are fastened to the bottom——"

"Yes, I know. They are made of catgut, like violin strings?"

"Certainly. We have even thicker ones, of a better grade of material, used for bass-fiddle strings."

All thoughts of sheet music forgotten, Rudolph purchased a substantial length of the drum-snare material, delighted to learn that its price was only five cents the foot. He could hardly wait until he reached his study before snipping off a short piece of it, bending it into a circle, and after a number of unsuccessful trials finally fitting the two ends into a short piece of rubber drainage tubing so that it retained its annular shape.

He and Paul Michinard were busy for weeks thereafter, ironing out various flaws in the technique of using absorbable rings of catgut instead of decalcified plates of bone in aiding the support of intestinal sutures. They found, for example, that moisture distorted the rings badly after they had been fastened into position; the cure for this was to boil the material first, letting it shrink on drying, and then remoistening it in a preservative solution, after which it no longer warped at all.

They were particularly enthusiastic about the fact that their catgut rings need not be made in advance but could be cut to size as needed. It was Rudolph who pointed out that by using these instead of the flat, oval Senn plates, they could make end-to-end sutures of severed intestines—circular enterorrhaphies—instead of the anastomoses by which blind ends were reconnected laterally.

All that winter of 1888–89 Rudolph demonstrated the drum-snare rings before his classes at Tulane and at the Polyclinic. He and Paul Michinard were already at work upon the paper whose publication would bring them the acclaim of their profession; then the blow fell. In an article published by the New York Medical Journal for March 23, 1889, Dr. Robert Abbé of New York suggested the substitution of rings made of heavy catgut for the Senn plates of decalcified bone. The Abbé rings were made of four strands of light catgut, wrapped around the ends of three fingers and then wound around with more gut of the same weight.

Rudolph had been preparing to present a paper reporting the results of his work and that of Paul Michinard before the Louisiana State Medical Society in New Orleans on April 10, 1889, only a little more than two weeks after Abbé's publication appeared. He presented his paper just the same, and with good grace; thereafter he engaged in no debate over priority, merely declaring that his development of the solid catgut ring had been made independently, and with no prior knowledge of Abbé's work. As late as 1890, when he demonstrated the Senn plates, the Abbé ring, his own ring, and various other catgut mats, plates, and the like, before a June meeting of the Orleans Parish Medical Society, he said:

"If I should adopt the order in which the various substitutes for the Senn bone plate have been presented to the medical public, I should next claim your attention with a discussion of the solid catgut ring, made of the heavy commercial gut known as 'drum-snare' material, which I thought of independently, and demonstrated in my classes at the Medical Department of Tulane University and in the New Orleans Polyclinic . . . before the publication of Abbé's paper."

The long, long hours, the trials and failures as well as the successes in devising improvements on the Senn principle had been good, he told himself, regardless of who might snatch after the laurels of renown. He said much the same thing to Adrienne, when she sought to console him for a disappointment.

"The real founder of this new art of aided sutures is not Abbé or Matas or Brokaw," he said, "but Senn. His is the work that is imperishable; and when you consider that the whole field is less than two years old, the important thing is that all of us keep right on trying to pick flaws or find improvements in his basic discovery, not which of us did this first or second or last."

Actually the question became academic in 1892, when Dr. John B. Murphy of Chicago demonstrated the first "Murphy button"—a metal two-piece snap of small size which held the surfaces of an anastomosis in close apposition until they united and then dropped into the channel to be passed out in the course of nature. The Murphy button replaced every earlier type of suture aid—bone plate, catgut ring, rubber disc, and all.

In the midst of the frantic rush to get the paper on his and Michinard's work before the Louisiana State Medical Society, Rudolph took time out on the spur of the moment to write to Lafcadio once more. In the letter, dispatched to Martinique on March 21, Rudolph blamed himself and not his friend for being "an irregular correspondent."

No one knows what inner need for the realities of shared affection compelled him write as he did. Perhaps it was the feeling that this was one empty loneliness that could be remedied. The solitary link that had maintained the semblance of communion with his father was gone; from his mother he received no word of tenderness, merely an occasional stilted acknowledgment of the letters he wrote once a month or so; Adrienne was and would continue to be unattainable in the only manner that could fulfill his need. But perhaps Lafcadio might be won back to a renewal of the precious companionship they had once known.

The answer to his letter of March 21, 1889 came not from Martinique, but from Philadelphia, from the home of Dr. George M. Gould where Hearn was living at the time.

"It seemed like tearing my heart out to leave Martinique"; Hearn wrote, "and though I am now in one of the most beautiful cities in the world, among dear friends, and with the splendid spectacle before me of man's grandest efforts—not the wild cyclone of electricity and iron like New York, but a great gentle peace—the tropical nature with all its memories haunts me perpetually—draws my thoughts back again over the azure sea and under the turquoise sky to the great palms and the volcanic hills and the beautiful brown women. . . .

"Thanks for news of Miss Queyrouze, and Mrs. Courtney. As for other people wondering what has become of me—that is just what I want. I don't care to have any one know what I am doing till it is done.

". . . I do not wonder you should be an irregular correspondent—considering the immensely busy life you live; and I shall never complain again—for I feel the difficulty of writing myself more and more with far less to do. But I want to know always where you are and where you are going for vacations, and what you are doing in a literary way. For you ought to become a very extraordinary man, if you can keep your health in a climate far more debilitating, let me assure you, than that of Martinique.

"I wish I were able to send you some pretty souvenirs of my voyage: but you will have to be content for the present with my books. I had to live on a scale of such economy as you would not believe if I told you, and returned as poor as I went—no, a good deal poorer. However, the harvest is yet to reap. Best love to you.

"Lafcadio Hearn."

And that was it! Rudolph answered the letter, of course. But he received no reply . . . ever.

CHAPTER XVIII

Rudolph Matas's life span fell short of a crowded century by less than three years. Yet if any one twelvemonth out of the ninety-seven should be designated as the turning point of his career, it would be 1894.

During the dawn of what came to be known as the Mauve Decade, his roster of patients was no longer restricted to charity cases shunted to his service at the hospital, the remnants of his early benevolent-society practice, or the old families clinging with stubborn determination to what was plainly a rapidly deteriorating residential area. Almost overnight, leaders of social, commercial, and financial New Orleans began in ever-increasing numbers to seek his professional services. Among them were such moneyed Titans as Augustus Wheeler, a financier whose counsel made it possible for Rudolph to invest his savings both securely and shrewdly; Alexander Hutchinson, the transportation nabob who had fought the state quarantine law with relentless intensity; Isaac Delgado, the Jamaica-born immigrant who became a multimillionaire as a sugar and molasses broker; James D. Houston, who had literally fought his way up from humble beginnings to such positions of power as administrator of state tax collectors, president of the waterworks company, and a high place among the leaders of the Louisiana Lottery.

None the less Dr. Matas's other work, notably his editorial and teaching commitments, was accorded a full meed of time and energy. His Polyclinic courses were eagerly sought, though some of the older matriculants grumbled about the multiplicity of authorities cited by their youthful instructor. They had no desire to know everything that had ever been written and done in the particular field under discussion, they said; all they sought was a working knowledge of salient developments to bring them up to date in the field. Some of his colleagues, on the other hand, complained that all too often he encroached on their time, running over his allotted hour without regard for what might be scheduled for the ensuing period.

Over and above his editorial stint for the *New Orleans Medical and Surgical Journal,* he also assumed in 1889 an associate editorship of the *Annual of Universal Medical Sciences,* published by Dr. Charles A. Sajous at Philadelphia. Naturally, it was inevitable that he should fall behind his scheduled assignments since he undertook more than could possibly be packed into even the longest working days. From that time on to the end of his life he never did succeed in clearing his docket, or in keeping what he wrote within the limits assigned to it. "Oblige me by not exceeding the number of words allotted to your department," Dr. Sajous wrote him testily in 1891. "Last year this evidently escaped your attention and gave us a mountain of trouble." During the same week he received a letter from Dr. Hobart A. Hare, acknowledging the year-late arrival of a manuscript on diseases of the pleura.

Swamped by more calls upon him than any one individual could have met, fashion's newest medical favorite in New Orleans was too preoccupied to be fully cognizant of the various pushes and pulls that were then setting faction against faction among the community's physicians.

On the one hand, the State Medical Society clamored for passage of a Medical Practices Act at Baton Rouge. The homeopaths opposed this. Most of the lay press supported them, but they were excoriated as "our brethren of the sugary pellet" by the *New Orleans Medical and Surgical Journal.*

At the same time the Lottery interests, whose franchise expired in 1892, bought enough votes to secure a twenty-five-year renewal and even to override the veto of Governor Francis Tillou Nicholls, an amputee Civil War hero, who wrote that he would not permit his right hand to sign away what he had sacrificed his left arm to preserve: "the honor of my native state."

The Tulane medical faculty was still more bitterly divided, as was the rest of the world of medicine at the time, by controversy over Robert Koch's triumphant but, alas, premature and erroneous announcement of serum for the cure of tuberculosis. Koch had sent five phials of this presumably priceless stuff to President Benjamin

Harrison for distribution to research centers in the United States. One of these had been allotted to Dr. Joseph Jones, head of Tulane's Department of Clinical Medicine;* he promptly became the target of bitter attacks by physicians to whom he doled out none of the wonder serum for experimental purposes.

The sharpest cleavage of all, however, concerned the selection of a professor of surgery for Tulane University. Because of progressively debilitating infirmities, the long-time head of this department, Tobias Richardson, had already relinquished the college's deanship to Dr. Chaillé. When it became necessary for him to give up all teaching activity as well, ailing and aging Dr. Samuel Logan reluctantly agreed to act as interim professor of surgery. While one faction actively championed the permanent appointment of Dr. Albert Baldwin Miles, theretofore professor of materia medica, another just as vigorously demanded that Dr. Edmond Souchon be chosen.

In short, espousal of and opposition to the proposed Medical Practices Act, the Lottery franchise renewal, the experimental distribution of Koch's tuberculin, and selection of a permanent appointee to succeed Tobias Richardson as professor of surgery at Tulane were all snarled into one vast tangle of disputation, in which factional support in one issue was freely bartered for alliance in the others.

Dr. Matas kept himself apart from these feuds—he was not even fully cognizant of their various ramifications—and when Dr. John B. Elliott was elected president of the State Society for 1892, a year when the legislature would once more be called into session, he was named vice-president, an honor in which Adrienne seems to have taken far more pride than he.

While he never did become wholly reconciled to their platonic relationship, he did find solace of a sort in the cherished serenity they shared, especially in each day's beginning. Long before Rudolph arose in his monastic first-floor apartment, Adrienne would be bustling about the kitchen, putting a measure of green coffee beans into a heavy iron skillet and roasting them to brown fragrance. Still hot, they were cascaded into the hopper of a small mill attached to the wall and ground fine. The aromatic grist filled the top of a drip pot, through which a few hissing tablespoons of boiling water at a time would be filtered. The first small cup was brought to the bedside of the head of the house, in conformity with the mores of that time and place.

Thereafter, while he retired to the bathroom and went through the ritual of cleansing himself and giving meticulous care to his fine beard

* Dr. Jones's grandson, another Joseph Jones, is today president of the Tulane University Board of Administrators.

237

and mustache, Adrienne put plain gold studs into the rigidly starched bosom of a fresh shirt, set out detachable cuffs and collar, and returned to the kitchen to prepare breakfast. By the time he had touched up beard and mustache with perfume, she was once more on hand to fasten his ready-tied cravat—an art he never did master—and then at length they would sit down to the morning meal.

During the course of the repast he would talk over the happenings of the day before and the schedule of events for the day to come. . . . Dr. Richardson's illness was taking an ominous turn for the worse; in fact, at her failing husband's insistence, Mrs. Richardson had presented a gift of $100,000 to Tulane's Medical Department, so that this institution might be properly housed. The site for a modern building had already been selected: Woods' Cotton Yard at Claiborne and Canal.* . . . Augustus McShane was going to buy the *New Orleans Medical and Surgical Journal;* he had requested Rudolph to serve as one of five permanent collaborators. . . . Dr. Edmond Souchon had been dispatched on a tour of all major medical centers in the country so that the latest developments in medical and educational architecture might be incorporated into the new building.

As a matter of course he and Adrienne discussed at length the *cause célèbre* that has gone down in New Orleans history as "Who killa da Chief?" Police Superintendent David Hennessy had been the first member of his profession to breach the secrecy that surrounded the Mafia's achievement of extending its crime cartel to the United States. He was shot down one night while walking from his office to his home. The assassins were brought to trial; but, through what was later shown to have been subornation, a hung jury professed itself unable to agree on a verdict, and a mistrial was ordered.

Some of the community's foremost citizens thereupon published a signed manifesto, calling a mass meeting which assembled at New Orleans' principal street intersection, St. Charles and Canal, where at

---

* In the first number of the *Journal* issued under the ownership of Dr. McShane (July 1891), Dr. Matas wrote a commentary on the selection of the Canal Street site for the proposed Richardson Memorial building, declaring that "we cannot repress a few reflections. . . . The numerous visitors that General Butler brought with him (in 1862) were quartered in various parts of the city, and one of the places selected was Woods' Cotton Yard. The writer was wearing the garments of infancy when Butler first enjoyed the hospitality of New Orleans; the General was warmly received but many people thought he stayed too long. . . . *Tempora mutantur!* On the ground where the rattle of invaders' bayonets was heard nearly thirty years ago will soon be heard the eloquent voices of teachers instructing ardent youth how to save human life and not to destroy it. In olden times the prophet urged the warriors to turn their swords into plowshares, and their spears into pruning hooks. Now the fancy lightly turns swords into amputating knives and muskets into bistouries; and where once the chilling clink of bayonets was heard, nothing more discordant than the cutting of the dissecting knife shall disturb the timid ear."

that time a statue of Henry Clay dominated the wide neutral ground. One of the signers of this manifesto was Dr. Henry Dickson Bruns, who, at the time, was still presiding editor of the *New Orleans Medical and Surgical Journal.* The assembly stormed the jail and lynched eleven of the Mafiosi who had been returned to their cells to await a new trial.

Chief among those who had called and led the mass meeting was James D. Houston whose big voice had boomed out at the gathering that "When we assemble in Lafayette Square, we meet to talk, but when we assemble at the Henry Clay monument, we meet to act!"

It was Houston's life that, soon thereafter, Rudolph Matas was called upon to save. Suffering from an attack of acute laryngitis, the burly politician—he was only forty-eight at the time of his death in 1894— had received what was the accepted therapy of the day: a plaster of cantharides was applied to his throat, and, when the resulting blister burst, powdered morphine was dusted over the exposed flesh. The practitioner who treated him on this occasion had been overgenerous in applying morphine. The patient went into so deep a stupor that Dr. Matas was summoned.

"I repeatedly aroused him by means of body flagellation with towels soaked in ice water and pleaded with him to stay awake or he would surely die," the surgeon declared in one of his last public addresses many years later. "I appealed to him to try and remember some piece of poetry he might have learned in school and to recite it as a means of keeping awake. The only poem he knew was Savile Clark's 'The Siege of Lucknow.'"

One must picture the strange scene: the high-ceilinged, second-floor bedroom, the long French windows, the full-length jalousies, the heavy rosewood armoire, the marble washstand, the four-poster with its filmy mosquito bar, the ormolu gasolier—and the small, dapper, bearded physician belaboring with icy towels the burly, somnolent figure that lurched back and forth across the flowered carpet, alternately mumbling and bellowing:

"I hear the wailing of children, and the moaning of men in pain . . . I see the siege of Lucknow burnt in upon my brain . . ." and so on and on, with periods of torpor until the blessed pipes of the rescuing Highlanders are heard: "and then the peril was ended, and the sorrow was overpassed . . . they had raised the siege of Lucknow, and we knew we were saved at last. . . ."

And, at last, Jim Houston too was rescued from the shadows closing in upon him. In gratitude he gave what he treasured as his most valued and valuable possession. A hard man was Jim Houston. In fighting his way up to wealth and eminence he had been directly implicated in at least three killing affrays. But the most precious gift he chose to give to the man who saved his life was two volumes of Boydell's *Illustrations of the Dramatic Works of Shakespeare,* complete with a specially fashioned table to hold them!

Naturally, his captaincy of the horde that wreaked summary vengeance on Hennessy's slayers was discussed by Rudolph and Adrienne over their *déjeuner à la fourchette.* Another of the topics of their conversation, no doubt, concerned the business difficulties in which his mother's clutching avarice had involved him. A dilapidated building, heavily encumbered by tax debts had been left to Teresa, as sole heir of her brother Tomás. Though nominally rented out as a barroom, it brought in nothing. Moreover, the structure's extreme disrepair was such that no tenant could be induced to pay for its occupancy. But it was not until 1890 or thereabouts, when the city surveyor officially condemned it as unsafe, that Teresa reluctantly agreed to its rehabilitation.

Such morning chats, all too brief, since Rudolph had to be about his hospital rounds, house calls, clinics, editorial work, and other professional duties, were almost the only opportunity vouchsafed them for undisturbed companionship. By night, at the close of his instruction period as demonstrator, McShane usually walked home with him. As often as not, they would go roundabout by way of Julia Street, where Patrick and Katy Sullivan kept a barroom and grocery.* In the friendly atmosphere of the living quarters behind the grocery the oddly assorted quartet—two Sullivans and a McShane, with a Louisiana-born Catalan named Matas (né Hereu)—would chat over beer or coffee until all hours. The Sullivans had a houseful of sons, one of whom, John, a brawny giant even at fifteen, would in the years to come make a descendant of McShane mayor of New Orleans. John's daughter, Marian, would marry one of Rudolph's inner coterie of future favorite students, Walter Peters Gardiner who, after helping pay his way through medical school by correcting quiz papers for his preceptor, in time became head of the New Orleans Board of Health.

It was no more than natural that Rudolph should envy the Sullivans' happy, one-for-all-and-all-for-one family life and find in their exuberant clannishness a wistful sort of transference for his own privation.

The oppressively hot summer seemed endless, but as the year wore to a close, and Dr. Souchon returned from his tour of medical centers, everyone connected with Tulane was caught up in a fever of excitement over plans, and later over ground breaking, and finally over cornerstone-

---

* Almost every neighborhood grocery in the New Orleans of that era, and up to the enactment of national prohibition, maintained two small, separate but adjoining barrooms in conjunction with its food distributing establishment, one for white and one for colored, as specified by state law.

laying ceremonies for the new Richardson Memorial Building. Scant heed was accorded even the formal announcement of the Board of Health that with the onset of cool weather another summer had waned without the incidence of a single case of yellow fever in New Orleans.

After spring had banished the brief semitropical winter the Louisiana State Medical Society, under the presidency of Dr. Elliott, began once more to stir up support for united presentation of a Medical Practices Act to the members of the incoming, newly elected legislature, which nonetheless promptly shelved the measure.

"It was killed with a celerity that was startling," lamented the *Journal* in its next issue. "For two long and weary years we will have to wait before we will be able to remove from Louisiana the reproach of being the dumping ground for the medical refuse of all the other states of the Union. . . . [Two years ago] several influences combined to defeat it: the opposition of our homeopathic friends, dissensions in our own ranks, and the crowding-out pressure exerted by the Louisiana Lottery Bill upon everything else. . . . The homeopaths in our midst are too strong to be ignored. The knights of the sugary pellet are well organized."

A day or two before the second effort to enact such legislation ended in failure, Tobias Richardson's memorable career as soldier, surgeon, and teacher was brought to a close. His name will always stand high among those who lifted medicine, as practiced in North America, out of the realm of medieval mumbo jumbo into that of science. He was the first Louisianian to become president of the American Medical Association, which he had helped to found; he crowned his career by donating, a year before his death, the funds with which the first really modern medical school building in the South was brought into being.

Three names were now heard in speculative discussions about the Richardson succession: Edmond Souchon, Albert Miles, and Rudolph Matas. The latter was no longer a boy prodigy, whose phenomenal store of information, manual dexterity, and daring ventures into new fields of medical and surgical technique won the admiration of his elders. He was nearing the middle thirties in an era when comparatively few mortals attained the Biblical allotment of threescore years and ten. He had walked sedately along the middle way since the icon-smashing forays of his novitiate, he had studiously refrained from offending any of the archangels among his preceptors, he was renowned and admired among the laiety as a great healer, and was esteemed among his students and their associates as a scholarly and inspiring teacher.

Edmond Souchon, professor of anatomy, was also "professor of clinical surgery." The distinction lay in the fact that only the head of a department was designated simply as its professor; his associates were "clinical" professors. However, in the case of Dr. Souchon, it was not to be denied that the transfer from professor of anatomy to professor of surgery would be a distinct step up; in an era when specialization had not yet restricted "the doctor" to one circumscribed field of practice, the head of a medical college's department of surgery was generally regarded as second in official status only to the dean.

Dr. Miles, though just turned forty, had served two years as student-resident at Charity Hospital and in 1882, though still a young practitioner, was unanimously appointed to the post of house surgeon. He had held this position ever since, subsequently coupling with it the duties of professor of materia medica and therapeutics on the faculty of his alma mater.

The sudden death of Dr. Logan, who had been serving as interim professor in Dr. Richardson's stead, forced an immediate decision on the Tulane faculty, which met at once and tendered the professorship of surgery to Dr. Miles. If Rudolph felt any disappointment it was not for himself, but for Dr. Souchon, whom he had hoped in time to succeed as professor of anatomy. Besides, a signal distinction was conferred on him in this same year—an invitation to address the Postgraduate Medical School and Hospital in Chicago. The assembly was being held in conjunction with the Columbian Quadricentennial exposition, and renowned physicians—men like Lawson Tait, Nicholas Senn, and William Osler—would be in attendance. Yet he, Rudolph Matas, would be given the entire evening of August 9 for the delivery and discussion of a paper on aneurisms of the vertebral artery.

There is no proof to buttress the assumption that the forthcoming journey to Chicago was discussed at any length with Adrienne, or that the burden of his part of such a discussion was that, if only they two were married, she could accompany him and to some degree share what was beyond question a major triumph, since he had never before been invited to address so distinguished a gathering. Yet the supposition that they must have engaged in some such colloquy is implicit in the fact that later Adrienne did accompany him on virtually all such journeys—and that without her to see to such matters as hotel reservations and the proper fastening of his shirt studs and cravat he felt lost. As it was, both he and Dr. Charles Chassaignac, who was his companion on the trip to Chicago, all but became homeless waifs on arrival.

Dr. Franklin S. Martin, secretary of the Postgraduate Medical School, had made the following request in issuing his invitation: "Please write about two weeks before leaving New Orleans so that we will have no difficulty in securing your accommodations." It goes almost without saying that when the time to prepare for his Chicago journey drew nigh, Dr. Matas gave the request for advance notice not so much as a second thought. His hosts' first intimation of his arrival was a wire informing them when his train would reach the Twelfth Street station. In a Chicago swarming with out-of-town and out-of-country visitors, some heroic measures were needed to provide hotel rooms on a moment's notice, but the miracle was finally achieved; it is to be presumed Dr. Chassaignac did the needful in the matter of shirt studs and cravat when the *costume de rigueur* was donned for the night session of August 9.

Meanwhile, back in New Orleans, preparations were busily under way to have some sort of acceptable Medical Practices Bill drafted for a third effort at enactment by the Legislature the following May. Dr. Miles, newly installed as president of the State Medical Society on the heels of his elevation to Tulane's chair of surgery, appointed a committee of one hundred physicians from all sections of Louisiana to establish and maintain contact with the legislators. He likewise named a smaller and less unwieldy committee to confer with the "prophets of *similia*" in working out draft legislation they, the homeopaths, would agree to support.

From the very outset, any step that might be construed to recognize homeopaths as men of science on a par with medical practitioners elicited indomitable protests from some members of the State Society; but the cold fact remained that without their active co-operation or, at the very least, passive acquiescence, no Louisiana law regulating the practice of medicine could possibly be enacted at that time. For one thing, the influential morning newspapers of New Orleans, the *Times-Democrat* and the *Picayune*, were both arrayed in opposition to any measure to which the homeopaths objected.

At a conference in the St. Charles Hotel that December, delegates of the contending factions met in an atmosphere of guarded neutrality. A draft bill submitted by the medical physicians was coldly received by the homeopaths; but they did go so far as to concede that if certain amendments they desired were incorporated into the measure, they might support it. On that note the conference was adjourned until sometime in January, when the changes to be specified by the homeopaths could be discussed.

As for general medical interest, it was focused more and more on efforts to conquer typhoid fever, now clearly recognized as an entity and not merely as a form of malaria which would not yield to treatment with quinine. It was Dr. Matas who advanced at a Parish Society discussion the thesis that some source other than drinking water alone must be regarded as carrying the typhoid infection, since New Orleans, which drank only pure rain—i.e., cistern—water, nonetheless had to face the fact that typhoid incidence was ominously on the increase. He pointed out that in his own practice he had noted frequently that three and sometimes more members of the same family would sicken with the vicious ailment which, ten years earlier, he had described in one of his first major papers as one of the "long continued (as distinguished from intermittent or remittent) fevers of Louisiana."

Within five months of this utterance, a typhoid-fever attack brought about the great turning point of Dr. Matas's career, the course of which would have been materially altered had the movement to provide New Orleans with subsurface sewerage disposal been launched a year or two before the elimination of open drains was actually begun.

CHAPTER XIX

As might have been foreseen, the only basis on which the homeopaths would agree to the proposed Medical Practices law was an amendment providing for two examining and licensing boards. One would be composed of physicians, the other of homeopaths and both would be empowered to pass upon the qualifications of whoever might apply to them for a permit to practice.

When Dr. Newton, chairman of the physicians' delegation to the conference group, accepted this proviso on behalf of his association, a number of committee members refused to go along with him. Among the most inflexible of these was Rudolph Matas. He not only declined to sign the majority report, but drafted a blistering minority report, signed by himself and six or seven other dissidents. It was rejected, and, possibly in an endeavor to smooth matters over, the convention's nominating committee placed the name of Dr. Matas at the head of its slate as unopposed candidate for president. He was not even present in the auditorium when the questions of endorsing the compromise Medical Practices Bill and election of officers for the ensuing year were taken up.

Compromisers and Irreconcilables argued bitterly, and at times intemperately, throughout the morning session; but once the question was put, the compromise bill was overwhelmingly endorsed.

Not until then did President Miles read a letter from Dr. Matas, declining the presidential nomination "for reasons that do not in the least affect my loyalty to and affection for this organization."

Dr. Miles explained that the letter had been in his possession for several hours, but that no opportunity to interrupt the debate over the Newton report seemed open for an earlier reading of the communication. Some members took offense at what they regarded as a snub to the Society, but the majority held that he should be waited on by a committee, which should at least try to persuade him to reconsider, since anything like a schism in medical circles at this time would only serve to invite a third defeat for regulatory legislation.

The bearers of olive branches succeeded so well in smoothing matters over that after the gathering's luncheon recess Dr. Matas returned to the hall. Thereupon he was elected to the presidency by acclamation and, in the briefest public address of his entire career, described himself as "very sensitive to the grave responsibilities of my position, and feel assured only in the thought that responsibility for the success of my administration rests equally as much on those who have elected me as upon myself."

Whatever his personal convictions, the Society's new president lost no time in implementing the Newton compromise, whose two-board medical bill was enacted without substantial opposition and was signed by Governor Foster on July 4, less than a week before the Legislature adjourned.

"Believing that so much of the future success of this Society will depend upon the success of this Board," President Matas told the special session of the State Medical Society on this occasion, "I can be excused for urging that your preference be given to those who combine with the best professional and ethical qualifications the greatest loyalty to this Society." Without receding from his unalterable stand on homeopathy in any respect, he thus bowed to the will of the majority with at least an outward show of grace. It was not long, as such things go, before the homeopaths, their numbers dwindling steadily, ceased to nominate a licensing board of their own, accepting the medical group as the proper body to pass upon their qualifications too.

For Rudolph, that August of 1894 was to stand as the most memorable month of his memorable year. True, four months earlier, in March, he had bought a magnificent home, a mansion occupying four lots of ground on the most exclusive section of St. Charles Avenue, next door to the Whitney residence. The price was $18,000; he paid $8000 cash and gave a one-year note for the balance, a circumstance which testifies eloquently to his financial standing. Mrs. Julia Catherine Smith, the seller, lived in Norfolk, Virginia; the house was occupied by tenants to whom she had rented it.

This was one reason why Rudolph waited nearly a year before

moving from a section whose blight was rapidly becoming total to the ultrafashionable Garden District. He could have overcome this obstacle easily enough by invoking a thirty-day cancellation clause in the deed of sale. But the transfer would have separated him and Adrienne. Even had she continued to keep house for him, she and her sons, her mother and her brothers would have had to be domiciled elsewhere, since the modern mansion was not divisible into separate establishments like the old-fashioned home in Rampart Street. Deserting it would have entailed the sacrifice of those early morning tête-à-têtes in which he and Adrienne sought in tranquil companionship a substitute for the rapturous unity which was denied them.

So the tenants were left in undisturbed possession of the St. Charles Avenue mansion, and Rudolph counted the fashionable world well lost for love. His practice continued to grow, his wealthy patients beat a pathway to his door through a jungle of cheap-John stores, pawnshops and dance halls. He was operating now not merely at Charity Hospital, but also at Hôtel-Dieu and at the New Orleans Sanitarium. Word-of-mouth repute hailed him as something of a miracle worker and made him hundreds of literally—not merely figuratively—devoted adherents.

There was, for example, an Italian baby, a nine-month-old hemophiliac boy, who had fallen face down and so cut the inner surface of his upper lip. Despite the use of astringents, the wound continued to ooze blood, especially while the infant was nursing at his mother's breast.

Alarmed by the tot's progressive weakness and anemia, the family physician called Dr. Matas in consultation. The latter immediately ordered spoon feeding instead of breast nursing to halt the obvious increase of hemorrhage brought on by suction; then, without further ado, he applied two deep sutures to the injury. However, noting the next morning that blood now oozed from the sutures, he hit upon the expedient of compression to close the punctured vessels long enough to permit them to heal; so he stripped the wide rubber band from his wallet and stretched it around the infant's head, from upper lip in front to occiput at the rear.

The band from his wallet, he noted later in a paper* about the Italian infant's case, "exercised just the pressure that was required and effectually stopped the bleeding. . . . Feeding was not interfered with by this simple hemostatic contrivance, and the child soon recovered from the extreme weakness and anemia that threatened its life." He cradled the little sufferer cherishingly in his thick, gentle arms and noted with great satisfaction that the baby, obviously relieved,

* "Notes of Cases Illustrating Surgical Lesions of the Vascular System." *New Orleans Medical and Surgical Journal*, vol. 22, p. 252ff.

snuggled confidingly against him. It is attested by all who ever watched or helped him operate, that he was invariably gentle in working with infants. No one spoke of this more eloquently than Adrienne's youngest son, Lucian Landry, who was associated with his stepfather in practice for many years, and whose son, Rudolph Matas Landry, is himself a surgeon of note today.

As an isolated instance of surgical ingenuity and resourcefulness, the episode would be interesting rather than significant; but Dr. Matas's ever-growing practice, crowded with cases that lent themselves to such word-of-mouth report, was making him one of the most talked-of individuals in New Orleans.

Specialization was still far from becoming the rule in medical practice. Only in the largest communities could a few outstanding physicians afford to restrict their professional activities to ophthalmology, let us say.* Thus Dr. Matas was not yet merely a surgeon but a general practitioner as well. As such, he was absorbed at this time in a special study of the ominous rise of typhoid-fever incidence at New Orleans during 1893–94. It was during the latter year that, on April 18, Dr. Joseph Holt, president of a newly organized New Orleans Sewerage and Drainage Company, turned the initial spade of earth to inaugurate the first subsurface sewerage disposal in the city's nearly two centuries of existence.

This had been a great occasion, with Mayor Fitzpatrick, ex-Mayor Shakespeare, and scores of other high dignitaries among those present. In his address Dr. Holt likened New Orleans to a gross living creature, explaining:

"It is without those natural passageways for cleansing and keeping pure . . . its own organism. . . . No marvel that offensive odors and disgusting sights repel! No wonder that [we suffer] a high annual death rate with all its implied sickness and industrial loss. . . . [Masterful surgery] is about to begin—without anesthesia—a brilliant operation in laparotomy, not restoring but actually creating an entire urinary and intestinal tract, and establishing—pardon, Your Honor— an artificial anus!"

But the work thus begun in April with oratorical ruffles and flourishes, was years away from reducing or even leveling off the dreadful rise of typhoid-fever cases. In June 1894, eight were reported, not to mention the strong probability that some, if not most, of the eleven deaths attributed to "unclassified" malarial fevers were likewise

---

* In this same year of 1894, Dr. Xavier Galezowski, one of the renowned ophthalmologists under whom Rudolph's father had studied in Paris during the early 1860's, received a $25,000 fee for a visit to Persia, where he was called to treat a son of the shah.

really typhoid fatalities. Vital statistics for the following month listed ten typhoid or typho-malarial deaths, and nine under the heading of "unclassified" malaria, i.e., any fevers that did not yield to treatment with quinine. The grim roster for August ascribed ten deaths to typhoid and typho-malaria and eleven more to unclassified malaria.

One of those August fatalities was the death of Dr. Albert Baldwin Miles, who had somehow contracted typhoid in the Charity Hospital where he was still house surgeon, after completing his term as Rudolph's predecessor in the presidency of the Louisiana State Medical Society and his first full year as professor of surgery on the Tulane faculty. His death certificate, signed by Dr. J. D. Bloom, cited as official cause, "typhoid fever and hemorrhage," and gave his age as forty-two. His untimely demise vacated Tulane's chair of surgery for the second time in less than eighteen months. Speculation as to who would be selected to fill what was regarded as, next to the deanship, the top post in the medical faculty was set off afresh.

Rudolph had no idea at the time of aspiring to the vacancy. As before, he told Adrienne, during one of their morning tête-à-têtes, Dr. Souchon was the logical man for the place. "Dr. Souchon's appointment to head the Department of Surgery," he continued, "would vacate the professorship of anatomy; and since I have been demonstrator now for ten unbroken years, I am the logical one to succeed Professor Souchon—unless——"

. . . . Unless Dean Chaillé still harbored resentment against Rudolph's intransigence in the matter of the Medical Practices compromise; unless Dean Chaillé still felt vindictively aggrieved over the refusal of a young man he had befriended to go along with a course his benevolent patron so trenchantly advocated; unless Dean Chaillé still held a grudge.

All too soon it became obvious that Dr. Chaillé not only opposed the transfer of Dr. Souchon from the Department of Anatomy but even vigorously opposed the appointment of his once-favored protégé to a professorship. There was ground for his stand in regard to Dr. Souchon, because he was almost beyond challenge the foremost American anatomist. To transfer him from the headship of that department to surgery would inevitably weaken the former without bettering the latter, since many others qualified to fill the chair of surgery were available.

Hence Dean Chaillé proposed that a leading surgeon from some other community be called to the Tulane faculty. Specifically he named, as his choice for the Miles succession, Dr. Louis McLane Tiffany, professor of surgery at the University of Maryland in Baltimore.

But he had not reckoned on the almost idolatrous devotion of lay New Orleans to one of the community's best known citizens. His suggestion of going to Baltimore for a professor of surgery touched off such a storm as had never before set either New Orleans or any other comparable community by the ears over so academic an issue as a faculty appointment. Newspaper editorials volleyed and thundered, even physicians wrote letters and gave interviews to the lay press, and the public at large simply bombarded the medical faculty and the editors of all daily newspapers with vehement letters of remonstrance; the Sullivan clan made a Third Ward issue of it, and that counted for something, since John was already courting Katherine, the beautiful daughter of Mayor John Fitzpatrick; grateful patients all but erected barricades in the streets; medical groups passed formal resolutions.

"I cannot refrain," said Dr. Frederick W. Parham, "from expressing the view that a serious mistake will be made if Dr. Tiffany be really asked to come to the surgical chair. . . . However well some of us may understand the reasons for this action, it will be . . . to the non-professional world an advertisement of the incapacity of New Orleans' men."

Dr. Andrew Smyth, legendary pioneer in aneurismal surgery, was more vehement:

"It is nothing short of an outrage," he informed the *Times-Democrat*, which quoted him to that effect in a strong editorial expression, "that the faculty of Tulane University should entertain the idea of going to Baltimore to fill the chair recently made vacant by the death of Dr. Miles."

Every one of the city's four newspapers (the *Times-Democrat* and *Picayune* in the morning field, and the *Item* and the *States* in the afternoon) had plumped for Matas uneqivocally from the beginning in their editorial columns. Moreover, an open letter, signed by no less than fifty of the city's best-known physicians, was printed in all the dailies. Among the signers were Smyth, Parham, Salomon, Scheppegrell and De Roaldes.

"Let the Matas wave roll on," rhapsodized one Charles Thompson in the *Times-Democrat*, "until, borne upon the gathering flow of un-limited popularity our distinquished surgeon and illustrious citizen is securely seated in the Chair of Surgery at Tulane."

The "gathering flow" thus gained such proportions as would brook no denial. A meeting of the medical faculty was called for September 28; returning from his summer residence at Asheville, Dean Chaillé dispatched the following letter by hand to his former protégé on September 27, with the word "Confidential" scrawled holographically across the top of the small sheet:

"Dear Dr.

"Please call without fail at my house tomorrow at 10 A.M. and oblige

"Yours truly

"Stanford E. Chaillé, M.D., Dean."

No documentation has come down to us about what was discussed during that hour of private conversation in Dean Chaillé's home on the morning of September 28. But from a letter the dean wrote in North Carolina immediately after the faculty meeting, it is safe to assume that certain criticisms of Dr. Matas's tardiness in meeting his classes, his proneness to overstay his allotted time, and perhaps his verbosity were mentioned. Presumably the popular clamor in behalf of Dr. Matas must have been touched upon, for the *States* had said editorially a day or two before that "it seems certain when [Dr. Chaillé] discovers [on his return] that so many of the prominent physicians and surgeons here are against the appointment of the Baltimore surgeon he will gracefully yield. . . . Not only have the physicians of the city taken a position in the matter, but the public itself has come forward with an expression of its views."

In all likelihood the discussion was followed by a sentimental and perhaps even emotional reconciliation. At the very least, Dr. Chaillé must have agreed to support his former favorite for the professorship, since at four o'clock that same afternoon Rudolph was unanimously designated professor pro tem by the Tulane faculty.

"Dr. Matas was a very busy man last night," reported the *Times-Democrat* the next morning, in describing the "steady stream" that literally poured through the modest office suite at 72 Rampart Street. Continued the *Times-Democrat*:

"The Professor tried in vain to stay the flow of compliments and praise showered upon him, and when permitted to speak, uttered broken fragments of sentences that would have made a continuous statement in this order:

"'Why wish me continued success? What can I hope for more than this? What honor could I desire greater than this? . . . . Of course the Chair of Surgery was my ambition but I did not think I was entitled to it. It was fortunate for me indeed that the faculty would not consent to have any but Dr. Souchon in the chair of anatomy, the chair to which I aspired because I thought he would be raised from it. When he found what were the wishes of the Faculty as regarded him he generously withdrew his name, and then the claims that my friends had made for me could be recognized.'"

However shining this triumph, Rudolph must have been keenly, perhaps agonizingly, conscious of the fact that no member of his family was present to share it with him. He had telegraphed his father in Tucson, but apparently received no direct reply, since all other letters of congratulation, press clippings, and the like were preserved by him in a cherished scrapbook. He had also written to his mother, but she would not receive the letter for at least a fortnight; and if that bitter, grasping old woman, then nearing her seventies, or her waspish spinster of a daughter ever acknowledged Rudolph's dazzling success, no evidence of the fact was preserved.

The poignancy of this lack is heavily underscored by the fact that in his scrapbook there remained indeed one telegram from a woman. The first teacher from whom he had learned American mores and speech wired him from Brownsville on October 5, just a week after his appointment: "Heartfelt congratulations on success in your professional career from your friend and exteacher Mary C. Butler."

Sharp pangs of loneliness on another score must have been in the background of his emotions throughout the great evening, while visitors filed in and out. As his housekeeper, Adrienne could not be present even to help serve the *'ti' noir* cups with which the kitchen kept the office-reception room supplied until the last visitor had left. This vitiated even the continuing enjoyment he found in reading newspaper editorials as these went on from day to day to laud the faculty for having chosen so wisely and so well.

In its October issue the *New Orleans Medical and Surgical Journal* used for its frontispiece a photograph of the new professor of surgery, a studio portrait showing to the best advantage his glossy, heavy mustache, the carefully barbered beard, the heavy shock of black hair meticulously parted along the left side, the ready-tied Ascot scarf about the stand-up collar, the small vee left by piped coat lapels, though scarf and beard effectively concealed any glimpse of stiff-bosomed shirt somewhere within this investiture. This same photograph was reproduced in the *Times-Democrat* of November 2, with cut lines identifying and describing it as a picture of Nicholas II, Czar of all the Russias —a circumstance Rudolph noted in his diary among other and more professional entries for the day.

The long letter Dr. Matas received from his dean in Asheville, on the other hand, was calculated to bring the one-sided eulogies into balance. Dr. Chaillé pointed out that one of the most frequent criticisms of his newest professor's teaching methods was to the effect that "Dr. Matas will never be able, 'certainly not in his first year, to be always on hand promptly when his bell strikes, and to finish promptly when the bell again strikes at the end of the hour. The Polyclinic complained of him much in these regards, and he will give you [the dean] trouble

which you will not stand.' About this last, he is certainly right, for
should you deserve such criticism as to our college, I would very surely
make your professorship a hell to you, as much as is in my power.

"As I have already warned you, I regard lack of punctuality at
assigned lectures, for which you have been amply paid . . . as down-
right dishonesty. The faculty order of lectures pledges you to certain
hours, and your obligations to your colleagues and to your students
binds you to certain hours. If you trespass over your hour, then you are
. . . guilty of the presumption that in your opinion your teaching is
more important to the students than is your colleagues'."

There were times when Rudolph sat in his coupé outside the
Richardson Memorial Building, engrossed in some newly arrived publication from among the papers with which the saddlebaglike recep-
tacles on the inner side of each buggy door were filled. On such occasions
one or another of his students would come down the broad steps of
the school to remind him that his class awaited the presence of their
mentor. It must also be confessed that despite his best effort to be
punctual in terminating his didactic discourses, he did occasionally
trespass upon the time of his colleagues. However, his instruction and
his operating technique were so inspiring to his students, his success
as a teacher so marked, that the Board of Administrators unanimously
confirmed the faculty's nomination of him to the professorship pro tem,
and on April 24, 1895, as the first scholastic term of his appointment
drew to a close, the faculty voted without dissent to make his appointment permanent. Rudolph Matas remained professor of surgery at
Tulane for 32 years.

Surrounded by well-wishers as he entered on his new duties, he was
yet prey to the gnawing dissatisfaction of being unable to share any
of these splendors, save in the privacy of the rapidly deteriorating
Rampart Street home, with the woman he loved. She was still to him
the same slim girl he had adored since he first caught a fleeting glimpse
of her. Those fine, dark eyes still met his with serene trust and understanding, just as they had looked upon him since their paths met, to
run side by side, even though they could not merge.

No one now knows just when, during the closing days of 1894 or at
the dawn of 1895, they discovered they were free to marry. Somehow,
somewhere, and somewhen, Adrienne's former husband, the father of
her two children, had remarried. His nuptials were sanctioned by the
Church; obviously the first marriage must have been annulled. This
meant that he and Adrienne were neither separated nor divorced, that
the Church would sanction her marriage too.

That must have been a tremendous moment when, perhaps during
one of their morning tête-à-têtes, after Adrienne brought him his coffee

and put studs in his shirt, and was adjusting the cravat he never learned how to fasten, Rudolph formally asked her to be his wife.

Admittedly, she could not yet publicly share either his new-won glories or his exalted social contacts, like the evening when he had dined at the home of Dr. de Roaldes along with Drs. Lewis, Parham, Souchon, Michinard and Bickham with their wives, and the entire party repaired to the French Opera House afterwards to hear *Rigoletto*. But within the very near future she could and should do so. Perhaps, during that evening at the opera, he felt a thrust of envy of the colleagues whose wives accompanied them while he could not yet have at his side the one woman whose image he had ever cherished as that of his beloved, the one with whom he most longed to share the joy and the exultation of being "the Professor." But now the barriers were down; before the current opera season was over Adrienne would attend such performances with him. He had asked his dearest one to be his wife.

One feels that despite her metamorphosis in figure and in years since the long-ago days of girlhood, "Dearest Adri"—as he addressed her throughout their marriage—the plump matron, verging on 35, gave as tremulous an assent to her sweetheart's proposal as though she had been a debutante dancing at her first Carnival ball. No doubt they laughed joyously then, in flooding awareness of long-deferred fulfillment, now at last attainable, and then turned to the task of making workaday, practical arrangements to be married.

A conventional wedding in New Orleans would obviously involve embarrassing revivals of an unhappy past. In this dilemma, Rudolph sought the aid of two close friends—General T. M. Miller, an attorney, and Dr. Arthur de Roaldes, the physician who had put a newly-graduated Dr. Matas, not yet twenty years old at the time, on the Charity Hospital staff as visiting surgeon. General Miller had connections among the leading attorneys in Vicksburg, and to one of them, Murray F. Smith, he wrote asking that all be made ready for a civil wedding on the night of January 19th, with licenses, certificates, and other essential documents provided in advance, against the arrival of the night train from New Orleans.

On that Saturday in January 1895, Rudolph held his clinic as usual from eleven to twelve, then repaired to the modest home—which could soon be vacated, at last!—in Rampart Street, where a radiant yet oddly shy Adrienne Goslee (she had used her maiden name in giving General Miller the data for the marriage license) awaited him. Together they walked sedately up Rampart Street to the Illinois Central depot, where General Miller and Dr. de Roaldes joined them as they boarded the Yazoo and Mississippi Valley local train that followed the Mississippi's meandering course upstream to Vicksburg.

The day had turned off chilly, and the coal stoves at either end of the parlor car shed a grateful warmth over the passengers. Darkness, falling early, shut out the smudgy vista of small river towns: Laplace, set amid cane fields newly denuded of their sweet harvest; Lutcher, surrounded by the neat-rowed plantations that produced the world's entire supply of perique tobacco. Night had brought "good dark" before they reached Baton Rouge; it was well past midnight when the train chugged into the grimy station of Vicksburg.

Murray Smith, beaming, welcomed them with a marriage license duly signed by Cooley Mann, circuit clerk, and J. B. Dabney, his deputy. They did not spare the horses as they drove to the home of F. W. Little, Justice of the Peace. Since it was well past midnight when they arrived, it was technically on Sunday, January 20, that Mr. Little pronounced Rudolph and Adrienne man and wife, regardless of the date on their previously prepared marriage certificate. There was not even time for a token wedding breakfast; their train left Vicksburg on its return trip at 1:15 A.M. Rudolph had reserved the only drawing room for the journey. General Miller and Dr. de Roaldes took seats forward in the smoker. The bridal party was back in New Orleans by 10 A.M.

That, at least, is the hour set down by Rudolph in the notebook diary he had kept ever since taking over the Chair of Surgery. In its pages he had entered under each date what lectures he had delivered, what patients he had seen, occasionally what theater he had visited, and with whom he had dined.

But for Sunday, January 20, 1895, his wedding day, only a five-word note was inscribed. It read: "Nothing much of special interest." He had to wait until the next day, Monday, to give the tenants in the Garden District mansion their formal notice to vacate.

CHAPTER XX

For the newlyweds there was no *lune de miel*. The day after his marriage Rudolph followed his accustomed routine of classroom, hospital, and patient calls. Arthur and Lucian, now his stepsons, had addressed him for years as *Teur*—a monosyllable to which their mother's formal *Monsieur le Docteur* had been reduced in the intimacy of the household; they continued so to address him. In view of the approaching transfer of the *ménage* to lordly St. Charles Avenue from down-at-the-heels Rampart Street, few alterations in established living arrangements were initiated at the old home.

Rudolph and Adrienne did go shopping together for furniture, once or twice a week, thriftily avoiding the golden-oak splendors of Grand Rapids modernity, as displayed by the big new furniture stores, and searching out what would one day be known as antique shops along Royal Street for disdained and abandoned four-posters of solid rosewood and mahogany, heavily carved sets of black walnut "parlor" furniture upholstered in fading brocade, and other such items of *démodé* Empire luxury. That was Adrienne's doing, of course; thus and only thus had the homes of people who mattered been furnished in the days of her girlhood under the tutelage of that classic scholar, her patrician grandfather.

Naturally, Rudolph had informed his parents at once of his marriage, writing to his father in Tucson and to his mother in San Felíu. Narciso, the ineradicably romantic dynast, was literally overjoyed; Teresa flew into a black and bitter fury. Though neither of the replies they sent their son was found among the latter's papers, it is abundantly clear from subsequent developments what the reaction of the twain had been.

Narciso, still enjoying a large and quite lucrative practice, was lonely. Louise and her daughter had never returned from Los Angeles. He had prospered moderately, and though yet dominated by the conviction that he would become Croesus-wealthy by day after next through the mining ventures he now backed, he also had some more solid investments, like stock in the Tucson Traction Company, which would keep him from want. The thought that his "dear little son"—the child prodigy who had joined him in endowing the gargoyles of Notre Dame with names and personalities—would now perpetuate his sire's Hereu lineage enthralled him. He, the individual, would die one day; but the flesh of his flesh would remain immortal, going on and ever on from one generation to the next.

Teresa and her testy daughter, who, though only twenty-four, seems to have been apprenticed at birth to shrewishly invincible spinsterhood, took ship for New Orleans at the earliest feasible moment. Their obvious determination to break up this unholy marriage, or in any case make Rudolph pay dearly for the privilege of keeping it intact, fits accurately into the sustained behavior pattern of their embittered lives. Ostensibly, Teresa justified her rancor to herself with pious references to the sacramental view of marriage, according to which a divorcée who remarried was simply living in open adultery.

But she was quite ready, even eager, to surrender such convictions for cash on the nail. That is precisely what she had done when her husband divorced her to marry Louisa Mallett Aphold, to whom he was already united at the time by civil ceremony, following an *ex parte* territorial divorce in Arizona.

Rudolph's first serene summer as a man of family had waned; the second year of his professorship, confirmed and made permanent the previous spring, had begun; Lucian and Arthur were enrolled in Dyer's exclusive private school for boys as day pupils, the St. Charles Avenue mansion was a settled and smoothly functioning household. But the idyllic season of contentment was abruptly terminated when word arrived in the early fall that Teresa and her daughter were returning to New Orleans. Apparently nothing was said to indicate whether this was to be a brief visit or an indefinite resumption of residence.

Rudolph told his wife the news late that night, in his second-floor study-living room, after the boys had retired. Adrienne spent a great deal of time there with him now, for she was learning to use the typewriter, a basket-model Remington whose carriage had to be raised every few minutes to enable the typist to read what had been imprinted on the paper. He was enormously proud of her and was coming to depend more and more on her secretarial aid, though the old taboo against "straightening up" the papers on his desk was still in force.

Adrienne remained thoughtfully silent for some moments, after hearing the news, then asked where Teresa and her daughter would stay. Taken aback by the idea that such a question should ever be raised, Rudolph replied that they would live with him and the other members of his family, just as he and his family, visiting San Felíu, would be expected to live with them.

For perhaps the only time during all the twenty-three happy years of their marriage, Adrienne, the gentle wife, ordinarily submissive to her husband's lightest wish, laid down an ultimatum. She had long been aware of the feelings Teresa had never troubled to conceal. Had not Mrs. Matas put it bluntly enough in 1886 when she sought to breach even the platonic relationship between her son and the girl he later married by putting the width of an ocean permanently between them? Let there be no mistake about it, therefore. She, Adrienne, would never live under the same roof with either or both of the women who, whatever their relationship to her husband, had made unforgivable references to her husband's wife. Either they or Adrienne would live somewhere else than in the St. Charles Avenue residence that had been the Matas home since April.

Rudolph was deeply troubled but worked out what to him seemed a reasonable compromise. Obviously, as a leading citizen and pillar of the community, he could not close the door of his home to his mother and sister. But on the ground that some essential remodeling and an already scheduled early departure for summer research in Washington necessitated it, he closed off part of the house, made Arthur and Lucian boarding pupils instead of day scholars at Dyer's, took a suite for himself and Adrienne at the Cosmopolitan Hotel in Royal Street, and was then ready to welcome his mother and sister to the habitable section of his home.

The Cosmopolitan's parlors, lobbies, bar, and smoke-filled rooms were the focal points of Louisiana's stormy politics. As 1895 drew to a close Rudolph and Adrienne found themselves engulfed among the participants of no less than three major engagements. Following the panic of 1893, William McKinley and Garret Hobart were to restore to the American workman the era of the full dinner pail. The Republicans of Louisiana—naturally a high-protection state by reason of its sugar interests—were moving heaven and earth to destroy the odious linkage between Republicanism and carpetbaggery. They even went so far as to organize a self-styled Lily White Republican party, from which Negroes were excluded as rigidly as they were banned from Democratic suffrage. The Lily Whites referred to the old-line Republican die-hards as the Black and Tans.

So much for the national stage. In New Orleans a reform crusade was seeking to unseat an entrenched municipal bossdom, and a number of prominent physicians were given places as candidates on the Citizens' League slate. Finally, in the state at large, the Lottery interests, plainly *in extremis,* were making a last-ditch fight to keep one of their archfoes, Governor Murphey J. Foster, from being re-elected.

Though the tactical maneuvers of all three conflicts swirled about him, Rudolph could have devoted little attention to their marches and countermarches, for he was offering his mother and sister the same sort of sop his father had used to such good purpose in purchasing peace from them years earlier: money, represented and secured by real estate. During the previous December he had gone to some lengths to make Teresa's rental property more attractive to tenants and thus more remunerative, by purchasing an adjoining building and renting the entire parcel as a unit for $1140 a year in place of the previous $700. Thus, within a fortnight of Teresa's arrival in October, Rudolph made to her and to Elvira the following offer:

He would sell the adjoining property to his sister Elvira for $1500 which was $500 less than he had paid for it the year before. He would then lease the combined parcel from his mother and sister for ten years at a rental of $1500 a year, payable in advance. This was substantially more than the property was bringing or could bring on the open market. He would additionally make his mother and sister the beneficiaries of a $10,000 life-insurance policy, to protect their interests in case death kept him from carrying out the terms of his lease. Moreover, in purchasing her portion of the package, Elvira need not put up a penny of cash, since he would consider payment in lieu of the first year's rental.

There was just one stipulation, which the lease, formally executed before Nicholas Browse Trist, Notary Public, on Novermber 18, 1895, set forth in the following words: "That the Lessee shall have the right, which he hereby reserves, to cancel the lease at any time upon the return of the Lessors, or either of them, to New Orleans, Louisiana." By way of still further inducement, Rudolph agreed to pay all taxes and special assessments and to maintain the property at his own ex-pense during the term of the lease, which was to be automatically renewable for an additional ten years at its expiration in 1905.

In sum, Rudolph offered his mother and sister $30,000, payable in twenty installments, plus ownership of a substantially valuable piece of urban realty, on the one condition that they leave New Orleans never to return. They accepted the offer in all haste, consummating it in

December. Then, without reasons other than that they wanted a larger cash payment in hand, they declared they would stay in New Orleans until it was received. Apparently the technicality that thus they did not "return" to New Orleans kept the lease from being canceled.

The final conference must have been a stormy one. It is clearly evident from subsequent developments that Rudolph, infuriated beyond endurance by some remarks his sister made—they must have concerned Adrienne—slapped her soundly. He regretted this, of course, and tried to bring about a reconciliation, but was inflexible on one point: he and his wife would spend the summer in Washington and during their absence his mother and sister might continue to reside at the St. Charles Avenue home; but on Rudolph's return in the fall, he would resume occupancy of this home with his family, and without house guests.

Teresa and Elvira did not give ground. Within a month after the Matas departure in April, they put up the Dryades Street property for sale at public auction, including the portion which had been sold to Elvira in November. It was purchased by one Henry Rooney for $10,577, subject to a lease which still had three years to run.

However, Rooney cannily insisted on a judical determination of the validity of Elvira's title to her part of the property, and so brought a friendly suit, which was adjudicated in his favor, the court holding that regardless of the circumstances, Rudolph's "sale" to his sister was good. The transaction was thus not finally consummated until August 18, 1896, which makes it almost certain that Rudolph, deep in his researches in Washington by that time, knew nothing of it until his return a month later.

He was now working from early morning till far into the night, utterly engrossed in a search for anything that had ever been published in any language, land, or era about the surgical creation of an artificial opening for the bowel of an infant in those rare cases when babies came into the world with an "imperforate anus." Two years earlier, during the summer of 1894, a wealthy young matron whose family physician Rudolph was, had been delivered of her third child, a daughter. The birth was apparently normal in every respect; but within some thirty hours it was discovered that the baby's digestive canal ended in a blind sac, with no external opening. Unless such an opening could be created by surgery, the infant was doomed.

Details of the operation Dr. Matas undertook constitute a classic of surgical literature. Rudolph devised hitherto untried techniques, labored and talked incessantly through a series of surgical interludes, rinsed his hands in his special font, emerged from the operating theater wiping his face on the hem of his gown, still talking. The baby's life was saved for the moment, but no one could say how long or how well the artificial duct would continue to function. It was for this reason that Rudolph decided to spend the summer of 1896 in research that should at least assemble into a single treatise anything ever previously published about such cases, even though this would make it impossible for him to attend the American Surgical Association's meeting in New York or the American Medical Association's annual convention in Atlanta.

Dr. Matas's almost fantastically daring surgery proved entirely successful. The newborn girl infant of August 1894 grew to normal adulthood and is, in this year of 1960, a happy, healthy grandmother. Dr. Matas's report, published late in 1896, incorporated not merely a meticulously worded and illustrated description of his procedures but the all-embracing review of the previous literature about such cases which he had been gathering.

"Dr. Matas is away for a much-needed rest," reported the Medical Items department of the *New Orleans Medical and Surgical Journal,* "and also, almost a paradox, to do some literary work in Washington." It was no paradox to him. Release from the nagging, rancorous greed of his mother and sister, freedom from the small interruptions of private practice and teaching, fascinating work—all this re-enforced by the beatific realization that in their suite at the old Willard his wife was waiting for him—who could desire a more pleasant way of life?

Adrienne, twiddling her thumbs all through the long, scorching hot days of a Washington midsummer, found the situation far less to her liking. She finally announced that she was bored with nothing to do and no one to talk to except during the few moments her husband would spare from his work. So she sent for Lucian, who, like his elder brother Arthur, had remained as a vacation boarder in the Dyer School, along with the sons of wealthy Latin American families who could not well make the long ocean journey home and return during the relatively brief weeks of summer release from classroom attendance.

Lucian's arrival left Rudolph all the more freedom to devote himself to the task in hand, for Adrienne and her son made sight-seeing trips about the capital each day and once reported excitedly that they had seen President Cleveland drive out from the White House to Capitol Hill in his fine carriage. On another wonderful day they took the Interurban to Mount Vernon and roamed through the grounds and buildings from which George Washington had gone forth to wrest colonial rule from Great Britain.

Rudolph usually took them to dinner at the Willard (American Plan), where lavish courses might follow one another indefinitely, among them such items as bear steaks, roast elk, wild turkey, and that epitome of the Mauve Decade's luxury dining, quail on toast. And once they were joined at dinner by Dr. Souchon, with whom Rudolph had planned to attend the surgical and medical conventions and who spoke with shining enthusiasm of the pilgrimage he had made to Montgomery, en route to New York, so that he could visit every place hallowed by association, in one fashion or another, with Dr. Marion Sims.

So the weeks slipped by, and before Rudolph was really aware of summer's passing, he was brought up short by the realization that Lucian must return to school and that the opening of his own courses at Tulane in mid-October was only a fortnight off. Adrienne reminded him also that much still remained to be done in the way of putting the St. Charles Avenue home in order. Heaven alone knew in what condition it had been left at the time of his mother's and sister's departure.

Upon his return, Rudolph learned to his shocked amazement that though they had left his home for a modest *pension* in the Esplanade Avenue area, his mother and sister had sold the Dryades property and felt no further concern with regard to the cancellation clause he had specifically reserved in executing his lease. Not only had they canceled it themselves but they were ready to confront him with an even more disagreeable ultimatum, as a letter from Benjamin E. Forman, counselor at law, made distressingly plain. Under date of December 8, it read:

"Dear Sir:

"Miss Elvira Matas has consulted me about her right to reparation for her injuries when you so far forgot yourself and lost control last January. She has waited and hoped for a private arrangement which will not make so disagreeable a matter public.

"But my instructions are to file suit unless this matter is satisfactorily arranged by 10 A.M. of the 10th Dec.

"I am, sir, respectfully,

"Your obedient servant,
Benjamin E. Forman."

What follows is to some degree a matter of conjectural reconstruction. In view of a subsequent letter from Forman it is quite obvious that Rudolph, with only one day of grace conceded to him, turned for advice to the man who had befriended him from the first and who had nonetheless threatened "to make your professorship a hell to you" if he were lax in meeting its commitments. This was Stanford Chaillé.

Dr. Chaillé would have been prosecutor, judge, jury and executioner if the facts had come to him from some other source, or if they had been bandied about the public prints. But as quasi confessor, he was kindness and understanding itself and took matters up directly with

Elvira's attorney. Naturally this gave him a terrific leverage, for the principal weapon on which a shrewd attorney would have relied was Rudolph's presumed readiness to do almost anything to keep the facts from coming to the knowledge of Tulane's authorities. Thus we find that on December 21 Forman wrote, not to Rudolph but to Dean Chaillé, as follows:

"My dear Sir:

"I have seen Miss M. and she is very firm in her ideas. She says she wishes the sum of $5000 for the support of her mother, and is satisfied if it is given to her mother. She will not accept anything less than $5000 of which $1000 is cash, the residue to be paid in one, two, three and four years, secured either by mortage or personal instrument and bearing 7 per cent interest. She is not willing for Davila to be the depository, but of course she will accept you as a depository. She will agree not to annoy the doctor or his family. The sum is not any more than he may reasonably be expected to pay for the support of his mother, and it will be taken in full satisfaction of all demands made for reparation."

"Very truly yours,
"Benjamin E. Forman."

To be sure, Rudolph's income had reached a point at which the additional $5000 his affectionate sister was thus sweating out of him on the shabby pretense that it was for their mother's support would deprive him of nothing except personal dignity. The conviction that this was less Elvira's idea than a scheme in which their mother was using her would not down. It seemed impossible that this Elvira was the same prim and studious darling to whom he had written so affectionately from Havana not many years ago.

"My dearest little sister," he had addressed her on Sept. 1, 1879, less than two weeks before his birthday. "Your charming little letter dated 29th ult. has just been received, and I must say that its perusal has been a source of the highest gratification to me, in fact, the remarkable excellency of your composition and the select French you write, which with the exception of two errors that I could find would be creditable to either a youthful Lamartine or a La Fontaine of whom you seem so justly fond, obliges me for fear of a just criticism to write to you this short answer in English, a language more familiar to me and one in which I may be better able to express my thoughts, besides, a letter in this language may also be somewhat instructive to you and I understand you are devoting your attention to the study of English as well as French.

"The last thoughts in your letter so full of tender sympathy and enchanting candor are mixed with a sympathy and grace that is incomparable and which I only could answer if I were near you by covering you with kisses, but alas I must satisfy myself by sending these to you by letter.

"My numerous occupations prevent me at present from giving you an account of the beautiful scenery and other pleasant things to be seen in Cuba, and I will be obliged to reserve my narrative till my return home, when I will chat with you and tell you all about my travels and adventures.

"Give Mama many thanks for me and you my little darling sister receive your brother's tenderest and most affectionate caresses."

Rodolfo."

This same darling sister whose letters had been so full of tender sympathy and enchanting candor was now letting herself be used by their embittered mother to mulct him of money over and above the demands he had already met. This was a bitter potion; but since the bargain was struck without further delay, one may assume that its outcome was the most welcome gift that Christmas season could have bestowed upon even the sorrowfully disillusioned head of a household.

Thus the year ended as benignly as its beginning had been ill-starred; but the twelvemonth that followed was one of omen. Classes entering Tulane's medical department were the smallest in years; the great depression of 1893 was still largely unrelieved; not yet had the Dingley protective tariff replenished the nation's shrinking gold reserves. Indeed, the inflationary trend of the times would not be halted until 1898, when the Klondike sent a fresh stream of gold into the national economy.

Threatening overflows and levee crevasses that spring of 1897 once again necessitated postponement for a year of the annual May Medical Society meetings. But eighty-three new physicians, graduating from Tulane in April, received diplomas; and these, incidentally, for the first time in the institution's history, were worded in English instead of Latin.

The climax of the year's disasters, however, was another major yellow-fever epidemic which swept the Gulf coast from Florida to Texas. It originated in Mississippi, probably in Ocean Springs, a small port. But this and all the other towns along that short stretch of coast—Pass Christian, Bay St. Louis, Gulfport, Biloxi—were crowded with New Orleans commuters, who traveled daily to and from their summer homes via unscreened suburban trains which thus bore both incipient fever patients and mosquitoes back and forth. By the time Mississippi's health authorities reluctantly admitted the visitation's true nature, Bronze John held New Orleans firmly in his grip.

Along with the rest of the coastal area, the city was isolated by a federal quarantine. As one collateral result, Rudolph was balked for the third successive year in his desire to attend a meeting of the Southern Surgical Congress, where he had planned to deliver his paper on the operation that had saved the life of a girl baby three years before. In November 1895, negotiations for purchasing peace from his mother and sister kept him in New Orleans; the following year his researches had held him in Washington, compelling absence from all professional meetings; in 1897 the federal yellow-fever quarantine barred both him and Dr. Souchon from leaving the city. It even delayed the opening of medical classes at Tulane until November 29. Hence the papers prepared by Drs. Souchon and Matas were read by title only at the Southern Surgical Congress in St. Louis and were never actually delivered.

All this while the *New Orleans Medical and Surgical Journal's* articles referred to the epidemic month after month as "the prevailing fever." Not until the December issue did it commit to print the previously shunned phrase, "yellow fever," except in the vital statistics issued by the City Board of Health, which had listed the following grim tabulation of deaths due to the epidemic: September, 28; October, 158, November, 105, and December, 7.

The death toll was nothing like the appalling casualty list of 1878, but its impact was multiplied by two factors. The first was general disappointment over failure of what had been hopefully regarded as invincible quarantine regulations; the second, had Mississippi's small ports maintained the same safeguards, the epidemic could have been averted. New Orleans therefore led the demand for united action, pointing out that its quarantine system had functioned admirably until nearby communities, less scrupulous in enforcing adequate precautions, had admitted Bronze John, who had then entered New Orleans by the back door. Even the Mississippians agreed that a joint conference of sanitarians representing all the Gulf and South Atlantic states should be called on to draw up a uniform code of quarantine regulations to be applied rigidly to *all* ports in which shipments from tropic harbors were received. Meanwhile the coy pretense that no such disease as yellow fever had devastated the coast was stripped away.

"Let's not quarrel over whether it was yellow fever, dengue, or malaria," urged an official proclamation by the public-health authorities of Mississippi's Hancock county, "but make sure that we don't have it next year." Householders from the affected area were urged to open their homes wide on every very cold day from November to March and particularly to carry all blankets and other bedding into the open on days when temperatures dropped near or even below the freezing point.

At the same time, Congress was memorialized to finance further fever researches, and finally did authorize President McKinley, by joint resolution, to take such steps, through treaties or otherwise, as "would induce the governments of tropical American ports to secure proper sanitation of these harbors and of vessels clearing thence for the United States."

Mr. McKinley was preparing to do this when, at 9:40 P.M., February 15, 1898, the battleship *Maine* was blown up while lying at anchor under the frowning battlements of Morro Castle in Havana harbor. "Remember the Maine!" thundered across the land. "You furnish the pictures and I'll furnish the war!" cabled William Randolph Hearst from New York to a somewhat bewildered staff artist, Frederic Remington, in Cuba.

And before the last boy in blue had quitted Cuban shores, further investigation into the causes of yellow fever had become academic, and the scorned theories of Carlos Juan Finlay, as well as Rudolph Matas's boyish faith in them, had been vindicated beyond all further doubt or challenge.

By that time Spain had lost its last remaining foothold in the Western hemisphere, and the United States had become a ranking world power. But the most bloodthirsty despot overthrown, through what today would hardly be classed as a police action, was Bronze John.

CHAPTER XXI

The Spanish-American War was too short and above all too one-sided to generate the amateur spy hunts so popular with home-front patriots during the First and Second World Wars. Admittedly, at the outbreak of hostilities, the Regular Army of the United States could have been tucked away in any of today's major football stadia; but the so-called Volunteers—Rough Riders under Colonel Theodore Roosevelt, Tennesseans under Colonel Cordell Hull, Mississippi Immunes under James K. Vardaman, and other units of the same genre—made up a recklessly audacious force which the Spaniards found irresistible in combat.

The result was a steady succession of sweeping victories, in the light of which no one charged Americans of Spanish blood with signaling troop information from Key West to the Boy King in Madrid. No chauvinist insisted on rechristening Spanish omelets as Liberty Eggs or hurled the epithet "pro-Spaniard" at men like Rudolph Matas, though the latter made it plain, then and thereafter, that "during the Spanish-American War, when the question came up of my enlisting in the United States Army of Invasion in Cuba, I said I wouldn't mind serving the United States Army as a doctor and would be ready at all times to treat the troops in my capacity as a physician and surgeon, but I should never go on the battlefield with a gun in hand prepared to shoot Spaniards."

There had naturally been an immediate call for immunes by all branches of the armed forces. In the United States, "Bronze John" was a periodic visitor, arriving unexpectedly from time to time during the late summer and autumn. But in Cuba there had not been a day since 1761 when the island was without yellow fever. Dr. Matas must have realized perfectly well that as a surgeon he would be a noncombatant. In fact, that very spring the Orleans Parish Medical Society sponsored a resolution to exempt surgeons in the field even from being held as prisoners of war when captured.

"What credit to us if we could announce to the world that we no longer deprive the enemy's wounded of their surgeons!" enthused the *Journal*. It also pointed out that "when a man on the way up the rounds of a very long ladder to success drops from his position and surrenders all he may have yet gained to take a place on the field of glory and of action for a nation's honor with only the opportunity of hard work, tempered with deprivation and with the hardships of camp life, he deserves laudation."

Rudolph Matas must also have been well aware of the incredible frustrations military service would impose on so relentless a medical perfectionist as himself. Dr. Hamilton Polk Jones enlarged on this in a fully documented account of his Cuban experiences* as an army surgeon. He had been among the first of more than fifty-three Tulane-graduated physicians to volunteer for service. When ordered to make up a hospital train he organized a remarkably equipped field unit in Tampa: twenty new ambulances, each with four sound mules and enough additional mules to replace battle casualties, all in charge of "a western wagon-train master." But five days prior to embarkation, orders were issued to abandon all ambulances and all tentage other than canvas "flies"; and when he landed at Siboney after nineteen days at sea——

"I was on foot and loaded with as much chloroform, instruments and drugs as I could stagger under, leading my horse which was also loaded with over 200 pounds of hospital supplies. Each of the five medical officers attached to this hospital did the same thing, as did the 39 hospital corpsmen, only the men in addition to their own rations and packs, carried litters loaded with hospital supplies." The unit was set up 1200 yards to the rear of the area where the bitterest fighting for El Caney occurred, and "the surgical staff of this hospital stood at the operating tables from 8:30 A.M., July 1, for 42 consecutive hours, and then got up at daybreak and began again . . . We ran out of splint material, but Dr. Kirkpatrick, surgeon of the 24th U. S. Infantry happily discovered that the stem of last year's leaf of the royal palm was an almost ideal splint material. . . . I (later) established what

* Son of the Dr. Joseph Jones who had been a stormy petrel of the profession in Louisiana in connection with such issues as the testing of Koch's tuberculin, the enactment of a Medical Practices Act, etc.

was known as the Jones Yellow Fever Hospital on the Siboney Road.
. . . The men for several days lay on the ground in water one or
two inches deep . . . my main soup pot was a stolen officers' bath tub.
. . . At one time I had at this hospital 150 cases of yellow fever,
one urinal, one chamber, one bed pan and several deaths as a result of
going to the sinks."

Meanwhile, for the second successive year, and despite unified
quarantine organization, yellow fever again became epidemic along
the Gulf coast. In all likelihood this was attributable to the stepped-
up maritime communication between Cuban ports, Miami, Key West,
and New Orleans. As in 1897, the first report came from Mississippi,
but this time without specious circumlocution. In McHenry, a small
sawmill settlement, twenty-three cases occurred, none of them terminating fatally. Nevertheless, Dr. Souchon, as head of the Louisiana
State Board of Health, declared an immediate quarantine against the
three coastal counties, where so many well-to-do residents of New Orleans maintained summer homes. He decreed that none of these commuters could enter Louisiana except after thorough disinfection and
ten days' detention in any city north of the fever zone, the nearest
one of these being Atlanta. Since this fiat virtually split any number of
New Orleans families, the breadwinner remaining in the city while
the distaff and nursery contingent abode in the coastal resort section
of neighboring Mississippi, it evoked a world of bitter protest.

The tenor of these objections was heightened, of course, when, in
spite of such precautions, yellow fever came to New Orleans anyway.
The first case was officially reported on September 17, and six deaths
from this cause occurred that same month in the city, forty-three in
October, and seven in November. Once more Tulane University's opening of medical classes was postponed for about six weeks, until the
quarantine which had promptly been imposed by other states against
New Orleans was lifted.

Apparently the welter of conflicting theories as to the cause and
cure of yellow fever was to continue unabated, as it had for a
century past. In Franklin, Louisiana, where two cases occurred during
this siege, they were soberly attributed to the fact that both were within
range of the dust given off when a house where a yellow-fever patient
had died during the preceding year was demolished.

In New Orleans there had been calls, as in Mississippi two years
earlier, to let winter's chill rid the community of Bronze John. The
winter of '99 brought the severest cold of which the city had any official
or unofficial record. On the bitterest morning, outside temperatures
dropped to a literally unprecedented 7 degrees; Dr. A. L. Metz
enclosed a registering thermometer in a trunk in the attic of his home

and got a recorded graph to prove that even there the low was 13 degrees. Dr. Quitman Kohnke, as the city's health chief, officially urged that houses, and more especially their bedrooms, be opened wide to the near-arctic blasts, and the *New Orleans Medical and Surgical Journal* backed him up in an editorial which declared:

"With outside temperatures ranging for three days from freezing to 25 degrees below (freezing), even asbestos-covered water pipes burst; so it would seem that, had any one tried, it would have been nigh impossible to coddle a few germs through the unprecedented spell."

And now a new voice was added to the dissonant chorus. Dr. Giuseppe Sanarelli, of the University of Bologna in Italy, working at Montevideo, announced that he had traced the cause of yellow fever definitely and specifically to a *Bacillus icteroides*, from attenuated cultures of which an "anti-amaryllic serum" which cured yellow fever had been produced. Dr. Paul E. Archinard* in New Orleans reported that he and his brother John had found *B. icteroides* in the blood of all yellow-fever patients and cadavers they had examined and had failed signally to find it anywhere else; but they went on to say that after administering Sanarelli's anti-amaryllic serum to twelve patients at the New Orleans Charity Hospital "this agent in our hands had shown no curative powers whatsoever, none of the important and dangerous symptoms of the disease having in any way been mitigated or prevented by its administration."

As late as the autumn of 1899, the Federal government's Marine Hospital Commission reported that the micro-organism of Sanarelli "is the cause of yellow fever" and that "the infection takes place by way of the respiratory tract." This dictum derives added interest from the fact that two other high government agencies categorically dissented.

One was Surgeon-General George M. Sternberg, who pinned the blame for yellow fever on a micro-organism he identified only as *"Bacillus X"*. The other was a Federal Yellow Fever Commission appointed by General Sternberg to work in Havana after the same fashion in which the Chaillé Commission of 1879, of which he had been a member, had worked. The new appointees were Walter Reed, James Carroll, Jesse Lazear, and Aristides Agramonte; and at long, late last they were deep in conference with a lanky, frock-coated Cuban physician of Scottish descent, who carried around with him dried rafts of mosquito eggs and insisted, as he had been insisting since 1881, that one genus of mosquito, referred to by him as *Culex fasciatus,* was the sole agent through which yellow-fever bacilli, whatever they might be, were transmitted from the sick to the well.

* Professor of diseases of the nervous system at the New Orleans Polyclinic and bacteriologist for the Louisiana State Board of Health.

This Commission no longer shrugged this aside as the *idée fixe* of a crackpot. Mosquitoes had been found definitely guilty, less than a twelvemonth earlier, of transmitting malaria. The Commission, therefore, outlined a series of tests which would prove or disprove Carlos Finlay's mosquito hypothesis of yellow fever, a plague to which American soldiers in Cuba were succumbing like flies as the summer advanced. Pending the outcome of these tests, they suspended judgment on the claims of Sanarelli and others.

Though Reed spent most of his time in Washington, the remaining commissioners and their aides scrupulously carried out the tests he had outlined. Volunteers, living in absolutely sanitary surroundings, coming into contact with no food or fomites—bed linen, clothing, blankets, towels, flour sacks, or whatever—that had not been unsparingly disinfected or sterilized, were bitten, under rigidly controlled laboratory conditions by caged female mosquitoes which had previously gorged on the blood of yellow-fever patients.

Meanwhile, at Las Animas Hospital, Navy Surgeon John W. Ross provided two completely screened wards, entry to which could be had only through a tightly screened lock chamber which was meticulously rid of mosquitoes before its inner door was opened. The volunteers in those wards lived first for a week in a clean and sanitary observation area, so that any possibility of their having already been infected with yellow fever could be ruled out. Then for another week they lived amid indescribably revolting filth, using bedding that was black with the vomit, blood, and excrement of victims who had recently died of yellow fever in homes or hospitals.

Moreover, from time to time they shook out other fomites of the same sort, until the dust of dried vomit and fecal matter that had clung to the filth-smeared fibers filled the room and danced down the slanting beams of sunlight streaming through the tightly screened windows. Yet not one of those men came down with yellow fever. Almost without exception, the patients living in sterile, hospital-clean surroundings, but bitten by envenomed mosquitoes, contracted the disease. One member of the commission, Jesse Lazear, died of it; another, James Carroll, fell ill with a "benign attack" from which he recovered.

Back in New Orleans the heretofore uncompromising exponents of fomites contagion, even that rock-ribbed conservative, Dr. Edmond Souchon, conceded the necessity of guarding the city against the omen of periodically recurrent yellow-fever epidemics not merely by quarantine and disinfection, as hitherto, but also by exterminating mosquitoes from the urban areas as far as this might be possible.

"If the remarkable reports of Drs. Reed, Carroll, and Agramonte are confirmed," editorialized the *Medical and Surgical Journal*, "the mosquito is the greatest foe mankind seems to have yet discovered. With malaria and yellow fever to condemn them, the *Culicides* of the future should become as rare as buffaloes." And again: "Enough has been demonstrated to create in the minds of thinking people the urgent necessity for destroying the mosquito and its breed."

But this was no longer enough to satisfy Carlos Finlay's first convert to the mosquito hypothesis. True, like many another disciple of an even more mystic faith, Rudolph Matas once turned his back on it as a youth, because "I had not mustered the courage to battle with tradition." But now a newer, bolder, and more fortunate commission had carried out its experiments, had summoned Major Gorgas to Havana, and had turned over to him the task of giving their experimental findings large-scale practical form.

Dr. Matas had demanded the same sort of large-scale mosquito campaign be waged in New Orleans, the city which, more than any other community in the United States, had been suffering from recurrent yellow-fever epidemics. On February 23, 1901, when the yellow-fever commission's general findings had just been made public in a report submitted to the Pan-American Medical Congress in Havana, he rose to address a meeting of the Orleans Parish Medical Society.

"The remarkable reports presented by Drs. Reed, Carroll, and Agramonte," he declared, "conveyed information which, if confirmed, will revolutionize all our ideas as to the mode of transmission of this disease, and will likewise radically transform our methods of sanitation and prophylaxis. As these conclusions by the commission emphatically declare that yellow fever is transmitted solely by a particular kind of mosquito (*Culex fasciatus* Fabr.) and that wearing apparel and fomites are incapable of communicating the disease, it behooves this society as the medical representative of a section of the country most interested in all yellow-fever questions, to take immediate steps to investigate the correctness of these conclusions and their applicability to our local situation. As a preliminary step, I move that a committee be appointed by our president to investigate and classify the mosquitoes found in New Orleans and vicinity, and to determine especially the presence and topographical distribution of the *Culex fasciatus*."*

The motion was carried unanimously; but the more reactionary bigwigs in the Society could not quite bring themselves to the point where they would permit so bumptious and relatively youthful a prophet to lead them away from the path they had followed for years. Hence, while the Matas motion was unanimously adopted,

* *Orleans Parish Medical Society Proceedings* (1901), Business Minutes Appendix, pp. vii & viii.

a number of queer technical objections were raised to keep it from being put into effect.

By way of illustration, the one Orleanian best qualified to carry out the proposed survey was Professor George E. Beyer, of the Tulane University Department of Biology. Yet a hue and cry was raised in the Society that Dr. Beyer was not a physician; this rendered him ineligible to become a member of the Orleans Parish Medical Society and consequently ineligible to conduct the Society's survey.

The knotty problem was not solved until nearly three months had passed, when Dr. Beyer was elected an "honorary" member; as such, he was made secretary of the commission, the chairmanship of which was tendered to Dr. Matas. But he was very much put out by the obstructionists' delays, and irritably declined the honor.

The Beyer findings were simple enough. A map showing which species of mosquitoes were most prevalent in each section of a community whose municipal boundaries included a sprawling wilderness of swamp and marsh between the Mississippi River and Lake Pontchartrain naturally showed that the fever-spreading insect—*Culex, Stegomyia, Aëdes*: it has borne a number of different names—was indeed concentrated in some of the closely built older sections of the city. A large-scale mosquito extermination campaign was set as an ultimate goal; as temporary expedients it was urged that cisterns be screened, gutters flushed out periodically, and enough oil poured into all privy vaults to cover the surface of fluid contents. It was further ordered that all malaria and yellow-fever patients henceforth be confined within screens as soon as their ailment was determined, to prevent mosquitoes from gaining access to them and thereby spreading the infection.

As a direct result, and for the first time in four years, not a single yellow-fever case was reported in New Orleans during 1901. But this was as nothing compared to the report made in December from Havana by Major Gorgas. During several months and for the first time in 140 years, not a single case of yellow fever had occurred in Havana.

Rudolph Matas might have made much of this and of his own youthful championship of Finlay. Actually, he gave the matter relatively little thought. For one thing, he was busily preparing for the American Surgical Association's forthcoming meeting in June, and not merely because he had been elected treasurer of the organization. He had decided to use this forum for the announcement of the dazzlingly successful results attending his resumption of sutures as a radical cure for aneurisms. Having defied the reactionaries in the matter of mosquito control, he was equally ready to battle with the Hunterian-Anel tradition of ligatures.

But not only this engrossed his thinking during the fall and early winter of 1901, for one September morning, after bringing early coffee to his bedside, Adrienne informed him that she was pregnant and would give birth to their child the following March.

CHAPTER XXII

When Bienville's intrepid band founded a new city at the gateway of a hemisphere, they placed their fortified settlement at the apical bend of a sharp river crescent, so that sentries might keep a vigilant lookout for approaching foes both upstream and down. Homesick, the newcomers bestowed on their alien environment names that had the nostalgic ring of the motherland they had quitted for a new world.

The streets of their walled *ville* were named after various members of the fourteenth Louis's royal household, including even some Bourbon scions conceived without benefit of prior wedlock. A broad promenade just beyond the downstream wall of the *ville* became the Champs-Elysées and is Elysian Fields Avenue to this day. A swamp trail to Gentilly is now a paved highway, but is still designated as the Paris Road.

Across the Mediterranean Sea from France lay Algiers. Hence the one *faubourg* of the original New Orleans which is on the west side of the Mississippi is known to this day as Algiers. And so it came about that in the kitchen of an Algiers butcher the Hunter-Anel ligature was finally superseded by the Matas intrasacular suture.

At no time during the mosquito campaign and its triumphant denouement had the doctor neglected his teaching duties, his private practice, his omnivorous and insatiable devouring of professional literature, and the meetings of medical societies. For example, he was instrumental in bringing to New Orleans Dr. Karl von Ruck of Asheville, North Carolina, where the latter's Winyah Sanitarium for tuberculars

277

was established. After the spectacular collapse of the claims originally made for Koch's tuberculin, von Ruck set out to refine a watery extract of attenuated tubercle bacilli (Koch's was a glycerin extract), calling it antiphthisin, a serum whose therapeutic value a committee of the Orleans Parish Association was instructed to investigate.

Over and above the fact that tuberculosis was the principal executioner among diseases to which the residents of large cities were then still heir, Rudolph Matas had a very special interest at this time in any condition affecting the human chest. His unremitting curiosity about what lay beyond medicine's known frontiers was driving him to a consideration of surgery as a remedial measure for thoracic affections of any sort; externally inflicted (that is to say, traumatic) injuries or internally generated mischief (abscesses, tumors, gangrenous tissue, tubercles, and the like).

Thanks to asepsis and rapidly improving instrumentation, surgical invasion of the abdomen (laparotomy) was no longer regarded as a last, desperate resort. But dreadful perils still attended any major surgical opening of the chest. An apparently insuperable difficulty lay in the fact that once the membrane lining the chest cavity was pierced or ruptured enough to allow external and internal air pressures to equalize, the lungs collapsed. Asphyxiation and death followed as a matter of course. Obviously some mechanism for keeping the lungs distended and supplied with freshly oxygenated air was the only conceivable defense against such an otherwise inevitably fatal termination.

Some experiments along this line had been made many years earlier on goats by a British surgeon at the Medical School of Cairo. Several other surgeons had wrestled with the problem. Modifying the two most promising sets of apparatus thus far devised, Dr. Matas came up with an ingenious positive-pressure device for passing a tube through the mouth and throat of an anesthetized patient (in other words, not through an additional tracheotomy incision), while a foot-operated bellows, attached to the tube, not merely kept the lungs from collapse but rhythmically supplied fresh air. His primitive apparatus has long since been superseded by some of the modern artificial heart-lung machines, but in a very real sense it opened the door to the fantastic advances made since that time by thoracic surgery, which now can repair a damaged heart valve or remove an entire cancerous lung.

Such pioneering achievements were rapidly gaining him recognition among the acknowledged leaders of his profession. One of these was his early idol, William Halsted of Baltimore, who visited New Orleans in 1898 to deliver before a meeting of the American Surgical Association a remarkable paper on the operative treatment of breast cancers. The convention's official journal notes that in the discussion that followed the Halsted paper, "Dr. Rudolph Matas . . . gave a lengthy synopsis of *twenty-seven* operative cases," and "spoke at length of 15 complete operations performed since November, 1894, and gave the results in detail." It should be considered that this was done extemporaneously and without reference to so much as a card of jotted notes. While the protracted recital no doubt engendered in the program chairman a progressively worsening morbidity, the other listeners were enthralled by what was beyond question an unparalleled feat of memory.

It is likewise a matter of record that in December 1899, Rudolph Matas performed the first operation ever attempted in America under spinal anesthesia. Earlier that year August Bier had performed such an operation in Kiel, Germany, having had the injection of cocaine into the spinal canal first tried out on himself. A few days after the Matas operation in New Orleans, Dr. John B. Murphy performed one in Chicago. But most of the experimenters abandoned spinal analgesia for a time, because of the severity of the reactions following the use of cocaine in this fashion. These involved almost intolerable headaches, severe chills, high fever, and uncontrollable vomiting. In one of Dr. Matas's patients the postoperative headache persisted for months.

All in all, he pointed out in a memoir on the subject, the aftereffects "made me realize that the dangers of spinal anesthesia with cocaine could not possibly be compensated by the simplicity of the technique or the effectiveness of the anesthesia, so much so that I, in company with many other pioneers, abandoned it altogether until novocain was introduced by Braun in 1905–6."

By the time he had held his professorship five years, his students had developed an attitude toward him that fell little short of veneration. They were well aware of his small foibles and of such handicaps as the high-pitched, bleating voice; but his apparently boundless fund of knowledge, his ability to cite chapter, book, and verse from memory in almost any field of medical literature, and the sheer artistry of his operating technique made them less his pupils than his fervent disciples.

The graduating class of 1899 was the first to present him with a special testimonial: a crayon portrait of himself. Twenty-six years later another graduating class made him a similar gift on the eve of his retirement from active instruction to become professor emeritus for life.*

* On this latter occasion he drew a whimsically rueful comparison between "thick hair, dark beard, and smooth face" as contrasting with "bleached gray whiskers, bespectacled eyes. . . ." Yet some of his most notable honors were still to be accorded him.

As the year drew to its close he was busily organizing his paper on the history of pulmonary insufflation and the positive-pressure apparatus he proposed to demonstrate before the Southern Surgical and Gynecological Congress, which was to hold its annual meeting in New Orleans that December. He was still aligned with the Hunter-Anel traditionalists in the treatment of aneurisms by ligation, when two such cases turned his thoughts once more and permanently, toward suture as a radical cure.

A white man, identified in Dr. Matas's subsequent report merely as "Sam P." accidentally suffered a gunshot wound while hunting deer in one of the still trackless swamps upstream from urban New Orleans. Passing through the thigh, a single buckshot pellet badly injured the main (femoral) artery so that blood, forced out of the damaged vessel by continued pulsations, did not simply diffuse in the surrounding tissue (as it does, for instance, in a "black eye" contusion) but accumulated in a tumorous swelling which continued to grow, to pulsate, and to become ever more painful.

Following standard practice, Dr. Matas ligated the femoral artery both above and below the wound. Pulsation was immediately arrested. To that extent, the operation was a success. But it became apparent almost at once that virtually no collateral circulation thereafter was capable of carrying blood to the foot. "Gangrene occurred immediately after the simple ligature," reported Dr. Matas later. It progressed so rapidly that only a hasty amputation of the leg saved the man's life.

Within a month, an almost identical situation developed in another case of femoral aneurism. "Gangrene of the toes occurred in a sequel to the ligation," Dr. Matas noted, "[and this] led me again to revert to the modified Antyllian operation as I had performed it in my first case."

The impact of this dual incidence of gangrene might not have proved so decisive, had not a third case of the same type of aneurism come to his attention almost at once. This was relatively commonplace during the hunting season, since firearms still had hammers, which were frequently caught by twigs or fence wires, thus accidentally discharging the weapon. As a result of the accidental discharge of a Colt's revolver, a .32-caliber bullet had passed through the upper arm of one F.C., grazing the bone, ranging upward, and emerging near the point of the shoulder.

Very little hemorrhage occurred at the time. When examining the wound later, Dr. Delaup made a point of the fact that "in spite of careless treatment the wound healed kindly." But within five weeks or so a pulsating swelling appeared near the armpit on the inner side.

"No serious attention was paid to the swelling until about three months after the accident," reported Dr. Matas to the American

Surgical Association's 1902 convention at Albany, New York.[*]
[Then,] "owing to the comparatively rapid growth of the tumor and the
painful symptoms that accompanied it, the patient consulted me
through the recommendation of his physician. I discovered a tumor
[which] had all the characteristics of an aneurism. The patient was
quite a stout man and it was not easy to apply digital compression, so
I decided to ligate the brachial [the main artery of the arm] as its
origin. This was done at the home of the patient. . . . All pulsation was
immediately arrested and the wound healed kindly *per primum.*"

Unfortunately, some two months later the tumor returned and was
once more pulsating as strongly, as painfully, and as ominously as
before. Accepted practice would now have ligated the artery below
the tumor as well as above it, along with such collateral blood vessels as
could be reached. But this would halt virtually all circulation to the
lower arm and the hand. Gangrene had promptly followed this type
of procedure in two cases Dr. Matas had just treated, and the patients'
lives had been saved only by immediate amputation of the affected
limbs.

F.C., white, 32, native of France, would be permanently handicapped
by the loss of an arm. And so, willy nilly, Rudolph Matas mustered
enough courage to battle with tradition and "I decided to incise the sac
and suture the orifices, as I had done in the previous case" (of Manuel
Harris, twelve years before).

However, the patient did not believe in hospitals, and in this instance
the operation would have to be performed in the kitchen of a small
home in Algiers, that over-the-river *faubourg* of small homes beyond
which Judah P. Benjamin had once dwelt in splendid luxury at Belle
Chasse, his plantation manor. No well-appointed operating room, fully
equipped to meet the unpredictable; no corps of trained nurses; and no
amphitheater crowded with admiring observers either. Just a pair of
blanket-covered ironing boards, laid side-by-side upon two sawhorses,
the patient strapped securely to them with twisted sheets from the
household supply of bed linen; he was, as Dr. Matas pointed out, "quite
a stout man," and no surgeon could chance his thrashing about in a
fashion that might topple him to the floor. Another board—a plain
1' × 12' piece of cypress planking covered with linen—would project
at right angles from beneath the patient's shoulders. To this the injured
arm would be firmly bound.

"We will have to operate by daylight too," Dr. Matas told his assistants

---

[*] *Transactions of the American Surgical Association,* vol. 20. The case was also
described in the *Annals of Surgery,* vol. 37, p. 197ff., and in a paper on "The Suture
in the Surgery of the Vascular System," read before the Medical Association of
Alabama, April 22, 1905.

while preparing for the world's second intrasacular suture. "Oh my, yes. True, we're not using ether for the simple reason that it is too inflammable for us to risk insurance-oil lamps or open gas flames. But Delaup tells me the house has no electricity, so we'll give ourselves plenty of daylight. Now"—he began to check off the various items on the stubby fingers of his left hand—"we'll have to bring with us every single thing we will need, except water. Sterile instruments, sterile swabs, sterile sheets, anesthetics, gauze, bichloride. Pack everything into a couple of army surgical trunks; we've got any number of surplus ones from the Cuban campaign around the place. My, my, my! There are even some Civil War ones, and they'll do just as well. We'll load them into an ambulance and take them across the river on the Canal Street ferry.

"We'll have Delaup for one assistant, Louis Genella can ride with the ambulance driver, and Gessner and Larue can come with me. My, my, my, this will be something for all of us to remember, like the time I assisted Dr. Richardson in operating on President Davis's sister. She was in the St. Charles Hotel, and we had to bring——"

The cavalcade moved down Canal Street and across the plaza where a panic-stricken schoolboy had fled from the crash of cannon and musketry fire as the White Leaguers recklessly charged the carpetbaggers' artillery nearly thirty years before. They clattered across the heavy wooden flooring of the levee, piled high with freight though but a handful of river packets were docked where once the largest inland fleet of steamboats the world has ever known jostled one another for wharfage. Shod hoofs thumped like muffled drumbeats against the deck planking of the *Thomas Pickles*, a catamaran stern-wheel ferry that plodded back and forth across the turbid, mile-wide current.

Dr. Delaup had scrubbed and shaved the stout patient by the time the Matas procession drew up at the modest cottage home. Little was said during the preliminaries, since each of those present knew in advance exactly what he had to do.

"Let's have plenty of hot normal saline before we start," directed Dr. Matas, "and then cover the embers in the range with ashes. It'll be too hot for comfort in here anyway. Oh my, yes, yes, indeed." Felix Larue would have been the one to measure out the water and weigh the common table salt, since Hermann Gessner served as anesthetist and Louis Genella was readying the rubber Esmarch and laying out towel-wrapped packets of sterile instruments. It was therefore Larue, too, who would have prepared in an ordinary washbasin a 1:2000 dilution of bichloride, setting this on a kitchen stool where the bearded surgeon could rinse his hands in it from time to time as the operation proceeded.

Then the patient was secured to the improvised operating table, and Dr. Gessner began the measured drip of chloroform upon the upper surface of the wire-gauze "cone," which was likewise an Esmarch contrivance, and Dr. Delaup, speaking in French, instructed the supine F.C. to count until *un, deux, trois* and their successors began to blur, falter, and finally cease.

"The Esmarch bandage was then applied from the fingers to a point about two inches below the lower limit of the tumor," we read. That would be to keep the forearm and hand from becoming engorged with blood as a tourniquet—"be sure it's compressing the artery or we'll all get a red bath"—was applied constrictively just below the shoulder. "A free incision was made over the tumor and the upper pole exposed. . . . The sac was incised longitudinally and a large mass of mixed clot was evacuated. . . . Two large orifices, one the inlet and the other the outlet of the artery were now seen in the interior of the sac. . . . Orifices large enough to admit the tip of the little finger"—which had just been thoroughly rinsed in the washbasin font atop the kitchen stool, one may be sure. Then, "without further preliminaries, the orifices were quickly sealed by a fine continuous silk suture which penetrated the entire thickness of the sac walls. . . . The sutures held perfectly."

After this, the elastic tourniquet which had kept the patient from "giving us all a red bath" was relaxed "and I was pleased to see that not a drop of blood escaped . . . and, after applying a copious antiseptic dressing, the arm was bandaged in the Desault position"— that is to say, arm at the side, elbow flexed, and forearm bandaged to the body as though in a sling—and "three weeks after the operation the wound had healed entirely. . . . The patient has since moved his residence to Honduras, Central America, and was, according to recent reports of his friends, enjoying excellent health."

That is part of the report Dr. Matas gave the American Surgical Association's delegates two years later, but it conveys no real picture of what went on in the small kitchen of an Algiers cottage that April afternoon; the steamy heat rising from a kettle of normal saline solution atop the stove in that enclosed place; Rudolph Matas's uninterrupted commentary giving the history of this procedure and of that, the reasons underlying Pierre Desault's innovations in surgical instruments and procedures, and the fashion in which Desault's disciple, Bichat, had recorded them; the oniony-sweet reek of chloroform, and at the end the escape into relatively cool, fresh air, with Dr. Matas scrubbing away at his beard, cheeks, and eyes with the hem of his white operating smock to rid himself of the smart of sticky perspiration.

Naturally, there was no longer any question of mustering enough courage to break with tradition. In November of that same year, 1900, a certain "A.P., white, married, a saloonkeeper, ae. 27," was cured of an aneurism back of the knee by the same sort of radical suture—"popliteal endoaneurismorrhaphy" in surgicalese.

The case had some interesting sidelights and one medically very significant feature. When A.P. first applied for relief, Charity Hospital residents treated him, in the traditional way, by elastic compression and flexure. This was so painful that the patient simply deserted. Yet his condition worsened so that he was compelled to apply for readmission and came to Dr. Genella's service. The latter submitted the case to Dr. Matas, who operated under local anesthesia by infiltrating the nerves—especially the main trunk of the sciatic nerve—with cocaine. At one time during the operation the patient became very nervous and restless, though not complaining of pain. A few drops of chloroform were applied to an inhaler and "had the effect of immediately quieting the patient without abolishing consciousness, as he was able to reply to questions and had a clear knowledge of his surroundings."

This popliteal—i.e., "back of the knee"—aneurism was just the sort which, when treated by ligation, so frequently either reappeared or resulted in gangrene. But in this case "the color of the limb and the foot was entirely normal. . . . The patient made a complete and uneventful recovery . . . [and] when last seen March 25, 1901, was walking on the street with good movement of the joint, except for a slight limp."

The next patient, suffering a femoral aneurism, was a Negro roustabout. The suture operation revealed that "the cavity of the aneurism was large enough to admit an adult fist." Once more: "The patient made an uneventful recovery but remained in the hospital [several weeks] as he served as help for some time after his convalescence."

Thus, beginning with Manuel Harris in 1888, and overleaping the twelve-year hiatus which followed, there were now five cases, every one of them spectacularly successful, to report to the 1902 convention of the American Surgical Association at Albany, together with many drawings by Dr. Kohnke, the gifted head of New Orleans' municipal health board, and by a Miss Fry, of 1041 Haley Street, Brooklyn, professional illustrator.

Therewith a new tradition was established by the glossily dark-bearded surgeon from New Orleans; a tradition others would henceforth need courage to oppose. Dr. William J. Mayo, of Rochester, Minnesota, validated this during the discussion that followed the delivery of Dr. Matas's paper.

"About two years ago," he said, "I assisted my brother in operating on a popliteal aneurism in which the dissection was very difficult. After getting down and turning out the clots from the sac, he put in strips of iodoform gauze . . . continuing the packing to the surface. The result was most excellent. The gauze checks the bleeding and closes all the open vessels, and the resulting granulation obliterates the sac. It is practically the method which Dr. Matas describes . . . [but] the Matas method is superior in that it leaves a perfectly closed wound which must heal by the open method. We [i.e., the Mayo Brothers' clinic at Rochester] will certainly adopt the most admirable technique which the doctor has marked out with his operation."

An even more significant memento of the immediate acceptance accorded the Matas operation, perhaps, is the recorded *volte-face* of opinion expressed by Dr. Frederick Parham. It is difficult to give on paper, and at this late day, an adequate yet fair presentation of the feeling between him and Dr. Matas. To say there was bad blood between them would be a complete overstatement; yet for some time they had not been on the best of terms.

Dr. Parham had hoped for the professorial appointment which Rudolph Matas received in 1894 but had to content himself with succeeding the latter on the faculty of the Polyclinic. There, in a sense, he regarded himself and his colleagues as rivals (or perhaps "competitors" would convey a more just connotation) of the Tulane faculty. Certainly, from the moment Drs. Charles Chassaignac and Isadore Dyer purchased the *New Orleans Medical and Surgical Journal,* placing Dr. Parham in charge of its surgical section, the overwhelming majority of those contributing original articles were identified as professors on the faculty of the Polyclinic, and the name of Dr. Matas all but disappeared from the index where it had been seen so frequently for two decades.

On the evening of June 14, 1902, the Orleans Parish Medical Society met. Dr. Matas, newly returned from Albany, and Dr. Parham were both present. The details of the Albany convention, which had met only the week before, had not yet been disseminated to the profession at large. In the discussion of various cases by members of the Parish Society, Dr. Parham happened to report one in which he had ligated certain arteries, only to find that a slight gangrene of one heel followed the operation.

Dr. S. M. D. Clark thereupon (and perhaps with a minim or two of malice aforethought) requested Dr. Matas to "state the method of curing aneurisms in his clinic." That was quite enough to launch a long and detailed lecture on the various steps involved in making endo-aneurismal sutures. One concludes that the atmosphere of the gathering became progressively less cordial as the recital went on and on and on. When Dr. Matas finally brought his discourse to an end, "Dr. Parham questioned the advisability of putting sutures into an already diseased vessel wall. He believed that the proposed method involved more traumatism than ligature above and below and packing. He did not admit that the collateral circulation was disturbed less by Dr. Matas's method than by the older one."*

In view of the foregoing, a report the same Dr. Parham made to the Southern Surgical and Gynecological Society three years later in describing two cases of aneurism is doubly revealing.

"In this case," he wrote, "the effect of suture in controlling hemorrhage which the proximal ligation had failed to do satisfactorily was both beautiful and striking. . . . In devising this operation and so clearly marking out its indications and its technique, Dr. Matas has done a most brilliant piece of work which is, without doubt, one of the most valuable contributions to surgery in recent years."

* *New Orleans Medical and Surgical Journal*, vol. 55, pp. 120–22.

CHAPTER XXIII

Rudolph Matas was short of stature, but the steely slenderness he inherited from his father masked this until the plumpness of well-nourished middle years overtook him. Nonetheless he walked as one ten feet tall during those closing days of 1901 when he knew that in March he would become a father—an ancestor—one who had perpetuated the Matas name and blood.

At home, to be sure, this triumphant exultation would vanish like a pricked bubble, for Adrienne confined him as much as possible to his study, more or less declaring the rest of the house off limits, except at mealtimes or the like. The forbidden areas were pre-empted by herself and her mother. Ermance Marc Goslee had taken over the more arduous phases of managing her daughter's household, though to look at her one would imagine such tasks well beyond her physical powers. Not more than five feet tall and girlishly slender still, she was actually dwarfed by her statuesque and buxom daughter. In appearance, she put one in mind of a Dresden doll or a Watteau shepherdess who, donning modern garb, had acquired the hue and sheen of well-polished silver; her complexion had translucence which heightened the general effect of a *grande dame* wrought in exquisite miniature.

Like Adrienne—in fact, like every well-brought-up Creole girl of that era—she was a superb needlewoman. Nearly twenty years had passed since Adrienne had last prepared for the advent of a baby. None of the essentials of an infant's proper *tenue* remained in her fastidiously kept armoires or cedar-lined chests. Everything would have to be provided

287

afresh. So she and her mother sewed endlessly, making microscopically small stitches, hemming soft cloth squares for diapers, trimming long cambric gowns with lace, embroidering ribboned caps and bonnets by the score, knitting dozens of small bootees and the like.

The two Landry youths were blessedly not underfoot during this gynecocratic regime. Both were occupied with the study of medicine, Lucian eagerly and Arthur listlessly. Such of the latter's classroom notes as were found among the Matas papers are mere disorganized hugger-muggers, jotted down indiscriminately and with no semblance of relation to one another, misspelled to a degree one would find incredible in a schoolboy, to say nothing of a professional student in his twenties.

Lucian, on the other hand, though inclined to adopt a certain pugnacious willfulness in his attitude toward the world, was an avid student in spite of the fact that engineering and not medicine had been his first choice of a career. To this end he had been enrolled in Louisiana State University, "the Old War Skule," so named because most of the student body and faculty resigned to join the Confederate army, so that the first president of the university (who also resigned to resume his federal commission as major) recorded in his memoirs that "the Seminary was dispersed by the war." Almost at once, however, in a band-saw mishap during a shop course, Lucian lost part of his right thumb and forefinger. Emergency surgery, much of it directed by Dr. Matas via long-distance telephone from New Orleans, succeeded in retaining for him complete mobility of the injured hand; and when fully recovered, he returned from Baton Rouge to enter the medical department of Tulane University.

About this time Arthur gave up the study of medicine to become a dentist. A new Orleans Dental College had recently been founded and had graduated three students with the degree of D.D.S. the previous spring. With his stepfather's consent, Arthur enrolled for the session of 1901–2 and was initiated into the college's newly organized "Stomatological Society of New Orleans."

Mrs. Matas and her mother pointedly continued to grant Rudolph no more than a sub-minimal voice in domestic affairs, save when it came to demands for money. Ordinarily frugal to the point of parsimony, he joyfully provided for "our child" on the most lavish scale imaginable; the layette of exquisite needlework should lack nothing that paternal pride and maternal skill could afford. On the score of Dr. Matas's extreme conservatism in money matters, two points should be emphasized. The first is that he did not let what was almost a passion for personal security influence his relationship to his patients; even after he was world renowned, his fees were still moderate. But the realization of what had happened to his father, when a tremendous fortune—

Matas and members of
Violet Hart Vascular Sur-
' Committee with Mont
l, first recipient of the
rd (January 22, 1934).
ed, from left to right:
t R. Reid (recipient), Dr.
as, and Mike Hart, who
blished the fund in mem-
of his sister, Violet Hart.
ding, from left to right:
Lucian H. Landry, Emile
ch (chairman), Isidore
n, and Alton Ochsner.

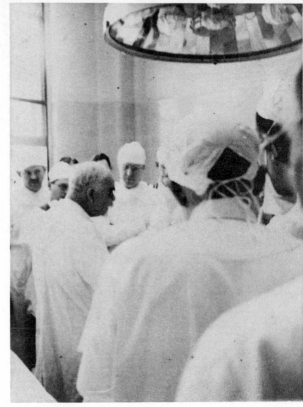

essor Matas gives "dry
ic" to visiting surgeons at
ro Infirmary (1935).

Dr. Matas at the home of Dr. Isidore Cohn (May 22, 1936). Dr. Matas inscribed the picture, "In memory of a delightful evening."

Dr. Matas invested with the Order of Carlos Finlay in Havana, Cuba (1941). Decoration presented by Dr. José Presno, president of the Academy of Science, Havana.

Dr. Matas in his library at home (1941).

Dr. Matas and members of the staff at Touro Infirmary who were on the staff when Dr. Matas was chief of service. Standing, from left to right: Drs. Hermann B. Gessner, Matas, Lucian H. Landry, Urban Maes, and Isidore Cohn.

Bronze plaque dedicated to Dr. Matas by Touro Infirmary (June 24, 1941). From left to right: Isidore Cohn, Mrs. Hilda Scudder Manning, sculptor, and Dr. Matas. Dr. Matas commented "Quite a solemn occasion looking at my epitaph."

esentation of plaque to Pro-
sor George Grey-Turner, of
ndon, during the Congress
the International Surgical
iety at New Orleans (1949).
. Matas is holding a gavel,
ich had been presented to
1 by the American Society
Vascular Surgeons, while
fessor Grey-Turner holds
plaque.

. Matas and Professor René
riche, of Paris, looking over
olume in the "Rudolph Ma-
Library" at Tulane Univer-
School of Medicine dur-
the Congress in New Or-
ns (1949).

Candid shot of Dr. Matas, age 90. (1950).

Dr. Matas in his library at home, age 92 (1952).

Television appearance of Dr. Matas on September 12, 1955, age
95. This was one of the last public appearances made by Dr.
Matas.

enough to have kept the family in affluence for the rest of their days —was dissipated in a single season of reckless speculation, engendered what became a fixed resolve never to lose sight of the value of financial security. Yet this passion manifested itself solely in the minutiae of personal expenditures and not in any larger matters involving the public weal.

To cite a specific contrast: in 1900 he launched a furious campaign against the Telephone Company, not merely because of a general rate increase it had put into effect but for charging physicians the substantially still higher "business" rate for their residential as well as for their office telephones. On the ground that this constituted indefensible discrimination, he carried his fight through the Parish Society to the Railroad Commission, which then regulated all Louisiana public utilities—and won his point!

On the other hand, during this selfsame season, he persuaded the ailing millionaire, Alexander Hutchinson, to bequeath almost his entire estate to Tulane University for the furtherance of medical education. Had Dr. Matas proposed it, the shipping magnate would just as readily have endowed a private hospital bearing Rudolph's name. But the physician who would haggle for weeks over a difference of a few pennies on an item of personal or household expenditure, saw to it that Hutchinson's wealth went to one institution whose administrators had it in their power to dismiss him at their pleasure, and to another—Charity Hospital—with whose directorate he was constantly at loggerheads because, so he charged, they kept for themselves and their aides the surgical cases most needed for instruction.*

The relation between Alexander Hutchinson and Dr. Matas who was nearly forty years his junior, was a curious manifestation of almost childlike trust on the part of the financier. He and his wife Josephine, who died in 1896, had been childless. After her death, he continued in her memory the practice she had begun some years earlier, of sending small gifts quite anonymously—merely "in the name of Josephine"—to patients in the children's wards of Charity Hospital. One of the members of the hospital's board, General William G. Vincent, had assisted Hutchinson in this and ultimately appealed to him to make a more substantial donation to the institution; enough in a single grant to construct and equip either a nurses' home or a badly needed separate building for the treatment of contagious diseases.

Hutchinson had called in Dr. Matas two or three years before for a very minor operation, the success of which impressed him so that he

* Two surviving members of the Hutchinson family—a brother, Edwin A., and a sister, Mrs. Emma Moore—contested the will. Dr. Matas was the only medical witness heard during the prolonged litigation that followed; and the will was declared valid.

retained the rising young surgeon as his personal physician. Professional contacts developed into close friendship. Thus, when in 1901 General Vincent made his appeal for a large gift to the hospital, the magnate put him off until he could consult Dr. Matas as to which of the two suggested projects he should endow.

The reply was all but immediate. Rudolph had been one of the first to agitate for the establishment of a School of Nursing, declaring that Charity Hospital's system of using otherwise untrained convalescent patients of both sexes for nursing service deprived other sufferers of whatever chance of recovery skilled care might have afforded. The school was established in 1894; any proposal to raise its effectiveness as a training center was bound to enlist Dr. Matas's cordial endorsement, especially when he had just engaged a trained and registered nurse to attend Mrs. Matas in her confinement the following March.

Naturally he recommended that Mr. Hutchinson earmark his gift for the establishment of a Nurses' Home, and this was done, with the added stipulation that the gift be anonymous. To this end the donor purchased in New York a bank draft payable to Dr. Matas, who was directed to endorse it to Charity Hospital without revealing its source. Unfortunately, the New York bank was keenly publicity conscious and gave a reporter on the Wall Street run enough of the details to provide just the sort of heart-tug chronicle Hutchinson abhorred. After all, this was the man who had helped Cornelius Vanderbilt make William Walker president of Nicaragua, so that the Vanderbilt Transit Line from Greytown through Lake Nicaragua could shorten the distance to California for gold seekers from the East. This was the man who had fought state, city, and federal governments tooth and nail in the matter of yellow-fever quarantine. Furious over the prospect of being portrayed as a sort of senile Big Lord Fauntleroy, he was on the verge of withdrawing his donation. Dr. Matas succeeded in dissuading him from such a course, on the ground that this would make the nurses, who were assuredly innocent of any complicity in the matter, suffer for the sins of a New York banker.

It appears that one of the conditions on which the ailing transportation executive agreed to let the donation stand was that his physician help draft a will for disposing of his estate to the benefit of medical practice in Louisiana. Quarantine had been Hutchinson's *bête noire* for years. He may have been utterly illogical in contending that the restraints thus imposed on shipping and travel did nothing to root out yellow fever, but he was enthusiastic in his appreciation of what medical men had just achieved, however tardily, by conquering Bronze John in a war of extermination. So he put the proposal unreservedly into his physician's hands. It is quite conceivable that the temptation to have a private hospital thus endowed, so that his surgical teaching would no longer depend on the whims of a politically appointed public-hospital staff and the leftover cases they might concede to his service, was strong. Nonetheless, he urged without qualification that the Medical Department of Tulane University be made the residual legatee of the Hutchinson estate.

"Draft that provision the way *you* think it ought to be," Hutchinson told him and thereafter left New Orleans for yet another ocean voyage. A hypertensive, he had suffered acutely from insomnia ever since his wife's death. In time he acquired a fixed conviction that only during sea voyages could he achieve the bodily restoration afforded by natural sleep. Psychosomatic or not, he did manage to sleep well on shipboard, though he remained wretchedly wakeful ashore. Meanwhile, Dr. Matas, in steady consultation with Dean Chaillé, composed a draft copy for the bequest which, through his attorneys, Hutchinson incorporated into his final testament on November 20, 1902, less than three weeks before his death on December 10.

By that time the cornerstone of the Nurses' Home had long since been laid, a ceremony which Hutchinson, still inflexibly anonymous as the building's donor, simply ignored. Not more than a fortnight before his death, his coachman drove him slowly past the newly completed building; he had this one and only glimpse of it to take with him. When the will was probated, Tulane's share of the estate proved to be in the neighborhood of $800,000, an enormous sum for that era in a region not yet recovered from the economic ravages of a losing war and the even more destructive rape of the carpetbaggers that followed. At the close of litigation, the funds were wisely invested, and the total was increased from time to time by other gifts, notably by a $30,000 legacy from General Vincent. Construction was not completed until the 1930's,* but to this day the Alexander and Josephine Hutchinson Memorial Building houses Tulane University's College of Medicine.

Otherwise, the latter part of 1901 dragged on for Rudolph Matas at a snail's pace. During the seemingly interminable period of waiting he kept himself under the anodyne of overwork to almost the same degree to which he had subjected himself to it during the years before he and "Dearest Adri" were married. So far as that might go, his services were in ever greater demand, anyway, not only by his patients but on the part of his fellow-practitioners. For example, Dr. R. J. Mainegra found himself in difficulties when he delivered an infant only to discover it had come into the world with a fractured thighbone. How to devise a splint? He called in Dr. Matas, who ingeniously fashioned one that

---

* The building has been greatly enlarged since that time by a number of additions to its space and facilities.

immobilized the infant in a monolithic plaster cast from shoulders to knee. . . . A young physician realized that one of his women patients was fated to die horribly unless a radical mastoid operation was performed, but she refused to permit this. Dr. Matas was summoned and, perhaps merely through some sort of magic attaching to his name —the same spell which aroused all the city when it was learned he was to be passed over by Tulane in the appointment of a new professor of surgery—persuaded the patient to go forthwith to the hospital and submit to the operation. . . . Dr. Louis Genella was called by a Mrs. Flynn five days after she boiled two boxes of parlor matches in sugar water, and then drank the potion, seeking to commit suicide. By the time Dr. Genella was summoned she was on the brink of death. Unsure of himself, he asked Dr. Matas for assistance. The latter dredged up from the inexhaustible storehouse of his memory the amount of phosphorus in each head of a common parlor match, counted the number of matches in a box, made a rapid calculation and announced that the total constituted an inevitably fatal dose which only immediate counteraction with antidotes and emetics might have helped. . . . Appalled by an official report of the field-hospital casualties in Cuba and the Philippines, Dr. Matas introduced into the Tulane medical curriculum a course in litter work, first aid, and minor surgery, with weekly drill sessions at Jackson Barracks.

The hectic overload mounted with each passing week as more and more calls were made on him by the professional organizations to which he belonged. The American Surgical Society had met that May of 1901 in Baltimore. William Halsted invited him to stay at his home in Eutaw Place, rather than at a hotel, and he was delighted to accept, for between the two men a firm friendship had sprung up which was to endure until Halsted's death. It was at this meeting that Dr. Matas was elected treasurer of the Society; it was in his friend's home that he outlined the aneurism paper he meant to deliver when the Society next met the following June at Albany.

Christmas came and went. There had never been a traditional tree with glittering adornments and radiant candles in the Matas household, and there was none this year. But there was the usual exchange of gifts, or rather an unusual one. In addition to the cut-glass flacons of imported perfume for Adrienne and an ornamental shawl for Mrs. Goslee, there was a fleecy small blanket of lamb's wool wrapped in tissue paper and red ribbon, with a card on which Papa-to-be Matas had written in his all but illegible prescription scrawl the address: For Baby, care of Dearest Mama Adri."

The Ball of the Twelfth Night Revelers on January 6, with a conventional Master Chef to cut the King's Cake, ushered in another

Carnival season; the State Board of Health, Dr. Edmond Souchon presiding, heard a plea from representatives of all the city's commercial interests asking that in view of the conquest of yellow fever by mosquito eradication, quarantine fees for vessels entering the port of New Orleans be halved. Rather grudgingly, the Board did finally reduce the fee by a mere $25; but President Souchon, as yielding as a steel girder, made a statement officially reported in the minutes as follows: "Speaking for the Board, the President said that the Board shall continue its work of protecting the public health on the *well-established* lines of safety."

This was in February, by which time Rudolph was as nervous and wrought-up as any other first-time father. In vain Adrienne tried to reassure him; she and her mother had never been compelled to endure a really difficult labor, and, for the love of God, he should certainly know better—a doctor to whom confinements were an old, old story— than to pace up and down like a caged panther, smoking too many cigarettes. Seeking to distract him she called on him to admire with her the trundle in which their child would so soon be sleeping—if, indeed, one did not have to walk the floor for hours with a fretful infant. . . . "Save your pacing for that, *mon cher;* you won't think being a father is such a shining wonder, then, I guarantee you!" Throughout February she continued to remind him that she had checked her calendar carefully and he would have to contain his impatience until another full change of the moon had run its course.

Time and again he sat down to write more about the coming miracle to his father, knowing the latter was likewise finding it difficult to contain his eagerness for a lineal descendent of the Areu line they had traced back two full centuries to that stout Catalonian warrior, José, son of Lorenzo. But time and again he gave over the effort, because there was nothing he could communicate to his sire except his own gnawing sense of anxiety against which Rudolph, the great physician, found himself impotent to armor Rudolph, the expectant father.

At length the change of the moon was accomplished; Rudolph sent for the trained nurse, who went rustling from kitchen to bedroom and back—her crisply starched blue uniform with its white apron and short, white oversleeves, to say nothing of who knew how many starched petticoats. On the afternoon of March 11 the first harsh clutch of pain launched the labor period, which proceeded normally, the intervals between pains gradually diminishing, as Rudolph raised a great to-do about making certain there would be plenty of hot water and seeing to it that the triple-refined olive oil be kept warm. The fire in the kitchen range was to be maintained until further orders from him. A fire was also kindled in the bedroom grate after nightfall, although the afternoon had been warm, for at sundown the weather turned off cool; the mercury dropped to 60 degrees. It was unthinkable that the child of Rudolph and Adrienne Matas should come into a world whose chill had not been moderated.

From time to time he bent over his wife, during remissions from the bleak tides of anguish which were now following one another ever more closely, and listened raptly through the stethoscope for the faint sound of *his* child's fetal heartbeat, no doubt murmuring "Fine, *maman!* Everything is coming along just fine!" with the professional heartiness that is the obstetrician's stock in trade. And no doubt she smiled up at him wanly and tried not to wince at the onset of the next searing throe. After that Rudolph would retire to his study, knowing he could really do nothing but await the great advent, the miracle of renewal in which life finds fulfillment. Beyond doubt, he picked up bulletins and reprints or perhaps even some of his students' written examination papers, accumulating on his desk now that their scholastic year was drawing to a close. But just as assuredly he must have cast them impatiently to one side, calling for one *'ti' noir*—but with sugar—after another.

Sometime after dawn the nurse rustled into the study, her face grave. Matters were not going well, she said haltingly. The pains—they seemed to have stopped. Suppressing an icy surge of panic he hurried to Adrienne's bedside, doing his best to look and sound confident and unworried, listening in fierce intensity through the stethoscope and trying not to betray the anguish that gripped him when he could no longer indentify the fetal heartbeats. Literally weak with fear, he cranked the telephone, gave Central Dr. Felix Larue's number, and after outlining the situation to him, also sent Dan and the carriage for old Dr. Ernest Lewis, the dean of southern gynecologists.

They came in all haste through the cool, blustery March morning and hurried up the staircase, black satchels in hand. As a basic preliminary, they exiled Rudolph to his study. He was still there when the nurse brought word from the physicians that Mrs. Matas had been delivered of a fine, large boy, with strong, straight back and beautifully formed features. The flooding relief weakened him more than had all the torture of doubt. He asked why he had not yet heard the baby—his son!—cry, and was told that the doctors were even then busily spanking him into the labor of drawing breath for himself. Was everything the doctors needed to hand? The hot water, the specially refined olive oil, the soft cloths, the bassinet? Smiling loftily, the nurse assured him all had been properly provided. Then she returned to the bedroom.

He waited in mounting impatience for the summons that would bid him behold his own begotten son, and as the minutes dragged by without such a call, doubt and trepidation returned to plague him. At length, unable longer to endure the suspense, he left the study and strode down the familiar hall to the room where Adrienne had been so long in labor, brushing past Mrs. Goslee who sat huddled in a large wing chair, a forlorn little figure, weeping silently. The instant he entered the bedroom, he read in the compassionate eyes of Dr. Lewis and in the swift movement with which Dr. Larue turned his back to stare at a curtained window, the appalling verdict. "Pappy" Lewis, the older physician was affectionately called among his juniors, and there was indeed something paternal in the gentle, pitying way in which he blighted Rudolph Matas's exultant sense of fulfillment: You know as well as anyone else, my boy, the many causes that can bring about peri-natal death. . . . The heart was beating at birth, and it continued to beat for eight minutes or so. . . . Respiration simply could not be initiated. We left nothing undone. . . .

Fiercely Rudolph took up the little body, pressed his bearded lips to the soft bud of a mouth and tried to inflate the baby chest with his own anguished breath. Gently, Dr. Lewis took the small corpse from him. . . . Please try to control yourself, son; we attempted mouth-to-mouth insufflation as long as there was any hope of . . . you have Mrs. Matas to think of . . . she is under sedation now but she will be conscious soon and you have to . . . she does not yet know. . . .

By a great effort he pulled himself together, thanked his friends brokenly, and assured them he knew they had done all that human skill and knowledge could achieve. He was master of himself now and would attend to all essential details; they need give themselves no further concern on that score. His first task, of course, was to bring what consolation he could to Mrs. Goslee, to convince her that Adri was in no danger, yet making it plain she would need the comfort of her mother's understanding presence. Arthur had left the house for his dental-college classes as usual, but Lucian remained at home and knew at once what had happened.

Thereafter Rudolph returned to his study to make two telephone calls. One was to the undertaker, ordering an infant's coffin to be delivered forthwith and a mortuary worker to bed the baby's body in it. The second, after some hesitation, was to his friend, Frank Moore, the portrait photographer who took all of Dr. Matas's medical photographs of patients before and after surgery. Narciso would have to be notified too; but bad news could keep, and he would send him a telegram from the city later in the day, or even tomorrow. He felt a surge of pity for his father's impending grief.

He returned quietly to the bedroom. Adrienne was not yet fully conscious, and Mrs. Goslee, the dainty little doll of a minuscule *grande dame* was beside her, having bathed her face in cold water, and touched her temples with eau de cologne to disguise as best she could the ravages wrought by sorrow. Rudolph nodded to her, complimented her in a few words of French on her splendid courage, then beckoned to the nurse to follow him into the hall. He directed her in whispers to bring to the study the baby's body, in its feather-quilt-lined basket, and the finest of the garments that had been prepared for its birth. There the dead infant was clad in the softest of flannel, and the most ornate of long, embroidered dresses, the best lace-collared jacket and beribboned cap. When Frank Moore arrived with his lights and his large portrait camera, his sensitizing and developing tanks and other equipment, Dr. Matas directed the nurse to a chair. Then he placed the tiny corpse in her arms tenderly, arranging its limbs and the finery in which it was clad, so that the casual observer might assume the baby was merely sleeping. He bade Moore take the picture, and turned swiftly away, for now tears welled from his eyes as he envisioned his child. O Absalom, my son, my son!

One copy of this picture he later sent to his father, and perhaps another to his mother and sister in Catalonia. The rest were found among his papers after his death. In all human probability Adrienne was never even told of its existence.

The undertaker arrived soon after Moore had developed the wet plate to make sure the photograph had turned out well. Once the body was placed in its tiny casket, this was permanently closed. Rudolph and Lucian carried it out to the barouche which Dan had brought around to the carriage block on St. Charles Avenue. Otherwise unattended, the equipage drove past the hospital, through what was known as "back-of-town," to the bridge across a then seventy-year-old "new" Basin Canal, and Metairie Cemetery along its far bank. Late that afternoon, the small casket was turned over to sextons to be placed in the Matas family tomb as first occupant of the cold, miniature marble temple, set in a silent city of similar above-ground structures.

Of the reunion between Adrienne and her husband there is no record other than the fact that for the future they were more consummately devoted to one another than ever. But there remains incontestable testimony of the dissolution of the last vestige of the old breach which in 1882 had estranged Rudolph from his father. On March 13, 1902, Narciso wrote:

"My dear son:

"After many days of anxiety I received at last your telegram announcing the severe confinement of your wife and the delivery of a still born male child. It is too bad that after going in so much trouble and conceiving such good hopes, and happiness, she should have had only a dead child. I imagine how much she has suffered and under what mental anxiety and nervous strain you have been many days before and during the confinement. I understand now the cause of your long silence and delay in writing. You have no idea how bad it made me feel. Sometimes I would imagine that you was dangerously ill and unable to write; and some others that your wife was the sick one, and that you didn't have tune even to think about anything else. This worked my spirit day and night and I could hardly relieve my mind from the worst imaginary predictions. Your telegram although sad in one respect put an end to my heartache and mental wonderings and I am glad that is now all over and I hope your poor dear wife will pull through all right.

"Tell her that I fully simpathize with her and regretted that for her own sake and the happiness of us all she could not be delivered of a living child. Still her life is more dear to us than a child upon whom the effections of the heart have not yet had time to root deep. Kiss her for me and tell her, that my heart and soul is now with her and that I hope and pray that she will soon recover and forget all her hard time and sufferings and become stronger and healthier than before.

"It is in these occasion, my good boy, that I feel sorry to live so far and separated from you. I know how much you have suffered morally and physically during the ordeal of the last weeks and especially during her confinement.

"Your official position and duties must have proved a terrible burden to you, on your sad hours of anxiety. I know that amongst all your friends and acquantences, there was no one on whom you could open your heart like you would have done with me, and receive in return the encouragement and consolation which your gloomy heart needed so badly! Oh how I wish I could sell the mines, so that we could see and be together once more and for ever.

"This is a letter of expansion to my heart and feelings, and will not disrespect its sacredness by introducing in it any other subject.

"So have courage my Dear boy and take good care of your Dear wife, give her my love and blessings and you my beloved son receive the heart and the blessings also of your loving father

"Matas."

If Teresa or Elvira sent any letter from which he might have gleaned some meed of consolation or sympathy, it was not found among the papers he kept through all the years until the lengthening shadows darkened into night.

CHAPTER XXIV

At the century's turn, Dr. Matas was called to treat a member of the prominent Wheeler family and thus met a son of the house, fifteen-year-old Augustus. Casually considered, that would be a matter of little moment; a busy and popular physician meets well-born teen-agers every day. But this meeting is distinguished by the fact that in time Gus Wheeler and John Woolfolk founded what became one of the greatest investment firms in New Orleans' financial history.

Rudolph was the new partnership's first client, and the association ultimately made him a millionaire. Moreover, he was still going to the safe-deposit vault of his bank every Saturday, checking securities, clipping and depositing coupons, and otherwise looking after his investments long after the firm had passed into other hands, following the death of its founders. Throughout the association, he had heeded Gus Wheeler's sage counsel in all matters of finance save one: during the 1929–33 debacle he flatly refused on purely sentimental grounds to sell any bonds of Spanish-speaking countries or their political subdivisions, even when these defaulted their interest payments. Paradoxically enough, this *beau geste* paid handsome dividends as, with the passage of time, south-of-the-border economies were stabilized.

Yet in 1902 Rudolph Matas gave no thought to the meeting between himself and that Wheeler boy other than to congratulate himself on adding so prominent and wealthy a family to his clientele. Certainly he accorded far more attention to the published accounts of Walter Reed's death of appendicitis in Washington that November. He felt an even more compelling interest in the arrival in New York of an Austrian orthopedist, Adolf Lorenz by name, a man who used manipulation instead of surgery to reduce and bring back to normal such deformities as clubfoot. So great was Lorenz's renown that a Chicago packing-house magnate, whose daughter had been born with a malformed hip, paid him a fabulous fee to correct this defect, if possible, by his so-called bloodless surgery.

The moment it became known that Lorenz was coming to this country in response to the Chicagoan's call, various professional organizations, New York's Academy of Medicine in the van, invited him to address them and demonstrate his techniques. The principal invitation was that of the American Medical Association, scheduled to meet at New Orleans in May 1903. By that time Lorenz had become a highly controversial figure. Glancing at contemporary newspaper chronicles of the New Orleans convention, one might gain the impression that the A.M.A. meeting was simply another adjunct to the Austrian's tour of the United States. Incensed by this, a number of delegates let it be known they were prepared to expose Dr. Lorenz's "pretensions."

The man's personality was certainly dominant, an effect he did nothing to minimize. In fact, he came to New Orleans two days before the convention opened and remained for three days after it adjourned. Even among the delegates, when these arrived, his appearance was arresting: tall, spare, very wide of shoulder, and bearded like an Assyrian king who had just been given a permanent wave, a luxurious growth of hair falling in dark, glossy ripples from chin to below the chest line. Small wonder that before the other notables arrived, the *Daily States* reported:

"The gaunt figure of Dr. Lorenz was very much in evidence in the rotunda [of the St. Charles Hotel] last evening. He stalked about, the observed of all. . . . 'I am only here as an observer,' he said in his [foreign accent]. 'I shall not operate here, I think. I shall not discuss.'"

Those who promised to expose him charged he was little better than a charlatan, whose methods were not new, not successful nor even his own, being exploited merely through the sort of personal publicity physicians were more and more determined to brand as unethical. Yet he had at least two major champions among the convention bigwigs. One was commandingly tall, well-knit, raspy-voiced Dr. John B. Murphy of Chicago, who bluntly told an inquiring reporter, "The men who are preparing and circulating these things are members of the Knockers' Club, that is all. . . . [Dr. Lorenz] operated on more than forty-one cases in Chicago, and they have hunted out only the occasional failures."

The other champion who hastened to the big Austrian's defense was short, plump, squeaky-voiced Rudolph Matas, whose neat, compact, meticulously trimmed Vandyke afforded so marked a contrast to Dr. Lorenz's Mosaic profusion of flowing whiskers. Dr. Matas was one of the more prominent convention figures. On the day before the principal meeting, he addressed the National Confederation of State Medical Examining and Licensing Boards, speaking as official representative of Tulane University.

His special interest in Adolf Lorenz stemmed from the fact that in spite of the orthopedist's public denials that he would operate in New Orleans, arrangements had already been made to have him demonstrate his techniques before the physicians and medical students of the city, as well as before the convention delegates. Dr. Matas was one of those directly concerned in making these arrangements, since he was anxious to have the clubfoot of eight-year-old Amédée Gaudet, nephew of Dr. Charles Gaudet, corrected. Indeed, Dr. Matas had sought unsuccessfully to rectify this little boy's deformity surgically some years earlier; it was through his instrumentality that Amédée was the first patient on whom Lorenz operated in the Miles amphitheater under the eyes of more spectators than had ever before crowded its galleries at any one time.

In addition, the hallways of Charity Hospital were thronged with parents of physically handicapped children, begging the great man to bring their babies the benison of one of his miracles. Among them, noted the *Picayune,* "were many richly dressed women with colored nurses who held the children in their arms"; the *Times-Democrat* additionally reported that Dr. Lorenz "operated before 400 to 500 of the leading medical men of this and other countries"; also that at the close of his demonstration "a mighty cheer went up by the throng assembled in the hallway. . . . He was given an ovation by those who failed to gain entrance to the amphitheater."

His first operation completely corrected small Amédée Gaudet's clubfoot. Dr. Matas made this statement unequivocally on September 13, four months later, before a meeting of the Orleans Parish Medical Society.

"Dr. Lorenz's brilliant demonstrations throughout the country," he declared, "roused the profession [once more] to a full recognition of [the method's] actual superiority to the surgical procedures then in vogue. . . . Two days ago I assisted in removing a cast from the clubfoot of a little boy operated on by Dr. Lorenz during his visit here." After relating how he had operated surgically on this same child some years earlier he went on to say that "a relapse had occurred and, looked at from the operative point of view, there would have been no way of reducing the deformity except by [extensive bone surgery].

301

. . . Yet after great efforts of more than an hour's duration, Professor Lorenz had succeeded in molding the foot into a position of over-correction. All resisting obstacles, even to the bones of the tarsus and metatarsus, which were fractured at resisting points . . . [were over-come and thereafter] the foot could be overcorrected without the least tension."

The unresisting member was then encased by a rigid plaster cast in its overcorrected position, the cast extending nearly to the knee; and the parents were told that within two days the lad should be en-couraged to walk about, with the cast still on his foot. It was this which Dr. Matas helped to remove four months later, as he related while showing the photograph of an apparently normal foot without any ob-vious sign of malformation.

However, the Matas statement before the Orleans Parish Medical Society gave none of the color that had made Lorenz's appearance at the Miles amphitheater in May so memorable. He said nothing, for in-stance, about the child's terrified weeping when approached by the anesthetist, as the gaunt, bearded figure of the orthopedist towered over him; that was left for a reporter of the *Daily States* to describe, with the addenda that the child was finally calmed when "his par-ents, standing near him, talked to him soothingly in French," and that "Lorenz talked incessantly during the operation, and many of his re-marks were highly humorous."

This last would seem to stand in need of semantic interpretation, if the one quoted example of the Austrian's "humor" is to be taken as typical: a statement by Dr. Lorenz after the cast had been applied and while a "window" was being chiseled into the hardened plaster down to the skin, so that the circulation of blood for the toes would not be impeded. "If the knife slips," the reporter quotes the operator as remarking humorously, "this will not be bloodless surgery."

It is a pity no news cameras were present, and that therefore no photographs of the scene have come down to us—the frock-coated physicians with their opera glasses in the tiered arcs of amphitheater seats, the straining, corded, and almost unbelievably muscular hands and forearms of the Mosaically bearded operator, the uniformed student nurses, and the Sisters of Charity in their dull, powder-blue investiture with white, wide-winged coronets, all working together to have ready to hand whatever the great man might desire in the way of supplies.

Summarizing his comments on the outcome of this operation four months later, Dr. Matas concluded with the flat declaration that "the result was beautiful [and] . . . could not be more gratifying, for no operative procedure could have been as satisfactory."*

* *New Orleans Medical and Surgical Journal,* vol. 56, pp. 337ff.; *Daily States, Picayune, Item,* and *Times-Democrat* files for May 6–12, 1903.

Incidentally, it must have cost Rudolph a very substantial effort to deliver so composed and well organized a report to his professional colleagues at their September meeting, for he and Adrienne were involved at the moment in one of their rare quarrels. The subject of the dispute was, of all things, Lucian's addiction to competitive sports—a trait of which both his mother and stepfather disapproved in almost equal measure.

In contrast to his older brother's apparently ingrained lassitude, Lucian had always been of an athletic bent; in fact, at the moment, he was one of three Tulane medical students trying out for the varsity football squad. Because of Dr. and Mrs. Matas's uncompromising disapproval, he had to do this surreptitiously. His mother placed a ban against rough contact sports because she was afraid of what might happen to one of her darlings; Teur regarded football, baseball, and the like as senseless interruptions to study and research. So Lucian said nothing of football practice and spoke vaguely instead of taking up tumbling at the Young Men's Gymnastic Club.

Adrienne's apprehension was intensified by fear of what might be in store for her first-born. Earlier that year Dr. Matas—already concerned over Arthur's distaste for anything that smacked of physical exertion—became specifically alarmed over a persistent cough which Ott, as he was called en famille, had developed. He finally insisted that the young man submit to a searching physical examination. It revealed beyond all question that Arthur was suffering from a well-developed case of pulmonary tuberculosis.

He was taken from dental college at once, given prolonged bed rest and put on a rich milk-and-egg diet. Meanwhile Dr. Matas entered into correspondence with Karl von Ruck at the Winyah Sanitarium in Asheville. Rudolph had been impressed with the report by von Ruck on results achieved through treatment with antiphthisin, a serum for which the claim was made that it had overcome the flaws which rendered Koch's tuberculin and tuberculin-R dangerous in the treatment of human patients.

At any rate, tuberculosis victims were sent to Winyah from all sections of the land and among them, in August 1903, was Arthur Landry. Unable at the moment to leave his practice and postpone other urgent professional commitments, Rudolph sent Adrienne and Arthur north by the Morgan Line's coastwise passenger ship, Louisiana, a soi-disant luxury liner of that era, plying regularly with its sister vessels between New Orleans and New York. They sailed on August 7, despite the fact that the late summer-early fall bracket on the calendar has never been the most auspicious time of year for a journey through the Caribbean and past the Virginia Capes, inasmuch as this is the spawning period of the Atlantic Ocean's "tropical disturbances." Sure enough, the *Louisiana* made rough weather of it.

In a sketchy journal* Arthur noted that on August 9 "at half past three we ran into two squalls, all the ladies sick and every body scared"; while the next day's entry recorded that "Ladies still sick but feeling a little better, I slept for half an hour in the morning we all felt dizzy, the ship was rolling like a barrel."

Debarking at last, and settled in a modest hotel, they took in the Bowery, Chinatown, Grant's Tomb, the "famous speedway" in Harlem, and other such divertissements, as a sort of rackety farewell by Arthur to indulgence of the flesh for a space. Then mother and son took train for Asheville, where she remained with him until he was reasonably conditioned to Winyah, a matter of several days. He was desperately lonely and perhaps more than a little frightened after seeing her off at the station, though the patients who had fallen under the spell of her captivating personality and radiant friendliness made quite a party of her farewell, so that Arthur might not feel deserted and alone after the train pulled out. But——

"We went right up to our rooms," he wrote that very night in penning his first letter to "Dear Ma" an hour or so after her departure, "as it was so lone some with out you, it seemed as if the light had gone out of the place and all was dark, I don't know how the Eucher turned out I was feeling to sad to play." But he soon grew a little more cheerful and within the fortnight wrote, "Oh! Ma I get my stick (i.e., the hypodermic injection of antiphthisin) every other day now, so I must be getting all right." At first he received an injection every day. The letter closed, as did almost all his missives to his mother:

"I still remain your dear boy with a thousand kisses for you, Teur and Lu. Ott." A postscript urged: "P.S. Don't write too much if it hurts your eyes. Your dear Ott."

September came on with a Labor Day celebration at Asheville and the beginning of classes for other and more fortunate collegians, but Arthur was still receiving his "sticks" and complaining about the food at Winyah and the lack of letters from his bevy of girl friends.

"Renee has not yet answered my letter eather," he lamented to his mother, "neather has Toney, Mollie writes me twice a week and always sends you her love but don't send me anything but best regards, I am glad she don't want to waste her time on me as I would rather stay

---

* He also kept a Matas-type expense account, beginning with the entry of "Cash—$30.00"; first disbursements listed against it were incurred in New York, among them "Keath's Theatere .50," "Brooklyn Bridge, .20," and "Fair" to the Bowery, 10 cents. Apparently the ship's cabin and dining-saloon stewards went untipped.

with you any how, and I know if I was to get married I would have to live apart from you which I wont do, so I guess it is best for me to have five or six girls as I have been having and that way I will keep out of truble, I guess Lu will get married as soon as he can so he can pay up for us both as I have seen to many marriages turn out bad . . . now if they were all like Toney it would be alright, if I had a wife I would not know what to do with her after I had her as I know I would want to go out with the boys and could not so I guess I will forget it and stay with my dear mama.

"Well, as I have no more to say I will close with love to all and a thousand kisses to you, Teur and Lu I remain your big boy   Ott."

When this letter reached New Orleans "Lu" had just precipitated the September quarrel between his mother and "Teur" over his participation in competitive sports. His surreptitious football practice had been bared when he emerged from the season's first scrimmage with one side of his face skinned. This was shrugged aside casually as a brush burn, implying without specifically saying so that it was incurred through a slip on the canvas tumbling mat at the Y.M.G.C.: but unfortunately, the next morning's *Picayune* gave an all too detailed account of the previous afternoon's football practice, mentioning one Lucian Landry by name. Dr. Matas promptly issued a football-or-medicine-but-not-both ukase, with a severe penalty clause, and though Adrienne wanted Lucian barred from perilous pastimes, she flew to her son's succor and there was a fine family row. Most of what followed is forever lost to posterity because the debate was carried on in Spanish,* but there is evidence in one of Arthur's letters from Winyah that Adrienne had taken the disagreement very much to heart, so much so, indeed, that she had written him about it in some detail. In reply he wrote:

"I am sorry you had a fuss with Teur about Lu try and do what Teur asks you ma for he has been very good in sending me up here to get well let Lu get a scolding once in a while you know Teur is doing all he can for him then Lu might think more of you."

He appended to this letter a special page addressed to "Teur," giving his eight-a-day temperature readings and twice-a-day pulse record for the entire week of September 16 and scrawling across the bottom "Do you like this chart Ott." He was looking forward eagerly at this time to his mother's impending visit, for she and Dr. Matas were planning a trip to Philadelphia, New York, and Baltimore in October. Adrienne had been troubled about her eyes, explaining particularly

* Dr. Landry recalled (1958) that "we spoke French or English at home, unless the Governor and my mother wanted to talk about something we boys were not supposed to know; then they spoke in Spanish. She had studied Spanish just the way she did typing, so as to be of help to him in every way she could."

to Arthur that this kept her from writing him oftener and at greater
length. Since George Gould in Philadelphia—Lafcadio Hearn's faithful
friend—had prescribed Rudolph's glasses some years earlier, it was decided that in the course of the October journey he should prescribe
glasses for Adrienne too.

From Philadelphia they took train for New York and a modest round
of theater and dinner parties by night, after Rudolph had visited hospitals and medical libraries by day. Then Adrienne went to Asheville
while her husband took a solitary jaunt to Baltimore. Precise details of
his visit to that city are lacking, save that he stayed at the home of
William S. Halsted and that the latter operated on him in one of the
third-floor rooms of his residence—not at a hospital. A few fragmentary
Matas diary notes make no mention of what this surgery involved
whereas there is an absolute welter of highly adjectived descriptive
material about a storm he and Adrienne encountered in the course
of a guided drive to a mountaintop resort near Asheville. Whatever
its precise nature, the operation was clearly a minor one; Rudolph left
Halsted's Eutaw Place residence for Asheville six days later, on October
29. The incident served still further to cement the cordial friendship
which had linked the two men since their first encounter years before.

By way of illustration: In 1921 Dr. Matas sought very actively to
assure for Dr. Halsted recognition by the National Dental Association
and bestowal of that body's gold medal as orginator of local anesthesia.
Several claimants had appeared for the coveted award. Head of the
Dental Association at this time was Dr. C. Edmond Kells of New Orleans,* to whom Dr. Matas submitted a spate of evidence in the way
of early reports and published papers, all validating Dr. Halsted's
priority. On the basis of his evidence, the award did go to Dr. Halsted,
who was notified of the Association's decision on his sixty-ninth birthday. He immediately dispatched an ecstatic letter to Dr. Matas, saying
among other things that "it is indeed a rich harvest that I have reaped
year after year from the little seed so joyfully sown on the third floor
of 1201 Eutaw Place long, long ago."

Later, when the medal was presented by Dr. Kells at a Baltimore
banquet given in Dr. Halsted's honor, he wrote Dr. Matas, who was
unable to attend: "Not a wink of sleep did I get during the night of
Saturday, I was too exhilarated for repose . . . How can I ever find

---

* Dr. Kells was himself one of the great pioneers of his profession, being among
the first to apply X-ray examination to dental diagnosis. As this was a new field
whose perils had not yet been charted, he became an early victim—certainly the
first in New Orleans—of radiation sickness. He lost all fingers of one hand; those
of the other were unmistakably affected too, when he put them to a final use by
shooting himself.

words to express my gratitude for an act of unparalleled kindness which has covered two years!" A short six months later, in the course of a memorial oration delivered after Halsted's death, Dr. Matas said:

"It was . . . fourteen years after I had known Prof. Halsted as a great, soulful surgeon, that I came to know him for the first time by personal contact. . . . As I was convalescing in his home, I learned to love the sound of his cautious footsteps as he approached my room late at night. . . . He would sit by my bedside and, relaxing after the arduous work of the day, indulge me with his commentaries on many of the questions and problems in which we were mutually interested."

Under such auspices, it is obvious that Rudolph would have been eager to prolong his 1903 six-day stay at the house in Eutaw Place; for that matter, he would have liked nothing better than to spend sometime in the cool of the Carolina mountains with "Dearest Adri." But inexorable commitments in New Orleans put this out of the question. For one thing, Adri very ardently longed to be in New Orleans on All Saints' Day, the traditional holiday of South Louisiana, when families make flower-laden pilgrimages to the cemeteries to brighten with blossoms the tombs of their dear ones. In view of the fact that Rudolph could not leave Baltimore before the 29th of October, she was doomed to disappointment in this; so she entrusted to Lucian the mission of decorating the tomb in Metairie cemetery where reposed the small casket of the stillborn child of which she had been delivered the year before.

Lucian wrote her a long and flawlessly typed letter in which he said: "I went today to Virgin's to order some flowers for Sunday; I wanted to get some white roses, but they were $4 a doz. and I knew six wouldn't look nice at all so I just had them make up a bouquet composed mostly of small sized white flowers which I think will make up a nice bunch." He added news of a record matriculation at Tulane, and of the lectures he had attended, closing:

"With much love to You, Teur and Ott, and assuring you that I am anxiously watching for your return, I am as ever your Baby Boy Lucian."

Dr. Matas was in two minds about leaving Arthur at Winyah any longer, for he was beginning to harbor serious doubts about the claims made for antiphthisin. These misgivings were underscored by an examination of Arthur's physical condition. But von Ruck importuned him not to prejudge the case without permitting the serum treatment to continue over a long enough period to provide an adequate test, and in the end he agreed to let his stepson remain. Arthur was deeply dejected by this decision. His letters during November were progressively more and more despondent, even though one postcard to Dear Ma proclaimed: "What do you think, we had snow yesterday and this morning the thermo. was 10° above zero." But two days later he wrote that "I have just had a long talk with the old Dr. and I guess I am in it up to my neck with no land in sight . . . He seems to have the impression that I am to stay all winter if I have to I know I shall die for want of proper food, as it is I don't know how I am going to stand it as long as I am here I don't think that you or Teur can blame me. . . ."

They did not blame him, of course. They sent for him to come home, and he arrived on Thanksgiving Day bringing with him a letter of instructions, Phial No. 100 T.B.E., and a blank chart with the rate of increase of extract dosage indicated. It is not of record, however, that the watery extract of tubercle bacilli was ever administered to him again. The returned invalid feasted on turkey and its traditional accompaniments the day of his arrival, though he felt little appetite; and the following day on *bacalao,* a dark and spicy Spanish stew of codfish, of which Dr. Matas and the boys were all inordinately fond and which Adri prepared for them almost every Friday.

But Arthur was bedfast before Christmas and obviously growing weaker each day during the short Carnival season that followed Twelfth Night. Shrove Tuesday fell on February 16 that year. As always, the major Carnival pageants, beginning with the parade of Momus on the Thursday before, moved up St. Charles Avenue on one side and down on the other, thus passing the Matas home twice. So did the biggest spectacle of all, the parade of Rex (who that year was Frank B. Hayne)—crowned, bearded, and clad in gold-embroidered white silk as he sat enthroned on the ornate float from which he toasted Mayor Capdevielle at City Hall, and greeted his Queen of the Carnival, Miss Josie Halliday, among the Maids of her Court on a special balcony before the Boston Club.

Urban Maes, one of Dr. Matas's inner circle of dedicated disciples, had attended Arthur ever since the latter's return from Winyah, offering what solace he could to Adrienne, whom, like the other members of that group, he addressed as "madame." It was he who signed the official certificate attesting that on February 16, 1904, (while gaily garbed maskers and the tinselly glitter of the pageant of Rex, Monarch of Mirth, held sway over a joyous city) Arthur Landry died of pulmonary tuberculosis.

But it was Lucian who made his way through the revelers down St. Charles Avenue to its intersection with Jackson Avenue, and there at the head of the parade halted his close friend Billy Fayssoux, captain of the Rex organization, and asked him to still the music of his dozen marching bands, as they passed before the doorway of 2255 St. Charles Avenue, explaining that his mother had just been prostrated by the death of her first-born; so that for perhaps the only time in all the long history of Rex, his pageantry moved in somber silence through one of the sections of his mad capital-for-a-day, until a house of mourning had been left far behind.

Within two months bereavement struck a yet heavier blow directly at Rudolph Matas when that blithe spirit of timeless romanticism, his father, succumbed to a stroke. Fate was kind to Narciso at the last, for he came to his end, as he would have wished, in the arms of the "dear little son," from whom he had been estranged for so many long and lonely years.

At the time Rudolph's baby was stillborn, Narciso set out to sell his Tucson holdings, as soon as he could find a buyer at a fair price, and then join his son's family in New Orleans. The Tucson properties were anything but inconsiderable. Not only had Narciso enjoyed a substantial private practice; he was medical examiner for nearly all the mutual societies and insurance companies represented in Tucson, he had served as pension examiner for one term, and as County Physician and Health Officer.

He owned a pleasant home on West Pennington Street and held title to a great deal of other valuable real estate, among other items half a block on Bennington Street and the Steward Hotel. He was a substantial shareholder in a number of gold, silver, and lead mines like the Mammoth and the Apollo. He had been one of the organizers of the Tucson Street Railway Company, of which he had been president for a time and was still a director. Naturally, these properties were all heavily pledged to secure extensive loans against them.

In other words, there was no compulsive pressure on him to sell out his holdings at a sacrifice—and he had fixed ideas of what constituted a fair price even for a mine which, though certain to be worth millions almost any day now, had never as yet been more than a marginal producer. Hence he found it difficult to liquidate his Tucson assets while considering the desirability of moving permanently to Louisiana. Then the decision was abruptly taken out of his hands.

For a number of months he had felt some concern over the condition of his left eye. No acute symptoms manifested themselves, no excruciating pain, no intermittent diminution or loss of vision. But every so often, looking at a light, as when examining the eyes of a patient, he would see a halo around the center of illumination, or spray of rainbow arcs. That rendered the diagnosis relatively simple for one who had studied in Paris under de Wecker and Galezowski and had emphasized the practice of ophthalmology throughout a medical career in which specialization had proved infeasible. He was suffering from glaucoma, an increasing pressure of fluid within the eyeball. Such a condition could be relieved only by an iridectomy, the selfsame operation he had first performed on the pet rabbit, the *cher 'ti' lapin* of his then three-year-old son in Paris.

Assuredly, Narciso could have been operated on in Tucson, Phoenix, or any other relatively large, nearby community. But he welcomed a pretext thus afforded for the long-deferred visit to Rudolph. He reached New Orleans only a few days after Arthur Landry's funeral. Still grief-stricken, Adrienne nonetheless made much of him, installing him in the best upstairs guest room and pampering him in every conceivable fashion. The sheer delight of his response was obvious; it had been so very long since any woman had devoted herself to showering him with the fussy attentions in which genuine fondness finds expression.

Rudolph had asked Dr. Paul L. Reiss rather than one of the older ophthalmologists like de Roaldes, who had all but wholly lost his sight, or Bruns, to take his father's case. Examination and diagnosis were equally clear-cut. Narciso was a co-operative patient who submitted willingly to having a few droplets of a cocaine dilution applied to his eye, so that a cuplike instrument could be fitted over the orb to measure the exact degree of internal pressure. He was equally tractable when the time came for Paul Reiss to perform the iridectomy at Touro Infirmary. Listed among his other attending physicians was his son Rudolph—the same prodigy who had capered so ecstatically about the apartment on the Boulevard St. Michel forty years earlier when praised for correctly identifying *la cornée, l'iris,* or *la pupille.* The operation was wholly successful.

Narciso was discharged from Touro the very next day, February 26, wearing a patch and dressing over his left eye to immobilize it as much as might be. His son's coachman Dan drove him home, and Adrienne made even more of a loving fuss over him than before, seeing to every little comfort that could possibly suggest itself to her. Paul Reiss called at the house later in the week to change the dressing and declared the healing progress nothing short of perfect. When the patch was finally removed, Narciso was to all seeming a well man once more.

But he put off from day to day his return to Tucson. Adrienne and Rudolph not only raised no objection to this; they urged him to dispose of his holdings, even at a loss, if need be, and make his home with them. If he wished he could practice medicine on a scale that would not overtax his energies; in any case, he would be free to enjoy at professional gatherings the stimulation of contact with some of the greatest medical practitioners of the day; he could seek and find diversion in almost countless ways.

Lucian joined the chorus. He would finish his medical course the next year but was determined to capture a Charity Hospital internship by competitive examination as his stepfather had done before him. Success would mean his diploma would be withheld for two years, although he would attend no further lectures, laboratory demonstrations, and the like.* He too urged Narciso to stay on, so that Adrienne might have company after he had become an intern, which would necessitate his leaving home to reside at the hospital. Rudolph drily told his stepson that "you have not won the examination yet," but cordially seconded his argument as an added inducement for his father to remain in New Orleans.

Under such circumstances, it was easy and natural for Narciso, basking in this solicitous atmosphere of warm family affection, to postpone his return to a lonely Tucson milieu, even—or perhaps especially—after he learned his wife Louise and their daughter Adelaide had recently returned from Los Angeles to resume permanent residence, though not under his roof. Moreover, March is the pleasantest month of the New Orleans year; camellias and azaleas turn every garden into a welter of flaming colors. . . .

It was Adrienne who found him that dreadful morning toward the end of March; found him where he had fallen, in the carpeted upper hallway. She tried vainly to reach Rudolph and finally did succeed in getting Lucian to the telephone and turning the task of finding his stepfather over to him. But when the two reached the house, Felix Larue and Urban Maes were already there. Narciso had suffered a massive cerebral hemorrhage. He was speechless, and his entire left side was paralyzed. There was practically no hope for his recovery. Yet he lingered on for a fortnight, during which time Rudolph was almost constantly at his side. When a second and final stroke put an end to Narciso's helplessness, "he died in my arms," as Dr. Matas wrote Dr. W. V. Whitmore, of Tucson, when the latter was compiling life sketches of pioneer residents for a state history of Arizona.

"In politics," he noted, "Dr. Matas was an independent. In religion, though a hereditary Catholic, he was a free thinker, unprejudiced and liberal toward all religious creeds. In his social relations he was a Mason, a member of the Benevolent and Protective Order of Elks, and of the Ancient Order of United Woodmen."

Funeral services were held on April 13, 1904, at Notre Dame Church, and were followed by interment at Metairie, in the same little marble mausoleum where reposed the bodies of Arthur Landry and of Narciso's stillborn grandson.

* In those days, medical students who qualified for internships were not given their diplomas until the end of their two-year hospital service, at which time they received their M.D. degrees along with their hospital certificates. During their internship, therefore, they were addressed as "Mister" and not as "Doctor." The same system had just been discontinued at Touro, where medical graduates, addressed as "Doctor," were thereafter accepted as interns.

CHAPTER XXV

In 1905, Honduras, where Columbus first set foot on the mainland of the Americas, reveled in a briefly peaceful interlude of general prosperity. At least three years were to pass before efforts to overthrow President Manuel Bonilla would return the country to a strife-torn and revolutionary norm.

At Puerto Cortés small banana steamers were loaded to the marks with green stems for a relatively fast trip to New Orleans. Between steamer departures and arrivals, the small port's dock laborers relaxed in *cantinas* along the single street, the *Calle de la Linea,* or lolled contentedly in their mud-floored hovels, with abundant supplies of plantains, coconuts, fish, *tortillas,* conchs, rice, and venison for the larder.

Of course there was sickness among them. But when was there a time in which no sickness occurred? When had it not been the case that every now and again one of the invalids died in the throes of *el vómito negro,* especially if he were a newcomer to the tropics?

Much the same sort of situation prevailed in and about Belize, farther up the coast toward Yucatán, principal port and governmental seat of the crown colony of British Honduras. And everywhere in the moist and steaming jungles the fruit companies had cleared for their vast banana plantations, mosquitoes swarmed in the twilight; not for nothing was the Honduranean wilderness adjoining Nicaragua known as The Mosquitia.

Quarantine physicians stationed at the banana ports rarely heard of these commonplace illnesses even in nearby inland settlements.

313

Steamers bearing banana stems to a railhead in New Orleans for fast transshipment to all the rich markets of the Colossus of the North, crossed the Gulf of Mexico in all haste, their forests of forward-opening funnels sweeping cool sea air through the filled cargo holds where an occasional deadly tarantula and many a more deadly mosquito, having gorged on the blood of a yellow-fever victim somewhere among the interior plantations, clung torpidly among the green "hands" of bananas during the brief three-day journey. A dozen days must elapse before it could implant Bronze John's lethal seed in another human host.

In New Orleans too, business was booming. Theodore Roosevelt's election was a guarantee for Louisiana's sugar planters that no assault would be made for the moment, at least, on the tariff which enabled them to compete with Cuba and the Philippines. A modern sewerage-disposal system was at last being extended throughout the built-up sections of the city, river water was being filtered and chlorinated before it was pumped into the mains which, block by block, were replacing open cypress cisterns; as a result, typhoid fever began to disappear from the New Orleans scene.

As another result, there was no lack of employment along the water-front and on the plantations. Cane cultivation was still carried on by mule and manual power; on the docks, work-along-shoremen loaded and unloaded ocean and river vessels. Aristocrats among these toilers were the screwmen, who used hand-operated jackscrews to compress cotton bales into the holds of cargo craft bound for Liverpool, Boston, or Yokohama. Most of the screwmen were Irish and the area in which they dwelt, hard by the cotton warehouses and compress yards, is known to this day as the Irish Channel. Many banana ships on the other hand docked downstream from Canal Street, near what was then and still is the Old French Market. Most of those who earned a meager living by shouldering the great green stems and transferring them thus to refrigerated freight cars were Latins, among whom Italians predominated. The French Market area, though in the very heart of the original *Vieux Carré* laid out by Bienville's engineers, thus became an Italian and Sicilian colony, with St. Mary's Italian Church as its communal center. Other Latin immigrants, born and bred in the rural soil of Sicily, moved into the truck-farming area that served the city and into the nearby sugar plantations as agricultural laborers.

Former produce warehouses, along Decatur, Gallatin, Barracks, and Hospital streets became teeming warrens where the Italians roomed and boarded with not even the most rudimentary provisions for sanitation. Macaroni factories sprang up in the vicinity, so that those who toiled along the docks, trudging across the levee with an apparently endless flow of heavy banana stems, could still their ravenous hunger by washing down steaming tangles of *pasta* and cheese with the sour red wine that cost so little. Under such circumstances, who paid any attention to a mosquito bite incurred while unloading a banana ship that was only three days out of Puerto Cortés or Belize, where the slight increase in local deaths from *el vómito negro* over what was normally the case had not yet come to official attention?

Meanwhile, in Terrebonne parish, where the fat, black soil—so say the natives—can be sacked and sold to northern farmers as fertilizer, the new cane crop's stubble grew tall in its raised rows. Along Bayous Du Large, Grand Caillou, Noir, L'Ourse, and other waterways, mellow plantation bells called plowhands at dawn to the yards where big sugar mules—the largest, most powerful of their sterile ilk—waited to be hitched to two-row cultivators. Luggers with sweeps and sails moved up the bayous from shallow coastal lakes—La Peur, Chien, Felicité—with cargoes of seafood, all of which found a ready market. On split-cypress racks black moss for the upholstery trade was drying. On gray cypress shakes which shingled shed and lean-to roofs, piles of pink boiled shrimp were curing under a blazing summer sun for winter gumbo pots. On Saturday nights, *faisdodo* dancers crowded the halls of bayou-side barrooms, for times were indeed good, and another fine crop seemed certain to make them even better.

Dr. Matas now operated one day each week at Touro Infirmary; within a year or so he would be chosen to head the surgical division of a reorganized Touro staff. Often he and his assistants, interns, and students—for he frequently made his Touro practice an adjunct to his teaching schedule now—ate lunch from trays sent up by the diet kitchen and then operated again through the afternoon and sometimes far into the night. Losing patience with the Charity Hospital administration where an all-powerful house surgeon still withheld from the Tulane faculty the very cases best suited for student training, Dr. Matas was preparing to shift a major segment of Tulane's surgical instruction from Charity to Touro.

For the present, however, he was still operating at Charity Hospital on all weekdays save Friday and taking advantage of the drive from his residence to Tulane to drill Lucian for the competitive examination that young man would have to survive in April before he could hope for appointment to one of the coveted Charity Hospital internships. Each weekday morning except Friday, therefore, they would leave the house together. En route, they passed of necessity through a section where a long-dead planter, subdividing his cane fields into city lots, named the newly laid out streets after the nine Muses.

As Dr. Matas and Lucian started for town a brisk oral quiz was begun. It continued until Lucian missed a question. If this happened before

Polymnia Street was reached, the test was scored a failure; if no question was missed until after the carriage had crossed Calliope Street or had passed beyond it around Lee Circle, it was scored a major success. When at last the hospital examinations were held in April, Lucian passed second only to George H. Applewhite among a host of ambitious applicants. But in anatomy, the subject in which Dr. Matas had coached him morning after morning while Dan drove them townward, he stood first. Lucian and Applewhite became firm friends throughout the two years of their tour of duty as interns. The initial service to which they were assigned was that of Dr. John B. Elliott, Sr., to whom all "suspicious" fever cases would be referred on admission.

So far as Louisiana and its bustling port metropolis were concerned, all was right with the world that late spring and early summer of 1905, when something secret and deadly among the green banana cargoes that came pitching up through the Yucatán channel from Puerto Cortés and Belize flitted ashore and disappeared among the overcrowded tenements where the banana loaders hived in the French Market area. Then it burst like a shrapnel shell's charge out from New Orleans into the bayou country.

Leon Lescale, an Italian field hand on Ardoyne plantation in Terrebonne parish, complained to Dr. C. M. Menville in Houma of trouble with his eyes and was sent to New Orleans on June 20 for treatment as an outpatient at Charity Hospital. He found rooms with fellow immigrants or kinsmen along Decatur Street. On July 2 his brothers Mario and Victor went to New Orleans to bring him home, assumably with time out for a weekend carouse in the congenial company of other Latin expatriates. They stayed with Leon in his tenement cubicle but returned on July 4 without him, reporting that he had taken sick and could not be moved. Two days later Victor fell sick and on July 14 he died, just three days after Leon returned from New Orleans, weak and jaundiced but convalescent.

From other parishes other Italians—a fruit vendor from Grosse Tete, a shrimp fisherman from Clark's Chênière, a pregnant young housewife from Lake Providence, a dairyman from Bayou Lafourche, a plantation hand from Iberville—returned to their homes after a sojourn at New Orleans to purchase supplies, visit relatives, seek medical attention for minor ailments, or find diversion. One by one they sickened of fever, as did more and ever more of the Sicilians along the banana-wharf enclave. Within two weeks, panic flight scattered the terrified foreigners, many of them unable to understand English and therefore deaf to sound medical and hygienic counsel. On August 8, when the United States Public Health and Marine Hospital Service took charge of the situation,* after an appeal direct to President Roosevelt, no less than 606 active yellow-fever cases were officially on record as being centered about 101 individual foci in New Orleans alone (counting the Sicilian quarter opposite the French Market as only one focus).

Prior to this time, on July 12, two "suspicious" cases had been reported by attending physicians to Dr. Souchon, president of the State Health Board. One was that of a boy, who died in the living quarters back of his father's grocery just two doors from the house in which the second patient, a woman, died. However, neither Dr. Souchon nor the attending physicians were willing to shoulder the responsibility of ascribing these deaths unequivocally to yellow fever, and therefore listed them simply as "suspicious"; but on July 17 two unmistakable yellow-fever deaths were reported to the Board of Health from Hôtel Dieu. Dr. Souchon visited the hospital the instant this report was received, then summoned public-health officials from neighboring states by telegram, so that a joint autopsy could be held. The findings of this grisly conference were that, beyond challenge, death had been caused by yellow fever.

A report was immediately wired to Surgeon-General Wyman in Washington, and he dispatched Surgeon Joseph H. White and a large staff to the Gulf area. Meantime New Orleans for once submerged all intramural differences and united on such a concerted program of self-help as few communities have ever known. The Rev. Dr. Beverly Warner of Trinity Episcopal Church called to his house of worship the first meeting; a city-wide meeting followed, and the directions of a specially appointed advisory group from the Orleans Parish Medical Society were swiftly and effectually translated into action.

An emergency hospital had to be provided, a crash mosquito eradication campaign had to be set in motion, and, above all, screening had to be undertaken without delay on a city-wide basis. The first essential was money. A $100,000 emergency appropriation was made by the state of Louisiana; the municipal treasury of New Orleans provided $60,000; but the citizens of New Orleans individually pledged —and put up in cash—$160,000 additional.

"No outside aid was accepted," reports Augustin's *History of Yellow Fever*, "and several offers of assistance were declined with gratitude."

The task of establishing an emergency hospital was confided to Dr. Hamilton Polk Jones, who as surgeon-volunteer with the Cuban Expeditionary Forces had established a yellow-fever hospital along the Siboney Road after the battle of San Juan. A three-story building at the very focal point of the original area of infection was summarily

* The transfer of authority to the Federal health services was consummated *de jure* on this date, but did not attain *de facto* status until August 14.

expropriated. Laboring around the clock, crews of workmen cleaned, screened, lighted, and equipped it while Dr. Jones assembled and organized a staff. Within thirty-six hours of the project's initiation the hospital was admitting patients—and even the ambulance (in charge of a resident Tulane medical student) was screened.

Ventilation of the hospital presented the most serious obstacles of all, since the structure had windows in only one of its four sides, namely the front wall. Circular openings were therefore cut one above the other in each floor as well as in the roof, each accommodating a large rotary electric fan. These were kept going night and day in an endeavor to clear the air and cut down the stifling heat of late summer along the New Orleans waterfront. Ventilation was impeded still further because originally inadequate supplies of wire screens, whose mesh was small enough to exclude mosquitoes,* were swiftly exhausted, so that cloth mosquito netting had to be used instead; moreover, the netting had to be applied both inside and outside of all street-level openings because cats, swarming in the vicinity of the French Market's seafood stalls, developed a passion for stretching hooked claws against the exterior fabric.

An apparently insuperable obstacle was raised by the problem of providing adequate laundry service. The mosquito theory was fine for the scientists; but too many persons had heard about fomites, and too many others felt an understandable revulsion against coming into contact with infected fabrics and bedding. But finally the Sisters of the Holy Family called for the soiled linens and took them, just as they came from the wards, smeared with the black vomit and bloody excrement of the dead and the dying, bore them to their convent and returned them, newly cleansed and ironed, to the hospital.

Ultimately, through the arbitrary but welcome offices of Mayor Behrman and others, a public-school building was commandeered. This had windows on four sides, so that adequate ventilation could be provided. It was transformed into a hospital where infinitely better care was given the patients brought to its wards.

In any case, the principal attack was not centered on medication or therapy of individual patients. For some years a great many authorities had contended that the best thing one could do for yellow-fever sufferers was exactly nothing. *Primum non nocere* young Rudolph Matas had adopted as his watchword during the epidemic at Mier in 1882; and *Noli me tangere*—the classical equivalent of "Hands off!" —should really be the name of yellow fever, according to a paper

---

* Virtually all metal screens of that era were gauged merely to exclude flies. Thus they presented no barrier to the free two-way passage of mosquitoes.

read by Dr. Joseph Holt in 1905 before a special meeting of the Orleans Parish Medical Society on July 29.

"Dr. Osler advises the administration of quinine," he continued ironically. "Yes, and he further advises us . . . when hemorrhage sets in to use perchloride of iron; all of which is enough to make a New Orleans physician collapse in fatal syncope. Let Dr. Osler pursue this course in Baltimore* where they have inhabitants perhaps over-crowded and to spare, but to advise it as permissible in New Orleans he merely declares to us that he has passed his forty mark by many decades and for the sake of his yellow-fever patients should have been chloroformed long ago."

The point was not debated at length during this meeting, but six weeks later the same Dr. Lucian F. Salomon with whom young Rudolph had shared on Baronne Street the modest office where he later met Lafcadio Hearn, took sharp issue with those who contended no medication could ameliorate or cure yellow fever. He even scored "my friend, Dr. Matas, who stated in his remarks at the last meeting that ergot was useless in yellow fever. . . ." For the rest, Dr. Salomon laid about him mightily, sparing no one, and detailing the ingredients of his prescription for administering potassium nitrate after a strong saline purgative, with a hypodermic injection of ergot if Black Vomit should set in. He concluded:

"I submit the foregoing remarks to you with the hope that you will cut loose from the dicta and dogmas of those who have little faith in the efficacy of drugs even when properly and intelligently applied . . . and I leave you with the scriptural injunction 'According to your faith be it unto you.'"

At this time those newly installed interns at Charity Hospital, Messrs.—not Doctors—Lucian Landry and George Applewhite, were likewise being indoctrinated by the first yellow-fever epidemic they had encountered as adults. Assigned to the elder Dr. Elliott's service, which handled all yellow-fever admissions, they were directed to make out case histories on every patient brought in from the various fever foci. With French Creoles from the Teche country they had no difficulty, for Lucian spoke their language fluently enough not to be baffled by occasional bits of bayou patois. Applewhite understood enough German to make out with those newly settled in the upriver Côte des Allemands.

But Dr. Elliott insisted on the inclusion of complete family back-grounds in the individual case histories; and when it came to the

---

* Dr. Osler was no longer at Baltimore or Johns Hopkins at this time, having accepted an appointment to Oxford University in England as Regius Professor of Medicine, a Chair founded in 1546 by King Henry VIII. A farewell dinner was tendered him by American physicians at the Waldorf Astoria on May 2, 1905.

Sicilians from Decatur Street, the Messrs. Landry and Applewhite found themselves up against a very blank wall indeed. They scurried around to find interpreters among the other patients; but when this could not be done, in desperation lest too sketchy a history bring them harsh rebukes, they simply drew on their imaginations to supply the causes of death for parents and grandparents in Randazzo or Palermo, even when such forebears were in all likelihood still hale and hearty among the living. Inasmuch as family background was known by that time to play no part in contracting yellow fever, no real harm was done; but Lucian had a lively dread of what his stepfather would say if the methods he and Applewhite employed in their researches were ever brought to light.

However, Dr. Matas was deeply absorbed in one of the major roles of the general campaign. By mid-August the citizens' organization had subdivided New Orleans into eighteen districts, each of which was put in charge of one of Surgeon White's assistant U.S.P.H. and Marine Hospital surgeons. Each such assistant had at command a group of physicians, nurses, and citizen volunteers to furnish food where needed and, above all, screens.

Of necessity, virtually each district maintained one or more screen wagons with crews. The very moment a fresh case of yellow fever was reported, the assistant surgeon-in-charge dispatched a screen wagon to the address, and it came dashing up much as fire-engine horses galloped recklessly to the site of a conflagration. In a trice a room was isolated, fumigated with sulphur and pyrethrum to kill whatever mosquitoes might be there at the time, and then securely screened. After that, the patient was moved into it, while the balance of the house was gassed with mosquito-killing fumes. If this were not feasible, the patient was moved out of his sickroom to a cot enclosed in a mosquito bar, while the room he had occupied was screened and rid of its mosquitoes so that he could be moved back. A sanitation squad followed to inspect and screen all cisterns in the vicinity, flush out gutters, empty carelessly left containers of standing water, and pour oil over the contents of vaults and privies. But in every case the major effort was devoted to keeping mosquitoes from getting at the patient and thus spreading the contamination.

The provision of medical and nursing service—especially the latter—posed one of the most vexing difficulties that had to be overcome. Hence, a paper Dr. Matas delivered, by request, before a special yellow-fever meeting of the Parish Medical Society on August 12, bore the rolling title: "New Duties and Responsibilities Imposed on Trained Nurses and Other Persons Entrusted with the Care of Yellow-Fever Patients, In Consequence of the Newly Acquired Knowledge of the Mode of Transmission of This Disease by the Mosquito." It was made up of a synopsis of detailed instructions on procedures to be followed under various sets of circumstances, as for instance: "If mosquitoes are found within the netting (of a bar over the patient's bed) they should be killed inside, not merely driven or shaken out."

Dr. Salomon may have been ready to do battle *à outrance* for the hypodermic injection of ergot and to smite objectors to this procedure hip and thigh. But he entertained no doubts about the value of the Matas synopsis and immediately took the floor with a motion that it be elaborated by its author into a pamphlet, this in turn to be printed and distributed by the Orleans Parish Medical Society to physicians and nurses throughout the city. The motion carried unanimously. Moreover, the Surgeon-in-Command for the U.S.P.H. and M.H.S., took up the matter of distributing the Matas instructional brochure throughout the South, wherever the omen of yellow fever was specially imminent. No less than 7000 copies of it were sent out, all told, during the battle against the 1905 epidemic.

Later, a still more detailed elaboration of the treatise was published in *The Trained Nurse and Hospital Review* for the last quarter of 1905. This still stands as "the" classic on "Nursing in Yellow Fever and the Duties of the Trained Nurse in Epidemics." It goes into the minutiae of such details as how to "clean the patient's teeth of the gummy saliva known as sordes"; how to give a hot mustard foot bath (referred to by Dr. Matas as "a pediluvium"); and the injunction that "mosquitoes can bite through mosquito nets if any part of the patient's body is in contact with the netting."

Curiously enough, though only once before in all its history had New Orleans suffered a yellow-fever epidemic that began in so virulent a form so early in the year, the community's spirits remained confident and high. Dr. Matas noted in a subsequent memoir that "when the yellow demon of the tropics came back, a new evangel had come to exorcise and banish it from our shores . . . the people of the city won the day with the battle cry 'Away with the mosquito! Down with Stegomyia!' . . . they won the victory in a desperate battle fought from house to house."

It was this fact which made the campaign, and Rudolph Matas's part in it, memorable and significant for all the world. For the first time since Colonel Gorgas's work in Havana* the antifever campaign was

---

* Those who sought to minify the significance of Gorgas's work in Havana insisted that the improvement in that city's appalling previous condition of general filth, contaminated water supply, etc., did as much as, if not more than, mosquito eradication to check yellow fever there. But New Orleans, though far from a model of municipal sanitation, was a veritable archangel of hygiene and cleanliness compared to what Havana had been prior to 1900. This endowed the New Orleans battle of 1905 with special significance.

directed solely against the mosquito, without therapy for the individual patient.

Running a typical course, the epidemic of 1905 should have become progressively more widespread and more lethal through August and September, by which time previous major epidemics numbered their fatalities in the thousands; it should not have disappeared until the onset of the year's first frost.

Yet the record showed 62 deaths during July in New Orleans, 217 during August, a sharp drop to 111 in September (which had been by far the worst month in all previous epidemics—the worst by more than 100 per cent in 1878); 60 deaths for October, 6 for November, and *none* for December. The total death toll was 456, though the epidemic began at the same time and with the same general degree of virulence as had previous epidemics which slew 7848 in 1853 and 4046 in 1878. The last fresh case was reported nearly two months before the first frost which did not come until December 5 that year. Above all, the 1905 epidemic gave every promise in its beginnings of setting an all-time record of fatalities because it struck after a swiftly expanding population of nonimmunes had enjoyed years of freedom from such pestilential visitations, not on the heels of a previous major epidemic, which would have left thousands of newly protected immunes in its wake.

Theodore Roosevelt made a typical "Our Teddy" gesture at this time. He offered to visit New Orleans to show the nation, in effect, that travelers had nothing to fear from sojourning in the Valley's gateway metropolis. He arrived by special train and was whisked from the riverfront station to the yacht *Comus*, traditional craft of Mardi Gras royalty, for a port inspection trip. It was on this vessel that he greeted cotton factor John M. Parker* with a booming "I've already got three bears this year; I'm coming down this winter to get some more with you in the cane brakes!" He congratulated Charles Janvier, one of the leaders of the Citizens' Yellow Fever Committee, on the magnificent achievement of that body and publicly pledged that Surgeon Joseph White would be detailed to New Orleans as long as he might be needed here. He was tendered a midafternoon banquet at the St. Charles Hotel and was hurried back to his train at five thirty for the return trip to Washington.

"The battle is over," rejoiced the *New Orleans Medical and Surgical Journal* in its next issue, heading its editorial with the single word:

---

* John Parker became one of the leaders of the Bull Moose movement in 1912; in 1916 he was nominated for Vice-President on that ticket, and when Roosevelt withdrew as Presidential candidate to support Hughes, ran for Vice-President on the headless Bull Moose ticket, supporting Woodrow Wilson.

"Victory!" "As we write there have been no deaths from yellow fever in six days. During that same period in 1878 there were 195, and even in 1897, the year the fever commenced very late and was considered so mild, there were 31 deaths from that cause during the corresponding time . . . Success is due chiefly to the destruction of mosquitoes . . . and the protection of the sick from the bites of these insects by means of screens."

In short, the battle against Bronze John was victoriously at an end. New Orleans never again suffered a yellow-fever epidemic.

Rudolph and Adrienne Matas took train for Washington and New York, and it is of record that in the capital they enjoyed, or at least experienced, their first automobile ride; an outing in the White Steamer of Colonel John Shaw Billings. The experience so unnerved Dr. Matas that three years passed before he mustered up courage enough to replace his carriage with a motorcar. This was a Chalmers phaeton to which he referred invariably as his John Chalmers Da Costa, in jocular tribute to the great Philadelphia teacher and medical encyclopedist. Unfortunately, he got little use or enjoyment from its possession. A short time after he acquired it he lost an eye; months were to pass before he could be sure he could ever again practice surgery.

CHAPTER XXVI

It must be taken for granted that in the career of even a truly great surgeon, one who is not without honor among his own kin, the interplay of life and death, the pushes and pulls of hospital administration, the unending study of current professional literature, attendance at medical meetings, and the preparation and delivery of original papers, inevitably tend to fall into a static routine. In 1906, Rudolph Matas's career still held nearly half a century of surgical practice; his instruction would continue to inspire collegiate generation after generation for more than two decades. But he made no really major contributions to the advancement of surgery as a science after this time. His role thenceforth was that of an artist whose matchless technique others would emulate. He continued to be a student, but he was no longer a pioneer; a searcher, but not a researcher.

To be sure, there were still individually memorable moments along the way where adventures in keeping the slender thread of life from being snapped had become commonplace. In 1906, for example, Dr. Matas brought his continuing feud with the administration of Charity Hospital to a head in a roster of complaints charging that "of the 281 cases assigned to me I was only able to utilize 76 (or 27%) for operative clinics, the large proportion of the remainder being operated or treated by the House officers. To teach surgery to medical students on the basis of 76 operative cases during an entire session . . . is manifestly not possible."

The situation had reached a state of crisis at which Dr. Matas was prepared to move his surgical classes to Touro Infirmary as soon as the enlargement of that institution, then in progress, had been completed. But a $200,000 bequest to Charity Hospital from Isaac Delgado was included among the latter's legacies, the sole stipulation being that the money be used to construct for the treatment of indigent patients of both sexes a surgical and gynecological building to which medical students would be admitted for clinical instruction, and that "the professors of Surgery and Gynecology of the Medical Department of the Tulane University of Louisiana, my friends Dr. Ernest Lewis and Dr. Rudolph Matas, and their successors in their respective chairs, should be given the privilege of attending the patients of the Delgado Memorial as members of the visiting staff at the Charity Hospital, and of conducting their operations in such a manner that their classes may profit by their teachings and example."

Two refinements of medico-surgical procedure were initiated by Dr. Matas at this time. One was a special preoperative dietary regimen for all patients about to undergo surgery at a point whose surface might be contaminated by intestinal discharges (e.g., for hemorrhoids). He did this after a second patient in his practice had died of postoperative tetanus. Reporting to the American Surgical Association at Philadelphia, seven or eight years later, he declared that "no patient should be brought to [such an] operation without antitetanic preparation . . . [which] is very simple and consists in (a) purgation three days before the operation; (b) the suppression of all raw, uncooked food, especially green vegetables, berries and other fruit for the same period of time."[*]

The second contribution was purely mechanical: a clamp for controlling the rate at which fluid was given a patient intravenously. Simple as it was, it may yet prove to have a wider and more lastingly beneficial, if less dramatic, effect on surgery than his monumental work on aneurisms. Theretofore the rate of intravenous infusions had been regulated solely by raising or lowering the height of the reservoir from which the fluid—glucose, normal saline, or whatever—was administered. Occasionally such an otherwise unchecked flow placed an overload on the right side of the patient's heart and thus brought about the collapse and death of the very individual whose life it was designed to prolong. The Matas clamp made it possible to control the rate of infusion, as viewed in a sight glass, at so and so many drops a minute, regardless of the reservoir's height.

Dr. and Mrs. Matas spent much of the summer of 1906 in the East. After attending the American Medical Association convention in Boston, they remained in Philadelphia, New York, and Washington, in each of

[*] *Annals of Surgery*, vol. 50, p. 341.

which cities Rudolph busied himself about the hospitals and libraries, leaving Adrienne bored and lonely without anything to occupy her but the trivia of travel management.

At the 1907 A.M.A. convention in Atlantic City Rudolph was made chairman of the surgical section before which such Titans as Crile and Mayo would deliver their papers the following year in Chicago. It turned out subsequently that Dr. Matas would deliver an address then too; a eulogy of Nicholas Senn, to whose legendary career death had just put an end.

Returning to New Orleans, he found himself swamped with detail work demanded by organization of the Touro surgical staff. In order to find more freedom for creative activities in addition to teaching, private practice, and association duties at the local, state, and national level, he persuaded Warren Stone Bickham to return from New York and join the Matas office, with Lucian Landry as junior associate. To this end a building was acquired directly across Prytania Street from Touro Infirmary, and the offices of Drs. Matas and Landry were transferred to it for the next half century.

Meanwhile, Dr. Matas neglected no opportunity to continue his altercation with the Charity Hospital house staff under Dr. Batchelor. At a meeting of the parish society the latter read a paper listing the eighteen gall-bladder operations performed on his service during the previous six years. By way of opening the general discussion which followed, Dr. Matas noted with some acerbity that the Charity Hospital statistics of 9000 ward patients and 20,000 outpatients treated annually, "with only eighteen operations for gallstones in six consecutive years by the house surgeon . . . is in itself a striking commentary upon the conservatism, so-called, of the practitioners in this section . . . my own practice exceeding over 80 cases operated in the same time."*

As before, Dr. and Mrs. Matas put in the summer "vacationing" among the libraries, hospitals, and hotels of New York, Philadelphia, Washington, and Baltimore, returning to New Orleans during the latter part of October, just in time for him to begin his year's course of lectures and clinics in the surgical department of Tulane. Lucian, now a full-fledged practitioner, became for nearly two years his stepfather's anesthetist. He finally rebelled, and not too subtly, by calling a young friend, Dr. Ansel Caine, to serve as anesthetist at the next scheduled operation, without first consulting Teur in the matter; when the latter became aware of the substitution the patient was already anesthetized, by which time it was too late to assert quasi-parental authority. Therewith Lucian was accepted as junior associate.

* New Orleans Medical and Surgical Journal, vol. 60, pp. 747–48.

It was during this year that the Louisiana State Medical Society devoted its annual session to a symposium on ophthalmology. The papers delivered at that time, along with summaries of the discussions that followed, were not printed until December. One of the most memorable contributions was a short report by Dr. Ernest A. Robin of New Orleans, proposing a new method for enucleating the eyeball under local anesthesia.

"The patient is conscious," he stressed, "and by that fact stands warded against the awful error of removing the wrong eye, an accident of which several instances have been reported within recent years."

Dr. Matas's interest in the specialty for which his father had prepared himself, even though the quirks of chance had made him a general practitioner in frontier settlements, found expression in the reorganization of the Touro staff. Each department save one was headed by a single chief. The sole exception bore the official title of "The Department of the Eye, Ear, Nose and Throat," which was placed under the joint directorship of Drs. Paul L. Reiss and Marcus Feingold. The former had operated on Dr. Matas's father; the latter became first chairman of the newly organized Clinical Society of the Touro Infirmary Staff, before which Dr. Matas made a number of his most significant reports and where he almost invariably led the discussions.

He never willingly absented himself from one of these meetings, where among other things he could talk to his heart's content, with no chairman to call time on him. If Dr. Sidney Simon, for instance, reported on several cases of hysterical hiccups and hemorrhages that had come to his attention, Dr. Matas could—and did—dredge up from the recesses of his memory the early history of stigmata, in which hemorrhages had appeared periodically in the palms of certain individuals without breaking the skin; he could quote Charcot and Velpeau and even recall the obstinate singultus which had kept one of his father's Mexican patients in Matamoros hiccuping violently for ten weeks.

"The peculiar, loud noises," he related, "heard at a very considerable distance from the patient, led [her] to be known as 'the clucking woman.' The singultus stopped promptly one day . . . In an ordinary individual it would have proved fatal by exhaustion."

A major event of the late spring of 1908 was Chaillé Jubilee Day, celebrated May 19 on the eve of the last commencement over which the venerable Dean would preside in that official capacity. On March 20, completing fifty years of service to the Tulane College of Medicine, he announced a bit wistfully that at the close of the current scholastic year he would retire. The Carnegie Foundation voted him an allowance of $3000 a year for life; and among other tributes, the Alumni

Association created a permanent fund to establish and maintain a chair of physiology on the Tulane faculty, named in his honor.

The formal Jubilee program was held at night in the Tulane Theater. Dr. Chaillé's acknowledgment of the various tributes was very moving. He confessed sadly that "few live long enough to realize how sore a trial it is for a lover of useful labor to be deprived by the increasing infirmities of age of the habitual occupation of a lifetime." But he also struck a sturdy note of confidence for the future when he told of the endowments by which the capacity of the Medical Department for continued progress would be increased, laying particular stress on the princely gift of Alexander Hutchinson "due to the solicited advice of his trusted friend and my grateful pupil and distinguished colleague, Professor Rudolph Matas, M.D." The medical college had grown from the thirteen students of its first year in 1835 to such an extent that, during the twenty-three years of his deanship, Dr. Chaillé had signed more than two thirds of all the diplomas issued in its entire seventy-three years of existence.

Within the week Dr. and Mrs. Matas left for Chicago, where the greatest convention ever held by the A.M.A. up to that time went into session on June 2, with no less than 6459 physicians and surgeons registered. The *New Orleans Medical and Surgical Journal* characterized as "DESERVED NOTICE" Rudolph Matas's eulogy on Dr. Senn, reporting that "the following paragraph . . . is so true and so well said in referring to the late Dr. Senn, that we cannot refrain from reproducing it:

"*Vir praeclarus et ornatus.*—Senn, the incomparable teacher, the peerless clinician, the scrutinizing pathologist, the perennial investigator, the faithful historian and charming raconteur; the world traveler, the philosopher, soldier, patriot and organizer; Senn, the philanthropist, the citizen of Chicago and of the world; Senn, one of the greatest masters of our art—will remain an imperishable name in the great pantheon of American surgery.'"

Rudolph and Adrienne remained in Chicago for four days after the convention adjourned, for he had been invited by the College of Physicians and Surgeons—the medical department of the University of Illinois—to deliver the doctorate address at its formal commencement exercises. Immediately thereafter, however, they hurried back to New Orleans, for while nominally Warren Bickham was looking after the Matas practice in his absence, a considerable backlog of operative cases which were not of an emergency nature had been set for future dates pending his return.

Incidentally, he had finally surrendered to the spirit of the times and acquired an automobile, replacing the aged Negro coachman, Dan, with one John Sutton, who was not only one of the new breed of young, professional chauffeurs from whom the "benzene buggy" hid no arcane secrets, but the father of a two-year-old daughter whom Adrienne spoiled shamelessly. Dan remained in service, of course, to putter about the grounds and do odd jobs around the house. No doubt he was staunch in the conviction, as were so many other coachmen, hostlers, and livery-stable proprietors, that as soon as the vogue of stinking, noisy, unreliable mechanical conveyances had passed, the horse would be restored to its proud and rightful place in the scheme of things. In all likelihood, his employer was in full agreement with him at the moment.

Dr. Matas planned to go East later in the summer. Meanwhile he kept office hours, visited patients at their homes, went about his duties as visiting surgeon at Charity Hospital, and put in the nights at his study table till all hours. On Fridays he operated at Touro with his assistants and his interns for as long as it might take them to finish whatever had been scheduled. After the day's surgery, however late the hour, he went to rooms and wards to check on the postoperative condition of the day's patients; he had hardly reached his house before he was telephoning the interns of his service, who had been on active duty throughout the day with him; he demanded a full report on each patient. Almost invariably he concluded the interview with the direction: "Call me in an hour to tell me what the situation is then."

So he came to Friday, July 3, three weeks after his return from Chicago. Among others scheduled for surgery this day was a woman from whose genitals a tubo-ovarian abscess was to be removed. Because of the nature of the infection, her name was placed at the bottom of the list as the last patient to be operated on that day. But for that, Rudolph Matas might not have lost his right eye three months later.

He had an odd Victorian fixation against appearing to disrobe in the presence of women. On busy days, therefore, he did not remove his gown in the presence of nurses after an operation before donning a fresh one. He simply discarded his gloves and mask, scrubbed up afresh, and put on a newly unwrapped sterile gown over the old one. Very occasionally, toward the end of a crowded day of surgery, a supervisor of nurses might succeed in divesting him of as many as seven gowns, leaving still another—the first one to have been donned early that morning—so that Dr. Matas could retire decorously. But usually he wore them all until he could take them off in the screened semiprivacy of the doctors' dressing room.

So it was that this Friday, on the eve of Independence Day, the outermost gown he wore on leaving the operating room was the one he had put on to excise a tubo-ovarian abscess whose infected area was so distended with pus that it ruptured during the operation. Thus released, internal pressure splattered its foul ichor onto the surgeon's gown. With his usual staccato "My, my, my!" Dr. Matas interrupted the steady stream of conversation, comment, and instruction to rinse his gloved hands in the disinfecting solution of his font and continued the day's final operation.

A steaming, hot July evening; his hands were pallid and wrinkled as he stripped off the rubber gloves in which the accumulated perspiration of the last hour was confined. Walking from the operating room he took off mask and glasses and, as was his custom, scrubbed the perspiration from his face with the hem of his outermost gown, a gown befouled with the corruption splashed out of a burst tubo-ovarian abscess. Had the operation been performed earlier that day, the gown would have been safely hulled within the other, he had donned later. . . .

The next morning brought with it the usual rackety Independence Day hullabaloo, but no medical or surgical emergencies. Remaining at home, Dr. Matas checked on the condition of his patients by telephone. To Adrienne he complained of discomfort in his right eye where what had begun as a mild itching early that morning rapidly grew more painful. He slept but little that night and early Sunday morning he called Marcus Feingold to diagnose and treat whatever might be amiss with the troublesome eye.

Dr. Feingold made a routine examination; then he telephoned to intern Isidore Cohn at Touro to bring glass slides and a platinum loop to the Matas home, prepared to make a smear of the matter the patient's right eye was freely discharging by that time. Still clad in his intern whites, Dr. Cohn made the trip by streetcar. Arriving at his suffering chief's bedside, he used the sterilized loop of fine platinum wire to dip from within the lid of the infected eye droplets of fluid, spreading these over the surface of individual glass microscope slides which were carefully housed in a slot-sided wooden box.

Returning to the hospital he followed what had become routine procedure for such bacteriological examinations; a dip into gorgeous Gentian violet to stain the smear, and finally the microscopic scrutiny under high magnification. Appalled by the unmistakable showing of twin-coupled, fatly curved organisms, each united pair presenting the aspect of the flat inner surface of a coffee bean, and unwilling to accept the obvious fact, he examined other slides. The evidence was beyond challenge or denial: these were gonococci or, in the more austere terminology of the bacteriologists, diplococci. This meant Rudolph Matas was suffering from a gonorrheal conjunctivitis.

The young intern called Dr. Feingold and said he would rather the latter came to Touro to see for himself what the microscope had revealed; he did not even want to mention the word over the telephone. But Dr. Feingold impatiently brushed this aside and, when he heard the report, accepted it as authentic. It was all tragically clear. The abscess he had extirpated two days earlier was venereal, the ichor that had splashed from it when it ruptured was gonorrheal pus, and Dr. Matas had wiped the perspiration from his eyes and forehead after the operation with the hem of a gown on which some of the venomous filth had found lodgment.

Thus began three months of mounting mental and physical anguish. Every resource known to medical science at the time was called into play in an effort to cure the infection by irrigation. Dr. Feingold's wife was out of the city, visiting her ailing mother; he virtually gave up his practice and all but lived at the Matas home. Night and day nurses were engaged. An enameled irrigating can hung from an iron bedside stand, with a flexible hose terminating in a small glass nozzle. Whenever the discharge from the infected eye became obvious, it was irrigated gently with permanganate for a few minutes, and this was followed by the installation of a little argyrol within the inflamed lid upon which, between irrigations, a pledget of cotton dampened with permanganate was kept.

Adrienne wanted to help nurse her husband, but was sternly forbidden to do so. As it was, the nurses wore sterile gloves whenever they irrigated or otherwise treated the infection and scrubbed up unsparingly after each contact.* The treatment went on and on and on, but except for one temporary remission, the condition of the eye worsened steadily, and the pain it caused grew so intense that at times sleep became difficult. Adrienne and Dr. Feingold took turns then, sitting up with the patient until far, far into the night. The physician read to him from professional magazines and reprints which accumulated mountainously as the weeks dragged by; Adrienne— Dearest Adri—read him the mystery novels he relished with such deep delight: Meredith Nicholson's *The House of a Thousand Candles*, Maurice LeBlanc's exploits of Arsène Lupin, and *The Mayor's Wife*, by Anna Katharine Green.

"Feingold's eternal and constant consideration, and the infinite pains he took to help me spoke volumes for his splendid conscience," Dr. Matas declared years later, when recalling the omen of this dark hour. "I must pay tribute to him. He was the most patient individual I have ever known. He never complained, and no one is more fully aware than

---

* Nothing could more graphically illustrate the progress of medicine during the half century that has elapsed since this incident; the treatment, the months of torturing doubt, the excruciating pain of a prolapsed iris—all these went for naught, since in the end the eye had to be sacrificed anyway. Nowadays, penicillin injections would clear the infection literally in a matter of hours, there would be no prolonged siege of suffering, and the eye would be saved.

I am of what a trial I must have been in those days to every one around me."

At one time there was hope that constant nursing and irrigation might bring about a cure; at least, the corrosive progress of the infection appeared to have been checked. A month or so after the inflammation had set in, the patient was allowed to leave his bed for a drive with Adrienne and Dr. Feingold as companions and with faithful John Sutton at the wheel. On August 7, and again on August 9, they made these excursions from the sickroom, driving beneath the arching live-oak boughs that formed a vaulted roof over sections of St. Charles Avenue, and with the deep cerise and watermelon pink of foaming crepe myrtle blossoms to line the way. But a marked turn for the worse put a prompt end to such outings. At September's beginning, glaucoma set in; pressure inside the diseased eye forced a part of the iris out through an ulcerated break in the cornea.

"I still remember how bad it was—how terribly painful—the night the cornea ulcerated and the iris prolapsed," he recalled nearly half a century later. The rupture relieved the eye's internal pressure only briefly. A second attack of glaucoma set in the following week, and the next day Dr. Feingold performed an iridectomy, late on the afternoon of September 10, exactly sixty-seven days after the original infection, according to penciled notes in a small memorandum book found among Dr. Matas's papers after his death. The iridectomy was again followed by a brief respite from intense pain, but on the "75th day [after infection], Friday, September 18th—downstairs for the first time since August 18th"; and again, "Staphyloma stops leaking after September 23."

Dr. Bruns, dean of the city's ophthalmologists, had been called into consultation early during the course of the illness, when Dr. Reiss had already left with his wife for a summer of study in Europe. "I remember Bruns came to see me during July—he left for Virginia on August 1," Dr. Matas noted among the penciled memoranda. "He was cold-blooded in professional attitude." Just what this meant is not clear; in all likelihood Dr. Bruns had proposed the immediate enucleation of the eye, and to this Dr. Matas refused to listen. Even two months later, after the iridectomy, when Dr. Ernest Robin was called into consultation and likewise gave it as his opinion and Dr. Feingold's that, in order to save the sight of the left eye the infected one would have to be removed by surgery, he was still reluctant to accept the verdict. Monocular vision was known to lack depth perception, and a surgeon must wield scalpel and bistoury within a hair's breadth of the very fount of life. How could he saddle his patients with the added hazard of an operator's imperfect vision?

Beyond doubt—though arguing against his own conviction rather than against the unanimous findings of his physicians—he reminded Dr. Robin of the latter's paper, published only a few months earlier, to the effect that several instances of the "awful error" of removing the wrong eye had been reported within recent years. On the other hand, one-eyed vision, however flat, was infinitely better than blindness, and so, decided Dr. Matas, he would go to Philadelphia to be examined by the acknowledged foremost American ophthalmologist in his day, Dr. George Edmund de Schweinitz, and by his associates. If these agreed that enucleation was inevitable, he would return to New Orleans for the operation.

"Arrived in Philadelphia Friday, 2 P.M., Q. & C., [Queen & Crescent], October 2nd 91st day of illness" continue the penciled memoranda in the small notebook; and next day "call on Dr. de Schweinitz 9:30 to 10:30 A.M., Dr. W. L. Pyle 11:00 to 12:00, Dr. Risley 11:40 to 1:00 P.M." The day after that was Sunday, October 4 —the ninety-fourth day of his illness as he was careful to note—and he spent it with Adrienne at Atlantic City. "Stopped at Marlborough. Light so intense that I had to remain in room greater part of day." Monday he called on Drs. de Schweinitz and Pyle again; their findings coincided on every point with those of Drs. Feingold and Robin: further efforts to save the infected eye would merely involve loss of sight in the other as well.

The final penciled entry in the little memorandum book reads: "Friday October 9th 1908 98th day—Enucleation at 8:30 A.M. Feingold, Robin, Weiss, Bickham, Landfried, Lucian. Return to active teaching and practice October 29th—112 days after infection."

He remained for some years very sensitive on the subject of his loss and was deeply angered by any reference to it, even by members of his family or by his closest professional intimates. He did not appear in public until an artificial eye, made by a Philadelphia firm, had been accepted as satisfactory.

When he returned to his teaching post, Tulane classes had been in progress for more than three weeks. First- and second-year courses were held for the first time that fall in the newly completed Richardson Memorial Building on the distant campus of Tulane University proper instead of in the old building near Charity Hospital. There were also other changes; two faculty members had replaced Dr. Chaillé, Isadore Dyer having been named to his post as Dean and Dr. Gustav Mann filling the chair of physiology. The latter was a German, born in East India, schooled in Goettingen, and university-trained at Edinburgh. He had taught at Oxford until called to Tulane, his selection having the endorsement of such figures as Osler, Ehrlich, and Jacques Loeb.

Dr. Matas rejoined the Touro staff meetings for the first time on November 6; his first operation after losing his eye was performed on November 27 for the removal of gallstones from a thirty-two-year-old housewife, a "Mrs. W.R.S.V." No one would ever know with what trepidation he approached this threshold to his future, or how many hours, in the long watches after midnight in his study, he had tested out his monocular adjustment to depth perception, finding it adequate —where the life or death of another human being did not depend on the outcome. To all outward seeming he was quite composed as he stepped to the side of the table where Mrs. W.R.S.V. lay in the inertia of surgical anesthesia and of utter trust in the surgeon who was about to put to the test the possibility of trusting himself. Mortality statistics on gall-bladder operations ran high in any case. Had he the moral right, then, to test himself with the odds already high against the patient who had confided her future to his two hands and one eye?

He rinsed gloved hands in the font and extended one of them for the scalpel. For a time he worked in strained silence, fearful of distracting his attention by even the slightest degree from the task in hand. Then gradually he began to speak, and before long he was chattering away as of old, interspersing among his comments the "My, my, my!" that had become second nature to him. His hands were deft and sure, the beautiful artistry of his surgery had never been more clearly apparent.

Mrs. W.R.S.V. made an uneventful recovery. So did the twelve-year-old girl who was his next patient. Rudolph Matas was seventy-nine years old when he performed his last aneurism operation, and during the preceding four decades the work load he carried was one few other individuals could have borne. It was rare for him to leave his study before three o'clock in the morning. A bibliography of his published works, compiled for the *New Orleans Medical and Surgical Journal* on the occasion of a banquet tendered him when he returned from Europe after becoming emeritus professor on the fiftieth anniversary of his matriculation, shows a phenomenal amount of writing and lecturing, all after he became monocular.

In time, what had been an almost morbid sensitiveness about the loss he had suffered, began to lessen. For one thing, during the December following the enucleation of his eye he was one of five New Orleans surgeons commissioned by President Theodore Roosevelt as first lieutenants in the Medical Reserve Corps of the United States Army.

At any rate, by 1915, when seven years had shown him he had lost none of his power to work, to write, and to teach, he wrote to his friend, Dr. J. Collins Warren of Boston, who had just lost an eye through enucleation, a cheery letter in which he said in part:

"I imagine we are both reconciled to our cyclopean state . . . and can say with composure—*tant pis!* to the binoculars and ask no odds of them. When I first realized I would have to lose one eye . . . seven years ago, I was submerged in a semi-stupor at the mere contemplation of the future . . . [but] I began to inquire into the relative frequency of monocular vision and the history of those who had gone through the same ordeal. I was then comforted, as misery always is, by finding that I was only a small part of a very large company . . . [which] had succeeded in stamping itself in some way upon every period of the world's history.

". . . I found the monocular individual not only holding his own, but often outstripping his binocular contemporaries in the race for usefulness and fame. And this is particularly true in our profession . . . While I make no pretense at special merit by the side of the monocular immortals, I am pleased to state in spite of the additional handicap of a marked myopia and astigmatism in my remaining eye, I have never done more minute and exacting work than in the seven years that have elapsed since the accident which deprived me of my right and best eye.

"In consequence of my practically perfect adaptation to the monocular state, I find myself tramping along life's journey with a sure step and pegging along as if nothing had happened. The fact that I have not been restrained in my professional activities and that I have been able to keep up with the procession is quite sufficient explanation of my cheerful acceptance of a situation which had become perforce normal to me. . . . My heartfelt congratulations on your splendid recovery—a recovery which will permit us, the cyclopeans, to enjoy the privilege of your conspicuous and inspiring example as a member of our band, just as the binoculars have been honored by your leadership in the past."

The fact that by 1915 he had emerged from his Gethsemane became obvious earlier in that same year, for it was then, before the annual meeting of the Mississippi State Medical Society, that he delivered the oration for which he is best remembered in medical literature. Its title:

"The Soul of the Surgeon."

CHAPTER XXVII

As if to make up for the meetings from which invalidism had compelled him to absent himself, Dr. Matas plunged into a veritable frenzy of work during the year that followed his loss of an eye. As soon as the 1908–9 term was brought to a close he left New Orleans for a convention of the American Surgical Association at Philadelphia in June, despite the staggering accumulation of unfinished manuscripts for whose delivery the deadlines had long since passed.

This was one session of the A.S.A. he would have made almost any sacrifice to attend, for he knew that at its close he would be elected to its presidency, the highest professional honor yet tendered him. However, he had no more than taken the gavel to adjourn the convention which would not meet again until the following year in Washington, than he had to speed with Adrienne to Atlantic City for the annual gathering of the American Medical Association which, as a member of the executive committee of the surgical section, he would represent that fall at an International Medical Congress in Budapest.

To make this possible he would have to return in all haste to New Orleans, where an unbroken succession of eighteen-hour days at his office, at his library desk, in the operating rooms, in consultation with Gus Wheeler on Saturdays concerning the steadily mounting complexity of his capital investment structure—and above all, at Tulane's Laboratory of Operative Surgery with one of his young assistants, Dr. Carroll Allen, in performing on dogs the experiments which would set the capstone on his contribution to the treatment of aneurisms.

337

The major problem was this: once tightly ligated or clamped, an artery was irreparably damaged through injury to its inner coating, the intima. Thus, if conventional procedures brought on an ominous reaction (one-sided paralysis, loss of sight, etc.), even abrupt release of the ligated vessel from closure would leave it permanently impaired.

Working with experimental dogs, Drs. Matas and Allen set out to devise some method for providing temporary compression of a major artery without damage to the intima. Their first resort was to thin bands of silver, but these were abandoned as unsuitable; for one thing, the bands had to be fastened at the right degree of closure with soft lead clips. But aluminum bands, sufficiently malleable to be worked with the fingers, functioned perfectly. Using the carotid and femoral arteries of dogs, these bands were left in place for periods ranging from one to eight days. Some of the dogs were then chloroformed and put painlessly to death, so that microscopic examination of the vessel walls could determine whether these had suffered any damage. In other cases, the bands were removed, and the dogs were allowed to recover, so that the degree of evil aftereffects, if any, could be determined.

The Budapest journey of 1909 was Rudolph's first trip to Europe since 1886, when he accompanied his mother and sister to Spain. He was in some doubt as to whether Adrienne would agree to go abroad with him, for she knew he would revisit San Felíu de Guixols, where his mother had died the year before and where his sister still lived. The bitterness Adrienne harbored toward Elvira was such that she might even forgo her first trip abroad rather than come into any sort of association with one she had vowed never to forgive.

Rudolph was also plagued by some misgivings as to his wife's health. To be sure, he tried to convince himself that her shortness of breath was due mostly to the excess weight she had gained; but while the husband was eager for such reassurance, the physician refused to dismiss the possibility that this obesity must be due to more direful causes.

Adrienne, on the other hand, was torn between rapture over the prospect of making the Grand Tour at long last, and unwillingness to leave New Orleans, where her mother could visit and comfort her. Even less, however, would she consider letting Rudolph, who was so deluged with work that they saw little enough of one another when they lived in the same house, put an ocean between them for an entire summer. What she really might have demanded was that he too give up the Budapest journey, but he won her over when he said that en route back from Hungary, they would visit the storied cities of Italy and France which Adrienne had so long dreamed of seeing.

Even while consenting to accompany her husband to Europe, however, Adrienne was inflexible in her reiterated declarations that she would not go to Spain with him. Moreover, she did not propose to be left alone in Switzerland or France while he went to visit his sister. After all, Lucian was entitled to a summer abroad by way of rounding out his medical education and cultural background; therefore, if Rudolph insisted on going to San Felíu, well and good, Lucian must go to Europe with them so that she—Adrienne—need not be left in a hotel room like an old trunk, awaiting her husband's return.

To all of this Rudolph agreed readily enough and, since a young man would not want to travel tied to his mother's apron strings, Lucian should go abroad by himself, joining them in Paris en route to Budapest and staying with Adrienne while her husband went to visit *his* mother's grave in the little cemetery overlooking the blue waters of the Costa Brava.

He said nothing about the fact that in thus freeing Lucian from the maternal apron strings he effected a substantial saving in money as well. For himself and Adrienne, he engaged luxury accommodations on the *Lusitania*, keeping meticulous accounts of the $895 he paid for their steamer passage, over and above the $104.80 for Pullman travel to New York via Queen & Crescent, $200 in cash for pocket money, a $2500 letter of credit and "called at Fried (in New York) at 2:30 P.M. and got two extra eyes made costing $25."

But Lucian traveled at the special rate offered to delegates, on a slow boat leaving a week before the *Lusitania* sailed. Under this arrangement, the package price for forty-one days, including transportation and one week's hotel accommodations and board in Budapest, was $395 for the round trip.

Rudolph and Adrienne sailed on August 18 and both kept sketchy diaries. The crossing appears to have been something of a bore, though Rudolph did find among his fellow passengers a Chilean physician, Dr. Barrancha, also en route to Budapest. Otherwise, the first other-than-routine entry in Adrienne's diary marked the *Lusitania*'s brief halt outside the harbor of Queenstown, where bumboat women with fine Irish laces and small souvenir knickknacks came aboard.

Lucian joined them in Paris, as planned, and accompanied them on a trip through Switzerland, Germany, and Budapest, where, as Adrienne noted in her diary, they "drove to Royal Hotel where we found that our room had never been retained although we had paid and sent telegrams. Were given one room with small bed for two and one room for Lucian away but it is on the same floor but, oh my can't get bath. Here we are filthy and no chance to wash all over, as we must rush to see the opening of the Congress. Returned to get some breakfast.

It is raining . . . Saw grand opening and it was beautiful. The Emperor in all his glory.*

"What can we do. Well here comes a car. We (Lucian and Adrienne) took a belt ride and saw a good deal of the streets. Lucian is so tired he is actually sleeping on his seat. The different people here and their odd costumes, their bare feet and in their Sunday clothes amuses me."

Up to the time the Congress adjourned, Adrienne seems to have possessed her soul in patience at her husband's absence; but when they started the promised journey through Europe it was obvious she now expected Rudolph to devote himself to her and squire her about. Lucian had left them to make a leisurely pilgrimage through Austria and Germany before rejoining his mother and stepfather in Berlin. All went well enough with Adrienne and Rudolph until they "arrived in Venice—had our first trip on gondola. Landed at Hotel Europa, high prices but poor accomodations—no bath."

Next day they went sightseeing and Adrienne "bought beautiful lace collar $15." One suspects this and some lace-edged handkerchiefs constituted a peace offering from her husband, for it becomes all too evident that despite these and other placative gifts the only truly bitter quarrel of their quarter century of marriage developed that night on the Grand Canal, where "at 9:30 took a gondola and rode on the canal to hear some singing going on on a barge, but could see nothing."

The disagreement? One can only surmise that Rudolph wanted Adrienne to recede from her fixed determination not to accompany him to San Felíu de Guixols. It would have been scandalous, he pointed out, to pass within a stone's throw of his parents' birthplace without pausing for a moment of meditation or prayer at the grave of the mother who had cherished him through infancy, had nursed him through yellow fever . . . but had never forgiven his refusal to renounce his love for Adrienne Landry, and his subsequent sundering of the silver cord of her dominance. This much Adrienne understood and accepted. But she also knew that Rudolph's only living blood relative, Elvira, she would never accept.

Rudolph, on the other hand, did not want to visit his homeland unaccompanied by his wife, since this was certain to be misinterpreted to his discredit. Either he was married to one who scorned his origins and his kinsfolk, or he was the sort of weakling whose household would not recognize him as its head. So, in the black night on the Grand Canal with nothing to see, and to the background of singing from an invisible barge, one word led to another until they returned in bleak

* The Emperor was not there. Archduke Joseph did the official honors for the House of Hapsburg.

silence to the Hotel Europa and apparently did not even bid one another good night. At least the entry for Friday, Sept. 17, in Adrienne's diary reads:

"Very blue today—cloudy day which tends to aggravate conditions —feel more like staying in my dark room and forgetting the world. Took breakfast—very quietly—not a word exchanged. R. is supposed to go to Padua. I am sitting in St. Mark's Plaza writing this and looking at the pigeons . . . R. had gone to the library to look up some references about Padua—gone one hour now. I have walked my fool self tired, cried myself sick."

It is obvious that brief conversational exchanges could not be avoided on the day after that, since it was necessary to pack and leave for Vienna, where Adrienne "visited St. Stephen's Church everything black to me. Back at hotel my heart about to break." But she and Rudolph that night "went out to opera to see Pagliacci. Beautiful. Ballet after like no other I ever saw." After the performance "took chocolate and cake at Cafe de l'Europa. Back at hotel at 12."

Evidently some sort of entente had been restored by that time, for while Rudolph visited the Wiener Krankenhaus clinics, Adrienne shopped and went to churches to see murals, and sipped chocolate with thick whipped cream atop. Together they wandered through the gardens at Schönbrunn and after dinner they crossed the street from the Hotel Bristol to the Staatsoper to attend a performance of *Manon Lescaut*.

Adrienne was happy over securing good *wagon-lit* accommodations for them on the train to Berlin, where Lucian awaited them at the station and where "my two docs visited beautiful Rudolph Virchow hospital." On the final evening of their stay they went to the Imperial Opera House for a performance of *Götterdämmerung* which, according to Rudolph's diary, "lasted until 11 P.M., a most exhausting performance," and according to Adrienne's was "a five-hour play—bored us to death, came back in taxi cab to our hotel where we all had supper and broke up at 1:00 A.M."

Rudolph and his family parted at Berlin, to meet later in Paris. He remained only two days in San Felíu, noting in his diary merely that "October 3, arrived at San Felíu visited mother's grave—visited the niece of Emilio Forto—dinner at the old home. On October 5th left San Felíu for Paris, left Paris for Cherbourg October 13th to arrive in New York October 20th—trip on Oceanic, it took six days, eight hours, forty-eight minutes for the Atlantic crossing."

One surmises that the obvious contrast between two days in San Felíu with the sister he had not seen for fourteen years and ten days squiring Adrienne about Paris—to the Panthéon, to the Père-Lachaise cemetery, to a small curio shop in the shadow of Notre Dame to purchase small replicas of gargoyles, to Pathé's Gramophone and to the Cinematographs at night—healed whatever rift had been opened by bitter words along the Grand Canal.

It is worth noting that Rudolph was particularly fascinated in Paris by the work of Dr. Eugène Doyen, whose *clinique* on the rue Piccini he visited during every free moment. He had met Dr. Doyen a month before in Budapest, where the latter displayed moving pictures of a number of operations. He was now arranging to have prints of these films made, each set to be accompanied by his text, as a special course in operative surgery.

Dr. Matas became an immediate and enthusiastic advocate of this project and arranged to purchase a set of the films when these were completed in a year or two, so that he could show them before medical and surgical meetings in the United States. He predicted that future surgical instruction would avail itself increasingly of this medium— and he lived long enough to witness the telecast of an operation over a closed circuit, which made all details of the procedure far more clearly visible than the observer's unaided eye could see them from the tiered seats of any operating-room amphitheater.

Rudolph had to hasten back to New Orleans, though he would have liked to put in some days with Colonel Billings in Washington and George Gould in Philadelphia. But Warren Bickham had already returned to New York, Tulane was opening a new scholastic year, and the Southern Medical Association was meeting in New Orleans on November 9. So he took the first train home with his family, though he remained in New Orleans only until the Southern Medical group adjourned. In response to a special invitation from Dr. Will Mayo to attend a session of the Society of Clinical Surgery at Rochester, he then left posthaste for Minnesota.

He and Adrienne made two more trips abroad in the years that followed. The first, in 1911, centered about a meeting of the International Surgical Congress in Brussels; the second, in 1913, about a convention of the International Medical Congress in London.

In each case Rudolph visited San Felíu in the course of their stay abroad, and on each such occasion Adrienne, who would not accompany him, became ill during his absence. In 1911 a small stone formed in one tear duct while she and Lucian were in Switzerland, an extremely painful condition that had to be relieved surgically after the party returned to Paris. In 1913 she developed an obscure digestive malady which confined her to her hotel a great part of the time during Rudolph's absence. Her general physical situation was undeniably deteriorating.

They crossed the Channel to Boulogne and thence to Paris, where Rudolph left for San Felíu, losing his overcoat on the train en route. He stayed at the old house, №9 Plaza Constitución. During the second night of his sojourn the "local band of the Ateneo serenaded under my balcony." He rejoined Adrienne after an absence of nineteen days.

The 1913 International Medical Congress was opened in the Albert Memorial by Prince Arthur of Connaught, who observed that the first such Congress had been opened in 1881 by the then Prince of Wales, later Edward VII, and that Louis Pasteur had been one of those in attendance. This did not impress Adrienne nearly as much, however, as the fact that she and Lucian had the good fortune to see one of the suffragette parades about which she had been reading so much, led by the militants who at other times chained themselves to gratings in front of Parliament.

Rudolph was more than a little put out by the reception accorded his paper, delivered under the title of "The Suture as Applied to the Surgical Cure of Aneurism." It was in a sense a polemic against the growing favor accorded to the field of arterial grafts, and more particularly against the traditionalists' insistence that the Hunterian ligature was a safer operation than the Matas internal suture. In fact, Charles A. Ballance, the surgeon who discussed Dr. Matas's paper, said in so many words: "I should limit the operation of Matas to those cases of aneurism in which the Hunterian operation is inapplicable."

True, he sugar-coated this dictum by adding that "we owe an immense debt to Dr. Matas, and I doubt not that there is a vast field of usefulness for the operation which he has designed and practised." Rudolph also sugar-coated his riposte by proclaiming himself one of Mr. Ballance's greatest debtors but "he feared that Mr. Ballance had been unduly impressed with the difficulties of the technique of the suture from purely theoretical considerations. He was confident that if Mr. Ballance would only abandon all preconceived notions and give endoaneurismorrhaphy a trial, he would find how thoroughly elementary in its simplicity this method of suture is."

His displeasure over the obvious reluctance of a large segment of the British surgical faculty to depart from what Dr. Souchon would still have called "the method of Anel" led him to seek out, nonetheless, the one man in all England who had been most lavish in his praise for the "Matasian operation." This was Sir William Osler, who had not attended the Congress; when Rudolph made a special trip to Oxford to meet him, he found that Sir William and Lady Osler were in Scotland for their holidays and, returning to London, he bundled Adrienne and Lucian off with him to the Continent.

Mrs. Matas was likewise not finding the 1913 trip abroad very enjoyable. Save for a few noteworthy exceptions, she had not even been impressed favorably by her fellow passengers on the North German Lloyd liner, the *Kronprinzessin Cäcilie,* on which they had made the eastward crossing. Among the exceptions was a Philadelphia couple, the J. J. Colliers, with whom Adrienne and Rudolph struck up an instant, warm, and as it turned out, lasting friendship. Mrs. Collier made an adequate and engaging fourth at the bridge-whist tables Adrienne and Mrs. Will J. Mayo organized. She and Mrs. Matas were to become regular correspondents and frequently exchanged gifts at Christmas, anniversaries, and the like.

Mr. Collier, a banker, had heard of Rudolph from both Dr. Keen and Dr. Gould, and let it be seen that he regarded the famous Dr. Matas as a personage, not merely as a casual shipboard acquaintance, and the latter responded genially to the implications of such an attitude. Nonetheless, in the diary she kept intermittently throughout the journey, Adrienne noted under the date of August 2 that: "there is a ball on board tonight, but I fear the crowd is not equal to it. They are too slow." Farther down on the otherwise blank page appears the simple notation, heavily underlined: *"I was right."*

But she also noted in her diary with mounting frequency the times when she found herself compelled to return to her hotel room to rest, and the nights of broken slumber and general malaise. Once back in New Orleans she began increasingly to remain in the house, wearing soft slippers and the loose, comfortable garments still known as Mother Hubbards. It was a rare occasion that brought her out in modish attire.

But the deterioration of Adrienne's health was not the only factor that put a stop to further trips abroad for the Matas family, as well as for others. The assassination of an Austrian archduke by a Serbian student in 1914 was followed by the sweep of German soldiers across neutral Belgium into France, thus triggering what has come down in history as the First World War. For more than four years thereafter, virtually all commercial transatlantic travel ceased.

But Adrienne made one more journey during this interval nonetheless. On September 16, 1916, she and Rudolph traveled to Columbia, Mississippi, to attend Lucian's wedding.

CHAPTER XXVIII

World-wide interest was focused on the controversy over endo-aneurismorrhaphy versus the Hunterian ligature following the Matas-Ballance debate before the 1913 Medical Congress in London. Returning to New Orleans, Rudolph thus found himself in wide demand as a speaker at medical assemblies in all sections of the United States. Since his practice also continued to grow, this greatly restricted the time he could devote to further original researches, a fact clearly reflected in the character of the few papers appearing under his name during and immediately following the war in Europe.

His schedule was lightened by the newly formed working partnership with Lucian, to whom he turned over much of the postoperative observation of surgical cases, and by his growing reliance on Kate Pruitt Hess, who had been a member of one of the earliest classes graduated by the Touro Infirmary School of Nursing. Her abilities had claimed Dr. Matas's favorable attention even during her student days. After she was capped, he had her assigned almost exclusively to his service, both in the operating room and in the care of his convalescents.

It happened that at this time his success in the surgical correction of a small child's cleft palate and harelip brought him a rush of similar cases, each of which involved a series of individually small operations. Some years later, in paying tribute to Miss Hess, he stressed the fact that in the nursing care of children she proved invaluable; apparently she had the knack of comforting frightened, suffering youngsters by her mere presence, to say nothing of the skill and faithfulness of her ministrations, or the voluminous, clearly expressed case notes she set down on the charts of her little charges. The upshot of it all was that Dr. Matas took her out of the hospital and made her his office nurse-receptionist-secretary. She was to remain in his personal employ for more than thirty years, becoming in time not only his secretary and accountant, but also his housekeeper.

To be sure, this was during the later years of his widowerhood. Adrienne, increasingly querulous as her physical powers were curtailed by progressive illness, became unreasoningly jealous when, little by little, her secretarial and bookkeeping duties were transferred to the younger hands of the nurse. Unfortunately this could not be avoided. Though finicky as ever in keeping penny-by-penny track of his personal disbursements, Dr. Matas had neither the time, inclination, nor ability to keep the accounts of his office. Ever since their marriage, Adrienne had always relieved him of this task. When invalidism made it impossible for her to keep pace with its growing demands, the routine of sending out bills, acknowledging receipts, banking funds, and the like became a shambles when he took it over from his ailing wife. Reluctantly, Adrienne at last agreed to have the books of account transferred to Miss Hess for the future, but wept disconsolately over her deprivation of this share in her husband's affairs and inflexibly refused to let Miss Hess come to the Matas home for dictation or other secretarial work. Yet she actually raged, at times, over Rudolph's absences from home which were due to the fact that, in compliance with her own ukase, so much of this work had to be done at his office.

Adrienne's occasional and quite reasonless onsets of jealousy were an old story, a sort of vestigial survival from the days before their marriage when she could not attend the social gatherings to which he was invited. Once when Emma Calvé came to sing at the French Opera House she suffered a touch of laryngitis, and Dr. Matas was summoned by the management to remain backstage during the performance to swab the diva's throat with silver nitrate between arias. Adrienne insisted that he take Lucian, then a first-year medical student, with him; otherwise she would not permit her husband to attend that painted actress in her dressing room.

As in the old days, Rudolph bore the ordeal of his wife's causeless jealousy of Kate Hess patiently enough, especially after Adrienne suffered her first heart attack. Thinking to please her by making outings from the house easier, he had specially low running boards installed on the new White motor car which in 1915 replaced faithful old "John Chalmers Da Costa." He jested with her about the paradox of a "White" which was red, and insisted that while he was at his classes or in his office or occupied by day-long operating schedules, John Sutton take Adrienne out driving on pleasant days.

Despite these claims on his time and attention, he accepted nearly every invitation to deliver a talk. Though swamped with work, he made the first annual oration in the spring of 1914 to the Stars and Bars honorary medical college society which, after the death of Dr. Isadore Dyer, one of its founders, was merged with the Tulane chapter of Alpha Omega Alpha, an honorary medical fraternity. The Stars and Bars oration was a characteristically high-flown effort in the Matas tradition and consisted pretty much of quoted poetry. Later in the same year he delivered the Mutter oration in Philadelphia. But his real renown as a public speaker stemmed from the annual oration he delivered in May 1915, before the forty-eighth convention of the Mississippi State Medical Association in Hattiesburg.

Its title and theme, "The Soul of the Surgeon," sprang full panoplied from the deep resentment he had conceived for those who did not recognize in modern surgery, surgery of the asepsis and anesthesia era, a high and holy priesthood in a temple profaned by a relatively few unscrupulous charlatans and desecrated principally by gibes of the laity, from George Bernard Shaw down to the writers of "cheap diatribes in the yellow journals."

He worded his protest in such phrases as:

". . . The Soul of the Surgeon—if we may define the soul as 'the ethical and emotional part of a man's nature, the seat of the sentiments and feelings, as distinguished from pure intellect'—is part of his make-up that is unknown to the masses; and the profound emotions which agitate him and with which he is rarely credited, can never be appreciated or analyzed save by one of the Guild who has lived them.

"It is an easy matter for the critic, the dramatists, the novelist, the cynic and the cartoonist to exercise their talents at the expense of the surgeon. Surgery has furnished and continues to furnish themes inexhaustible for humorous dissertations in the comic papers and cheap diatribes in the yellow journals. This has been so from the days of Aristophanes to Bernard Shaw. Nothing easier than to sneer or rail at surgery by those who are not in need of its good offices. But in the presence of the cynical and grossly material concept of the surgeon's role in the social fabric, it is only fair that something should be said to prove the baselessness of the charge that he is mercenary, soulless, indifferent to the fate of his fellows, greedy of gold and thirsting for publicity and notoriety."

This was one of the first lusty, widely quoted blows at the sort of gibe typified by the cartoonists' text of:

"What did the patient have?"

"Four hundred dollars."

"I mean, what did you operate on him for?"

"For four hundred dollars."

It was in the nature of a revolt against the British custom that even to this day speaks of a surgeon not as "Dr." So-and-So, but as "Mr." Even so, Dr. Matas conceded that where unscrupulous practitioners are concerned "it is wonderful how sometimes the urgency and perils of a patient's pathology shrivel into a negligible quantity when it is discovered that the pocketbook is empty and that there are no stakes to rake off from the game."

Publishers of transactions of the Mississippi State Medical Society were literally deluged with demands for reprints of the paper appearing on pages 140–75 of the volume for 1915. The Society had to confess itself unequal to the demand. The oration was therefore widely reprinted in many sections of the country as a separate brochure. In New Orleans, for example, the Board of Managers of Touro Infirmary made a de luxe reprint of it for Christmas distribution to the physicians and nurses of the community in 1921, six years after its delivery.

However, this had not been Rudolph Matas's only address to the Mississippi State Medical Convention of 1915. He also read a professional paper. One of its sections was to play a great role in the Matas future. Its title: "Stereopticon Clinic."* The first case reported therein was that of a "Miss B.S.," whose real name was Lowell Sedgwick. She was the seventeen-year-old daughter of a lumber-company executive, L. B. Sedgwick of Columbia, Mississippi, and had been named for her father; but from virtually the moment of her birth she was called "Bunny" by everyone. Hence Dr. Matas's reference to "a Miss B.S."

For no immediately apparent reason she had gradually become unable to retain food. This condition had worsened during the course of the previous year. By the time a Mississippi physician referred her to Dr. Joseph Weiss in New Orleans, she had lost some thirty-five pounds. A radiological examination by Dr. Weiss at Touro Infirmary disclosed that a blind pouch had formed at the point where the oesophagus normally opens into the stomach; obviously this malformation was due to an obstruction. Food, accumulating in the pouch and unable to pass into the stomach, was regurgitated in nightly spasms which culminated in choking spells; lack of nutrition had thus brought an otherwise perfectly normal, healthy, and very attractive girl to a critical stage of weakness.

* It was published that fall in vol. 68 of the *New Orleans Medical and Surgical Journal*, pp. 215ff., under the title: "Clinical Reports of Cases Presenting Features of Unusual Surgical Interest."

The cause of the obstruction was finally traced to something that had happened when, as a two-year-old, Bunny had swallowed a very small quantity of lye—a familiar childhood mishap of that era. Because the quantity of ingested lye was so minimal, and the accident was discovered and treated immediately, no perceptible ill effects appeared at the time. But fifteen years later its consequences were threatening Bunny Sedgwick's life.

Efforts to pass either an ordinary stomach tube or an olive-pointed bougie beyond the obstruction failed, because these simply entered the blind pouch and continued to coil there, without ever entering the stomach. So the girl—blessedly cheerful and co-operative—was directed to swallow one end of a long, stout silk thread. In time this filament did pass the obstruction, entering the stomach whence its still free lower end moved on into the intestine, so that after a couple of days it held taut when the upper end was pulled. Perforated olive-pointed bougies, threaded upon this lifeline, bypassed the oesophageal pouch and entered the stomach "guided by the thread which acted as a pilot . . . [after which] the stomach was washed out and three eggs and a pint of milk introduced into it through the gastric tube on the pilot thread which was left in place . . . After this the pouch was washed out daily before the patient retired at night and on rising by the patient herself, who gave the most intelligent co-operation . . . [Later she] fed herself three times a day by the gastric tube with a variety of liquid and soft foodstuffs."

Finally it became evident that the blind pouch, having been kept clean and empty, was gradually disappearing, permitting the oesophagus to return to normal proportions, as food stuffs introduced into the stomach restored the young patient's strength. Then the constricting obstruction was gently dilated; further improvement in the girl's condition followed at once. Six such dilations were undertaken at intervals of some weeks, the last one only two days before Dr. Matas reported the case in his Mississippi paper. By that time, "The patient had gained 36 pounds and has returned to her boarding school. As a precautionary measure, she has been advised to return for examination every six weeks. . . ."

Just how essential from a medico-surgical point of view this precaution was is open to question, since Lucian was taking the N.O. and G.N. local train to Columbia on those weekends when Bunny was not being brought to New Orleans for check-ups. During the early stages of her treatment, routine passage of "bougies tipped with metal olives" had been turned over to him by his stepfather. On one such occasion, when the instrument was withdrawn he noticed what appeared to be bloodstains at its tip. In an agony of apprehension he thought: "My God, I've punctured her stomach, I've killed her!"

Concealing his agitation, he hurried across Prytania Street from the hospital to the building he and Dr. Matas shared and demanded of Miss Hess that she call "the Governor" from his sanctum immediately for an emergency consultation. When he explained what had happened, Dr. Matas, his eye twinkling behind the gold-rimmed glasses which also served to conceal from casual notice the fact that one of the eyes was artificial, said:

"Well, let's remain calm. No harm can be done by waiting a few days to see what develops. . . . By the way, she *is* a pretty one, isn't she?"

Forty years later, when he was himself a patient at Touro, with the same Bunny Sedgwick (by that time a graying grandmother) tending to *his* wants, Lucian confessed that "it wasn't till the moment I thought I'd killed her that I realized how deeply in love with her I was."

He and Bunny were married, after a courtship and engagement interval of a year and a half, in September 1916. Despite the difference in religious faiths—the Sedgwicks were Presbyterians—there had been no parental objection to the match from either side.

Because of the large number of guests, the Presbyterian wedding ceremony was held in Columbia's much larger Methodist church, borrowed for the occasion. Dr. and Mrs. Matas were in attendance, Adrienne in stiffly rustling brown silk, making an occasion not merely of her only child's marriage, but of what she must have recognized as her last journey from New Orleans. Her mother, Mrs. Goslee, had been left in charge of the St. Charles Avenue household, so that Rudolph and Adrienne could spend the night with the Sedgwicks, because no return train would leave for New Orleans until the next day. Dr. and Mrs. Landry were taken by car over dreadful country roads, not even graveled for the most part, to McComb, where they entrained on the Illinois Central's main line for Chicago and ultimately for Niagara Falls.

They continued to live for a time at the Matas home, after their return to New Orleans, but soon set up a small residence for themselves. It was some time before Lowell, visiting her mother-in-law, could bring herself to admit that she was *enceinte*. But rejoicing in both houses was brought to a tragic halt by a miscarriage. Adrienne was the only one who could comfort Lowell in that dark hour, assuring her that "you are young, you will have other opportunities for motherhood. When this happened to Rudolph and me—oh, if I could only make you understand how I longed to give him a son!—I had to bear the added knowledge that I would never again bear a child. Mark my words, you will carry the next baby full term, and if it is a boy you must promise me to name him Rudolph Matas Landry to make up for my inability to give my husband a son to carry on his name."

By this time Rudolph Matas was deep in the medical war work that was to absorb him for more than three years. Except for two minor papers, previously written but not published until 1916, the only major contribution he made at this time to medical literature was a surprisingly brief report on "What the National Committee of American Physicians is doing for Medical Preparedness and what it Expects to do in Cooperation with the American Red Cross."

He had been commissioned a lieutenant in the Medical Reserve in 1909, and ever since the outbreak of war in 1914 had followed with keen interest the organization of base hospital and ambulance units under Red Cross sponsorship. By July 1916, when Mrs. George B. Penrose called a meeting at her home for the purpose of organizing a New Orleans chapter of the Red Cross, twenty-two such base-hospital units had been organized in the United States for service with the Allied forces, and Rudolph Matas was busily organizing the nucleus of another, with himself as director, the first one to be set up south of Baltimore.

This became known at the end of the 1915–16 academic year and almost depopulated the Tulane Medical College overnight. The sophomore class volunteered in a body, and the freshmen countered by beginning to organize an ambulance unit. Dr. Matas had already enlisted almost the entire junior class; many of the newly graduated seniors were commissioned as staff officers; Dr. Matas was promoted to major. But the proposed hospital needed not merely to be staffed. It also had to be financed. That led to the organization of a Red Cross chapter which, under the direction of Mrs. Penrose, raised nearly $30,000 through public subscription to equip the proposed base hospital as a 500-bed unit under the official designation of Red Cross Base Hospital Unit No. 24 of Tulane University.

But Major Matas was destined not to lead his organization overseas, and it must be conceded that this was not due merely to a policy decision by the National Council of Defense. Undeniably, he had looked forward to adding a military chapter to his life's story. But with each passing day his anxiety over Adrienne's condition mounted. This sense of omen was intensified, one may be sure, when her hitherto growing captiousness suddenly yielded to an obviously conscious effort to radiate cheer and affection, in short to become in every sense the "Dearest Adri" of their early years of marriage. Lucian and his wife gave up their separate little ménage and returned to the Matas home, so that Bunny, though only nineteen years old, might relieve Adrienne of the need to make decisions and exert herself over household duties;

also to assist her in caring for the brightly colored songbirds with which she had surrounded herself, help her to receive the small coterie of friends who dropped in for chatty, intimate visits: Miss Ethel Hutson who wrote for various New Orleans dailies; Harry Brunswick Loeb, head of a piano company, impresario, and occasional music critic for the New Orleans *Item;* Dr. Isidore Cohn and his wife Elsie—Adrienne still addressed him as Busy Izzy, an affectionate nickname she had bestowed on him in the days of his internship; Urban Maes, resplendent in his major's uniform, having succeeded Dr. Matas as chief of Base Hospital 24's surgical staff, while Dr. John B. Elliott, also a major, succeeded him as unit director.

Rudolph rarely wore his uniform, though occasionally he had to be chivvied into it for publicity photographs, official occasions, and the like; but he did revel in the special license plate he could now affix to the scarlet White automobile—a patent-leather tag which proclaimed the car's owner to be MRCUSA, a member of the Medical Reserve Corps of the United States Army. He kept this plate on his car for some years after the war had been won, since he was not formally separated from the service until April 1922.*

While he would have been reluctant to leave ailing Adrienne in any case, the decision was taken out of his hands in 1916, when the Surgeon-General's office notified the national director of the Red Cross that certain key base staffers would be urgently needed in the United States for instructional service. Moreover, the Council of National Defense decided that medical, engineering, and certain other technical and professional students already matriculated in institutions of higher education should not be conscripted into service. Most of the Tulane medical juniors were thus discharged from the Base Hospital 24 organization, and Major Matas was directed to turn command of the unit over to Major Elliott.

Rudolph Matas's services, it developed, were urgently in demand for organizing a special course of instruction at Tulane, at Charity Hospital, and at Touro for the treatment of war traumata, especially war fractures, which constituted more than a fourth of all battle casualties.

Military physicians, some with long regular-army service and others

---

* A freak clerical error kept him from promotion to a colonelcy. In March 1922, Surgeon-General M. W. Ireland wrote him on the assumption that his Reserve commission would expire as of April 23 and urged him to write immediately to Fort McPherson, requesting authority to appear before an examining board for promotion. He did so. A board was appointed on March 31, and on April 18 he received a stricken letter from General Ireland, confessing that the information furnished him to the effect that April 23 was the expiration date of the Matas commission had been a clerical error and that the commission had expired on April 9. Since it was not permitted to reappoint any officer who was more than sixty years old, promotion was no longer legally possible.

newly inducted into the reserves, were sent to these classes from all
parts of the country, while a 1000-bed fracture hospital, with a famous
New York surgeon, Dr. J. B. Walker, at its head, was established in
France, as close to the front as it could safely be placed.

"It is desired," pointed out the original directive, "to standardize
the treatment of complicated gunshot fractures by instructing medical
officers in the use of typical forms of stock splints for the various
fractures, so that when these officers return to their various cantonments
they can, in turn, instruct those who have not had the opportunity of
receiving this special course . . . By order of the Surgeon-General
and through the courtesy of the administrators of the Charity Hospital,
Touro Infirmary, and the Medical School of Tulane University, such
a course shall be inaugurated at the Charity Hospital on Nov. 5, under
the direction of Dr. Matas, Major MRC."

In all, eight successive courses, each of four weeks' duration, were
held in New Orleans, with a total of 134 medical officers as trainees.
The final course was completed in July of 1918, by which time the
German retreat toward the Rhineland had begun. The victorious advance of the Allies, launched at Belleau Woods, proceeded without interruption. A false armistice report, given out in October by a press-
association mogul, set off a brief outburst of mass hysteria; the final
proclamation, *La guerre est gagnée,* precipitated the most uninhibited
celebration the world had ever known. Its wildest manifestation was
in New York where Rudolph, immured in the small, inexpensive Hotel
Flanders, had penned to Sir William Osler a compassionate letter which
read in part:

"I was just about to write you in regard to our Tulane Base Hospital
Unit No. 24 . . . when I was shocked by news of the death of your
heroic son while on duty at the front. I cannot tell you how deeply
I have felt for you and Lady Osler in this immeasurable sorrow . . .
but on second thought, it occurred to me that the loss of this precious life, irreparable and overwhelming as it is, would only add to
the warmth of your generous sympathies and insure, even more, your
unfailing interest in the band of patriotic young men (the majority
of them about the age of your son), who have left their homes and
anxious parents to serve the country at the front."

He was a refugee, at the time, from the demands of a practice swollen
far beyond even its peacetime dimensions by the shortage of physicians
for civilian life, seeking time and solitude to complete a long overdue
addendum on war aneurisms to his section of a new edition of Keen's
Surgery.

Another factor that drove him to seek seclusion at a little-known

New York hotel the following summer was that in July 1918, just at
the close of the eighth and last of his special courses in the treatment
of war fractures, what became known as Spanish flu started its swift
and lethal sweep across the United States.

CHAPTER XXIX

A generation grown to maturity in an era of antibiotics inevitably finds it difficult to realize or to understand the near-panic brought on by the flu epidemic of 1918–19. In time the discovery was made that deaths were not due to influenza but to pneumonia, contracted secondarily by flu convalescents who left the sickbed too early. Thereupon the originally frightful mortality rate began to decline, but the chaotic scramble for protection or cure continued.

In crowded cantonments, in troop transports proceeding eastward toward Brest and St. Nazaire, even in the isolated spruce-production camps of the fir-clad fastnesses along the northwest Pacific slopes, Spanish flu struck without warning and without discernible cause. Cities passed emergency ordinances forbidding public assembly. Some of them even closed all theaters, schools, and movie palaces. Many made it unlawful to appear in public without a gauze mask tied over mouth and nostrils. Brisk profiteering in the sale of masks immediately sprang into being, especially as concerned the more elaborate ones, which provided pierced-metal discs, half an inch or so in diameter, pivoting over or away from a conveniently placed ring-rimmed opening, for those who desired to smoke without violating the masking law.

Serums were spawned almost like sea urchins; the more promising ones were tried out in army cantonments where the resident populace was in no position to implement its objections effectively. Some of these serums had the consistency of what was called "lube" in that uncomplicated era of dawning mechanization. Their injection promptly swelled the upper arms of recipients to approximately double the normal circumference but had no other appreciable effect. Neither had the zinc-sulphate sprays applied to the throats and nostrils of civilians and soldiery. The epidemic spread regardless of medications, just as had the yellow-fever plagues of an earlier day.

In New Orleans the local Lodge of Elks was headed by a dynamic onetime Grand Exalted Ruler of the Order, Colonel John P. Sullivan, in whose parents' home young Rudolph Matas had been a frequent visitor. When it was suggested that fresh citrus fruits might aid flu sufferers to recover, Colonel Sullivan organized his Lodge to turn school gymnasiums and auditoriums into emergency hospitals and commandeer every orange in the city for distribution among the sick. The fruit was paid for with notes which were later redeemed to the last penny out of the avails of a special membership drive which made New Orleans Lodge No. 30 second in size only to the Brooklyn lodge of the B.P.O.E.

Relatively few physicians were still in civilian practice and these were swamped by calls for their services, a situation that obtained throughout the country, not merely in New Orleans. Like all other healers, Rudolph Matas and Lucian Landry simply worked until exhaustion overtook them, slept as and when they could, and rose to work again until they could work no longer. This was a special ordeal for both.

Dr. Matas was, as usual, a year or more late in submitting a promised revision of his section on vascular surgery for a new edition of Keen's multi-volume text. But his concern for Adrienne would have kept him from consistent labor at such a task in any case. She had suffered her first heart attack that year; angina pectoris, as it was termed then. This was followed by nocturnal dyspnea: choking spells during her slumbers. She had long been suffering from chronic nephritis. Only the previous September Dr. Matas had written Sir William Osler that "I had resolved to offer my services to the British government when the illness of my wife kept me home . . . She, most unfortunately and sadly, has failed to improve, and is now so helplessly dependent upon me that I cannot leave her, and must confine my efforts to serve the Country to this locality."

There had been only a quiet family Christmas that December of 1917, though the usual remembrances to such friends as the Colliers in Philadelphia had not been overlooked. Moreover, intimate friends dropped in with little offerings of affection; but the state of Mrs. Matas's health and Bunny's miscarriage of the first child she had expected to bear to Lucian were enough to keep the holiday on a plane of moderation.

These were not the only gaieties subdued or postponed by the catastrophic pressure of the times. The previous spring—that is, in early 1917, months before America's entry into the war—Bunny and Adrienne had watched the gaudy pageantry of Carnival from the gallery of the Matas home. But the following year, on January 6, 1918, there was no Ball of the Twelfth Night Revelers, though for decades the Carnival season had been inaugurated at this gala affair when an artificial Kings' Cake was cut by a Master Chef; nor were any other Carnival parades or tableau balls held that year. True, some sporadic masquerading was indulged in on Mardi Gras, but even this was frowned on by the majority of Orleanians, who remained soberly intent upon the business of backing the war effort.

Lucian's anxiety for Bunny in the autumn of 1918 stemmed from the fact that she was once more with child. Each morning, before departing on his rounds, he left as complete an itinerary as he could; in addition, he telephoned the house and the office at regular intervals throughout the day, so that Miss Hess could summon him if anything went amiss. Moreover, he was under instructions from "the Governor"—a title he had long since substituted for Teur in addressing or referring to his stepfather—to notify him in New York at the first symptom of adverse developments. But Bunny's pregnancy proceeded quite normally. Adrienne beamed when she assured her daughter-in-law that nothing would go amiss, reminding her over and over that if the baby was a boy she must have him baptized Rudolph Matas Landry.

Dr. Matas's stay in New York was to have afforded him sufficient solitude and leisure to complete the Keen manuscript, but Dr. A. B. Dinwiddie, newly elevated to the Tulane presidency, urged him to use his good offices with his friends at the General Education Board and the Carnegie Foundation to secure favorable action on the Tulane Medical School's plea for financial aid. His efforts in both directions were abruptly terminated by a telegram from Lucian with the dire message that Adrienne's condition had taken a turn for the worse. Already weakened by chronic nephritis, she had been infected by the all-pervading flu epidemic and was not responding to treatment. He took the first train south, chafing at the inevitable thirty-eight hours of travel time, only to learn on arrival, from his old friend Felix Larue, the attending physician, that pneumonia had set in after Adrienne had failed to rally from the influenza attack. He, Mrs. Goslee, Bunny, and Lucian were never far from the patient's bedside. She died on the morning of December 10; Rudolph had not yet unwrapped the ornate

357

cut-crystal flacon of perfume he had brought from New York for his Dearest Adri's Christmas gift.

He moved in a sort of vacuum during the ensuing days, though he had insisted on arranging by himself every detail of the funeral. He had even managed to secure permission from Archbishop Shaw to have certain selections of Adrienne's favorite secular music played during the services at Notre Dame Church. Receipt of the Colliers' usual Christmas package for Adrienne, a week or so after she was buried, shocked him out of the dull narcosis of grief. Not until then did he take up the interrupted course of his existence. To the Colliers he wrote in fullest detail about what had befallen:

"Dear Friends—

"Nineteen days have now elapsed since my dearly beloved Adrienne passed away & I have been so crushed and overpowered by the overwhelming sorrow that has come into my life that I have not had the strength of will to write to any one. It was only yesterday when your ever thoughtful reminder of your constant friendship came to rouse me to the realization of my neglected duties that I decided I could not allow the sadness of this Christmastide and the New Year that is dawning so somberly before me, to interpose itself farther in the discharge of what, at other times, would have been a joyous obligation. Immediately after my wife's death I had copies of the daily papers mailed to you, but they were addressed to Ridley Park and I presume you never received them, as your box of Christmas presents with your good wishes to us both and to Dr. Landry would no doubt have come with a different message.

"She surrendered her sweet soul to the Almighty on the morning of Dec. 10 at 10:15 and expired in my arms and Lucian's, with her dear face bathed in our tears and her cold lips covered with our kisses. The end came suddenly in a final paroxysm of angina pectoris, though we all realized that the final parting could not be long delayed, as she had reached the limit of her endurance and that even her heroic soul and indomitable will could not survive the frightful strain that she had labored under in the previous week, when sudden pneumonia set in with the grippe; a super-added complication to the angina which had confined her to her home during the last six months.

"After a sleepless night of horrible suffering from air hunger and inability to rest, the dawn of the 10th brought with it a temporary lull in the general strain, and about 9 A.M. she seemed to rally, sipped a little coffee as was her custom, followed by the usual hot foot-bath and gentle scrub which comforted her. After bathing her feet and hands, and brushing her hair, which always remained beautiful and luxurious to the end, she received the attention of her faithful hairdresser. She then called for fresh linens and a pink gown which she selected herself. She looked wonderfully well and we all admired her superb courage and unconquerable spirit, and I told her as I kissed her that she had never looked more beautiful. Lu said she had dressed herself carefully as if primping for an evening reception. She smiled, but there was a strange spiritual light in her eyes as if her soul were looking to heaven—such as we see in the faces of the dying who are within sight of the Infinite Presence—a few minutes after, she fell back, after a slight effort to move from her chair and in our quiet group expired without immediate consciousness of the end.

"How sweet she looked in her pink gown and how perfectly she had set the final act of tragedy. With what uncanny foresight and prophetic vision she saw herself after death and prepared herself that she might look beautiful even in Death! And all that we might keep her in our hearts as a last vision, as an admirably holy vision, beatified but not distorted by her cruel martyrdom.

"The fact that our Christmas and New Year's greetings did not reach you must have been suggestive of some trouble at this end, as you know that Adrienne always anticipated that festival with much pleasure, as it gave her an opportunity to show her unfailing remembrance and appreciation of her faithful friends. The marked copies of the daily papers which I have recently mailed to your Philadelphia address will have reached you by this time and informed you of the frightful void that has been created in my life, and will account, I think, for my silence and seeming neglect in not extending to you and yours the cheerful message of good will which she would have been so happy to transmit to you had she been here.

"And so the parting came, leaving me alone, isolated and desolate, with only her sweet memory and the companionship of her child, her flowers, her books, her beautiful birds, her garments and everything that she touched and loved, undisturbed as she left it. Everything seems still warm with her presence and her breath, but I look vainly around for her coming. The hours pass, the sun sets and with the darkness I feel the chill that tells me she has gone forever.

"She spoke of you often, expressing her regret that her prolonged illness prevented her from writing to Mrs. Collier as she loved to do. Mrs. Collier's last letter, of Dec. 8th, reached me on December 10th, shortly after she had expired, and remained unopened until today.

"You now know all the essential facts, and it has been a relief to my pent-up feelings to write to you. I trust you will pardon the intrusion of my emotions, which is almost unavoidable in writing to such good and loved friends who I know will cherish her sweet memory.

"Dr. Landry and his wife join me in extending to you our thanks for all your kindness and good wishes which you know are now and will always be most cordially reciprocated.

"Faithfully yours
Rudolph Matas."

Numbed by the irrevocable finality of his Dearest Adri's death, Rudolph none the less insisted on performing for her whatever services the situation demanded. He notified the undertakers after Dr. Larue had filled out the death certificate: Immediate cause, influenza pnemonia; contributory, chronic nephritis; secondary, angina pectoris. When the undertaker arrived with his assistants, he showed them the negligée of lilac silk and the other articles of clothing she had selected for her burial garb and then went to his study so that he need not witness the manipulation by alien hands of the body he had cherished. He selected the twelve pallbearers; only two—Bunny's father and Harry Brunswick Loeb—were not physicians.

He busied himself then in drawing up on a scratch pad in a shaky penciled scrawl a selection of what had been Adrienne's favorite musical compositions: Ketterer's *Beaux Jours, Vous n'Etes Plus; Mon Coeur s'Ouvre à ta Voix* from Saint-Saëns's *Samson and Delilah;* Gounod's *Ave Maria;* Delibes's *Le Pas de Fleurs* from Naila; Gottschalk's *The Last Hope.*

He wandered from the study, knocked at the bedroom door to inquire if the morticians were in need of anything, chose volumes of poetry from the bookcases that lined the upper hallway, evidently intent upon selecting a verse to be carved on the marble that would seal Adrienne's crypt. Then he set himself to writing a special verse for her, patterned upon some of her favorites among the classics of sorrow and serenity. To the meter and form of Elizabeth Barrett Browning's *The Sleep* he wrote this stanza under the title *She Rests:*

> Nay, doth she not? Nor day nor night
> She resteth not from praise;
> Her spirit, winged with rapture, knows
> No more earth's weary ways;
> But ever toward the Infinite
> Her flight on, upward, doth she keep,
> For he gives active tirelessness
> Who "giveth His beloved sleep."

To the musical cadence of Rose Terry Cooke's, "The Two Villages," he set this quatrain:

"Over the River" so near it seems
To drift away to the starlit dreams!
To fear no more the face o' night
"Over the River" where "Love is light."

On and on he wrote, sometimes copying long excerpts from
Tennyson's *In Memoriam,* once drawing a design, flanked on each side
by a cross and reading:

"Thou Shalt be Missed": I Sam. 20:18

In Memoriam
Adrienne Goslee, beloved wife of
Rudolph Matas
April 23, 1860–Dec. 10, 1918

"Thou Shalt be Missed": I Sam. 20:18

Forty years earlier, young Rudolph Matas confessed that during the
lonely watches of his yellow-fever duty at the foot of the Vicksburg
bluffs he read Draper's *History of the Conflict Between Religion and
Science* and pondered it until "my faiths became attenuated and I
almost became an agnostic." Now the desolate man of science searched
the works of mankind's poets, from the Psalmist to William Watson, for
some sort of assurance that death is not an irrevocable parting. In shaky,
penciled script he set down the words:

Thy day has come, not gone,
Thy sun has risen, not set.
Thy life is now beyond
The reach of death or change,
Not ended—but begun,
O, noble soul! O, gentle heart! Hail, farewell!

He had taken no nourishment since his small cup of freshly dripped
morning coffee. From time to time Mrs. Goslee brought him a cup of
broth, which went untasted. After the undertakers left, he tiptoed into
the bedroom where Adrienne, clad in the negligee of lilac silk, had been
laid upon the daybed until she could be coffined in the morning.

Friends came to the house after nightfall to bear him company in his
bereavement: Isidore and Elsie Cohn, Marcus and Birdie Feingold,
Felix Larue, Henry Menage, Charles Landfried, Harry Loeb. He
remained with these visitors in the dining room until late that night,
but there was little conversation. From time to time he would withdraw
briefly, go upstairs to the bedroom and look in sorrowful bereavement
upon the still form that only this morning had been, and now would
never again be, his Dearest Adri. He did not retire after the callers

left, though both Lucian and Mrs. Goslee urged him to seek rest. He sat through the night, reading from the poets whose works she had loved and perhaps thinking of the old days, of the girl who had put up with all Lafcadio Hearn's vagaries for his sake and had prepared midnight suppers for them when they came home from long walks through the gaslit streets of a New Orleans much of which had vanished.

He dressed carefully the next morning and waited in his room while the undertakers carried the rigid, unyielding body he had held so dear down the long stairway to the casket placed on its black-draped stand before the mantel in the rarely used parlor. Those who had come to pay their last respects had already crowded the lower floor, the gallery, the small enclosure before the house, and the St. Charles Avenue banquette when he asked that the parlor be cleared. He and his devoted disciple, Isidore Cohn, were the only ones who entered the room where he was now to bid the unmoving, unchanging form farewell. He had brought with him a wisp of lace, the handkerchief he had given her in Venice nearly a decade before, when he sought to appease her after their quarrel on the Grand Canal, and an atomizer filled with perfume from the flacon he had bought in New York only a few days earlier. He sprayed the attar onto the handkerchief, placed it tenderly within the unyielding clasp of the cold fingers, then signed to the undertakers that the casket was to be closed.

He rode in solitude to the Requiem at Notre Dame, and thence to Metairie where the bodies of his stillborn son and his father occupied the tomb within which all that was mortal of Adrienne would repose in perpetuity. But he did not ride in the funereal black limousine provided for him by the undertaker. He rode instead in the scarlet White. It was perhaps as incongruous a sight as New Orleans had ever witnessed: the black limousine for the priest and his acolytes, the black limousine for the pallbearers, the black hearse, the scarlet limousine, and then the black automobiles for the other mourners, as the procession threaded its way slowly once more past the house on St. Charles Avenue.

It is beyond question that Rudolph wrote Elvira of Adrienne's passing, for he seems to have dreaded the possibility, suggested by the posthumous arrival of Christmas gifts from the Colliers, that other letters to Adrienne might continue to be delivered. He even wrote to the editor of the A.M.A. *Journal*, asking that a note be printed in the columns of that publication chronicling his bereavement.

"Dear Dr. Simmons," his letter read in part. "My dearly beloved wife, Adrienne, the sweetest companion of my life, passed away from this life Tuesday, Dec. 10th . . . She lived exclusively for her household, her husband and her son, Dr. Lucian Landry . . . whose lives she made

bright and happy by the inextinguishable radiance of her great love
. . . She was a regular reader of the *Journal* during the nearly quarter
of a century that our lives were united . . . Many of our good friends
in the fellowship of the Association, who doubtless remember her
constant companionship and who have missed her presence and mine
from the meetings of the last few years, should know the cause of our
absence; and I know of no better way to convey to them this sad
intelligence than by a notice in the volume of the *Journal* which she
perused so faithfully and regularly, even up to the last week before the
end . . . Thanking you in anticipation of this final act of gracious
courtesy to the memory of one who was so long your faithful
reader. . . ."

Thus one cannot escape the conclusion that he must have communicated the sad intelligence also to his only surviving blood relative; but
if Elvira sent him any message of condolence or sympathy in the hour
of his great bereavement the letter has as yet not been found among
the papers he was so zealous to preserve.

Lucian's young wife, just turned twenty, carried her child full term
and was delivered that February of a son. He was baptized Rudolph
Matas Landry.

CHAPTER XXX

The desolation left by Adrienne's death was eased but little by the birth of Bunny's son. Each passing day still heightened the realization that his Dearest Adri's absence was a permanent fact of his entire future; yet his professional and personal routine was not altered. Mrs. Goslee quietly moved in and took up in their entirety the household duties she had long been helping her invalid daughter to discharge. Miss Hess not only continued with the accounting, typing, and other secretarial work Adrienne had once been so zealous to perform; she could now come to the residence in the mornings and go about her work there until Dr. Matas left for Charity, Touro, or his office.

An ever-increasing proportion of the hours not pre-empted by his practice was now devoted to writing, for he could never resist a flattering request for contributions to "systems" of surgery: multi-volume pandects for which he was asked to write the sections on vascular operations. Appeals for monographs of a historical nature, or tributes to some of the great physicians of the past rarely went unheeded, and at national, regional, or local medico-surgical meetings he was always being called on for papers by harried program chairmen. Moreover he had it in mind to compile out of the mountainous accumulation of data he had gathered over nearly half a century a complete history of medicine in Louisiana, a magnum opus he would begin as soon as he had cleared his schedule of more pressing obligations: perhaps after 1925 when he would become professor emeritus, under Tulane's long-standing custom of retiring faculty members at age 65.

At the same time he fell victim to an almost obsessive interest in the movies. When there was no Touro staff meeting or other professional claim on his time, night after night would find him at one of the big new Canal Street cinema palaces or at some neighborhood shrine of the silent films. This was a form of diversion he had never before been able to enjoy, originally because of almost total absorption in his work and of late because it was impossible for Adrienne to accompany him. Now, dreading the long and lonely evenings, he fled to the movie theaters, occasionally accompanied by Lucian and Bunny, when the infant Ruddie could be left with Mrs. Goslee for a few hours.

Strangely enough, this scholar who could quote from memory page on page of the classics of literature and who collected rare editions on his trips abroad, naïvely included sober appraisals of the films in his diaries, even to the extent of making laudatory comments about such cloud-cuckoo absurdities as an opus in which Theda Bara saved Paris singlehandedly.

More and more of his teaching duties were already being divided between Drs. Maes and Gessner, so that he could leave for various medical assemblies or for more immurement in the Surgeon-General's library in Washington, or at the Academy of Medicine in New York. Perhaps the most memorable of the professional gatherings he attended at this time was that held in Montreal by the still relatively young American College of Surgeons.

Such excursions from New Orleans were matters of but a few days. Far more protracted were Dr. Matas's absences at the libraries where he was frantically endeavoring to catch up with long-neglected commitments to furnish articles or textbook material to various editors and publishers. His relations with these became hopelessly snarled time after time, so that much of his laboriously completed writings actually never appeared in print. For one thing, his memory was so unrelentingly tenacious that no fact entrusted to its keeping ever escaped; and he seemed helpless to exclude any such fact from his treatises.

At times, and especially during extemporaneous observations about papers read by his colleagues, this gift stood him in good stead. For example, early during the spring term of 1920, he addressed the student body of the Medical College at Tulane on "A Tour of the European Battle Fronts." When he finished, a student committee asked him to expand this eyewitness dissertation on medical war work in a future address, only to be informed that he had not been abroad since 1913 and that the tour he had described so vividly was taken in the library of the Academy of Medicine in New York.

However, when it came to encompassing textual material within the relatively inflexible bounds of a given number of pages or within a preset number of minutes of platform allowance, he had no valid concept whatever of space or time. In February of 1920 Dr. Albert J. Ochsner of Chicago, who five years later would install Dr. Matas as president of the American College of Surgeons, importuned him for the manuscript of a section he had promised to deliver for a new work on *Surgical Diagnosis and Treatment.*

"The first volume will appear shortly," wrote Dr. Ochsner. "Will you kindly send me your manuscript within the next ten days or two weeks in order that it may not prevent the prompt appearance of the book?" Other letters, increasingly peremptory, arrived throughout the ensuing spring and summer. Finally, on September 21, came a brusque reminder from Lea and Febiger, publishers, that "Volume III is now being held up for want of your MSS."

At this selfsame time Dr. Matas found himself involved in an almost identical dilemma with his great friend, Dr. W. W. Keen of Philadelphia, who had asked for a revision of the original Matas section on vascular operations for a new edition of Keen's compendium on surgery, setting aside a maximum of thirty printed pages for it. Months late, Dr. Matas delivered his material in a manuscript which would fill 127 pages of text, plus 15 more of illustrations: Dr. Keen suggested mildly that the inclusion of a mass of statistical material occupied "a great deal of space even in small type" and made "dry reading even for the most addicted statistician, and will be skipped by ninety to ninety-five per cent of your readers, if not by 99."

The necessary abridgment was finally achieved in great travail of spirit, which evoked this stricken lament in a letter to that ever sympathetic friend, Dr. William Halsted:

"Unfortunately the publishers found that I had already exceeded the limits of the space assigned to me, and the whole chapter was trimmed off. What a fearful waste of time and energy these composite systems and text books involve. It is not the midnight oil but the wick of one's own life that is consumed and wasted by these procrustean efforts to fit the measure of editors and publishers. All to no purpose, except to flicker for a speeding moment and then to follow the trail of a long funeral train of dead and forgotten text books that cumber the path of medical history."

Bitterly as he complained against procrustean efforts directed against him, he was completely impervious to the feelings of others upon whose space or time allotments he trespassed. At a meeting of the Southern Surgical Association in 1926, in Biloxi, one part of the program was set aside for papers by Dr. Matas and Dr. Vilray Blair of St. Louis. The latter was widely regarded as the world's foremost plastic surgeon and had come from Missouri to deliver his paper; but because of urgent engagements, he would have to leave almost in the very moment when his section of the program was completed. Fortunately, railroad schedules would allow him just enough margin to catch a return train.

But when his allotted time had expired Dr. Matas calmly declared he had not yet finished even his introductory remarks, and that the important bulk of his material was still to be delivered. Dr. Hubert Royster, presiding, could do no less than put to the assembly the question of whether or not Dr. Matas should be granted an extension of time, and the speaker then continued for another hour. Dr. Blair's commitments in St. Louis would brook no delay; so he returned without reading the paper he had been invited to come all the way from his Missouri home to deliver.

At this time Dr. Matas was preparing to leave for an extended stay abroad, his first trip to Europe in almost a decade. He had been invited to address the French College of Surgeons, meeting in Paris, "on behalf of the suture method of aneurismal surgery" as compared to ligation in any of its several guises and designations. He accepted with alacrity, turning his classes over to Urban Maes and Hermann Gessner; they and Lucian were also to carry on such of his surgical practice as could not be postponed against his return some three months later.

Little as this might have been expected, one of the factors most strongly drawing him abroad was a desired reunion with Elvira. Her disposition was no better than it had been of old. In her middle fifties she was still inflexibly a spinster, maintaining herself, a servant named Victorina, and the latter's little niece, who was Elvira's godchild and namesake, on the legacy bequeathed by her mother and the monthly allowance sent by her brother.

Though the Adrienne he had worshiped as sweetheart and wife hated Elvira and was in turn cordially hated by her, he clung to this one remaining tie of blood with a tenacity that was beyond all logic. The moment he accepted the invitation extended to him on behalf of the Congress by Dr. René Leriche, professor of surgery at the Sorbonne, he wrote Elvira, enclosing an additional bank draft and directing her to meet him in Paris, so that after the Congress had been adjourned they might travel together through the Swiss lake country, Italy, the Riviera, the Cote d'Azur, and so at length to San Felíu de Guixols. He hoped this might bring about a warm brother-and-sister intimacy neither of them had known since her childhood.

The Congress was only a five-day affair, but matters associated with it would claim Rudolph's time and attention for at least two days more. He delivered not merely his aneurism paper (in French, of course) on the same program with Sir George Makin, Dr. Paul Moure, and Dr. Leriche; he addressed a formal banquet on Louisiana's medical history, tracing this to the state's French heritage and prefacing it with a high-flown tribute couched in the florid style he had acquired forty years earlier through his almost idolatrous association with Lafcadio Hearn.

The ovation that greeted it was a triumph, and he was made an honorary president of the French Surgical Congress. Both addresses had been delivered in French, and he put in a great many hours having them transcribed by a typist. Elvira would not reach Paris until the following day, so, being at loose ends, he took in the bill of five one-act plays at the Grand Guignol. Returning to his hotel he spent hours setting down in the most meticulous detail on the scratch pad he was using as a diary the prurient plot of each playlet, prefacing his critique with a statement that these "show the typical aptitude of the French for this sort of play."

Elvira, arriving the next day, was entertained first by a visit to the "splendid free opening of the Dufayel stores" and later at a performance of *Die Walküre* in the Opera House, while Rudolph went to the establishment of Dr. Coulomb, an optician, to try on for size and fit a new artificial eye the latter had made for him. It was not satisfactory, so Dr. Matas left 100 francs as a deposit against the 200-franc fee agreed on for each well-fitting eye, with instructions to have others sent to him at Nice.

That night Rudolph took Elvira to the Folies Bergère. She had never seen or imagined anything of the sort, but the performance "turned out to be far better than I expected 35 fr. for each equals 70 fr. for the night; 11:30 stopped to take a glass of orgeat syrup at the Restaurant de la Paix and go home."

The journey to Milan via Simplon-Orient express was rich in incident, Rudolph, as usual, leaving most of the arrangements to Providence, with an occasional assist from various travel agencies. At Iselle, for instance, one Francisco Cavallo, a border guard (*agènte investigatóre*) "gives me the cheery news that I would have to return to Brigue in Switzerland, as my passport had not been visa'd by the Italian Consul. I let Elvira go on to Domodossola with the baggage and walk back with Cavallo . . . after running around for ½ hour I finally got the Italian Consul to stamp his visa on my passport and then on sister's. He charged 62 francs (Swiss) for my Amer. visa and 10 for sister's Spanish visa, showing strong discrimination against Americans generally."

In Milan brother and sister conscientiously went sight-seeing, not neglecting the Duòmo, the Galleria Vittorio Emanuele, Leonardo Da Vinci's fresco of the Last Supper—and a cinema, showing what today is called a double feature, but "these were all serials and a great nuisance." They did the same thing the next day, after sight-seeing till night, when "we took in a movie at Guersi's Cinema on the via Rome to see Linda Pini in the Deshonesti, not much of a play, a guilty wife tempted by her husband's small salary, the husband a defaulting clerk. . . .

Next day in Genoa they secured a double room with bath in a hotel opposite the monument to Columbus, rode around town in a horse taximeter, marveled at the seemingly innumerable cinemas, "stopped at the Orfeo and saw Theda Bara playing Salome, an American film, one of the best we have seen in Italy."

Then on to Nice where their first stop was at the American Express agency to see whether two additional eyes had been sent on by Coulomb. They had, but this was scant comfort in view of the fact that both proved too large to fit the orbit. They dined then in the Casino on the Promenade des Anglais. Next day they "took the tram to Monte Carlo and visited the Casino with its magnificent gambling house. Had to be identified, and showed a letter of credit to prove my identity. A curious recourse to insure, no doubt, against the admission of unfriendly or impossible people who would not pay their losses in the gambling house . . . With gambling go the fast women, champagne, fine toggery, millinery, and above all expensive jewelry, anything that can fascinate and charm women and make men prodigal spendthrifts to please them . . . Every inducement to vice, license and extravagance is here. Took the tram back to Nice after 7 P.M., and went to the hotel. Light supper and up to the room."

On the whole the trip must have been grievously frustrating. Only once before had he taken a leisurely sight-seeing jaunt; that was the return journey with Adrienne from the International Society meeting in Budapest. True, they had quarreled bitterly along the route, though he had made peace betimes. But there had been shared responses to the wonder and strange beauty of the panorama through which they moved: the harlots' houses in Pompeii, the hushed twilight of Notre Dame, the fountains of Trafalgar Square and the tumultuous prodigality of Fifth Avenue, the little curiosity shop in Paris where he bought chimères. He must remember to buy some more before returning to New Orleans, one of those customarily installed on his office desk had been broken when pamphlets and unanswered mail had finally pushed it to the floor. . . .

At Elvira's side, he found no naïve thrill at mingling for the first time with fast women and prodigal spendthrifts along the Elysian Riviera, no childlike enjoyment of the cinema, no shared response of any sort. One can see him yawning over his scratch-pad diaries as he copies out of Baedeker the names of the little railroad stations they passed en route from Genoa to Nice or pencils in the floor plans of a two-bed single room he occupied with Elvira, showing the exact location of bath, bidet, and other appurtenances. Elvira's stolid and occasionally disapproving acceptance of the Grand Tour only intensified the mounting sense of irreparable loss in Adrienne's absence.

It must have been this which was responsible for the tedious, guide-book details with which he crowded his diaries; for such notations as that on the excursion to the Château D'If the guide pointed out the cell in which Edmond Dantès was imprisoned, "but it is all pure fiction and nonsense, of course."

He was doing his best to capture something of warm gaiety at Marseilles, for from this port he and Elvira would take the train to Barcelona; once back in her domain, even the token affection of being thrown together among strangers would vanish. So he took her to the famous Restaurant Bosso on the Cannebière, and there "we indulged in a delicious bouillabaisse with langouste and white wine, a very enjoyable dish . . . Bosso's is known all over the world . . . fair day and colorful crowd from Marseilles and all parts made the occasion extremely enjoyable." But it was no good, for "after this the day, though short, was spent merely walking about. . . ."

This is the journal of a man valiantly striving to conceal from himself the stark fact of his boredom. But there was yet one more wearisome day of sightseeing to be got through before the costs of the hotel bill, railroad tickets, *pourboires* and incidentals were itemized in francs and their dollar equivalents. Then they boarded the night train for Port Bou and Barcelona. A Eugène Sue movie they had attended in Marseilles brought vividly to mind the image of his father, that sparklingly vital romantic from whom Elvira had turned in loathing, and whose last days had been made bright by the encompassing warmth of Adrienne's boundless affection. Straight from *The Mysteries of Paris* had come the very name—Rodolphe—which had been sacramentally bestowed on his "dear little son" in the old Jesuit Church in Baronne Street. Over these same rails from Port Bou to Barcelona he and his parents had traveled years before Elvira was born.

With something akin to relief he gave up sightseeing once they reached Catalonia and devoted himself to visiting hospitals, clinics, and the homes of famous physicians; but on All Saints' Day he called on various distant kinsfolk, especially the surviving Forto *gente*. He even paid a call on Consuela Ferriol, née Pareta, a cousin on the Matas side, noting that "her mother was Carmen Barquina de Pareta, she died in 1921 at the age of 85 years. She had helped to nurse me as a child and always remembered me."

Later they attended "a performance of Don Juan Tenorio at the Goya theater. It is customary to give this performance on All Saints', as it exhibits the hope of redemption and divine mercy toward the worst sinners. After the performance which began at 10 P.M. and ended at 1:30 A.M., stopped at a confectionery and took chocolate with marzipan cake. Back to hotel at 3 A.M."

Finally he and his sister left for San Felíu, via Gerona, arriving late in the evening, when Victorina welcomed them with supper well prepared. He spent a fortnight then, seeking—it seems clear—to identify himself more and more with his father. He strolled for many hours along the Paseo del Mar where on the early morning of his wedding day, as Rudolph had read in Narciso's fragmentary autobiography, his father had been torn between a desire to flee and a sense of honor which bade him fulfill his pledge to marry a girl he had just discovered to be ten years his senior. He searched Gerona in vain for the drugstore of Dr. Vivas di Colonnas, his father's uncle-by-marriage, where first Narciso was apprenticed to the healing sciences. He deposited with a Dr. Pascual the sum of $100 with which to establish a prize at the College of San Felipe Neri in his father's memory.

He visited the San Felíu cemetery on Saturday, bringing flowers to place on the tombs of his kinsfolk, and noted in his diary that he "saw the niche and epitaph on tombstone of Roberta Par Jorda, cousin who died at 15, March 28, 1866—a favorite of my father who took great interest in her. This date of her death fixes the period when father had established himself in Barcelona after his post-graduate year in Paris and return from the U.S. I was then 6 yr. old."

For the rest he continued to visit friends and distant connections of the Matas, Hereu, Jorda and Forto families; at least every other night he took Elvira and her godchild—"the little maid, Elvira"—to the movies. He bought rope-soled sandals for himself and had a tailor make for him, from cloth woven in Catalonia of Australian wool, a heavy suit and a light overcoat. And finally, as the day of departure arrived, unwilling yet to admit even to himself the disappointments he had experienced in renewing the fraternal bonds between himself and Elvira, he gave his sister 1000 pesetas as a parting present and left 250 pesetas for Victorina and 50 more for her niece.

He was back in Paris on November 16 and almost immediately visited the establishment of Dr. Coulomb, the oculist, to try still another artificial eye; but even this one did not yet fit, so he made an appointment for the following late afternoon. He found letters from Lucian, Miss Hess, and Jane Grey Rogers, librarian of the Tulane Medical College, enclosing newspaper clippings from the *Times-Picayune*, the *Item* and the *States* about his appearance before the French Congress and his elevation to an honorary presidency of that body.

He roamed the Boulevard St.-Germain next morning, apparently still seeking to materialize the vague image of a small boy trudging confidingly at Narciso's side. Failing to recognize the *pension* where he had cherished his *cher 'ti' lapin*, he crossed from the Left Bank to Notre Dame Cathedral where "a burial service was in progress. As I tramped on the old polished stones, polished by the feet of millions of worshippers, I thought that I too had helped to wear out the old stones a few times with my tiny feet nearly 60 years ago. This reflection only added to the emotion and romance that always stirs me when I visit the dear old Cathedral. Every time I come I am more impressed with wonderful architecture. I walked up the tower on the right (1 franc) and stirred up my heart and pulse considerably by the time I had climbed all 260 stairs up the old spiral stairway (pure stone, most of it carved work) as alone in the belfry I came in touch with the curious *chimères* who greeted me in the usual droll and fantastic way, evidently recognizing me as an old habitué. I am rewarded for my tiresome climb by a magnificent panoramic view of Paris too wonderful and beautiful to describe, but it is a lasting picture. I walked over to the Old Curiosity Shop 'Aux Chimères de Notre Dame,' which I invariably patronize when I visit Paris. I bought two more *chimères* (one named the *Penseur*), a small reproduction in plaster of the Nike of Samothrace, and another small *chimère* to replace the broken one at the office."

He spent much of the next day shopping at the Lafayette store, and did not neglect to note in his diary that "as a whole the young shop girls compared very favorably in looks with the best in N.O. and N.Y. The department stores are the best places to judge of the average physical features of the young women of the middle class."

Two days later he was on the boat train and at 6 P.M. of November 22 aboard the *Olympic*. Lucian met him at the station in New Orleans and he was made welcome by Bunny and Ruddie, now nearly four years old, and by Mrs. Goslee at the home which was just as empty as it had been when he left it three months earlier. He remained there only long enough to prepare for a meeting of the Southern Surgical Association at Memphis, less than a week later.

The years fled into the past at a steadily accelerating pace as the day of his retirement from the Tulane faculty approached. One must marvel that he got through as much work as he did, especially in compiling ever more detailed and voluminous material for the history of medicine in Louisiana into which he fully intended to expand the sketchy outline he had delivered before the annual banquet of the French College of Surgeons in 1922. Yet his commitments were forever in conflict with one another. For example, in the late fall of 1923, he had promised Dr. Hubert Royster of Raleigh, North Carolina, to send him, before December 13, a paper on the secondary effect of arterio-venous fistulae upon the heart and general circulation. But he was also preparing to deliver in mid-December the principal eulogy at a Halsted memorial meeting in Baltimore. So he did not even get the title of his paper to Dr. Royster in time to have it included in the printed program of the assembly before which it was to be read.

The following year he added to his already crowded schedule a medico-surgical development suggested by the success of his pioneering experiments with the continuous intravenous drip: a continuous gastro-duodenal irrigation by a Jutte tube introduced through the nose. "The duodenal tube," he reported in Volume 79 of the *Annals of Surgery* for May 1924, "as an adjunct to the continuous intra-venous drip, is simply of priceless value. It is easily introduced through the nose into the stomach with little difficulty. Once in the stomach, it is allowed to remain permanently in situ and held to the nose externally by strips of adhesive plaster . . . [It] empties the upper intestine of its toxic content and diminishes the abdominal tension caused by the pent up gases, thus adding enormously to the comfort of the patient." *

In this same year he was made president-elect of the American College of Surgeons at that body's New York City convention, with Dr. A. J. Ochsner presiding. The College has a unique system of selecting presiding officers. The member to be thus honored is elected one year, but is not inaugurated until the very close of the following year's convention, so that he does not actually preside until two years after his election. Thus Dr. Matas was chosen in 1924, at New York, just before the presiding officer, Dr. Ochsner, inaugurated Dr. Charles Mayo of Rochester. In 1925 Dr. Mayo presided over the convention in Philadelphia, his last official act being the inauguration of Dr. Matas to preside over the meeting to be held in Montreal during October 1926.

That was the year preceding the celebration in London of the centennial of Lord Lister's birth: as president of the American College of Surgeons, Dr. Matas had been invited to attend the exercises to be held by the Royal College of Surgeons. He was enormously pleased by the invitation and devoted much of his Montreal address as retiring president to a glowing tribute to "Pasteur, the father of modern scientific medicine, and Lister, the father of modern scientific surgery."

"The progress of surgery and the universal acceptance of the principles of surgical cleanliness laid down by Lister," he went on, "tend to give the surgeon a more objective evidence of his world citizenship than in

---

* During the last eighteen months of his life, Dr. Matas himself received no nourishment except through such a tube, "left permanently in situ," except that it was changed every six weeks or so for a fresh one.

any previous age. Dressed in white, immaculate, gloved, capped . . . to the visitor in any of the surgical clinics of the world, this uniformity is almost monotonous and . . . challenges the most expert observer to discover the nationality of the operator. Whether in Tokyo, New York, Paris, Cape Town, Calcutta, it matters not where, the surgeon to outward appearances . . . claims no nationality when in action, and only recognizes the world as his birthplace."

This was nearly a year after he had taken up with the Tulane authorities the matter of his retirement and the selection of his successor. The University of Alabama had just conferred upon him an honorary LL.D. degree, Dr. L. L. Hill, father of Senator Lister Hill, declaring that "it is the rule of the Board of Trustees that action on such a nomination be postponed for a year after the name has been proposed, but in your case, by unanimous vote of the Board, this rule was suspended."

The year was to bring him yet other joys and triumphs. In November the Boston Surgical Society bestowed upon him the Bigelow Medal, established in 1911 as a memorial to Henry Jacob Bigelow and awarded for distinguished service to surgery only three times in the ensuing fifteen years. The first one went to Dr. Will J. Mayo in 1921, the second to Dr. W. W. Keen in 1922.

The public tribute thus paid their fellow citizen so delighted the leaders of the New Orleans community that a "surprise party" was tendered Dr. Matas in the auditorium of the Hutchinson Memorial Building on his return from Boston. Miss Hess, who kept his engagement book for him, had left the night of November 11 free, and Lucian called him to attend a fictitious but important committee meeting. Climax of the ceremonies was the presentation of a watch by Miss Grace King, New Orleans' leading poet and writer on behalf of the entire assembly, the case being engraved: "From those who know you best and love you most." Deeply moved, he responded extemporaneously stressing the conviction that "an ounce of taffy to the living is worth tons of epitaphy for the dead."

He was rejoiced by yet one other announcement that year. It came from Bunny. She was once more with child; she and Lucian were praying there would be no mishaps and that in 1927 Ruddie would have a baby sister. To celebrate the glad tidings, Dr. Matas promptly took Ruddie to the movies.

CHAPTER XXXI

Retirement from the chair of surgery at Tulane marked for Professor Emeritus Rudolph Matas the beginning of a new way of life. He still maintained an undiminished and very lucrative private practice. But the unresting intellectualism that had formerly driven him to the exploration of one new field of research after another was now focused on a consuming desire to write.

He was still revered as the genius who had fathered the entire concept of latter-day vascular surgery. Indeed the honors yet to be bestowed on him were the highest of his long career. Not for another decade would he be elected to the presidency of the International Society of Surgery, receive the first Finlay Order conferred on a United States physician by Cuba, or be awarded the American Medical Association's first Distinguished Service Medal. But his contributions to medical literature and practice would thenceforth be confined almost entirely to reviews of what had been done in the past; his "research" became a quest for and compilation of statistical material.

Nearly a third of his ninety-seven years yet remained to him, he became progressively more than ever a prototype of the traditional absent-minded savant, forever mislaying important documents, forgetting room keys, losing baggage checks, and overlooking essential details of even his workaday routine.

Normally, he would have been retired from his professorship in May 1925, since he would have reached sixty-five, Tulane's mandatory retirement age for faculty members, just prior to the opening of the next scholastic term. But it was not until the spring of 1927 that his successor was chosen. He was pleased by this proof that the task of replacing him was obviously not easy.

One of the elements making the choice difficult was a major change in policy on the part of Tulane's administrators. In conformity with views held by the General Education Board in New York, it was decided that the professor of surgery must henceforth give his full time to instruction and be not merely a practicing surgeon, a part of whose work was devoted to a teaching schedule. Urban Maes had expressed a willingness to turn the fees from his practice back to the University, retaining no income aside from his professorial salary, and Dr. Matas endorsed the Maes appointment. But for the moment Tulane's Board members remained adamant in the matter of replacing part-time department heads in the College of Medicine with full-time successors. They finally appointed Alton Ochsner to the chair of surgery in March 1927,* just in time to let the newly fledged professor emeritus ask and receive a leave of absence that would enable him to attend, in London, the Lister Centennial session of Britain's Royal College of Surgeons.

He was as naïvely casual as ever in preparing for a journey, even though he now had the full-time assistance of Miss Hess, who took over the additional portfolio of resident housekeeper after Mrs. Goslee succumbed to a cardiac seizure on January 25, 1927. Ever since her daughter's death, the frail little *grande dame* had ruled the great house with its staff of half a dozen servants though, as year followed year, Miss Hess had found it necessary to relieve her of more and ever more of these duties.

Ermance Marie, daughter of the savant, Charles Edmond Marc, widow of a riverboat captain, outlived Mrs. Matas by a full decade and was eighty-three years old when, on a quiet Sunday afternoon, she suffered a heart attack and died early the next morning.

However, even with Miss Hess to aid in preparations for his first journey abroad as emeritus professor, Dr. Matas managed to involve himself in one dilemma after another. He had been sent a program, along with his credentials as a special guest upon whom an honorary fellowship would be conferred in the course of the Centennial ceremonies. The program included a notation that "delegates"—i.e., members of the College—would be received by His Majesty at Buckingham

---

* The arrangement ultimately proved unworkable. In October 1928, the Tulane authorities modified their ukase to permit the professor of surgery to engage in private practice, stipulating that the fees for such service be turned over to the Dean's office for the benefit of the Department of Surgery; then, in October 1934, after consultation with the General Education Board, Tulane modified the original ruling still further by adding the words: "with the exception that full-time heads of departments may retain the fees collected by them."

Palace on the afternoon before formal sessions were scheduled to begin.

Assuming that he too was among those invited to the palace, Dr. Matas lost no time in sharing the great tidings with his friend Hudson Grunewald, an *Item* reporter, whose story promptly found a place under a three-column headline on Page One to the effect that "Dr. Matas Will Be Presented to Royalty."

Unfortunately, the Doctor discovered upon reaching London no official documents that could be construed in any sense as invitations to Buckingham Palace. There was a place for him on the subsequent program as representative of the American College of Surgeons, in which capacity he would deliver an address and lay a wreath on Lister's tomb. In the course of another ceremony he would receive the ornately illuminated diploma of honorary fellowship in the college, along with Archibald of Montreal, Allessandri of Rome, Leriche of Strasbourg, and Lecene of Paris. But that was all.

Regarding this as an oversight, he referred it in mounting tribulation to one knighted surgeon after another, and to the College Secretariat itself. In the midst of this, realizing suddenly that he had neglected to include any item of formal afternoon *tenue* in his luggage, he purchased a top hat and placed a rush order with a Bond Street tailor for morning coat and striped trousers; as a matter of fact he discovered that he had also forgotten his visiting cards and even his credentials as a member of the Tulane University faculty. Losing hope, he noted disconsolately in his diary that "if Hudson Grunewald had not made an announcement in the *Item* that I was to be received by the King, I wouldn't bother about the reception, but he has communicated to the Press and I must try to attend."

His efforts to make Grunewald's story good were futile. The friends to whom he applied were probably more profoundly embarrassed than he was, for it was difficult indeed to explain to the Great Man why he could not attend His Majesty's reception. Ultimately he resigned himself to the inevitable and sought a measure of consolation in cabling Elvira twenty pounds sterling, so that she might take first-class passage to London and meet him there for the beginning of a long and leisurely summer's family reunion. Pending her arrival, he worked on a manuscript he had been commissioned to write two years earlier—that is to say, in 1925—by Dr. Dean Lewis of Johns Hopkins, for a new *System of Surgery*. Three years later—that is to say, in 1930—Dr. Lewis and his publishers, W. R. Prior & Co., would still be inquiring when he expected to send them the promised manuscript. The correspondence was couched in the most diplomatic terms, though it would become brusque enough after the lapse of two more years. T. J. Carroll of the Prior organization still flatteringly pointed out that "there is no surgeon in the world who is more highly respected and beloved than you are. You have done work on blood-vascular surgery that has made your name synonymous with the subject."

Replying, Dr. Matas explained that he had just returned to the United States after an absence of many months abroad. He had participated in the deliberations of the 1929 International Society of Surgery meeting in Warsaw; an adventurous interlude, incidentally, since in addition to his absent-minded disregard of routine matters he spoke no language the average Polish citizen could understand and was reduced to communicating with hotel employees through pictures he drew on a pad.

He had also journeyed on to Moscow from Warsaw, before returning to Western Europe, and was unfavorably impressed with what he saw of Communist living even in 1929, long before the Soviet regime sent its Iron Curtain clanking down. But he did buy a Muscovite doll for the collection of puppets he was making as a Christmas present to Ruddie's sister, Amelie, and each of these dolls—Japanese, Spanish, Indian Squaw, and the like—was accompanied by an individual document, in prose or in rather dreadful verse. With the Russian doll, for example, was a letter which read in part:

"My name is Sonia Rhonia Landrioff and I have come to America to be the Russian maid of Miss Amelie Landry. I met with a railroad collision on the way and lost my sight, but Dr. Matas who paid my way to New Orleans took me to the Hospital in New York where I was operated, and now I can see again . . . I am a little peasant girl and an orphan, but I can work and . . . oh! I am so glad to be with you for Christmas. It is so nice and warm and everything is so lovely and beautiful. Won't you kiss me?"

The dolls were sent on to New Orleans from New York because, on his return in 1929 Dr. Matas remained in the North, eating a solitary Christmas dinner at his hotel, to work on his latest literary undertaking. Hence, in reply to Mr. Carroll's plea for information as to when the Prior firm might expect the manuscript on blood-vascular surgery which Dr. Matas had been commissioned to write five years before, he confessed that he was now facing "three formidable literary contracts." These were the vascular section of Lewis's Surgery; an illustrated History of Medicine in Louisiana which, in 1926, the State Medical Society had commissioned him to write; and, finally, a treatise on Post-Operative Embolism and Thrombosis. This had been the topic of a worldwide symposium before the International Society of Surgery in Warsaw.

Yet not one of these three "formidable literary" works was ever published. The Louisiana history was begun in a feverish burst of enthusiasm two years after he had agreed to supply Dr. Lewis and the

Prior Company with the vascular section; a symposium on thrombosis and postoperative embolism was launched four years after the Lewis contract had been signed in 1925. Yet he unhesitatingly signed a contract with Paul V. Hoeber, Inc. for publication of the symposium on the understanding that the completed manuscript was to be delivered by August 1, 1930, just as he received the Carroll letter of inquiry about the manuscript, now nearly five years overdue, contracted for in 1925.

The medical history of Louisiana had not yet emerged from the material-gathering stage at the time of Dr. Matas's death in 1957. By then the accumulation of data had reached so prodigious a volume that the State Medical Society could not possibly have published it in any case.*

The vascular surgery monograph for the Lewis *System* was not in the publisher's hands until March 4, 1932, approximately seven years after the contract to undertake the work had been signed. At the outset, some three hundred pages in Volume IV had been set apart for the Matas contribution, but by the time seven years had run their course, only some forty pages in the final volume—No. XII—remained open. The publishers necessarily had to ask him to cut his manuscript or to omit reams of tabular matter. To this he flatly refused to accede. Thus, in the end, the section on vascular surgery was assigned to Dr. Raymond McNealy of Northwestern University to write.

Unfortunately, by that time a prospectus for the final volume of the Lewis work had been issued, announcing that the section on aneurisms, by Dr. Rudolph Matas, would appear therein. He furiously protested this indignity "when you knew that some one else was in fact writing the work," and remained deaf to all explanations, thus managing to convince at least himself that it was he who had been the aggrieved party in the transaction.

The symposium on thrombosis and embolism, in the newborn zeal for which all earlier commitments were relegated to the background, was ill-starred from the outset. Returning from Europe in November,†

* In 1953 Dr. Matas created a $40,000 trust fund, out of which the *History* was published by the Louisiana State University Press, in two volumes, which were edited by John Duffy, who reduced the Matas material to approximately one tenth of the mass of documents and other data submitted to him. The sum was likewise intended to defray publishing costs of a 1000-copy edition of the History of the state medical society as a separate and distinct enterprise. Both were scheduled for posthumous publication.

† He had interrupted the return journey for a two-month visit with his sister in San Felíu, from mid-August to early October, noting in his diary that on stopping at the French-Spanish frontier station at Port Bou for customs inspection, "I discovered that my trunks had all been left behind at Belgrade, and that I would have to leave my keys with a Spanish customs agent. He is to attend to the business of for-

he remained in New York to work up his travel notes and his report of the Warsaw discussion on thrombosis for the published proceedings of the International Society. He then went to Philadelphia as one of the three principal speakers at a banquet tendered by his colleagues to the great John Chalmers Da Costa, now immobilized in a wheel chair by arthritis.

While there it occurred to him to take up with W. B. Saunders & Co. the question of publishing an English translation of all the Warsaw thrombosis and embolism papers and discussions. The Saunders firm seemed disinclined even to consider this proposal. In fact, when Dr. Matas asked them to give him a definitive reply so that he could take the matter up with other publishers who might make him a better offer, a Saunders spokesman volunteered to introduce him to Lea & Febiger as well as other presumably competing medical publishers. After a fortnight of negotiations, the proposal was rejected on the ground that it would be too difficult to market such a volume profitably.

Dr. Matas's next disappointment was a letter from one of his collaborators, Dr. Paul Govaerts, professor of clinical medicine at the University of Brussels, in February of 1930:

"It seems to me that interest in the subject has lessened," wrote Dr. Govaerts, "and I deem the best thing is to drop the matter." Dr. Matas cabled his colleague a strong protest and confided to his diary that "I feel all disconcerted about his action and cannot account for the cool, irresponsible way he has acted."

However, at this time a magnificently bound anniversary volume was being prepared at a cost of thousands of dollars, a veritable *Festschrift* to be presented to him on his seventieth birthday.* It was produced by the New York firm of Paul V. Hoeber, Inc., which also published the *American Journal of Surgery*. The guarantee of payment for this lavishly bound and printed publication naturally made the enterprise profitable. Hence, when Mr. Hoeber was approached by the subject in whose honor the work had been undertaken, he lent a receptive ear to Dr. Matas's proposal for publishing the symposium too. In fact, he entered into a contract, not merely to publish it but to pay Dr. Matas a royalty of 10 per cent on all copies sold after the first thousand had been purchased. This was in May of 1930.

---

warding the trunks from Belgrade to Gerona and San Felíu" . . . After a further stopover in Paris, he reached New York on November 2—four days after the market crash in which he lost substantial interest payments from defaulted bonds and some paper profits on earlier investments.

*It was not presented until December 17, 1931, fifteen months after the Seventieth birthday it had been intended to mark. However, even then the presentation highlighted a great occasion, whose details were widely heralded in both the lay and the medical press.

With his precious contract in his brief case, Dr. Matas jubilantly returned to New Orleans after an absence of 349 days. He had remained in New York primarily to work on his report for the proceedings of the International Society, eating his Christmas dinner at the hotel, sending presents to his family—even Amelie's dolls—by mail, and leading a generally hermitlike existence. Now the report for the Society's proceedings was relegated to the background along with all other earlier commitments. In New Orleans he set to work on the symposium, and the longer he worked, the greater and more detailed became the nascent manuscript.

Meanwhile a great backlog of cases had awaited his return and for a year he enjoyed perhaps his busiest and most demanding season of private practice, writing at nights on his embolism symposium and adding new chapters to it from time to time: a separate chapter on thrombosis and embolism following abdominal surgery—even a set of comparative statistical tables on thrombosis and embolism in Germany and in the United States.

He devoted himself tirelessly to this task throughout the year 1930 and was still hard at it in 1931 when he left New Orleans in October to attend a session of the American College of Surgeons in New York. But he took with him the great bulk of his manuscript and after the College meetings were adjourned, he immured himself once more in his hotel room, leaving it only for the library of the Academy of Medicine, mealtime excursions to lunch counters and delicatessen stores, and almost nightly attendance at one or another of New York's modern movie palaces.

The mass of material on thrombosis and embolism grew and grew and grew. He was still dictating new chapters in New York in November 1931—the completed manuscript had been promised for August 1 1930!—but finally, on November 25, the typed sheets were bundled up for delivery the next day to Paul Hoeber at the latter's office.

"Get to Hoeber's at 11 A.M.," chronicles the diary, "and finally get to the business of counting the pages of manuscript and illustrations for the book . . . Decide that I have to return to the hotel [He had forgotten to bring the index section with him] . . . The book is estimated to be between 500 and 600 pages." Then comes an ominous note. Hoeber has "decided not to hurry" about publishing it. He suggests "it might appear in installments in the *American Journal of Surgery* . . . wanted me to leave the manuscript with him so that he could consider the affair until next Sunday. I decided to take the manuscript home."

After an interval of five days more, Dr. Matas left New York for his home, stopping in Baltimore to go over the aneurism treatise which had been promised to Dr. Lewis at Johns Hopkins and which he would now engage to deliver before March. And finally this diary note for November 30:

"Cloudy. A sad and ill fated day . . . Drive to Hoeber's, then realize definitely that if I wanted the symposium published it would cost me $5000!—He backed out of the signed agreement to publish the book in 1929 [sic!] but conditions had changed since that time, and he could not afford the risk of the loss on the book and since two years had elapsed, the agreement or contract no longer existed . . . We discussed several plans, but none seemed satisfactory . . . I left Hoeber's completely demoralized and disgusted . . . But Lewis's *System* and the Louisiana *History* are still waiting."

He had thus managed to convince himself once more that he was the aggrieved party, that he had fulfilled his side of a bargain on which the other party had defaulted after signing a contract. To the fact that between the date on which he had promised delivery and the date, more than fifteen months tardy, when he carried out this agreement, the worst depression in the nation's history had blighted virtually all prospects for the outlay of venture capital he gave not so much as a thought.

He was immensely cheered, however, by the homage paid him on the occasion of the *Festschrift's* formal presentation within a fortnight after his return to New Orleans from the Hoeber debacle. Heartened by this, he gave Ruddie and Bunny a Christmas gift of money to cover the cost of a trip with Lucian to Pasadena to see Tulane play in the Rose Bowl. Lucian accompanied the players as team physician.

Thereafter his literary efforts were devoted to the accumulation of an ever-growing mountain of material for the history of medicine in Louisiana, in which he had enlisted the assistance of Dr. Daniel N. Silverman, Dr. John T. Nix, the latter's secretary, Mrs. Hathaway Aleman, and Miss Mary Louise Marshall, assistant librarian of the Orleans Parish Medical Society. To be sure, he continued to turn out *tours-de-force* for special occasions—the Donald C. Balfour Lecture in Surgery (on thrombosis and embolism) he delivered in Toronto, the presidential address he gave in Brussels before the International Society of Surgery, the address he delivered in Havana when he was inducted with a world of pomp and circumstance into the Grand Council of the Order of Carlos Finlay.

He initiated one more notable essay at original research during this period. Harking back to his first scientific labors in connection with yellow fever, he wrote to Dr. Simon Flexner at the Rockefeller Institute, suggesting that his blood be examined to determine whether the immunity conferred on him seventy-five years previously by surviving a benign attack of yellow fever was permanent and hence still effective. To test this, he proposed that a sample of his blood be rushed to the Rockefeller Institute by plane and injected into mice which would then be inoculated with active yellow-fever virus.

Dr. Flexner did not reply in person, but his Director of Laboratories, Dr. J. H. Bauer, wrote at once, saying the test would be made as soon as a sample of Dr. Matas's blood, taken aseptically, could be sent to him.

Dr. Ernest Carroll Faust, professor of tropical medicine at Tulane, thereupon drew five cubic centimeters of blood from the veins of the eighty-three-year-old pioneer in the battle against yellow fever. This was done in the animal laboratory at Tulane's new Hutchinson Memorial Building. In New York, Dr. Max Theiler was assigned to use this sample in a "mouse-protection test" in which 36 mice became subjects. Serum from Dr. Matas's blood was mixed with known yellow-fever virus of a French strain, and twelve mice were injected with what had previously been ascertained to be fifty times the minimum dosage of this deadly material. Twelve other mice were then injected with identical dosages, in which the virulent material was mixed with normal, nonimmune blood serum. The third dozen mice were injected with the same virulent dosage mixed with a known immunizing serum from a recent yellow-fever convalescent.

The results were conclusive. All mice injected with yellow-fever virus and no protection died. In each of the other series, where twelve mice were injected with virus mixed with the Matas serum and twelve others with known fever-immune serum, 11 of the 12 little animals lived. Thus the "lifelong immunity" hypothesis was further buttressed by a test of serum whose immunity factor had been acquired from a primary yellow-fever infection occurring more than three-fourths of a century before.

In this same era of the early 1930's Dr. Matas developed two consuming hatreds that became possessively fixed convictions. One was for Huey Long; the other for a recently formed International "College" of Surgeons, which sought to have the established International "Society" of Surgeons amalgamate with it. Headquarters of the Society had long been in Brussels; those of the College were established in Geneva. Dr. Matas's bitterness toward the College became so intense that years later, when one of his devoted friends, who had delivered an address before the College, addressed a New Orleans meeting, he refused on the plea of illness to attend the lecture or even to receive the visitor in his home.

As for Huey Long, Dr. Matas's natural hostility toward authoritarianism and political interference in medical matters was made permanent and irrevocable when Long decided to add to Louisana State University's facilities a College of Medicine to rival Tulane's. That the L.S.U. college ultimately became an institution of great distinction cannot be denied. It is no less true, however, that the *raison d'être* for its establishment by Long was the spite the latter harbored against Tulane; the patricians who made up its Board of Governors were likewise leaders of anti-Long sentiment in social and civic affairs. They were the "sweet-scented silk hat" brigade he ridiculed from every stump; the cachet conferred upon Tulane because it had the only college of medicine in the tristate enclave of Louisiana, Mississippi, and Arkansas would cease to be a distinction the moment another medical college—especially one backed by the almost limitless financing he was prepared to lavish on it from the public treasury—stood cheek by jowl with it in New Orleans.

The financial abracadabra by which funds were made available for this purpose without legislative authorization was child's play for Long's adroit mastery of manipulation. A dozen years earlier, Louisiana State University had been moved by Governor John M. Parker from its old quarters to a 1200-acre plantation estate some miles downstream from Baton Rouge. Governor Long had erected a new, thirty-two-story state capitol on part of the old campus. He now had the Highway Department, whose treasury bulged with the avails of a newly doubled gasoline tax, buy two of the University's old buildings and a portion of the old campus for more than enough to erect a magnificent Medical School on ground already owned by the state for Charity Hospital use in New Orleans.

The new college was staffed by physicians, selected from among Long supporters, of course, with a brilliant young practitioner, Emmett Lee Irwin by name, as professor of surgery, and the superintendent of Charity Hospital, Dr. Arthur Vidrine, doubling in cap and gown as dean. Almost at once, Dr. Alton Ochsner, Dr. Matas's successor as professor of surgery, was summarily stripped of his status as visiting surgeon at Charity Hospital and denied any use of that institution's facilities. This was done by the Long-appointed Hospital Board, with but one member voicing a protest, on the ground that Dr. Ochsner had violated the loyalty every member of the hospital staff was supposed to maintain by writing a sharply critical letter about its "politicalization" to a friend in Baltimore. The exact details of the hanky-panky through which a carbon copy of this letter came into Huey Long's hands have never been revealed. But his riposte was characteristic; in effect, it left Tulane University's professor of surgery without clinical facilities for instruction. He would thenceforth be able to teach only by using laboratory animal subjects and delivering didactic lectures.

That satisfied the Kingfish's rancorous desire to harass the Tulane

Brahmins, but it likewise left him on the horns of a distressing dilemma. The accreditation committee of the Association of Southern Universities promptly denied L.S.U.'s new medical center the "A" rating without which its graduates would not receive recognition by other academic institutions and medical boards. To overcome this obvious and galling handicap, Long finally offered the professorship of surgery at his new school to Dr. Maes, who had long been one of Dr. Matas's favorite disciples. In making this tender, Senator Long (who had no official connection with the state administration of Louisiana, to be sure) dismissed Dr. Irwin by a casual ipse dixit.

Dr. Maes predicated his acceptance of the tendered professorship on a number of inflexible conditions. One was an immediate lifting of the ban against Alton Ochsner's use of Charity Hospital facilities as visiting surgeon and Tulane professor. He also demanded a firm agreement that at no time would Tulane University be denied equal access to the great hospital's clinical and teaching facilities. It is not to be gainsaid that this freed Tulane's teaching of surgery from the constricting limitation of ten beds the University had taken at Touro Infirmary. On the other hand, the practical demonstration thus given of nonpolitical future conduct of the new school certainly helped to win for it the "A" rating it received soon thereafter. Yet Rudolph Matas never forgave Urban Maes for his share in aiding Long to set the new Medical College on a sound foundation. Relations between the two men were thereafter professional and not cordial.

By one of the curious quirks with which cause and effect are sometimes continuingly bound in the course of human events, Rudolph Matas unwittingly had a hand in forging one of the first links in the chain of circumstance that ultimately led to Huey Long's assassination. As a member of the committee to select Louisiana winners of French Government scholarships, he met with that body on June 9, 1931, and voted with his colleagues to award the prize for that year to Yvonne Pavy, daughter of District Judge Ben Pavy of Opelousas.

As a Romance language major she began her studies abroad that fall and, during the course of the ensuing year, met another Louisiana student, young Dr. Carl Austin Weiss, Jr., who had been one of Rudolph Matas's favorite interns at Touro the year before. He was the son of a Baton Rouge otolaryngologist, who had sent him to Paris for a year's graduate study in this field. Yvonne and Carl fell in love and were married. The first and only child of their union—a third Carl—was about eight months old in September 1936, when Dr. Weiss learned that in a final drive to defeat Yvonne's father for re-election, Long had dragooned a gerrymander through the Legislature which would to all intents and purposes be certain to terminate Judge Pavy's forty-year tenure. Long further announced that he would take the stump against Pavy, using certain scurrilities which would reflect not only on the judge, but on all members of his family, one of these being Mrs. Carl Austin Weiss, Jr., to say nothing of her infant son.

So Dr. Weiss took his wife and baby to the Amite River for a Sunday afternoon picnic, knowing—as they could not know—that this would be their final day of tenderly shared devotion to one another. Returning with his family to their home, he left almost at once for the state capitol where the Legislature was assembled in special session. There he fired a single small-caliber bullet through Huey's abdomen and was promptly gunned down, as he had known he would be, by a hail of fire from Long's heavily armed bodyguards. The day was September 8, 1935. . . . Had some other prize winner been awarded the French scholarship in June, 1931, Yvonne and Carl might never have met in romantic Paris. Who can say how different a climax might then have been written to Huey Long's impact on the American scene?

Dr. Matas had not attended the meeting of the International Society of Surgery at Madrid in 1932. That was the year in which he was frantically trying to make up for the fiasco of his symposium plans by finishing the vascular surgery section for Dr. Lewis's *System of Surgery;* this was followed by delivery of the Balfour lecture in Toronto, and finally by a meeting of the American Medical Association in St. Louis. Having missed the Madrid convention of the International Society, he would ordinarily have been doubly eager to attend the next triennial session at Cairo in 1935–36. There has never been any authoritative explanation of his failure to do so.

But if conjecture be permitted, certain facts could well be considered. First of all, Long's assassination in September of 1935 occurred on the eve of a state campaign and naturally touched off a flaming political conflict. Anti-Long leaders called their slate of candidates the "Home Rule Ticket"; the slain Kingfish's crusading followers dubbed them the "Assassination Ticket," and called on the voters to avenge Huey's death by their ballots. The Democratic primary (whose outcome still is tantamount to election in local campaigns throughout the South) was set for January 22. Had he attended the Cairo Congress of the International Society, Rudolph Matas could have taken no part in the anti-Long campaign; indeed, since the Cairo meeting was not adjourned until January 4, he might not even have been able to return in time to vote. The intensity of his hostility to the Long cause was certainly no secret. It is confirmed by his diary entries for these dates:

"January 22nd. Election date go to the polls to vote for the Home Rule Cleveland Dear Ticket and against all Huey Long candidates."

"January 23rd. Election returns show sweeping victory for the Leche

Allen Long Ticket with immediate downfall of the Home Rule principles and party. Once more the stupidity of the herd is confirmed."

It may well have been, therefore, that an almost fanatic determination to help overthrow the Long regime kept him from Cairo's session of the International Society. Moreover, there was then no idea that he might be named to its presidency. At the Madrid meeting three years earlier, a Viennese surgeon, von Eiselsberg by name, had been elected to this office; under ordinary circumstances, he would have presided at the Cairo gathering. But illness prevented his attendance there, and a Hollander, Dr. Jan Schoemaker, presided in his stead. Schoemaker had been slated to become von Eiselsberg's successor, but inasmuch as he had already officiated, some other nominee was desired.

In conformity with the policy of rotating the presidential accolade among the various nations represented by the membership, it was agreed that the next president should be an American. From among the various names submitted by the nominating committee, that of Rudolph Matas was selected. On January 2, 1936, J. Shelton Horsley cabled him from Cairo: "CONGRATULATIONS PRESIDENT." Within the hour he cabled this reply:"HORSLEY SURGICAL CONGRESS CAIRO DIZZY BUT GRATEFUL MATAS."

The next convention of the Society was to be held in Vienna, during the latter months of 1938. But in March of that year, Hitler's Nazi legions goose-stepped into Vienna to validate the *Anschluss*. On the heels of this, Dr. Matas began to receive anonymous threats from Munich and other German cities, promising that he would be driven out of Germany if he dared to bring to the Reich Jewish physicians as delegates to a convention of which, with typical Jewish cunning, he had made himself president. He turned these letters over to the German consulate in New Orleans, which expressed appreciation for his thoughtfulness in not having made them public out-of-hand.

In mid-June he received a communication from Leopold Mayer, permanent secretary of the International Society, to the effect that the Nazi government had "taken the Congress under its patronage and will do all it can to assure its success." It was a relief to have the issue settled, and heightened the enjoyment of what had already begun as a pleasant year. In March Dr. Matas had been showered with congratulatory messages on the fiftieth anniversary of his first arteriorrhaphy operation, the one that had saved the life and the arm of Manuel Harris, plantation laborer.

In June, the American Medical Association, meeting in San Francisco, selected him as first recipient of its Distinguished Service Medal, an award whose annual bestowal for signal service to scientific medicine had been authorized only the year before. Drs. Simon Flexner and

Ludwig Hektoen had been the only other nominees whose names were submitted to the San Francisco convention. Yet, according to a diary note in June, the most welcome tidings arrived on June 2 in a letter from Leopold Mayer in Brussels "with the glad news that the Nazis have decided the Congress at Vienna shall not take place. Mayer trying to shift the Congress to Brussels, enclosed letter . . . which gives no explanation of the sudden *volte-face* of the Nazi government." Dr. Matas had to appeal to Miss Lydia Frotscher, professor of English at Newcomb College, to translate the Nazi letters.

In any event, the I.S.S. Congress was held at Brussels in September, and Dr. Matas celebrated his seventy-eighth birthday aboard the *Ile de France* en route. In consultation with Dr. Elliott Cutler, professor of surgery at Harvard, and in great anguish of spirit, he cut the original draft of his presidential address by half; and ultimately he made note of the fact that the cost of the luncheon he gave in Dr. Cutler's honor and of the *Soirée du President*, at which he was host, with an orchestra for the ballet directed by M. Katchovisk, came to $1555 in American currency.

Lucian, Bunny, Amelie, and Ruddie, who would enter Tulane's Medical School in a fortnight, had all come to Brussels to attend the Congress over which Dr. Matas presided. It was the Society's last convention for a decade. By the time another September had taken its place on the calendar, history's largest, costliest, and bloodiest war had begun; Belgium, where the I.S.S. maintained permanent headquarters, was the first West European nation to surrender to the Nazis. Dr. Matas, however, was determined the Society must be continued as an "organization in being," and that under no circumstances should it merge with the International College of Surgeons, with headquarters in neutral Switzerland, a nation untouched by war.

Throughout the tormented 1940's he would call meetings of all American members of the International Society of Surgery at every gathering of the American College of Surgeons, the American Medical Association, and other national and regional groups. He took on the duties and responsibilities of secretary-treasurer, collecting dues and keeping a meticulous account of such moneys, which he turned over to the revived international secretariat just prior to the first world-wide postwar session of the organization, held in London during 1947. It was at this time that the Society decided to meet biennially in the future, and, largely in tribute to Dr. Matas, that the next international gathering be held in New Orleans.

All this, of course, still lay far in the future at the time of the Brussels meeting, when Rudolph was confronted by a much more pressing personal problem. From the moment Spain had proclaimed the Second

Republic in 1931, exiling Alfonso XIII, disestablishing the Church and confiscating its properties, he had been deeply concerned about his sister Elvira's welfare. She had been writing him regularly during 1926, 1927, and 1928, acknowledging his remittance and congratulating him on his birthdays.

His anxiety had been heightened ever since 1933 when she wrote to ask an extra remittance of thirty dollars with which to purchase a little food in France, to be brought somehow across the border for San Felíu.

CHAPTER XXXII

Forty years had passed since Elvira had left Spain for anything but a brief excursion at whose end she would return to San Felíu. During those four decades she had lost the mother with whom she had lived throughout her spinster life; her brother had also lost his father, his son, and his wife. She and Rudolph were alone in the world. As awareness of this solitude became ever more demanding, the latter clung with growing intensity to the image of his sister as the one other human being he could truly call kin. To be sure, there were hosts of cousins of varying degree: Forto, Jorda, Villardell, and Matas *gente*. There was even a stepniece, the granddaughter of Narciso and Louisa Mallett Aphold, a girl who lived in California and whom Rudolph had never seen.

Forgotten now was the bitterness in which he had paid his sister and his mother to leave New Orleans under a solemn obligation never to return. Painstakingly he had searched through the hoard of letters and other documents in his files, consigning to the flames anything that might reflect upon any member of his family. In the brief autobiographical profiles he wrote for various publications, and in reply to a searching questionnaire sent out by Dr. Elliott Cutler in the middle 1930's, he included not so much as a syllable about the rift between his parents, his father's remarriage, or the efforts his mother and sister made to disrupt his marriage to Adrienne. In fact, he even went so far as to write in one of these sketches, that neither his mother nor his sister

393

ever returned to the United States after leaving the country for San Felíu in 1886.

Time and again he spoke of his debt to his parents, to the examples of piety and upright living they had set, to their earnest teaching, and to the tender home environment they had provided for him and for his sister. Gradually, the symbolic affection in which he had enshrined Elvira became real to him. He felt there had always been an indissoluble bond of tenderness to link them, one to the other.

Thus the establishment in Spain of the Second Republic alarmed him as a portent of unsettled conditions which might imperil his sister. As a first essential step toward assuring her safety and bringing her to the security of his home, he set out to validate her status as a United States national. In 1936, when the Falangist counterrevolution burst from Morocco into the Spanish mainland, when the siege of Madrid gave to the world a new concept clothed in the words "Fifth Column," the urge to come to his sister's defense became an overmastering purpose.

The most baffling phase of the difficulties he encountered was the fact that the only recognized diplomatic channels through which he could operate were those of the self-styled "Loyalist Government" which had been defeated at Madrid, at Toledo, Cadiz, Huelva, Seville, and Granada. It had been driven back into a small section of Catalonia. Its capital was Barcelona. Yet Franco's regime would not be officially recognized by the United States until 1939. Only the Barcelona splinter maintained consular offices in this country. Our State Department could deal with no other Spanish government, even though the Falange occupied and ruled nine tenths of Spain.

During the first weeks of October 1936, Dr. Matas therefore called on the Spanish consulate in New Orleans, and in the acting consul's diplomatic pouch dispatched to the Barcelona government sworn certificates attesting to Elvira's birth in Brownsville. These documents were accompanied by a recommendation from the acting consul, requesting that Elvira be permitted to leave Spain so that she—a citizen and national of the United States—could return to this country.

Elvira did not want to agree to this. One reason may well have been the religiocentric passion she had inherited from her mother; she was in complete sympathy with General Franco's announced program for re-establishing the Church as an arm of the State. At least, she and Rudolph quarreled bitterly over this point almost as soon as, two years later, he finally succeeded in getting not only her, but her faithful maid-housekeeper-companion, Victorina Comas, out of Spain.

Despite her reluctance, Dr. Matas continued his efforts to repatriate her, working through the State Department until, in 1938, he himself went abroad once more to preside over the Brussels Congress of the International Society of Surgery. Before his departure for Belgium he deposited with Secretary of State Cordell Hull $500, to be transmitted through diplomatic channels to the credit of his sister with the United States consulate general in Barcelona, so that funds for her journey back to the United States might be instantly available to her if the need arose.

At his suggestion, moreover, Elvira raised an American flag over the roof of her two-story, stone-walled residence. Rudolph's hope that this would protect the structure from Franco's German and Italian bombing planes, as these launched their missions of destruction from Mallorca, was obviously shared, not only by Elvira but by the rest of San Felíu, many of whose citizens fled to her home at the first note of an air-raid alarm.

Dr. Matas would have traveled directly to the Costa Brava the moment the convention over which he presided was adjourned, had he been able to secure authorization for such a journey from his own government. Unfortunately, all general United States passports that year specified that these documents did not authorize travel in Spain, Germany, or Austria. Dr. Matas, Lucian, Bunny, and Amelie were still in Paris when the Munich pact was signed. For the time being he could do nothing but wait for notification by Dr. Crespi, a San Felíu surgeon on military duty with the Republican army hospital, that Elvira's exit permit had been issued.

In October he finally secured from the American Embassy in Paris authorization for entry into and travel through Spain, left for Cerbère with enough American Express travelers' checks and United States currency for an extended stay. Elvira had evidently made it plain she would not return to the United States with or without him. Inasmuch as her American passport permitted her merely to leave Spain for what was technically her homeland, and made no provision for Victorina, both would need Spanish passports now to enter France. Even Rudolph knew by this time that this would involve long-drawn negotiations with every official echelon in the Republican government.

So, with gifts of chocolate and toilet soap, he arrived at Cerbère and crossed the border to Port Bou, where Dr. and Mrs. Robert Crespi were waiting with Elvira to greet him and drive him to San Felíu.

That was October 7, 1938. It was December before he, his sister, and Victorina could leave Spain. For one thing, the ineradicable faith that sent him off to crowded convention cities without a precautionary hotel reservation, still sustained him in the conviction that somehow Destiny was certain to provide. For another, his prodigious memory was a paradox. It never relinquished even the most trivial professional item entrusted to it, but strewed the trail of his world-wanderings with for-gotten belongings that ranged in dimension from a room key to a ward-robe trunk, and in importance from a spectacle case to the major section of a book manuscript.

By now, however, even he realized that simple faith was not enough for the battle against bureaucratic gobbledygook. Complicate the situation by almost daily bombing raids on the governmental seat of a rapidly disintegrating administration which realized it faced inevitable, ultimate defeat, and the wonder is that Dr. Matas ever got into Spain to begin with. That in no longer than two months thereafter he achieved his purpose is a still greater wonder. Yet he did bring both his sister and faithful Victorina with him into a Free France which Hitler's *Wehrmacht* would not overrun for another two years, opposing only his naïve trust to the harassments of petty officialdom.

The world was whirling madly out of a systemic orbit into who knew what chaotic future. That was no time for logic or efficiency; not when San Felíu, a coastal resort of approximately the same strategic importance as the weekly rehearsal night of a village church choir, was being subjected to no less than sixteen full-scale air-raid alerts and five actual bombings in the space of a few weeks; bombings that slew and injured an unconscionable number of civilians the Stuka pilots of a reborn *Luftwaffe* were using as practice targets.

Naturally, official pettifoggery welcomed an opportunity for a show of the dominance denied it elsewhere by the Falange's unbroken series of military victories. For example, Elvira who had lived in San Felíu more than forty years, had established herself technically as still a citizen of the United States. On the basis of this, she and Rudolph were each fined 50 pesetas for failing to report their presence as foreigners to the police at Gerona within forty-eight hours of "their" arrival in a Spain Elvira had not left—or even been permitted to leave—for years.

However, the American flag above Elvira's house was responsible for other and more agreeable developments too. Food was in distressingly short supply since Catalonia was encircled effectively both by land and by sea. But the residents who, during the many air-raid alarms, flocked for safety to the stout-walled home above which the flag of the United States was raised, expressed their appreciation tangibly with gifts of edibles; individually small, these offerings nonetheless represented what little treasure the donors possessed.

Dr. Matas noted in his diary that at 5 P.M. of the day after he reached San Felíu he walked with Elvira and Victorina to see the damage done by the forty-eight or more bombs which up to then had been dropped on the village. The next afternoon, following another such sightseeing stroll, "we came back to lunch-and-dinner which Victorina had cooked on her little stove—rabbit and *patole* stew, onions and a bread soup, anchovies, coffee and condensed milk. Dr. Crespi and wife called later and brought a big loaf of fresh bread and meat. Ferrada brought a dozen apples and two eggs (precious gifts these days) . . . Sirens scream the alarm of bombers approaching."

For yet another day the entry reads: "Levino, the old mountaineer, brings one dozen fine ripe figs, plundered from some neighbor's tree." There is even a complacently professional note to the effect that "the figs have been acting kindly"; and an equally appreciative notation that the surgical ward of the military hospital at Gerona is officially "the Rudolph Matas Surgical Ward, with my picture framed and my name inscribed in large characters on the wall."

Volunteers came forward with offers of assistance in the struggle against official double talk. A Sr. Durand, owner of the cork factory and related to President Isla of the Catalan assembly, promised to introduce Dr. Matas to this distinguished kinsman the first time the latter visited San Felíu. Assuredly, so influential a public figure could speed the issuance of passports for Elvira and Victorina. Meanwhile, three packages of foodstuffs ordered from a wholesaler at Cerbère were delivered, thus averting the immediate threat of actual hunger. The boxes were "a great contribution to our comfort. Now, with firewood cut from the pine forest by Carlos the Mountaineer, the fire has brought much cheer to the household . . . some of the foodstuffs have been distributed among friends who helped make the general scarcity more bearable."

But week followed weary week, without action on the passport applications. Food became something of a problem once more. "Celso the tailor comes with presents from Dr. Casals—three huge green peppers and a large cut of tender veal meat. We send him two cakes of soap."

The problem of returning to New Orleans became pressing as official inaction gave no signs of abating. The idea of inducing Elvira to make her home in New Orleans had been abandoned; but "if passports available," reads the diary, "Elvira and Victorina will remain in France until war is over. If passports not available, Elvira and Victorina will remain in San Felíu and I will leave for the United States, providing for their comfort as well as possible."

Early in November two bombing attacks were launched directly at San Felíu. Among other things, they wrecked the mains of the municipal waterworks. Fortunately, Dr. Matas, Elvira, and Victorina were all in Barcelona at the time, seeking to confer with the American consul general and if possible with Sr. Durand's distinguished relative, Assembly President Isla. However, Barcelona did not go unscathed either. Franco's bombers strafed it for two hours. "The mortality was fearful,"

Dr. Matas confided to his diary. "Dr. Joaquin Trias Pujol was kept busy all day attending the wounded . . . Barcelona is a thoroughly neglected metropolis: filthy, foul smelling and desolate, plunged into cavernous darkness at night when all lights are extinguished for fear of the bombers."

Late in November another bombing attack on San Felíu killed several persons and wounded some forty others. At the Red Cross station "I saw three bodies, one old woman and two old men. One expired from shock and fractured skull, one decapitated, and one from a bomb-fragment wound of the belly . . . The amount of destruction these bombs are capable of is something indescribable. At least thirty to forty buildings in various districts have been ruined by bombs this morning . . . Dr. Crespi picked me up to take me to the city hospital where the former director, a very old friend, Mr. Massor, lay in state. He had been killed about noon while he was putting a stamp on a letter in the post office. He had not finished attaching the stamp when a bomb exploded directly above him and he was buried instantly in the debris."

And then, with almost bewildering suddenness, the picture changed. Sr. Durand's influential kinsman, the Assembly President, waved his wand in the right quarter, and the difficulties vanished like wind-blown mist.

"A happy day!" rejoices the diary on November 28. "At last the business of the passports has come to an end . . . We were also excused from a fine of fifty pesetas each for failure to report as foreigners on arrival in Spain. I had planned to go to Barcelona in quest of these passports, but Mr. Isla gave us a very pleasant surprise when he handed me the passports with the remark 'It is all done, the permit is granted, you can leave now at any time.'"

So Dr. Crespi drove them to Port Bou in his ambulance, which waited on the Spanish side of the border, so that it could return with half a dozen boxes of foodstuffs for San Felíu as a parting gift from Dr. Matas. They were in Paris the next morning and it is worth noting (as Dr. Matas did) that Elvira and Victorina went straight from the hotel to the hairdresser before unpacking their luggage.

During all the next week Rudolph searched the highways and byways of Paris for a *pension* where Elvira and Victorina could live adequately and inexpensively on the $500 he had deposited to his sister's credit with the American State Department. Then the following note appears in the diary:

"December 8 . . . Very unpleasant dispute with Elvira. She has been planning surreptitiously to leave Paris and cross the frontier to the Franco side and is counting on the money that I would leave to her credit here in Paris after my departure to the United States."

There was a fine row, indeed; Rudolph insisted that Elvira cash the $500 deposit and turn the money over to him, so that he could have it banked where a trustee would pay it out to her at the rate of so much a month, as long as she remained in Paris to receive it; Elvira pleaded that he take the money and send it to her in her regular monthly allowance from New Orleans wherever she might be. Of course, there was a reconciliation.

He took his sister and Victorina to the prefecture to arrange an extension of their permits to remain in France beyond January 15, when the original visas expired; and he made the disgruntled notation that he had to pay 400 francs for his sister's additional permit because she was technically an American citizen, whereas Victorina's extension was issued without cost "as the exchange of passports with Republican Spain in France is free."

All this while he was encountering difficulties in securing any sort of reservation on westbound vessels out of France or England. Tourists and others apparently did not share the conviction that the Munich pact had assured "peace in our time." Refugees streamed out of the Reich. At length he managed to reserve passage on the *Paris* for January 4; but before leaving the City of Light he paid a last, brief courtesy call on his friends, the gargoyles of Notre Dame, and at the familiar old curio shop he bought figurines of Don Quixote and Sancho Panza.

He saw Elvira only once more. That was in 1947, after he had flown across the Atlantic with Isidore and Elsie Cohn to take part in the first truly international meeting the Society of Surgery held after the Brussels Congress of 1938 was adjourned. He enjoyed the plane crossing enormously, puckishly announced midway over the Atlantic that "I believe I have fractured my temporal neck!"—meaning, as he later chuckled, the neck of the temporal side bar of his eyeglasses. He landed in London sans baggage checks, these having been left behind or lost in transit, and without a confirmed hotel reservation, so that Isidore and Elsie Cohn gave up their room to him and made do in temporary quarters until proper accommodations could be provided.

That was early in September 1947. Five weeks previously, on August 1, he had received a cable from Victorina with the tidings that Elvira was critically ill and under the care of Drs. Casals and Planas. He replied by cable announcing that he had intended to visit San Felíu at the close of the London meeting in September and asking for details of the situation as it stood at the moment.

He waited vainly almost a week for an answer; then Dr. Planas cabled: "Circulation poor, gastro-intestinal hemorrhage, prognosis grave." Deeply distressed, he began to suggest treatments by cable, especially after Dr. Planas called in as consultant a Dr. Pinas who diagnosed the case as one of carcinoma of the liver, with a prognosis of fatal termination in a matter of weeks. He also doubled the amount of his sister's remittance, to cover whatever additional expenditure proper care and treatment might entail. While inquiring as to the possibility of securing an immediate passport through the aid of the State Department's Walton Butterworth, son of a New Orleans physician, he recorded in his diary, under date of August 11, that "I urged blood drip, digitalin, Vitamin K with protein and amino acids to diminish the hyperproteinemia." A few days later Dr. Planas cabled that the blood-drip infusion "was being better tolerated" and that some slight improvement in Elvira's general condition was apparent.

But the next diary entry bore the following note of omen: "Reports from the consultants indicate that efforts are being made to have Elvira take last sacraments . . . Planas' long letter makes it very positive that the diagnosis of Ca of the liver is correct. Elvira herself feels very confident that she is getting well and expects to have recovered completely by the time I reach Spain. Exitus would according to Pinas' belief be in about fifteen days from the day of his examination . . . or at most about a month and a half longer, or as late as October 31. Planas believes Pinas' prognosis is too short. Sent a cable to Elvira telling her I had heard from Planas the good news. Glad she is improving and I mailed her a letter."

He was torn between two conflicting conclusions. His immediate desire to rush to Elvira's side stemmed, not merely from fraternal affection but from the honest belief that as a great physician he could do more to help her than lay within the power of others. Yet, if he turned up in San Felíu weeks ahead of schedule and gave up an international meeting of surgeons to be with Elvira, she would inevitably be convinced her condition must be critical. Better to let her keep the conviction that she was on the mend, even though "exitus" could not be long deferred.

Then he chronicled on August 29: "Letter from Elvira in her own handwriting arrived today. She apparently feels very much better despite her swollen leg. She imagines she is on her way to complete recovery. She acknowledges receipt of my increased allowance for the month." The next sentence seems to blend fraternal gladness with professional pride: "Continuous intravenous drip saved her."

The "family" party that saw him off for Europe by plane now included Mrs. Hathaway Gibbens Aleman, who had become a permanent member of Dr. Matas's staff. At first Dr. Matas engaged her on a part-time basis, at the outset, to do the sort of statistical work in which experience had given her exceptional training. She later became a full-time research worker on his literary team.

From that it was but a step to taking over part of his general secretarial work, when this became too heavy for Miss Hess to handle without assistance. Thus, when he left New Orleans in the early autumn of 1947 with the dual objective of attending the first postwar Congress of the International Society of Surgery and then visiting his sister in Catalonia to make his own determinations concerning her ailment and its portents, he had reason to feel that the work of amassing material for the history would not lag during his absence. Moreover the news from San Felíu had certainly been on the hopeful side of late. Consequently, it was in a cheerful, actually gay, frame of mind that he celebrated his eighty-seventh birthday in London, receiving congratulatory cables from Lucian, Ruddie, Mrs. Feingold, and others, a fine new brief case as the joint gift of Isidore Cohn and the Touro Infirmary board, and "Mrs. Cohn presents me with a box of fine perfumed soap. Both very welcome gifts."

A happy and memorable day, all things considered, even though it lifted the curtain on his final year as an actively practicing surgeon. He must have realized something of this, for his evaluation of his physical condition was completely realistic—a much stronger and more readily perceptible pulse in his right foot than in his left, too much sleep during the day and too little by night, and so on. Yet he jested, on his return from a walk along the Mall, that certain phases of London life had certainly deteriorated as a result of the war; but for his cane, he said, he would have been utterly unable to ward off the importunities of the streetwalkers, despite his years.

However, when the sessions of the International Society began two days later, he attended few of its purely social functions. An intestinal malady was intensified by nervous worry over the difficulty of securing plane reservations for Madrid, for he was anxious to be on his way to Elvira at the first possible moment. So he kept to his room most of the time.

But he did finally manage a reservation on a flight to Madrid September 19. Though adverse weather conditions forced the plane back to Bordeaux at one time, he reached Barcelona only a day behind schedule. Dr. Planas met him there, and from him he learned with delight that Elvira's condition was truly and remarkably improved. Drs. Planas and Julio Altabas accompanied him on the drive to San Felíu, where the good tidings were confirmed by Elvira herself. Apparently quite well and active, she was up and about with the friends and kinsfolk who had gathered to welcome him with a champagne dinner to mark the auspicious reunion.

Dr. Matas proposed one toast in token of "gratitude for the kindness and help of medical friends, especially Altabas, Planas, Casals, Arice and others"; another toast to Victorina and her relatives; "and finally," the diary reads, "a toast to the central figure of the dinner, Elvira herself, who was seated at the head of the table." The dinner did not break up till six thirty, when the physicians had to leave on their return drive to Barcelona.

Next morning Dr. Matas breakfasted on fresh, ripe figs, and *café au lait* in Elvira's room, after which he subjected her to a searching professional examination. His conclusions: Elvira's illness stemmed not from carcinoma, but from a long-standing—probably since 1937—duodenal ulcer, whose hemorrhages had become acute in July, threatening her life until transfusions of whole blood by continuous intravenous drip supplied enough strength to maintain her until recovery could set in.

He stayed in San Felíu until the end of October, foregoing what would have been a great occasion for him in New Orleans—the fourth presentation of a Matas medal, an award instituted in 1933 by surviving relatives of Miss Violet Hart, who for years had been one of his patients. It was the custom, of course, to let Dr. Matas make these presentations, since the recipients would esteem the Matas Medal all the more if it came to them from the very hands of him in whose honor it was established.

On this occasion, it was manifestly impossible for him to be in New Orleans to present to Dr. Robert R. Gross, surgeon of the Children's Hospital in Boston, the medal and its citation, bestowed for an outstanding contribution to vascular surgery. So he wrote a brief speech in San Felíu, air-mailed it to New Orleans, and Dr. Isidore Cohn read it and made the presentation in his name.

He prolonged his San Felíu sojourn until Elvira was sufficiently restored to accompany him on relatively long walks by the seaside on the ancient Paseo del Mar, and when he finally departed on the first leg of his journey home, Elvira and Victorina accompanied him in a taxi as far as Barcelona: "Arrived Barcelona 6:30 P.M., where friends are waiting to accompany us to the hotel. Bid last farewell to Elvira and Victorina, who are returning in the same car to San Felíu."

His reason must have told him that in view of his sister's state of health—and of his own advanced age—this probably was in truth their "last farewell." No extrasensory premonition was needed to point up this conjecture. The next entry he made about Elvira in his diary was posted only fourteen months later, on January 8, 1949, when in a shaky scrawl he set down the words:

"Sad news from San Felíu has depressed me all day . . . Telephoned

Parsons I could not attend the banquet because I was in mourning for my sister in Spain, who had died on Friday, January 7th, at 6 P.M. . . ." At night he wrote notices of Elvira's death for publication in the *Times-Picayune* and *States*, making much of the fact that "Miss Matas had been educated in New Orleans." The banquet he did not attend was one celebrating the anniversary of Jackson's victory in the Battle of New Orleans. By coincidence, Louise Darling, granddaughter of Narciso Matas by his second marriage, the daughter of Rudolph's deceased stepsister, was visiting New Orleans and had just met her step-uncle for the first time, when the cable announcing Elvira's passing was delivered.

CHAPTER XXXIII

During the last conscious years of his life Rudolph Matas was perturbed, not so much by diminution of his physical vigor as by the loneliness which inevitably engulfs those who outlive their contemporaries by a generation. He was, in effect, totally* blind during nearly five years; but even this was not as cruel as the deepening realization that with each passing day there remained fewer to whom his name meant anything more personal than casual awareness that, like "Taj Mahal," the words "Rudolph Matas" stood for something notable.

In the past, he had been less deeply affected by the deaths of those he knew, as, one by one, these were gathered to their fathers. Most of them were his elders, and at the height of a crowded career, when there were not enough hours in a day or minutes in an hour to allow time for a tithe of what he wanted to accomplish, such events were taken in stride as regrettable but natural phenomena. The first loss outside of the immediate circle of his family that dealt him a truly shattering blow was the passing of Felix Larue, who had been his family physician and, in a sense, his secular confessor. Larue had been taken to the hospital and placed in an oxygen tent on September 30, 1935. Four days later we find this entry in the Matas diaries:

* "Totality" is absolute, and in that sense Dr. Matas was not "totally blind." The ophthalmologist who treated him reported that up to the last his patient could distinguish between light and darkness; but even under glaringly bright light and with the aid of high magnification he could not read, nor could he recognize and identify the features of those about him. For a man like Dr. Matas, that was tantamount to total blindness.

"Call at Touro to see Larue who is growing worse under repeated attacks of cardio-pulmonary failure . . . relieved only by morphine which puts him to sleep. When awake he is delirious. Suppository of amytal sodium succeeds in bringing about a deep sleep which ends in stupor from which he cannot be roused. Henniger inserts nasal tube into stomach through which he is given slowly a quart of solution of coffee and glucose. Leave him at 11:30 P.M. apparently quiet with fair pulse and respiration but in deep stupor. Called to see him again at 4 A.M., find him sinking in stupor. Always under oxygen, but at 8:46 he expired with pulse gradually failing. Breathing a few gasps at the end. Remain with him and close his eyes at 8:55 A.M."

With steadily increasing frequency he began to chronicle in his diaries the deaths of former friends and associates, some with plainly perfunctory interest, some with poignant and very real grief. An instance of the latter sort was his reaction to the letter from Miss Hess, informing him of Augustus Wheeler's death in November 1938, while he—Rudolph—was sweating out air raids in San Felíu.

He had been the Wheeler family physician since the 1890's, and Augustus had been his financial adviser ever since the partnership of Wheeler and Woolfolk was formed. "Gus Wheeler—53—died November 1," he set down sorrowfully in his diary, "following a spinal operation for tumor. This news received at 3 P.M. today via an airmail letter 15 days on the way. Gus died on the day of my arrival in Spain at Port Bou. Cabled Miss Hess 'Overwhelmed.' Sleepless night thinking of Gus Wheeler's death and what he meant to me. Mail letter to Mrs. Gladys Wheeler by air post . . . [Later] Letter from Lucian dated November 1, written while Gus was still alive and apparently rallying."

On the other hand there were deaths which severed the last remaining ties linking him to his youth. One of these was the passing of a nonagenarian St. Charles Avenue neighbor, John Walker Phillips, in 1937. This was the I. L. Lyons drug-firm executive to whom Ben Hibbard, manager of Brayda's pharmacy in Matamoros, had written a letter of introduction for Rudolph when he came to New Orleans as a freshman medical student in 1877. The same sort of pang followed the announcement from Rudolph Matas Krausse in Houston that his father, Louis, a classmate of Dr. Matas in the College of St. John at Matamoros, had died that morning.

These incidents punctuated a very busy career, for almost up to his eightieth birthday Rudolph Matas continued the active practice of surgery. In June 1939, the newspapers of New Orleans noted that "seventy-nine-year-old surgeon operates on seventy-eight-year-old patient." The latter was Charles B. Greenwood of Miami, whose aneurism of the right common carotid artery was of forty years' standing. The injury which brought it about had been incurred in Oklahoma, where a surgeon, believing it to be a tumor, operated, but later pronounced the aneurism inoperable as soon as he recognized it for what it was. It had then remained quiescent, for many years, but suddenly began once more to increase tremendously in size. At the time Dr. Matas operated, it extended from the collarbone to the angle of the jaw. He ligated the common carotid and thereby cured the aneurism, enabling the patient to speak and eat again without undue difficulty. Mr. Greenwood died a year or so later in Miami from other and unrelated causes.

Dr. Matas's last aneurism operation was performed that same year. It too was successful, though the chart records the surgeon was engaged thereon from eleven in the morning until two-thirty that afternoon. At the close of this ordeal Dr. Matas announced he had performed his last operation and would thenceforth confine his professional activities to consultations and office examinations.

Yet on one subsequent occasion he was prevailed upon to make an exception. In June 1940, Mrs. Birdie Feingold, widow of the Marcus Feingold who had virtually suspended all other practice in 1908 to devote himself to a prolonged effort to save Dr. Matas's infected right eye, pleaded with him to operate on her daughter, Rose, a school teacher. The latter had recently become aware of an enlargement in the thyroid region. One must assume that not only the memory of Marcus Feingold's selfless service in 1908 impelled Dr. Matas to break for this one occasion his resolve to retire from active surgery; Mrs. Feingold had been one of Adrienne's oldest and most devoted friends— the two had known one another affectionately long before Adrienne and Rudolph were married.

So, at Mrs. Feingold's urging, he scrubbed up for the last time as surgeon in charge, directed the placing of his famous "font of holy water," carried on a steady, clucking monologue, punctuated by a succession of "my-my-my!" exclamations while he worked with the old skill and care. The operation, technically a subtotal thyroidectomy, was performed without incident and was followed by the patient's complete and uneventful recovery.

So far as can be ascertained, he entered an operating theater, even as minor participant, but twice thereafter. In September 1946, just after his eighty-sixth birthday, he assisted one of his favorite pupils, Dr. Mims Gage, in an amputation. A month later he assisted Lucian in another amputation, the patient in this instance being Dr. Charles Landfried, who was perhaps the most intimate professional friend of Rudolph Matas's maturity. Though seventeen years younger, Landfried was the only associate who ever addressed him as Rudolph. To others he was always "Doctor," "Dr. Matas," or "Governor." For years they both operated at Touro on Fridays. When their schedules were crowded, which was virtually always, they had lunch together in one of the operating rooms.

A warty growth appearing on the sole of Dr. Landfried's foot had been treated by X-ray. A radiation burn that followed became malignant, and amputation was deemed essential. With his great stepfather as assistant, Lucian performed this operation, taking off the leg midway between ankle and knee. Dr. Landfried left the hospital five days later, well on the road to recovery. But he was readmitted thereafter at frequent intervals, because of other systemic disturbances, and a year later he died, only a few days after having been discharged from the hospital again.

Dr. Matas's attitude toward the encroaching weaknesses which would henceforth bar him from the exacting physical tax surgery levies on its practitioners was quite philosophical. He accepted this as one of the penalities imposed by longevity and occasionally quoted a Greek proverb to the effect that the old age of an eagle is better than the youth of a sparrow. Far harder to bear, however, were the slights—often quite unintentional—growing out of the fact that on occasion it did not occur to younger physicians, rising in the ranks of the profession, to accord him the consideration that for half a century had been his portion. The first such instance occurred in 1932, when the Mayo brothers, Will and Charles, visited New Orleans for a day or so. Beyond doubt what happened was due to an oversight, but it took place during the very week when Dr. Matas learned that the assignment of writing the vascular section for Dean Lewis's *Surgery* had been turned over to someone else, following his refusal to cut his manuscript to forty pages.

After all, he was still the modern Antyllus; the idea that someone else could replace him as "the" authority in this field must have left him keenly sensitized to the erosive changes wrought by time. His diary entry on this occasion reads: "Will and Charles Mayo in town, leaving today for Boston. Have not seen them—not notified of their arrival, although entertained by Ochsner and others. Work all day on Bibliography for Lewis." Since Dr. Matas had succeeded Charles Mayo as president of the American College of Surgeons and had been inducted into office by him, it is simply unthinkable that such a slight as this could have been intended either by the Mayos or their hosts.

More bitterly tinged with resentment was his 1947 comment on one phase of the American Surgical Association's convention in Hot Springs, Virginia. Actually, he referred to it as a meeting of the International Society of Surgery, since he called the American members of the latter organization into session before the American Association convention opened. His diary report of the incident reads in part:

"March 26: . . . Nothing sensational about the dinner except Gage's Rabelaisian jokes or stories borrowed from the bayous of Louisiana. Not fit to be heard by ladies but universally popular with the men. After the dinner I returned to my room which I was able to get into after a considerable delay, as I had forgotten my key in my room in the trousers which I had taken off. I had brought with me a little speech, but the arrangements committee have not given me a thought. As a whole, the day was a depressing one, and gave me a deprecating impression of the fellows making the arrangements."

It was because of such incidents, no doubt, that he treasured more and more the distinctions that came his way, not merely the great spotlighted awards: the Bigelow Medal, the Distinguished Service Medal of the A.M.A., the first elevation to the Grand Council of the Order of Carlos Finlay bestowed on him by President Batista in Havana.

His delight in being placed at the head table or in the front row was unfeigned. Confiding to his diary the circumstances attendant upon the ceremonies of conferring honorary fellowships on three members of the International Society of Surgery during that organization's 1947 Congress in London, he related how the Royal College of Surgeons went into session: "I am invested with the gown of my honorary fellowship," he wrote, "and form part of the procession leading to the main hall, where I am seated in the front row with the other Honorary Fellows." Or again, speaking of the elaborate inaugural ceremonies: "I arrived a little late, but was called to the platform with the official roster . . . I sat at one end of the front row near young Elston Turner, son of Grey-Turner."* At the Ogilvie dinner "I am conducted to one of the head tables."

Nonetheless he assayed his physical catabasis quite objectively. On January 1, 1946, he made the following entry on the first page of his new scratch pad: "Personal observation regarding difference between last New Year's day and Jan. 1st, 1945. Less weight this year, 184 pounds. More stooping, less height. Losing hair fast—approaching frontal baldness; loss of four teeth, compelled to use dental plate, now undergoing adjustment with Hava, the dentist; the media still clear, but slowing pupillary reflex to light and darkness, and now to reading, despite new glass in my left eye; more easily tired on slight exertion, sleep too little at night and too much during the day. As a whole, marked general decline in 1945."

Gradually he stopped keeping regular office hours, leaving most of this routine to Lucian. Occasionally, however, he made himself

---

* Newly elected president of the International Society, Grey-Turner was about to be inaugurated and would preside at the next meeting, to be held in New Orleans in 1949.

available to old friends who demanded he continue to minister professionally to their needs. Among these, for example, was Mrs. Elizabeth Meriwether Gilmer, only six years his junior, who "calls for annual examination and check-up with special reference to cramps and pains . . . the cramps are unquestionably ischemic . . . Hearing impaired, eyes good with glasses. Diabetic, injects herself with insulin, and diets." Then, as now, Mrs. Gilmer was more widely known under her pen name of Dorothy Dix.

Except for such demands on old friendship, he began more and more to spend his days at home, with servants to attend his wants and Miss Hess's companionship. The staff was headed in seniority by Nathaniel Givens, the chauffeur who doubled as valet and who, for some obscure reason, was called "Sam"; Annie Smith Bloom, who served as maid for more than twenty years, a Josephine, a Celeste, and a Selina, one of whom was cook and one of whom was a laundress, who, twice a week, took the wash out to her home and returned it cleaned and ironed. Miss Miriam Hale came in to do typing occasionally, and Miss Hess's grandniece, Marjorie Kister, who had helped at one time with her great-aunt's secretarial duties, now dropped in occasionally as a physician to check Dr. Matas's blood pressure, pulse, and the like.

Marjorie had lived in the Matas home with Miss Hess while she studied medicine at Tulane, but immediately after her graduation had announced she would marry a fellow student, Dr. William Charles Miller. Dr. Matas took this with bad grace, declaring she was wasting the education she had so painstakingly acquired; but he became reconciled to the situation, as all concerned knew he would, and consulted Dr. Miller as his physician to the end of his conscious days.

Another marriage brightened his declining years, the wedding of his namesake, Ruddie Matas Landry, the little boy he used to delight in taking to the movies. Ruddie had left Brussels, where he saw Teur preside over the International Society of Surgery, a fortnight before his parents and sister returned to the United States because, as a freshman medic about to enter Tulane, he could not afford to miss the opening classes.

Thus it happened that he returned from abroad on the same boat with the family of Dr. Frederick A. Willius, head of the heart department of the Mayo Clinic in Rochester. As associate professor in the University of Minnesota College of Medicine, he too had to return from the Brussels Congress early. Traveling with him was his daughter Jane.

That Christmas Ruddie approached his father and asked if his holiday gift might be a trip to Rochester. He explained why this seemed important. Jane did not visit the Matas-Landry families in New Orleans until 1942, when Ruddie, having been graduated the year before, was serving as an intern at Touro, and when Dr. Matas took the happy young pair "to the Saenger Theater after dinner to see a movie with Tyrone Power and Gene Tierney."

The following year Ruddie and Jane were married in Rochester. Dr. Matas confessed himself unable to make this trip to Minnesota in midwinter, but when his young namesake came to bid him farewell, he gave him a $1000 war bond as a wedding present. He also tried to wire the bride and groom his congratulations, but Western Union refused the message on the ground it was not an essential communication and thus fell within one of the classifications proscribed by wartime regulations.

As soon as Ruddie finished his internship in July 1943, he entered Navy service, being commissioned a lieutenant (j.g.). He was assigned to the Marine Corps as medical officer and was dispatched to California for training, taking with him a $50 viaticum from Dr. Matas. His bride returned to her parents' home in Rochester where, while Ruddie was in California, Rudolph Matas Landry II was born. As a combat medical officer, Lieutenant (j.g.) Landry took part in the invasions of Saipan and Tinian. Dr. Matas had his Christmas dinner that year at Lucian's— ducks and a fine Sauternes—and had the Landry clan at his home for New Year's Eve wassail, enlivened by letters from Ruddie on Saipan and a "new portrait of baby Ruddie just received from Jane."

Young Ruddie was home before the next Christmas and went to Rochester, where he was attached to the Mayo Clinic for four and a half years. He then returned to New Orleans and served a year on the staff of the Ochsner Clinic, when he received a flattering offer from the Newell Clinic in Chattanooga, an institution of which, before Dr. Matas's death, he became a full partner. Dr. Matas was told of his namesake's swift rise to eminence but in all likelihood he was no longer able to grasp the full import of the news.

Most of the stigmata of progressive debility left him relatively unperturbed, but the steady loss of visual power in his only eye distressed him keenly. For some time he had been annoyed—at first it was nothing more than annoyance—by an occasional floating dimness that briefly obscured his vision while reading; he would rub the eye in an effort to drive the misty film away. One must assume he knew what this portended. He had read widely about such afflictions, not only in connection with his own "cyclopean estate," as he liked to call it, but in connection with his father's special studies and his final attack of glaucoma. Thus it is likely he put off a visit to the ophthalmologist lest his fears be confirmed.

But in June 1946, he finally approached his moment of truth, admitting the situation to himself by making a full report of the incident in his diary.

"Called on Dr. [George] Hardin," he wrote, "to examine my left eye for localization of floating nebula which moves with the eye, like a mucoid film which flashes over the cornea and appears on blinking the eye. The film has been bothering my eye for quite a while, but much more so in the last few weeks. I have been under the impression that it is purely a mucus film, as it appears to improve after blinking and rubbing the conjunctiva with the lids. I am now afraid the film is intra-ocular and not conjunctival. Hardin examines attentively and believes that the film is in the vitreous humor. The film is very movable and follows the movement of the eye, always falls back on the pupillary field of vision, causing at times a transparent veil which is sometimes magnified to show its structure, like a very thin amorphous mucoid film. Hardin orders a weak astringent with sulphate of zinc and other simple lavages with boric acid lotion. The eye wash does good, cleaning the conjunctiva, but does not change the floating nebula. Clearly an intra-ocular phenomenon and not conjunctival. Apart from the nebula my vision is excellent. No headache or pain, no sign of glaucoma—low blood pressure."

The dire implications of such an evaluation lay in the stark realization of helplessness when confronted by inevitability. Complete familiarity with all the known answers would make any monocular physician only too well aware of the fact that the sight of his sole remaining eye was far along on the road to extinction. Yet Rudolph Matas did not flinch from the knowledge that shadows were drawing in, that no mortal hand could hold them back. He strove for amelioration and relief, noting in the summer of 1949, at a time when the need to prepare an address for the approaching New Orleans convention of the International Society of Surgery was "riding me like a nightmare" that "I find it difficult to concentrate on mental work. Eye worrying me. Headache, left hemicrania, follows attempt to read smaller print and attempts at reading in poor light cause headache. Accommodation of vision to reading at short distance without lenses impossible, accommodation from long to short distance very slow. Vision is only good and clear at a distance, with lenses. Vision made foggy at times by increased conjunctival secretion, improved by washing the eye."

A year later, when the sight of his eye was becoming ever more restricted, he reported that "at the suggestion of Mr. Sol Rosenthal, a neighbor, I called on Mr. W. A. Ferillian . . . to examine and try a patented floating magnifier as a visual aid in connection with my extreme myopia caused by senile impairment of my ciliary lenticular power of accommodation, which makes it impossible to read the usual small type newspaper print with any clearness. Decide after inspection of the apparatus to take it home. I have experimented with it and it appears to make my reading easier. I will keep the apparatus on trial."

As the shadows continued to draw in and he and the workaday world drew ever further apart, Rudolph Matas retired more and more into the past with whose events and experiences his matchless memory was replete. With its assistance he and Lafcadio Hearn walked again by night along the stilled, gaslit streets, ending their rambles but not their interminable discussions at the house on Rampart Street where Adrienne waited with a big bowl of gumbo or a dish of shrimp-stuffed *mirlitons,* a jellied *daube glacé* or other delicacy. . . . Lafcadio would wheedle the recipes from her for his cookbook. . . .

For nearly seventy years he had refused to permit publication of any of Lafcadio's letters even in expurgated versions. Perhaps he had been wrong in withholding these gems from print. . . . He took this up with various publishers, with newspaper friends, and with Edward Larocque Tinker, a writer for whom he entertained genuine affection and respect. But even this esteemed friend echoed the views previously voiced by publishers with whom the subject had been taken up. There was no longer enough interest in Hearn, who had died half a century before, to justify the publication of these letters as a commercial venture.

They were finally published, nonetheless, in Japan, being included among *Studies in Arts and Culture,* a multilingual, paperbound belletristic collection making up the eightieth anniversary volume released in 1956 by Ochanomizu University. The letters appear under an eight-line introductory paragraph by Ichiro Nishizaki, which reads in part:

"During his stay in New Orleans, Lafcadio Hearn found a most intimate friend in the 'brilliant young Spaniard, Rodolfo Matas,' a graduate of the College of Physics and Surgeons, and editor of the *Medical Journal.*"*

When the Boydell volumes† and a plaster cast of the bust of Homer purchased at the Louvre in 1909 were presented to Tulane University, Dr. Matas explained: "It is with deep regret that I am forced by my disabilities, especially visual, to have these remarks read for me. Even though I had found it possible to attend these exercises . . . my vision is so seriously impaired that I would not have been able to read this message which I have dictated."

---

* The Hearn letters were also scheduled to be published in Japan in a limited facsimile edition, with introduction and notes by the Messrs. Tinker and Nishizaki.

† The illustrations for the works of Shakespeare, which City Boss Jim Houston had given him in the early 1890's for saving him from a morphine coma in almost certain death.

It had been typed for him by Mrs. Aleman, for faithful, devoted Kate Pruitt Hess had died early in 1952. The house seemed very empty without her; she had lived there for more than thirty years. But Mrs. Aleman quietly and efficiently took over the duties of managing it, of seeing to the marketing, the laundry, the cleaning, the preparation and service of meals, during the day. By night, Rudolph was alone with Andrew Segrow, who knew whom to summon in case of emergency. He was no longer able to see the moving-picture show in which he had always taken such delight; it had been years since he could keep a diary, though for a time he had maintained one by clipping and pasting newspaper articles, especially the movie reviews.

In his ninety-second year, his visual ailment reached the point of crisis. Both Dr. W. B. Clark and Dr. Victor Smith, who had examined him three years before, declared he was suffering from a cataract, and Dr. Matas himself admitted at the time: "My field of vision very much contracted since last consultation in September." Dr. Clark found that Dr. Matas was also suffering from glaucoma and urged an operation. In discussing this at the Eye, Ear, Nose and Throat Hospital, Dr. Matas asked:

"Will the operation succeed or fail? If one had two eyes, there would be no question, of course. But if I am operated on and lose this eye, there will be nothing but darkness for me. I know that one thing cannot be changed: the senility of my 92 years . . . and I have several things I still want to do, several messages that I want to leave. I can still see my hands as matters stand."

It was beyond doubt a heart-tearing choice, but he made his decision calmly. On March 5, 1952, Dr. Clark performed an iridectomy and a cataract extraction—the same operation Rudolph's father had performed nearly ninety years earlier on his son's *cher 'ti' lapin* in Paris. Three months later Dr. Matas dictated to a friend the sorrowful tidings that "I am still living in a world of shadows which, while not seriously affecting my general health, has deprived me of practically all my visual efficiency. While no one can be very cheerful living in the penumbra of a ghost world, I am not rehearsing the lamentations of Job, and still manage to live in fairly good comfort, through the kindness and assistance of friends and the stimulating and encouraging messages which come to me through the radio."

The ravages of senility made rapid inroads upon what remained of his physique and his health. From 1954 on he used a wheel chair, except for occasional flashes of revolt, when he refused even to use the elevator he had installed for Adrienne four decades before, but insisted on walking up and down the stairs. Sporadically he still directed research for his medical history of Louisiana, the magnum opus whose appearance in book form would not be left to the crass whims of commercial publishers, but would be assured by the trust fund he had set up for the purpose.

Mrs. Aleman could and did read to him, of course, and he could listen to the radio; Amelie, the wife of Peter Walmsley now, would visit him from time to time. But the shadows which had already drawn a dark curtain across the field of his vision now began to close in on his mind, as the result of a generalized arterial sclerosis.

The last time he appeared in public was at the McAlister auditorium of Tulane University, where the famous Moscow correspondent of the Associated Press, Eddy Gilmore, was delivering a Lyceum lecture. Mrs. Aleman brought him there in his wheel chair, with the solicitous help of Nathaniel Givens. By the beginning of 1956 it became obvious that the ailing surgeon, who had passed his ninety-fifth birthday the previous September, should be hospitalized. In a formal consultation, Dr. Charles Miller, Dr. Isidore Cohn, Dr. Lucian Landry, and Dr. W. A. Reed, the urologist who was treating Dr. Matas for a prostatic affection, impressed this decision on him.

He demurred, but finally gave reluctant assent. Then, when the ambulance called to transfer him to the best room in Touro, he abruptly changed his mind and declined to leave his home. Later that same afternoon, however, the persuasion of friends and family prevailed, the ambulance returned, and on January 15 he entered the hospital where he lived for the next year and a half. He made only one condition: the house was to be kept open, the servants retained, with Mrs. Aleman in charge of maintaining it as a functioning residence—and for one reason only. When the time for final rites came, he must be buried, not from a mortuary morgue but from the home from which his Dearest Adri had been buried, the home he had bought so that he could install her there as his bride.

During nearly four months after his admission to the hospital he was not wholly helpless; he recognized his intimates, and at times, though at ever more infrequent intervals, spoke rationally. In May of 1956, the last spark of reason in what had been "one of" the great intellects of the three generations his lifetime spanned, flickered and went out. From then until 9:39 P.M. September 23, 1957, ten days after his ninety-seventh birthday, he remained incapable of performing even the simplest bodily function; he did not take so much as a bite of food by mouth.

During those final fifteen months, he was fed through a nasal tube which Dr. Harold Leslie Kearney renewed every six weeks or so; he discharged body wastes through catheters that were left in place except during the brief interludes when they were changed for fresh ones by Dr. Reed. He recognized no one, spoke no coherent words. Yet his body vegetated remarkably. Pulse, respiration, and temperature remained virtually normal, beginning to fade from time to time, but returning to almost incredible vigor after each such lapse, until the end came.

In the afternoon of that last day the nurse, Mrs. Mary Henderson, set down upon the chart from time to time who was present: Dr. Charles Miller, Dr. Cohn, Mac Wheeler, Dr. Landry . . . respiration shallow, pulse thready and barely perceptible. After supper, when the physicians returned, they could see that the end was near. From time to time one or another of them would feel the faint pulse still throbbing weakly; it became slower and slower . . . and then what had been Rudolph Matas ceased to breathe.

More than forty years earlier he had said in his memorable 1915 address before the Mississippi State Medical Society, the address entitled "The Soul of the Surgeon":

"Infirmity, disease and death in the aged are natural phenomena. They present a fateful and unavoidable character that causes them to be accepted as the natural consequences of the usure of time, of the degenerative and atrophic changes of senility. The transition between life and death should be gentle in the winter of life. Death, under those conditions, is invested with a certain grandeur and poetry, if it comes to a man when he has completed his mission. He reaches home with the sunset, and with the departing day lies down on his couch and folds himself to rest and sleep, after the long day's work is over. There is nothing to fear, nothing to dread, except by those poor souls that approach the problems of the unknown and unknowable eternity with fear and trembling; who see before them a long night of terror; those in whom the imprint of ancestral superstitions and the seal of puerile dogmas have not been effaced and who, rocked in the cradle with fantastic legends, still entertain visions of everlasting punishment; those who, in fine, look upon death as an eternal and terrifying ordeal, rather than a supreme and restful slumber.'"

The Great Transition was indeed gentle in the winter of Rudolph Matas's long life. He who had witnessed the beginnings of the Civil War had also been present at the birth of the Atomic Era. He had completed his mission. Kind destiny guided him in crossing, without fear or struggle, the threshold from a life that was no longer sentient to the couch of supreme and restful slumber he had envisioned many years before—or to whatever else he might encounter beyond finite existence.

APPENDIX

RUDOLPH MATAS

1880   Granted M.D. Degree by the University of Louisiana, (now Tulane University).

1880   Diploma from Charity Hospital, New Orleans, for Service as Resident Student 1878–80.

HONORARY DEGREES

1915   Doctor of Laws, Washington University, St. Louis.

1925   Doctor of Science, University of Pennsylvania.

1926   Doctor of Laws, University of Alabama.

1928   Doctor of Laws, Tulane University.

1928   Doctor of Science, Princeton University.

1933   Doctor of Laws, University of Guatemala.

OFFICIAL POSITIONS HELD IN MEDICAL SOCIETIES

1885   President New Orleans Medical and Surgical Society.

1894   President Louisiana State Medical Society.

1909   President American Surgical Association.

1911   President Southern Surgical Association.

1920   President American Society for Thoracic Surgery.

1925   President American College of Surgeons.

1931–32   Vice-President American Medical Association.

1935–36   Elected President of the International Society of Surgery (Brussels) at its meeting in Cairo, Egypt (*in absentia*).

1938   Presided at the Congress of the International Society at Brussels.

HONORARY FELLOWSHIPS IN MEDICAL SOCIETIES IN THE UNITED STATES

1920   New York Academy of Medicine.

1920   American Association of Industrial Physicians and Surgeons.

1923   American Society of Regional Anesthesia.

1926   Boston Surgical Society.

1926   Presented Bigelow Medal by the Boston Surgical Society.

1927   Honorary Fellowship Southern Surgical Association.

1929   Philadelphia Academy of Surgery.

1931   Medical Library Association.

1931   Southeastern Surgical Association.

1934   Louisiana State Medical Society.

1935   New Orleans Academy of Science.

1937   American Association for the History of Medicine.

1939   American Association for the Surgery of Trauma.

1939   New Orleans Graduate Assembly.

1941   Life Membership Association of Military Surgeons.

1948   Louisiana Academy of Science.

1948   American Society of Anesthesiologists.

1948   American Heart Association.

1948   American Society of Vascular Surgeons.

1948   Louisiana Surgical Association.

1948   American Society of University Surgeons.

1951   First Honorary Member of the New Orleans Surgical Association.

1952   American College of Surgeons.

LOCAL HONORS

1905 Loving cup presented by friends and faculty of Tulane School of Medicine, on the occasion of his twenty-fifth anniversary of graduation.

1926 Gold watch presented as a testimonial of appreciation after he had served as president, American College of Surgeons, and after he had received the Bigelow Medal.

1931 Anniversary volume issued in honor of Dr. Matas's seventieth birthday (1930). The contributors to this volume were surgeons from the United States and several foreign countries.

1934 Violet Hart Award, created by Mike Hart in memory of his sister: the Rudolph Matas Vascular Surgery Medal.

1937 Dedication of the library at the Medical School of Tulane University to Rudolph Matas.
NOTE: By his will (1957), Dr. Matas endowed the library with a legacy of $1,000,000. He also gave his complete medical library to the Rudolph Matas Library at Tulane University.

1938 Dr. Matas received the first Distinguished Service Medal created by the American Medical Association.

1940 *Times-Picayune* loving cup. Award for community service.

1941 Touro Infirmary dedicated a bronze medallion plaque to Rudolph Matas (Chief Surgeon from 1906–35—Emeritus Chief Surgeon 1935–57).

1941 Represented the City of New Orleans at the Carlos Finlay Celebration in Havana, Cuba.

1948 Nu Sigma Nu medical fraternity created the Rudolph Matas Lectureship.

FOREIGN DECORATIONS

1920 Honorary Member of the Surgical Society of Peru.

1927 Honorary Fellowship, Royal College of Surgeons of England.

1927 Chirurgo Praeclaro, Italy.

1928 Comendador, Order of Carlos Finlay (Havana).

1929 Corresponding Member, Medical Society of Copenhagen.

1930 Honorary Member Reále Accadèmia di Roma.

1930   Member, Société Internationale Histoire de la Medicine, Paris.

1931   Membership, Asociacion Medica, Mexicana.

1931   Membership, Polish Surgical Society.

1932   Legion of Honor, France.

1932   Foreign Associate, Société Nationale de Chirurgie de Paris.

1932   Honorary Member of Medical Society of Havana.

1933   Membre Associé, Académie Nationale de Chirurgie. (Membre Correspondant, 1922.)

1934   Medal of Honor (Venezuela).

1936   Foreign Corresponding Member, Academia de Ciencias, Medicas, Fisicas y Naturales de la Habana. (Also 1941).

1938   Corresponding Member, Havana Academy of Medical Sciences.

SOCIETE INTERNATIONALE DE CHIRURGIE

1929   Rapporteur by invitation, Congress at Warsaw.

1936–38   President.

1947   *Membre d'honneur*, 12th Congress, London.

1949   Congress held in New Orleans in his honor.

1939   Order of Leopold of Belgium conferred.

1941   Diploma of Federation of Cuba conferred.

1941   Corresponding Member of the National Society of Surgery of Cuba.

1941   Medal of the City of Havana (guest of honor).
Official guest as delegate from the City of New Orleans to National Finlay Celebration, November 1941.

1941   Finlay Medal, Cuban Medical Federation.

1941   Grand Order of Carlos Finlay conferred by Cuban Government. Jewel of the Order of Carlos Finlay was presented to Dr. Matas during a meeting of the International Lions Club, July 22–25, 1941, as the sole survivor of the Chaillé Yellow Fever Commission of 1879.

1943   Member of the Mexican Academy of Surgery.

1944   Honorary Professor of Surgery, University of Guadalajara.

1947   Honorary Fellow, Greek Surgical Society of Athens.

1948   Honorary Fellow, Belgian Surgical Society.

1948   Honorary Member, Royal Academy of Medicine, Belgium.

1948   Associate Member, French National Academy of Medicine. Medal as corresponding member received in 1950.

1948   Honorary Member, Surgical Society of Lyons, France.

HONORS RECEIVED FROM SPAIN

1923   Honorary Membership, Royal Academy of Medicine and Surgery, Barcelona.

1926   Testimonial diploma from the Institute of the Practice of Medicine, Barcelona.

1927   Corresponding Member of the Academia y Laboratori de Ciencias Medicales de Cataluña.

1927   Honorary Member and lecturer by invitation at the Spanish National Congress of Medical Sciences, held in Madrid.

1928   Corresponding Foreign Member, Real Academia Nacional de Medicine.

1929   Certificate as Caballero, Order of Alfonso XII (decoration).

1929   Honorary Fellow, Catalonian Academy of Medicine, Barcelona.

1933   Certificate of the Order of Isabella the Catholic from El Presidente de la Republica Espanola (decoration).

1933   Associate Member of the Society of Surgery of Madrid.

1934   Certificate of Testimonial Academia Nacional de Medicina.

1947   Honorary Diploma, Gerona (Spain).

INDEX

Bemiss, Dr. Samuel, 86–87, 99, 100, 102,
  114, 120, 127, 138
Bemiss, Dr. J. H., 221
Benjamin, Judah P., 281
Beriberi, 109–10
Beyer, George E., 275
Bickman, Dr. Warren Stone, 254, 327,
  329, 342
Bier, August, 279
Bigelow, Henry Jacob, 375
Billings, Colonel John Shaw, 323, 342
Biloxi, 184
Bishop, Stanhope, 192
Bisland, Elizabeth, 188
Black, Hardy, 202
Blair, Dr. Vilray, 367–68
Blanc, Dr., 221
Blanco, Ramón, 107, 108, 114
Bloom, Dr. J. D., 249
Bonilla, Manuel, 313
Borde, Mr., 226, 227
Boston Surgical Society, 375
Boyer, Dr. F. C., 89
Brayda, Vittorio, 75
Browne, Sir Thomas, 214
Browning, Elizabeth Barrett, 360
Brownsville, 24, 28, 29, 45, 59, 67, 69,
  140, 146–47
Bruns, Dr. Henry Dickson, 184, 220,
  221, 239, 333
Buell, Victor, 91
Burgaria, Narcisa, 15
Burgess, Dr. Daniel M. 108, 111
Butler, Colonel Andrew J., 25, 26–27,
  30
Butler, General Benjamin Franklin, 24,
  25, 27, 29, 30, 74 fn., 238 fn.
Butler, Mary, 68, 252
Butterworth, Walton, 400

Cabell, Dr. James L., 105, 110
Cable, George W., 166–67
Caine, Dr. Ansel, 327
Calvé, Emma, 346
Canada, Dr., 108
Canal Street, Battle of, 73–75
Canonge, M. Placide, 188
Capdevielle, Mayor, 308
Carcassonne, 43
Carlist wars, 46
Carmone y Valle, Dr. M., 185
Carnegie Foundation, 328
Carpetbaggers, 59, 65, 66, 68, 72, 73
Carroll, Dr. James, 272, 273
Carroll, T. J., 379
Carson, Dr. William, 95–96, 97

Carter, Henry Whinry, 71, 74
Casals, Manuel Areu, 14, 399
Catalonia, 14, 42
Catgut rings, 232–33
Cepere, Dr. Gilberte, 115, 116
Chaillé, Dr. Stanford E., 61, 62, 67, 86,
  99, 100, 102–3, 105, 106, 107, 109,
  114, 120, 121, 123, 125, 134, 138,
  144, 145, 147, 161, 185, 213–14,
  221, 237, 249, 250–51, 252, 263–64,
  291, 329, 334
Chaillé Commission, 105–17, 127
Chaillé Jubilee Day, 328–29
Chapman, Mrs., 84
Charity Hospital, 77, 80, 83, 85–88, 91,
  95, 126, 129, 140, 183, 199, 222,
  225, 247, 289, 301, 315, 325, 327,
  386
Chase, Salmon P., 24
Chassaignac, Dr. Charles, 129, 221, 242,
  243, 285
Cherbourg, 175
Chicago, 242–43, 329
Choppin, Dr. Samuel, 94
Clark, Dr. S. M. D., 285
Clark, Dr. W. B., 414
Clemenceau, Georges, 36, 42
Cleveland, Grover, 262
Clovis, Emperor, 46
Cohn, Elsie, 352, 361, 399, 401
Cohn, Dr. Isidore, 331–32, 352, 361,
  362, 399, 401, 402, 415, 416
Colliers, J. J., 344
Colon, 145, 146
Comas, Victorina, 394, 395, 396, 398,
  402
Congress of American Physicians and
  Surgeons, 224
Cooke, Rose Terry, 360
Corday, Charlotte, 43
Corpus Christi, 28
Cotton Centennial Exposition, 159
Coulomb, Dr., 369, 372
Crawcour, Dr. Isaac L., 18
Crespi, Dr. Robert, 395, 397, 398
Culex mosquito. *See* Mosquitoes
Cupples, Dr., 151–52
Cutler, Dr. Elliott, 390, 393

Dabney, J. B., 255
Da Costa, John Chalmers, 382
Darling, Louise, 402
Davidson, J. O., 166, 167
Davis, Jefferson, 97, 98, 148 fn.
Delaney, John Thomas, 202
Delaup, Dr., 280, 282, 283

225, 236, 238, 252, 262, 266, 272, 273, 285, 329
New Orleans Pathologic Society, 183
New Orleans Polyclinic, 221, 235
New Orleans Sanitarium, 247
New Orleans School of Medicine, 75
New Orleans Sewerage and Drainage Company, 248
Newton, Dr., 245
New York City, 32, 173, 174, 180, 306
Nicholls, Governor Francis Tillou, 85, 120, 236
Nishizaki, Ichiro, 413
Nix, Dr. John T., 384
Nixon, Dr. F. I., 144
Nott, Dr. Joseph C., 63

Ochanomizu University, 413
Ochsner, Dr. Albert J., 367, 374
Ochsner, Dr. Alton, 378, 386
O'Connor, Jimmy, 164
Opelousas, 25, 26
Orleans Parish Medical Society, 270, 274, 285, 302, 319
Orthopaedic Institute, 94
Osler, Sir William, 181, 214–15, 242, 319, 334, 343, 353, 356

Palmer, Dr. Benajmin M., 123
Panama Canal, 60 fn.
Panama Canal Zone, 63 fn.
Pan-American Medical Congress, 274
Parham, Dr. Frederick W., 185, 220, 221, 224, 250, 254, 285–86
Paris, 33–34, 35–44, 175–76, 180, 339, 341–42, 368, 372–73
Parker, Governor John M., 322, 386
Pasteur, Louis, 106, 110, 113, 221, 343
Pasteur Institute, 106
Pathological Society, 220
Pavy, Ben, 387–88
Pavy, Yvonne, 387
Penrose, Mrs. George B., 351
Pepper, James, 91, 100–2
Periosat, Padre, 71
Perityphlitis, 161–62
Perpignan, 43
Perry, Dr. Alfred, 64
Phillips, John Walker, 79, 406
Pinchback, Pinkney Benton Steward, 72–73, 74 fn.
Piver, L. T., 180
Planas, Dr., 399–400, 401
Plateau, Joseph Antoine, 70
Pont Major, 14, 15
Port Bou, 43
Port Isabel, 78

Pothier, Oliver, 202
Pratt, Dr. George K., 85, 102
Prevost, François Marie, 20
Puerto Cortés, 313
Puig, Esperanza, 14
Pujol, Dr. Joaquin Trias, 398
Pyle, Dr. W. L., 334

Queyrouze, Leona, 158, 188–91, 234

Radcliffe Infirmary, 214
Red Cross, New Orleans chapter, 351
Reed, Dr. Walter, 63 fn., 117, 213, 272, 273, 299
Reed, Dr. W. A., 415
Reilly, Dr. W. F., 134
Reiss, Dr. Paul L., 310, 328
Revueltas, General, 75, 77
Richardson, Dr. Tobias G., 80, 83, 84 fn., 86, 94, 97–98, 99, 122, 123, 124, 138, 161, 221, 237, 238
Rimbau, Rita, 15, 16
Roberts, Governor Oran, 146
Robin, Dr. Ernest A., 328, 333, 334
Rockefeller Institute, 384
Rocquet, Albert, 202
Rodriques, Dr. Felipe, 108
Rogers, Jane Grey, 372
Rooney, Henry, 261
Roosevelt, Theodore, 269, 214, 317, 322, 335
Rosenthal, Sol, 412
Ross, Dr. John W., 273
Royal College of Surgeons, 374
Royster, Dr. Hubert, 368, 374
Rush Medical College, 192

Sabatier, Dr., 226, 227
St. John's Collegiate Institute, 75
Salic law, 46
Salomon, Dr. Lucian F., 127, 139, 153, 250, 319, 321
Sambola, Anthony, 53
Sambola, Francisco, 17, 65, 66, 126
San Antonio, 151
Sanarelli, Dr. Giuseppe, 272
San Felíu de Guixols, 15, 44, 176, 177, 341, 372, 381 fn. 396, 397, 398, 401–2
San Román, José and Luis, 29, 41, 65, 66
Sax, Adolphe, 232
Scalawags, 72
Scheppegrell, Dr., 250
Scherck, Henry, 199, 202, 205, 207, 226
Schmidt, Dr. H. D., 161, 183, 185, 220
Schoemaker, Dr. Jan, 389
Schuppert, Dr. Charles, 96